Prejudice

Prejudice

Attitudes about Race, Class, and Gender

Von Bakanic, Ph.D.

College of Charleston

Upper Saddle River, New Jersey 07458

Library of Congress Cataloging-in-Publication Data

Bakanic, Von.
  Prejudice : attitudes about race, class, and gender / Von Bakanic.
    p. cm.
  Includes bibliographical references and index.
  ISBN 0-13-045330-7
  1. Prejudices. I. Title.
  HM1091.B35 2009
  303.3'850973—dc22   2007043888

Editorial Director: Leah Jewell
Editorial Supervisor/Assistant: Christina Walker
Full Service Production Liaison: Joanne Hakim
Marketing Manager: Lindsey Prudhomme
Marketing Assistant: Jessica Muraviov
Operations Specialist: Christina Amato
Cover Art Director: Jayne Conte
Cover Design: Bruce Kenselaar
Full-Service Project Management: Bharath Parthasarathy/TexTech International
Composition: TexTech International
Printer/Binder: RR Donnelley & Sons Company

Credits and acknowledgments borrowed from other sources and reproduced, with permission, in this textbook
appear on appropriate page within text.

Pearson Education LTD., London
Pearson Education Singapore, Pte. Ltd
Pearson Education, Canada, Ltd
Pearson Education–Japan
Pearson Education Australia PTY, Limited

Pearson Education North Asia Ltd
Pearson Educación de Mexico, S.A. de C.V.
Pearson Education Malaysia, Pte. Ltd
Pearson Education, Upper Saddle River, New Jersey

10 9 8 7 6 5 4 3 2 1
ISBN 13: 978-0-13-045330-3
ISBN 10: 0-13-045330-7

To my parents, Nelda Richard Bakanic and Edward Bakanic,
you gave me my foundation.
And to my husband, Floyd A. Roberts,
you helped me recognize my advantages and see the world beyond
"my raising."

Contents

SECTION II   STEREOTYPES, DISCRIMINATION, AND THE "ISMS"

Preface

As the twenty-first century begins, the United States has entered an era of increased reaction and attention to diversity. The new century had scarcely begun when terrorists hijacked four aircraft and succeeded in destroying the Trade Towers in New York and severely damaging the Pentagon. Only the intervention of passengers and crew prevented the fourth aircraft from reaching its intended target. Prejudices targeting people of Middle Eastern ancestry and members of the Islamic faith ballooned in the months following these attacks. Hate crimes rose dramatically. Bumper stickers and T-shirts expressing hatred and anger toward Arabs and Muslims sold almost as quickly as American flags. Prejudices increased as politicians appealed to the fear of their constituents in an effort to garner support for the PATRIOT Act and later the invasion of Iraq. The spread of terrorist activity did nothing to dispel the rising tide of anti-Muslim prejudices.

Other prejudices are increasing as well. After decades of increasing tolerance for gays and lesbians, reaction to political gains by the gay rights movement caused a widespread political and social backlash. The brutal torture and death of Matthew Shepard in 1999 was a harbinger of a rapid rise in antigay prejudices. In 2002 the murder of transgendered teenager, Gwen Araujo, became a focal issue for the GLBT community. Two of her attackers were convicted of second-degree murder. The jury, however, concluded that no hate crime was committed, because federal hate-crime protections do not extend to gay, lesbian, bisexual, and transgendered people. Civil rights gains that extended privileges and protections to GLBT people during the late 1990s were reversed during the next decade. Constitutional amendments banning gay marriage, antigay demonstrations, and condemnation of gay clergy are part of a widespread rise in homophobic prejudices.

Anti-immigrant, especially anti-Latino, prejudices rival the anti-immigrant movements of the nineteenth and early twentieth centuries. The political solutions to the immigrant crisis offered by contemporary politicians are strikingly reminiscent of the infamous "Know-Nothing Party" of the nineteenth century. The Know-Nothing Party was based on strong anti-immigrant views and was associated with the patriotism and nationalism. It advocated that government policies and legislation be framed by native-born Americans for native-born Americans. By native-born Americans the party meant white men of Northern European ancestry born in the United States. The party name reflects an early example of what has become a common contemporary strategy of denying or dismissing prejudice while at the same time advocating discrimination. Rather than arguing publicly about their racist views, members of the party were told to say they "knew nothing."

The patriotism revived after the September 11 attacks fueled public support for the wars in Afghanistan and Iraq. But, as those wars drag on, patriotism has turned to issues closer to home. An organization called the Minutemen has incorporated patriotism into a new anti-immigrant movement. Ordinary citizens have gathered along the border with Mexico to watch for illegal immigrants crossing the desert into the United States. According to their Web site, the Minutemen claims to be a vigilante group but disavow affiliation to any separatist, racist, or supremacy groups. However, the group also warns that unless immigration is curtailed "Future generations will inherit a tangle of rancorous, unassimilated, squabbling cultures." They claim immigration will result in political, economic, and social mayhem.

Technology has also played a part in the rise of prejudice. Web sites and online recruitment to hate organizations have increased the visibility of hate speech and swelled both the membership and the coffers of both established and neophyte hate groups. The Simon Wiesenthal Center's 2006 report on Internet hate groups identified more than 5,000 hate sites available to Internet users. The southern Poverty Law center reported a 33 percent increase in hate groups in the United States since 2000. Because the United States embraces freedom of speech, U.S. Internet servers have become a way to circumvent laws that censure hate speech in other countries. The Internet has become a hotbed of racist, sexist, and anti-Semitic bigotry.

There is ample evidence that prejudices based on race, ethnicity, religion, social class, gender, and sexual orientation are proliferating at a horrific rate. The irony of this explosion of prejudice is that the vast majority of individuals in the United States continue to claim that they hold no prejudices. How can groups and individuals disavow prejudices while in the same breath expressing them? What factors have facilitated the widespread denial of prejudice while allowing increases in the expression of prejudices and hate speech? What can be done to expose the prejudice problem and to curb the growth of prejudices?

This book examines theories and research on prejudice stemming from the interdisciplinary field of social psychology. Both sociologists and psychologists have contributed to the literature on prejudice, stereotyping, and intergroup dynamics. The problem of prejudice is not limited to bigoted individuals nor is it only a product of an abstract, impersonal entity generically referred to as "society." By building on the theoretical foundations and research traditions of both social psychologies, I hope to explain the phenomenon of contemporary prejudices and understand how the denial of prejudice fits into the proliferation of prejudices. Hopefully, increasing the understanding of what prejudices are and how people use them will lead to a motivation to reduce them.

GOALS OF THIS BOOK

The primary goal of this book is to understand what prejudices are, how they are formed and changed, and what purposes they serve. Particular attention will be paid to three types of prejudices: race, class, and gender. In Section I, I will define prejudice, examine the consequences of prejudice, and analyze the purposes it serves in American society. Each of the three types of prejudices will be described. This section will address both commonly held widely recognized prejudices and more-subtle or hidden prejudices. The symbolic value of prejudice and its relationship to other values will also be addressed. Section II will examine the relationship between prejudice, stereotypes, and discrimination. These terms are often used as if they were interchangeable or synonymous. Differences in these phenomena are explained, and the links between them are critically explored. Trends in the rise and decline of prejudice and the treatment of minority groups have followed changes in how groups fit into the social stratification system. Thus, macrochanges in antidiscrimination law and government policies are essential to the understanding of prejudice. The section then explains how prejudices become embedded in social structures. I refer to this phenomenon as the "isms"—racism, sexism, and classism.

Section III will focus on the dynamics of prejudice. Social psychologists have a long tradition of working in intragroup and intergroup relations. Understanding group dynamics is integral to the understanding of the circumstances in which prejudice occurs. Contrary to popular beliefs, prejudices are not merely dysfunctional attitudes. People use their prejudices every day to make judgments quickly during fast-paced interactions. Chapter 8 explores why complete elimination of prejudices is an unrealistic goal. This does not mean that prejudices should be encouraged or allowed to multiply unchecked. Chapter 9, the final chapter, addresses strategies that reduce prejudice. Is it possible for people to suppress their own prejudice? If so, how can individuals be motivated to reduce their reliance on prejudice? Group-level interventions, such as strategies that promote intergroup contact, are examined. Macro-level pressures for social conformity, such as assimilation, are contrasted with multicultural diversity. The inconsistent and sometimes contradictory policies that the United States has implemented help explain the irony of contemporary prejudices. Although prejudice is inevitable, the amount of prejudice and the problems associated with prejudice can be reduced if we acknowledge the important role prejudice plays within individuals' development, as part of the process of social interaction and how it becomes embedded in our social structures.

Well-intentioned educators and journalists have convinced most people that prejudices are bad and that the key to solving problems of racial, gender, or class conflict is to rid us of prejudice. This is an oversimplified and impossible solution. It has resulted in an almost total public disavowal of prejudice. The primary goal of this text is to present prejudice as an integral part of how we make sense of the everyday world. That does not mean that I endorse or condone prejudices; rather I contend that the denial of prejudices compounds the problems associated with them and impedes both an understanding of their role in interaction and the development of strategies to reduce them. The consequences of prejudice, both good and bad, will be explained as a complex and inescapable part of human society. By explaining the processes behind our prejudices, students will be able to recognize their own prejudices and make sense out of our increasingly diverse, rapidly changing society.

Acknowledgments

I am greatly indebted to Rita J., and Julian Simon who sparked my interest in this subject and provided the funds for the very first study of prejudice I conducted while I was a junior faculty member at the University of Southern Mississippi. Living in Mississippi and my experiences with the good people there were very important because I had to confront my own prejudices while studying theirs. They taught me humility and the value of introspection.

Many thanks to my colleagues at the College of Charleston who made valuable comments and suggestions as I wrote this book. Special thanks to my husband, Floyd Roberts, who has been my gofer, research assistant, and sounding board. Thanks to my daughter, Torie Roberts, who could have been a professional editor, but provided her services to me out of the goodness of her heart. My sister, Barbara Bakanic, endured many telephone calls that began "How does this sound . . ." I also owe a great debt to my grandchildren, Rodney, Zachary, Bryanna, and Charlize. Because they are children and have not yet fully mastered the art of denying and hiding their prejudices, they allowed me to observe how we acquire and use prejudices.

My thanks to the following reviewers for their helpful suggestions: Marguerite Martin, Gonzaga University, Karen A. Callaghan, Barry University, Linda J. Olson, Castleton State College, Abby Ferber, University of Colorado, Theresa A. Martinez, University of Utah, Valerie Moore, University of Vermont, and Douglas V. Davidson, Western Michigan University.

I have saved the most important thanks for last. My parents, Nelda Richard Bakanic and Edward Bakanic, have blessed me with their love and unconditional support. They made me believe I could accomplish anything!

Prejudice

CHAPTER 1

Introduction

What Is Prejudice?

The introduction includes an explanation of the perspective used in the text and an explanation of the major terms and concepts developed throughout the text.

Some time ago I was dining with friends and family at a local Japanese restaurant. There were people from a variety of racial and ethnic backgrounds seated around a hibachi enjoying the Japanese cuisine and culture. Out of the blue, my seven-year-old grandson said in a loud voice, "It's illegal for black people and white people to get married." Immediately his parents corrected him and quizzed him about where he had heard such a thing. Sensing a no-win situation, he refused to tell them, and eventually the conversation returned to other less-disturbing topics.

From this exchange, my grandson learned more than information about the current marriage laws. He learned that his statement was socially inappropriate and that it was obviously embarrassing to his parents. By observing the reactions around the table, he learned that talking about race upsets adults. But probably the most significant lesson he learned was to censure his comments about race.

According to survey researchers my grandson is not the only one who has learned to be silent on the subject of race. Self-reported racial prejudice in the United States has declined to the point that people no longer reveal their own racial prejudices (Schuman, Steeh, and Bobo 1985). Yet though we deny being prejudiced ourselves, we are not so naive as to believe racial equality has been achieved. A study conducted by the National Conference for Community and Justice (NCCJ) found that people in the United States are very aware of racism. In a national telephone survey of 2,584 people, 83 percent identified blacks as victims of discrimination (NCCJ 2000). A substantial majority of respondents also identified Hispanics, Native Americans, and women as victims of discrimination.

As with so many other problems Americans are in denial about their own prejudices. We recognize prejudice and discrimination as social problems, but we deny any personal culpability. Pretending that we harbor no prejudices may make us feel better about ourselves, but it makes frank conversation about inequality impossible. By denying the existence of prejudice within ourselves, we cannot address it. This presents social researchers with an ironic and perplexing problem: How can prejudices be investigated when most people are unwilling to acknowledge that they even have them?

An underlying assumption of this book is that whether we admit them or not, everyone has prejudices. Many times we are aware of our prejudices, but perhaps just as often, we don't pay attention to the prejudiced attitudes that influence our judgments. Some researchers argue that people who consider themselves nonprejudiced but nonetheless make prejudiced responses during interactions simply are not practiced enough at generating nonprejudiced responses (Monteith et al. 1994). Patricia Devine (1989) has shown that racial stereotypes affect both prejudiced and nonprejudiced people. Unless they are drawn to our attention, we uncritically use prejudices and stereotypes along with other information to make sense of our social world. Whether we are aware of them or not, whether we admit them or not, we all sometimes make prejudiced decisions affecting our own behavior in evaluating the behaviors of others.

COMMON SENSE AND SOCIAL PSYCHOLOGY

Prejudice is part of the "common sense" we use to interpret the world around us. Most people conceive common sense as simple ideas and meanings that everyone knows and accepts. But, common sense is neither common nor simple. Common sense is an illusion of consensus. It assumes that there are shared meanings known to all members of a culture or subculture. Try to pin down just what constitutes common sense and you will find it elusive. It varies from community to community, person to person, and from one time to another. Fortunately, it's not important whether we can come up with definitive examples of common sense. It doesn't even matter whether commonsense meanings are accurate. It matters only that people act upon them as true.

In this text *common sense* is understood as a way that people refer to "making sense" out of dynamic, ambiguous, sometimes conflicting social interactions. In an attempt to make sense out of what we experience in our daily lives we use pieces of information and experience pulled from countless sources, even though much of the information we use is unverified, unreliable, inaccurate and, many times, unfair. The process of making sense occurs rapidly and continually. Even if we wanted to, we could reflect only on a small portion of the ideas and meanings we draw upon to understand what happens around us. In a flash, meanings occur to us and we either act upon them or discard them.

Prejudices and stereotypes contribute to this process far more often than most people would care to admit. Far from being simple or obvious, commonsense prejudices are part of the complex process of human interaction. People use their prejudices to construct their social reality and make sense out of their own behavior and the behavior of others. Throughout this text, common sense explanations will be examined and compared with sociological explanations. Exposing common sense ideas to critical analysis reveals oversimplifications that distort people's understanding of prejudice.

RACE, GENDER, AND CLASS PREJUDICES

Research into prejudice, until recently, has focused on individuals and groups that hold prejudice toward others (e.g., Brown 1995). Currently efforts to study prejudice from the targeted group's perspective have increased (e.g., Swim and Strangor 1998). This book will encompass both perspectives—of perpetrators and of targets of prejudice. To understand how prejudice operates and is understood in interaction, we must identify prejudiced attitudes, assess their effect on behaviors, and figure out how they emerge during interactions between people.

Although the book begins with racial prejudice, gender and class prejudices will receive equal treatment. I begin with racial prejudices because in some ways they are easier to pinpoint. Despite widespread denial of racial prejudice, it is something most Americans are aware of and can easily recognize. Gender and class prejudices are, in some respects, more insidious.

Racial Prejudices

How people define race varies geographically and historically. Biologically, race is not a useful concept (cf. Olson 2002). This is because our concept of race is based on a variety of visible physical traits that people use to categorize others into groups. Although members of a group have physical similarities, using these traits to define a race is not a reliable way to determine whether people are genetically similar. There may be more genetic variation within a race than there is between races. For example, two people may share eye, skin, and hair color; however, that does not mean that they will be genetically more similar than two individuals with different skin, eye, and hair color. The study of human genetics has revealed that all human beings are very closely related. We are a single species. The only biologically definable race is the human race. Yet we continue to use physical characteristics to classify people into races.

At times in the history of our society we have used nationality and ethnicity as if they were synonymous with race. People spoke of the Irish race, the Italian race, and the Slavic race as if there were biological distinctions that paralleled national boundaries. We have even used religion as a racial designation. Although Jewish people come in every color and live on every continent, they have nonetheless been defined as a race and subjected to some of the most virulent racism of any group in human history. The definition of race has changed so frequently that the U.S. Census Bureau has changed how it measures race almost as often as the census has been collected. Currently the Bureau allows self-identification by people according to the race or races to which they believe they belong (Box 1-1).

Once we decide to group people into races we use racial prejudices to create and maintain boundaries between groups. Racial prejudices have a variety of uses. They define and distinguish groups; they justify differential treatment and social inequality between groups; they provide a rationale for quick decisions and cognitive shortcuts; and

BOX 1-1

Racial Classifications Used by the Census Bureau

The concept of race as used by the Census Bureau reflects self-identification by people according to the race or races with which they most closely identify. These categories are sociopolitical constructs and should not be interpreted as being scientific or anthropological in nature. Furthermore, the race categories include both racial and national-origin groups.

The racial classifications used by the Census Bureau adhere to the October 30, 1997, Federal Register Notice entitled "Revisions to the Standards for the Classification of Federal Data on Race and Ethnicity" issued by the Office of Management and Budget (OMB). The OMB requires five minimum categories (White; Black or African American; American Indian and Alaska Native; Asian; and Native Hawaiian or Other Pacific Islander) for race. The race categories are described below with a sixth category "Some other race," added with OMB approval. The OMB also states that respondents should be offered the option of selecting one or more races in addition to these five race groups.

White. A person having origins in any of the original peoples of Europe, the Middle East, or North Africa. It includes people who indicate their race as "White" or report entries such as Irish, German, Italian, Lebanese, Near Easterner, Arab, or Polish.

Black or African American. A person having origins in any of the black racial groups of Africa. It includes people who indicate their race as "Black, African American, or Negro," or provide written entries such as African American, Afro American, Kenyan, Nigerian, or Haitian.

American Indian and Alaska Native. A person having origins in any of the original peoples of North and South America (including Central America) and who maintain tribal affiliation or community attachment.

Asian. A person having origins in any of the original peoples of the Far East, Southeast Asia, or the Indian subcontinent, including, for example, Cambodia, China, India, Japan, Korea, Malaysia, Pakistan, the Philippine Islands, Thailand, and Vietnam. It includes "Asian Indian," "Chinese," "Filipino," "Korean," "Japanese," "Vietnamese," and "Other Asian."

Native Hawaiian or Other Pacific Islander. A person having origins in any of the original peoples of Hawaii, Guam, Samoa, or other Pacific Islands. It includes people who indicate their race as "Native Hawaiian," "Guamanian or Chamorro," "Samoan," and "Other Pacific Islander."

Some other race. Includes all other responses not included in the "White," "Black or African American," "American Indian and Alaska Native," "Asian," and "Native Hawaiian or Other Pacific Islander" race categories described above. Respondents providing write-in entries such as multiracial, mixed, interracial, or a Hispanic/Latino group (e.g., Mexican, Puerto Rican, or Cuban) in the "Some other race" write-in space are included in this category. Estimates for years after 2000 reflect an allocation of this category among the other categories.

Two or more races. People may have chosen to provide two or more races either by checking two or more race-response check boxes, by providing multiple write-in responses, or by some combination of check boxes and write-in responses.

Comparability. The data on race in Census 2000 are not directly comparable to those collected in previous censuses because of the introduction of recording of persons of two or more races. The data on race in the estimates after 2000 differ from Census 2000 figures in that respondents reporting "some other race" have been allocated to the other five categories.

The concept of race is separate from the concept of Hispanic origin. Percentages for the various race categories add to 100 percent and should not be combined with the Hispanic percentage.

Non-Hispanic White alone. It includes individuals who responded "No, not Spanish/ Hispanic/Latino" and who reported "White" as their only entry in the race question. Tallies that show race categories for Hispanics and non-Hispanics separately are also available.

SOURCE: http://quickfacts.census.gov/qfd/meta/long_ASR151205.htm.

they support and perpetuate racist social structures. Despite the fact that racial prejudices are currently politically sensitive, people use racial prejudices both deliberately and inadvertently every day in interactions and reactions. Despite the current social pressure to deny having racial prejudices, they surface in all of us as we negotiate interactions in an increasingly heterogeneous society.

Gender Prejudices

Gender prejudices are not always considered socially inappropriate. Indeed, sometimes people revel in them. Popular radio shows such as the nationally syndicated *Bob and Tom Show* enjoy high ratings primarily because of the sexist banter of the cast and guests. Even among people committed to equality between women and men, differences between men and women are a source of inexhaustible comic material. Male-bashing humor thrives alongside blonde jokes. Although often dismissed as harmless, sexist humor is rife with gender prejudice and has been shown to be associated with rape and other forms of aggression toward women (Moore, Griffiths, and Payne 1987; Ryan and Kanjorski 1998).

One of the fascinating aspects about gender prejudice is the prejudice we hold against our own gender. We may avoid tasks or pursuits associated with the other gender believing that we would have no aptitude or inclination for it. For example, I call for my husband to repair the vacuum cleaner rather than attempting the simple repair myself because I assume he is more mechanically inclined. Regardless of whether one's gender role ideology is feminist or traditional, sexism is entrenched in our responses (cf. Theriault and Holmberg 1998). Gender roles are embedded in our culture, in the socialization process, and, ultimately, in all people. Gender identity is internalized very early, and our gender responses become so habitual that they are considered innate.

Gender prejudices are so much a part of common sense that we often aren't aware of them. Whether intentional or not, when someone is called a sissy, a gender prejudice is invoked. Without reflecting on the gender implication of the term *sissy*, we equate cowardice with things female. If we happen to reflect on a gender prejudice, we may rationalize it as a "natural" sex difference. Gender prejudices are so much a part of how we view the world that they are often not recognized as a prejudice and instead are taken as fact.

Social-Class Prejudices

Class prejudices are perhaps the most difficult to recognize because social-class inequality is legitimate in our society. The very essence of capitalism is inequality. Those who have access to more monetary resources have both the privilege and the right to exclude others. Our civil rights laws are designed to protect citizens against discrimination in the public sector, but private clubs and communities may discriminate in whatever way they choose. In other words, not only is social class legally exempt from antidiscrimination legislation, but those with the resources to form private clubs and schools can use exclusiveness to exempt themselves from legislation prohibiting discrimination based on race, creed, color, national origin, or sex. Unlike race and gender discrimination, exclusion based on social class is neither legally nor socially objectionable. Whereas discrimination has negative connotations, exclusivity connotes high status and achievement.

Class prejudices are an integral part of American values. For example, meritocracy is a strongly supported value. It is the belief that one's social position should reflect one's ability and effort. According to the General Social Survey, about 96.5 percent of respondents agreed that the poor were poor because of lack of effort (NORC 1988–1991), whereas almost 72 percent agreed that the differences in social standing between people are acceptable because they reflect what people did with the opportunity they had (NORC 1983–1987). The prejudice implicit in meritocracy is that the poor are poor because they are lazy and stupid. Thus, they—not the affluent—are to blame for their own dismal living conditions.

Class prejudice extends to the working and middle classes as well. We see the working class often as uneducated and often stereotypically demean middle-class tastes as tacky or in poor imitation of the superior taste displayed by the affluent. Even the recently wealthy are subject to stereotypes of the nouveau riche. The attempts of those with newly acquired wealth to pass for wealthy are held up to ridicule. Etiquette books, newspaper columnists, and a seemingly endless parade of popular magazine articles capitalize on the insecurity generated by class prejudices and stereotypes.

PREJUDICE, DISCRIMINATION, AND THREE "ISMS"

Prejudice

Often people in our culture use prejudice, discrimination, and the "isms" (i.e., racism, sexism, and classism) as if they meant the same thing. Sociologists use these terms differently. Though prejudice and discrimination are certainly part of racism, sexism, and classism, it is imperative that we define the terms clearly and use them precisely so that we can see the contribution of each phenomenon to the process.

Prejudice is literally a prejudgment. It is a negative attitude about a person, group, issue, or thing. Prejudice is often based on stereotypes and overgeneralizations rather than on direct experience. The word *stereotype* was borrowed from journalism by Walter Lippman in 1922 (Marger 2000). Lippman described stereotypes as "pictures in our head" that allow us to quickly categorize people and make sense of them (Lippman

1922). In social psychology *stereotype* refers to an exaggerated belief associated with a group or category of people (Allport 1954). The trouble with stereotypes is that there is often "a kernel of truth" in them. But, that little bit of truth is exaggerated or overgeneralized so that the cultural variation within and between groups is ignored and individual differences are discounted.

Not all prejudices and stereotypes are negative. Positive prejudices, or **predilections,** are positive attitudes and preferences toward a particular group. We often hold positive prejudices and stereotypes about our own group. Although common sense might suggest that positive prejudices and stereotypes are beneficial, they are sometimes as harmful as negative ones. For example, the model minority stereotype has led many people to judge Asian Americans as hard working, industrious, and smarter than other groups. These assumptions heighten expectations of the performance of Asian Americans and lead to increases in racial tensions between Asians and other racial and ethnic groups. Similarly, the predilection for women as caregivers puts a disproportionate burden on women for the daily care of children, elderly parents, and other family members needing protracted care.

Prejudice and stereotypes are part of a larger ideology that is used to justify inequality. Prejudice ideology, in turn, is embodied in social structure. That is, prejudice stems from the policies, organizations, and institutions that comprise our society. So although prejudices are negative attitudes held by individuals, they are also deeply embedded in all levels of our culture. For example, the seeds of class prejudice are deeply embedded in our education system. Students with high grades and test scores are assumed to be intelligent and hardworking; this also implies those with low marks are stupid or lazy. A quick reflection on your own experience should bring to mind numerous anecdotes that point out the flaws in this assumption. Nonetheless if we are fortunate enough to receive high marks, it is tempting to justify our success with merit. The acceptance of merit-based grading in schools is mirrored in the job market and in the explanations used to justify advantaged social and economic position. Most people believe those with higher degrees should receive higher pay. But if merit were to truly determine position and salary, how does one explain the dismal salaries of teachers, social workers, and other college-educated service professions? We use meritocracy as an ideology to justify our own advantages and to blame the disadvantaged for their low social status. We feel proud of our own accomplishments and disdain for the lower classes even if we are aware of fallacies in our own reasoning.

A commonsense understanding of prejudice contends that if we could just eliminate prejudices, we would be able to reduce or perhaps even eliminate group conflict and social inequality. Taking this approach, many programs for prejudice reduction have focused on education and sensitivity training (e.g., Angele and Llweellyn 1997). Although these attempts to reduce prejudice are laudable, such approaches greatly oversimplify the complex way prejudices stem from and reinforce our system of race, gender, and social-class inequality.

Prejudice is more than a personal deficiency that can be overcome with education and resocialization. There is some evidence suggesting that prejudice reflects, rather than causes, the unequal treatment of various groups (Hughes 1997). This is consistent with Herbert Blumer's early argument (1958) that prejudice is a reflection of group position. As prejudices change, so do the relative positions of various groups. Group position theory assumes that members of the privileged group feel entitled to greater

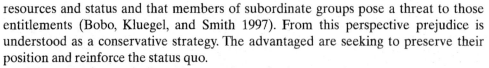

resources and status and that members of subordinate groups pose a threat to those entitlements (Bobo, Kluegel, and Smith 1997). From this perspective prejudice is understood as a conservative strategy. The advantaged are seeking to preserve their position and reinforce the status quo.

To summarize, prejudices are negative attitudes toward a group or category of people. They are often based on stereotypes that are by definition inaccurate. Prejudice and stereotypes are part of an ideology that is used to justify inequality. Even if we are aware of the flaws in our own reasoning, it's tempting to justify our advantages using prejudices. The prejudices we use to justify our position reflect the position of groups within our stratification system. So whereas prejudiced attitudes are espoused by individuals, they are deeply embedded in the structure of our society. Finally, whether we acknowledge them or not, everyone has prejudices. Denial of prejudice only makes it more difficult to address.

Discrimination

Discrimination refers to treating people unequally based on their identification or association with a group or category of people. Whereas prejudice is an attitude and therefore cognitive, discrimination must involve an action or behavior. Common sense tells us that prejudice causes people to discriminate. In actuality, prejudiced attitudes and discrimination do not always occur together. To understand this, we must be clear about how and when people discriminate.

Discrimination involves making choices that affect others. How our behavior impacts others is in part tied to our social position. For example, as a professor I award grades that affect my students. Hypothetically, I could use my authority to discriminate against students. My students, however, have little or no authority over me. Thus they don't have the power to discriminate against me. So to discriminate, a person must have some authority or control over others.

For most people authority isn't ubiquitous or universal. Authority stems from a social role or a position they occupy. That authority is constrained by the rules and regulations associated with the position or the institution that grants the authority. To return to my earlier example my authority over students is limited to scope and duration of the class they take with me. I don't have the authority to directly affect their employment or housing or any other aspect of their lives. So though everyone has prejudices, not everyone has the power to discriminate. Even when a person can discriminate, the scope of their ability to discriminate is limited by the role that gives them their authority.

Sometimes policies are written explicitly to make some kinds of discrimination less likely. For example, the goal of Affirmative Action policy is to reduce and eventually eliminate educational and employment discrimination. In other cases, policies can cause us to discriminate regardless of our own attitudes about a person or group. *Institutional discrimination* occurs when polices and regulations, rather than personal prejudices, compel a person to discriminate.

One example of institutional discrimination is ***Bona Fide Occupational Qualification*** (BFOQ). If an occupation requires a special trait possessed only by members of a particular group or category, then employers can legally discriminate. For instance, age is a BFOQ for jobs requiring an employee to sell alcohol. An employer in such a case must restrict consideration of applicants based on their age. A BFOQ is an example of a legal, and thus intentional, form of discrimination. However, institutional discrimination is sometimes a latent by-product of policy. As a remedy for discrimination against a minority group we may try to set aside a number or percentage of positions for the members of that group, but it is actually a requirement that discriminates all other groups. This is called *reverse discrimination.* In the United States both primary and reverse discrimination are illegal.

Unlike prejudice, discrimination involves behavior or action. Though a person might be able to hide their prejudices, discrimination is more observable. To discriminate, a person must have the authority to make decisions affecting others. Not everyone has the authority to discriminate, and the scope of the discrimination is limited by the source of that authority. Finally, discrimination is not necessarily motivated by prejudice. Institutional discrimination occurs when policies require discrimination or inadvertently produce a discriminatory result.

The Three "isms"

Racism, sexism, and classism refer to extensive complexes of attitudes, behaviors, ideas, norms, policies, and forms of organization that give one group advantages over other groups. They are part of the *social structure.* This means that racism, sexism, and classism are built into the patterns of social relationships and social institutions. Prejudices are part of the ideology that justifies and supports racism, sexism, and classism. For the sake of clarity, I will explain each term separately later in this section. However, racism, sexism, and classism are not entirely discrete phenomena. They intersect in a multitude of ways. Perhaps this is why no single unifying theory of prejudice can account for how prejudices are formed and combined when directed at different target groups. In later chapters we will explore variants of racism/classism, sexism/racism, and sexism/classism to understand how they intersect.

Racism is a structure that ranks racial and ethnic groups in a hierarchy of advantage. In the United States "whites" are currently the most advantaged race. Like all other races, how whiteness is defined has varied over time. The descendants of Caucasian Europeans have gradually assimilated into the advantaged white race as they shed their cultural distinctiveness in favor of blending into the privileged group. The racist structure that perpetuates white advantage is pervasive in our culture, but ironically those most advantaged by racism are less likely to be aware of it. In her essay on white privilege, Peggy McIntosh (1989) recounts the difficulty she had in listing her advantages as a white person. Although she eventually created a long list of advantages, her initial problem was that before attempting this exercise, she had not considered the lack of obstacles as an advantage (Box 1-2).

Consider this analogy. Two horses are in a race. Both horses are fitted with blinders to keep them focused on their lane. But one horse's lane has hurdles placed at intervals, whereas the other horse has a clear path. The outcome of the race is obvious. The winning horse is unaware that the other horse had obstacles, and of course the horses did not set up the unequal track. Like the racehorses, people must put forth efforts to accomplish their goals, but the obstacles people face are not equal. If an obstacle is not in our path, we may not be aware that such an obstacle exists for other people. Though white people may be aware of and perhaps even opposed to racism, they still don't

BOX 1-2

How Are You Privileged?

While teaching a women's studies course, Professor Peggy MacIntosh was lecturing about male privilege. One of her students asked about the privileges she as a white woman enjoyed. That triggered Professor MacIntosh's thinking. Back at her office, she began generating a list of the privileges she enjoyed as a member of the dominant racial group. Although it was difficult at first, she soon generated a list of forty white privileges. Try generating a list of your own advantages. Most people in U.S. colleges fall into at least one advantaged position. For example, by virtue of being in the United States even those in the lower classes enjoy a level of affluence unmatched by most other countries. Identify a privileged status you hold and list the advantages it brings.

Lists should include both micro- and macro-advantages. Most students will be able to identify micro-advantages. For example, white people have no difficulty finding "flesh" colored band aids that approximate their skin color. However, the macro-advantages may present more difficulty. A macro-advantage for white would be the high probability that homes in neighborhoods where whites are the majority will increase in value over time. You can generate a list of advantages by yourself or with a small group of friends or classmates. After generating your list, compare your advantages with advantages enjoyed by different groups. Is it easier to list your own advantages or those of other groups?

Your group:_____

Micro-Advantages	Macro-Advantages
1	1
2	2
3	3
4	4
5	5
6	6
7	7
8	8
9	9
10	10

experience racist obstacles in the same way as nonwhites experience them. Whether they are aware or not, whether they approve or not, whites are advantaged by racism.

Now let us consider racism from the minority race's perspective. What is it like to be immersed in a racist social structure? What effort does it take to overcome everyday prejudice and discrimination? Because racism is ongoing and pervasive, racial minorities become aware of racism at a young age. Evidence suggests that minorities develop the ability to anticipate and cope with racism (Aspinwall and Taylor 1997; Crocker, Major, and Steele 1998). The anticipation of racism may have as much effect on the lives of minorities as racist experiences. Once the possibility of encountering a racial obstacle is identified, individuals may choose a strategy to minimize the difficulty: avoiding the situation entirely or confronting the perceived perpetrator. Though such strategies may be a proactive way of controlling one's experience with racism, they also place constraints on the lives of minorities (Swim et al. 1998).

The perpetrators of the prejudice and discrimination range from strangers to long-term relationships. Even well-meaning friends can subject a minority group member to prejudice and discrimination. Racist experiences can be anything from street remarks made in passing to those involving long-term roles such as a student or employee. Commonly identified racist experiences include being watched, racial slurs, experiencing bad service, threats (including police threats), harassment, employment problems, and physical attack (Feagin 1991; Feagin and Sikes 1994; Swim et al. 1998).

There are relatively few studies on the prevalence of everyday racism. Between a third and half of minority respondents report experiencing some form of prejudice or discrimination over the previous year (cf. Sigelman and Welch 1991; D'Augelli and Herschberger 1993; Landrine and Klonoff 1996). Perhaps the most striking finding regarding everyday experience with racism is the gap between the perception of blacks and whites. Though a majority of African Americans report recent experience with racism, whites are much more likely to discount racism as a problem (Hacker 1995). People of different races experience the world and make sense of the world from different perspectives and with different perceptions.

In an attempt to learn firsthand what racism was like, a white journalist, John Howard Griffin, darkened his skin and shaved his head. In *Black Like Me* (1961) Griffin describes his sojourn in the Deep South experiencing life as a black man. Short of emulating Griffin's experience, it is difficult for members of the dominant racial group to fully appreciate the pervasiveness of racism. Racism affects every institution in our society and is experienced in a multitude of ways in everyday lives of racial and ethnic minorities.

Sexism refers to a social structure that gives advantages to men, relegating women to subservient positions. The complexity of sexism and its intersection with race and class make it more difficult to characterize sexism as a discrete system. More so than with racism, the targets and perpetrators of sexism are not easily distinguishable. In a sexist society women suffer oppression not only from men but also from other women. Further confusing the issue is the fact that men also suffer from gender limitations. For example, whereas women earn less money and constitute fewer elected officials, men are more often separated from their children by custody decisions. Another limitation that men in our culture suffer is an emotional one. The emotions men are allowed to express are severely constrained by gender norms. Men and boys are ridiculed if they cry or express tender or nurturing emotions. (See Box 1-3.)

Even though sexism harms men as well as women, it doesn't just silence women but practically erases their existence. In history, language, and culture the male experience is used as the neutral, common, or normative experience. If women's experiences are attended to at all, they are addendums, or worse, deviations. At its worst, sexism literally obliterates women's identity. For example, in some cultures neither birth records nor

---

BOX 1-3

Smile, Pretty Lady

According to Arlie Hochschild (1979, 1983) emotion creates, monitors, and preserves social bonds, but it's also an important component in social conflict and change. Thus, managing emotions is extremely important for both individuals and society. Hochschild calls the emotion management of one's self and others *emotional work.* Because women are in subordinate social positions, they have a special relationship to emotional work. Women are expected to manage and suppress their negative emotions, such as anger and aggression. In addition, because they are often dependent on men for financial support, women often engage in bolstering the emotional well-being of their husbands, boyfriends, and children.

The emotional management skills they learn in family relationships are often employed in their paid work. Women are more likely to work in nurturing professions, such as nursing, social work, and teaching. Hochschild refers to paid emotion work as the commercialization of feeling. She contends that when people are required to do emotion work as part of their job, there are consequences for their private lives. If one is required to sooth and cajole customers or clients all day at work, what happens to her ability to perform unpaid emotion work at home? If one is required to smile patiently and talk soothingly at work, the energy to genuinely feel those emotions is exhausted.

---

death records are kept for females. Women are legally barred from being seen or heard outside of their homes. They can own nothing, even the wages from their own labor. In its most extreme form, a husband or father has the authority to condemn a wife or daughter to death.

World governments have been extremely slow to interfere with gender oppression. It was not until 1993 that the denial of basic rights to women was declared a human rights violation by the United Nations. Two notorious examples of the denial of rights to women include gender apartheid and female genital mutilation (FGM). Though South Africa's racial apartheid was universally condemned, gender apartheid is still tolerated throughout the world. Female suffrage is far from universal, and most governments have laws that are applied differently to women and men. Even the United States has few such laws. For example, U.S. military draft laws apply to men only and some military career paths still legally exclude women.

Female Genital Mutilation is a cultural practice in many countries. Although the surgical procedure varies, FGM involves the partial or complete removal of the clitoris and the partial closure of the vaginal orifice. FGM is sometimes preformed without anesthetics on girls as young as two years of age. Perhaps the most shocking revelation about FGM is that some women in cultures practicing it defend the practice. They argue that their daughters would not be fit to marry if left intact. (See Box 1-4.)

How can women support practices that limit their opportunities and even physically harm them? To understand this phenomenon, you must remember that sexism is part of the social structure. The ideas, norms, and values that justify and perpetuate it

BOX 1-4

Female Genital Mutilation

Female genital mutilation is the term used to refer to the removal of part, or all, of the female genitalia. The most severe form is infibulation, also known as pharaonic circumcision. An estimated 15 percent of all mutilations in Africa are infibulations. The procedure consists of clitoridectomy (where all, or part of, the clitoris is removed), excision (removal of all, or part of, the labia minora), and cutting of the labia majora to create raw surfaces, which are then stitched or held together to form a cover over the vagina when they heal. A small hole is left to allow urine and menstrual blood to escape. In some less conventional forms of infibulation, less tissue is removed and a larger opening is left.

The vast majority (85 percent) of genital mutilations performed in Africa consist of clitoridectomy or excision. The least radical procedure consists of the removal of the clitoral hood. In some traditions a ceremony is held, but no mutilation of the genitals occurs. The ritual may include holding a knife next to the genitals, pricking the clitoris, cutting some pubic hair, or light scarification in the genital or upper thigh area.

The procedure is carried out at a variety of ages, ranging from shortly after birth to some time during the first pregnancy, but most commonly occurs between the ages of four and eight. According to the World Health Organization, the average age is falling. This indicates that the practice is decreasingly associated with initiation into adulthood, and this is believed to be particularly the case in urban areas. Some girls undergo genital mutilation alone, but mutilation is more often undergone as a group of, for example, sisters, other close female

relatives, or neighbors. Where FGM is carried out as part of an initiation ceremony, as is the case in societies in eastern, central, and western Africa, it is more likely to be carried out on all the girls in the community who belong to a particular age group. The procedure may be carried out in the girl's home or at the home of a relative or neighbor or in a health centre or, especially if associated with initiation, at a specially designated site, such as a particular tree or river. The person performing the mutilation may be an older woman, a traditional midwife or healer, a barber, or a qualified midwife or doctor. Girls undergoing the procedure have varying degrees of knowledge about what will happen to them. Sometimes the event is associated with festivities and gifts. Girls are exhorted to be brave. Where the mutilation is part of an initiation rite, the festivities may be major events for the community. Usually only women are allowed to be present. Sometimes a trained midwife will be available to give a local anesthetic. In some cultures, girls will be told to sit beforehand in cold water, to numb the area and reduce the likelihood of bleeding. More commonly, however, no steps are taken to reduce the pain. The girl is immobilized, held, usually by older women, with her legs open. Mutilation may be carried out using broken glass, a tin lid, scissors, a razor blade, or some other cutting instrument. When infibulation takes place, thorns or stitches may be used to hold the two sides of the labia majora together, and the legs may be bound together for up to 40 days. Antiseptic powder may be applied, or, more usually, pastes—containing herbs, milk, eggs, ashes,

(Continued)

BOX 1-4 (Continued)

or dung—which are believed to facilitate healing. The girl may be taken to a specially designated place to recover, where if the mutilation has been carried out as part of an initiation ceremony, traditional teaching is imparted. For the very rich, the mutilation procedure may be performed by a qualified doctor in hospital under local or general anesthetic.

SOURCE: © Amnesty International Publications, 1 Easton Street, London WC1X 0DW, United Kingdom. http://www.amnesty.org

are culturally pervasive. Sexism is not something men do to women; instead both sexes are socialized into and perpetuate sexism.

Though extreme variants of sexism shock and dismay most of us, everyday sexism is much more subtle and seemingly harmless. What, you may ask, is the problem with men opening doors for women? What harm can there be in an occasional wolf whistle? Who cares if mowing lawns, taking out the garbage, and changing the oil are men's work, and dishes and laundry are women's work? After all, "common sense" tells us that men and women are physically, psychologically, and intellectually suited to different roles. Though *everybody knows* that men and women are different, how they become different is the important issue for social scientists.

Sexism also encompasses prejudice against homosexuals. ***Heterosexism*** is part of the structure of sexism. It includes attitudes, behaviors, ideas, norms, policies, and forms of organization that derogates any nonheterosexual behavior or identity (Bem 1993; Jones 2002). Though discrimination based on sex is illegal owing to the 1964 Civil Rights Act, discrimination against gays, lesbians, and bisexuals is not illegal. Laws against sodomy were upheld by the U.S. Supreme Court until a 1986 court ruling was reversed in 2003. In almost every state, marriage is legally limited to heterosexuals only.[1] Openly identified homosexuals cannot remain in any branch of the U.S. military services. These are but a few of the examples of how heterosexism is enmeshed in our social institutions.

Heterosexism and ***homophobia*** (the fear and loathing of homosexuals) are important in understanding sexism because homosexuality blurs the distinctions between the genders. In our culture we expend a great deal of time, energy, and effort creating and maintaining distinctions between male and female behavior. Learning appropriate gender roles is one of the earliest and most comprehensive socialization processes we use to produce and maintain distinct social groups. Men and women learn different and somewhat complementary roles. However, those roles are not equally valued. Same-sex couples challenge the naturalness and legitimacy of gender and gender inequality.

---

[1]Since 2004 Massachusetts has recognized same-sex marriage. Connecticut, Vermont, New Jersey, California, and New Hampshire (from January 1, 2008) have created legal partnerships that offer all the rights and responsibilities of marriage. Maine, Hawaii, the District of Columbia, Oregon (from January 1, 2008) and Washington have enacted legal partnerships for same-sex couples that offer some, but not all, of the rights and responsibilities of marriage. Twenty-six states have constitutional amendments prohibiting same-sex marriage and explicitly banning the recognition of same-sex marriages performed by other states and jurisdictions.

In Chapters 5 and 6 we will discuss in detail the social construction of sexuality and the role of heterosexism in maintaining our patriarchal structure.

If we tried to eliminate the everyday forms of sexism from our behavior, we would have to be constantly vigilant. Remember, you couldn't just confine your attention to how you treat the other sex; you would have to attend to all your interactions with everyone. Sexism is so pervasive that it seems "natural." Therein lies one of the problems for social scientists studying sexism — gender prejudice and sexism are often not perceived as problems by those perpetuating them.

Recently while participating in a panel discussion on sexism, a well-dressed woman from the audience inquired, "What do you mean by oppression? I'm a woman and I don't feel oppressed?" She was an educated, intelligent woman from an affluent family. The advantages of her social class muted the effects of gender oppression. Differences in the way men and women are treated did not have the same consequences for her as they did for poor or working-class women. All three social structures — racism, sexism, and classism — can interact in ways that either dampen or amplify each other. This makes it difficult for people to recognize and understand their effects.

Classism refers to the entire structure of ideas, norms, values, policies, and forms of organization that results in advantages for the upper classes at the expense of the lower classes. In the postindustrial class system of the United States, classism is supported by capitalism. Unlike racism and sexism, class inequality is a legitimate part of our legal and economic system. Though laws protect us from discrimination based on race, religion, national origin, and sex, it is perfectly legal to use monetary resources and social status to exclude people from opportunities and desirable commodities. Social-class exclusiveness is seen as a hallmark of status, rather than a form of discrimination.

In the United States the denial of social classes is part of our history and value system. Opposition to the European class systems of the seventeenth to nineteenth centuries led to the popular idea that America was a land of opportunity where social classes did not exist. Differences in social and economic position were explained because of effort, intelligence, and talent. Rather than condemning great wealth as unfair hoarding of power and resources, it was celebrated as the realization of the American Dream.

Perhaps one of the best representations of the American Dream was the rags-to-riches stories made popular by Horatio Alger (1832–1898). Alger wrote over 134 books that featured stories about young boys from poor, disadvantaged families who overcame obstacles to achieve the American Dream (Nackenoff 1994). His immensely popular books were meant to inspire hard work and perseverance. His message was the same in all his books — success and riches were available to all who were honest and worked hard enough. Most people today are aware that social-class advantages have affects on education, careers, and finances, but the rags-to-riches ideology is still powerful. Ironically, in the land of equality for all, we dream of inequality — that is, we desire a larger share of resources for ourselves.

It has been argued that Americans have very low levels of class consciousness. *Class consciousness* is an awareness that a class structure exists and an awareness of one's place in that structure. The alleged openness of the class system, the hope of upward mobility, and difficulty assessing the social class of others have contributed to generally low levels of class consciousness among Americans. This, in turn, has contributed to the widespread myth that America is a classless society. Despite the myth, people do recognize class divisions and opposing class interests. Benjamin DeMott (1990) argues that although we maintain the classless delusion, awareness of and reference to social-class differences turns up regularly, especially in the commentary of politicians, pundits, and talk-show hosts.

There are few immediately observable differences in appearance or speech from which to infer social class. Mass marketing, mass education, and mass media have obscured social class beneath an enormous middle-class façade. Though we have difficulty determining the social class of casual acquaintances, we are capable of judging our own place in the class structure. The kind of work a person does is the way most people in the United States locate themselves in the social-class structure (Vanneman and Cannon 1987).

Whether people are aware of social class or not, class prejudices and stereotypes pervade the culture. Often mixed with regional and racial prejudices stereotypes such as "poor white trash," "rednecks," and "welfare queens" convey powerful attitudes about social class. Judgments about tastes in art, music, or clothing as "tacky" are also infused with class attitudes. Even though examples are less plentiful, the upper classes are also stereotyped. "Trophy wives," "preppies," and "rich snobs" are examples of a few of the stereotypes aimed at the affluent.

Parents teach class values to their children that ensure the replication and stability of the class structure. For example, the working class teaches the value of hard work by assigning chores to their children and encouraging after-school jobs. Middle-class parents teach the importance of education by stressing study over employment. But parents don't necessarily identify — or even know — their values as social-class values. The frequent intermarriage between members of poor and working classes and between working-class and middle-class families may also blur and blend class values.

In summary, there are three factors that make classism more difficult to recognize and comprehend. First, discrimination based on social class is legally and socially legitimate. Social-class exclusiveness is revered rather than chastised. Second, Americans have low class consciousness. The myth of a classless society combined with few visible social-class distinctions de-emphasizes the importance of social class (DeMott 1990). Third, people living in the United States blend, blur, and largely fail to recognize class prejudices and values. Thus unlike racism and sexism, classism is not a commonly recognized concept. In many ways classism is the least recognized, but most powerful of the three "isms."

OVERVIEW OF THE BOOK

The primary goal of this book is to understand what prejudices are, how they are formed and changed, and what purposes they serve. This will be accomplished by examining three types of prejudice: race, class, and gender. Section I defines prejudice and examines the consequences of prejudice and the purposes it serves in everyday interaction and at the societal level. The section will describe and examine each of the three types of prejudices.

Chapter 2 approaches prejudice as a type of attitude. The chapter describes the process of attitude formation and presents brief overview of attitude research. It goes on to describe the relationship between prejudice (as an attitude) and discrimination (as a behavior) and explores the reasons for the relatively weak link between the two. The chapter reviews and evaluates the methods used to measure prejudice in both sociology and psychology. Chapter 3 reviews major theories accounting for prejudice and attitude

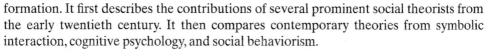

formation. It first describes the contributions of several prominent social theorists from the early twentieth century. It then compares contemporary theories from symbolic interaction, cognitive psychology, and social behaviorism.

Section II explores the relationships between prejudice, stereotypes, discrimination, and social structure are explored. Chapter 4 examines the role of stereotypes. The chapter first clarifies the difference between prejudice and stereotypes and then explores the relationship between the two phenomena. The chapter then analyzes the commonly held, widely recognized prejudices and stereotypes as well as prejudices that are more subtle or hidden. Finally, the chapter explores the symbolic value of prejudice and stereotypes and their relationship to other values.

Chapter 5 considers the link between prejudice, discrimination, and the social structure. Prejudice has been blamed for the discrimination and the persistence of racism and sexism, but the presence of racist and sexist structures in our society creates a greater and more rigid social inertia. Because social-class discrimination is legitimate, it presents a more insidious puzzle. Although Americans like to deny that they have social classes, some not-so-subtle class prejudices are used to support inequality and support the status quo. Chapter 6 explores the intersection of racism, sexism, and classism. The chapter addresses the role of social structure in the maintenance of prejudices. One of the defining differences between sociological social psychology and psychological social psychology concerns the role of social structure in prejudices. Sociologists contend that because prejudice is embedded in the social structure, attempts to alter the attitudes of individuals will have little impact on the levels of prejudice in the society. Prejudices are part of the ideology that justifies and supports systems of social inequality. The chapter also describes the differences and similarities between the processes used to create and maintain racial inequality, gender inequality and social-class inequality.

Section III will focus on the dynamics of prejudice. It addresses how prejudices are used at both the individual and group level. Social psychologists have a long tradition of work in intragroup and intergroup relations. If prejudices do not predict our behavior toward others, what do they accomplish? Chapter 7 begins with a discussion on how prejudice contributes to our sense of self. Prejudices help establish both individual and social identities. The chapter next explores different types of groups and explains differences in intragroup and intergroup dynamics. Prejudices are one of the ways with which groups create boundaries and promote homogeneity within groups. Finally, the role of leaders in the promotion or suppression of prejudice is explained.

Chapter 8 scrutinizes the role of prejudice in interaction. It describes how people use prejudice to anticipate the behavior of others, ascertain meaning, and interpret situations. Readers learn how people use prejudice as a rationale for their own behavior and as an explanation for the behavior of others. This includes a discussion on how people use prejudices to justify their social position and rationalize their advantages. Chapter 9 will focus on conditions under which changes in prejudice occur. It explores the strategies for prejudice reduction on the micro-, mezzo-, and macro-level and examines the plausibility of such strategies. Students will explore changes induced by education, pressures for social conformity, and antidiscrimination legislation. The chapter also explores what happens to subverted prejudice. When prejudice is hidden, denied, or recast as predilection, there are still consequences for both individuals and the entire society.

One goal of this book is to expose the denial of prejudice as both a self-deception and societal misrepresentation. It is *not* the aim of this book to justify or approve of prejudice. Although I argue that prejudice cannot be entirely eliminated because of its role in the process of making sense of the people and situations we encounter in every-day interaction, it can be reduced at the individual, group, and structural levels. I hope that a better understanding of its complexity will increase awareness of prejudices by individuals, further the understanding of the role of prejudice in intergroup relations, and lead to a greater understanding of the role of prejudice in interaction, group dynamics, and maintaining structural inequality and the status quo. Only by becoming aware of and acknowledging our prejudices can we, as a society, decrease the negative consequences of unbounded prejudice, misinformation, and unequal treatment.

Key Terms

- Classism
- Discrimination
- Heterosexism
- Homophobia

- Institutional discrimination
- Predilection
- Prejudice
- Racism

- Reverse discrimination
- Sexism
- Social structure
- Stereotype

Taking It Further — Class Exercises and Interesting Web Sites

How much do you know about your racial and ethnic heritage?

Race is a social phenomenon rather than a biological one. This exercise helps people understand how little of our own racial composition we know. Make a chart tracing your ancestry. Start with you, then your parents, then identify your maternal and paternal grandparents, then identify the four pairs of great-grandparents, then the eight pairs of great-great-grandparents. Go back as far as you can, identifying your ancestors by name, race, and ethnicity. Few people can complete every entry on the chart for more than a few generations.

You _____

Mother   Father
_____   _____

Grandparents   Grandparents
_____ _____   _____ _____
_____ _____   _____ _____

Great-Grandparents   Great-Grandparents
_____ _____   _____ _____
_____ _____   _____ _____

Great-Great-Grandparents   Great-Great-Grandparents
_____ _____   _____ _____
_____ _____   _____ _____
_____ _____   _____ _____
_____ _____   _____ _____

For more information about the social construction of race see the PBS Web site for their series Race the Power of Illusion (http://www.pbs.org/race/000_General/000_00-Home.htm)

Play the sorting game or learn more about what constitutes a race from the resources accompanying the films.

What social class am I?

Identify the social class to which you belong without reading the rest of this exercise? How did you place yourself in that class?

My social class is _____.

I decided I was in this class based on my _____.

Sociologists use multiple indicators to locate people in the class structure. Most use a combination of occupation, education, and income. The most important of these is occupation.

The wealthy don't usually have occupation because their income comes from interest, dividends, and sales of capital assets. You are wealthy if most or all of your income comes from your stocks, bonds, and other accumulated assets.

Jobs that require higher education, that are paid a salary rather than an hourly wage, and that require continual career development are classified as middle-class occupations.

The working-class work at skilled trades. They are usually paid an hourly wage and advance in their jobs through seniority. Carpenters, truck drivers, administrative assistants, and licensed practical nurses are examples of working-class jobs.

Poor people work at low-skill jobs that do not pay enough to support a family beyond minimal subsistence. The working poor often work multiple part-time jobs with few or no benefits. Unemployment hits this class first and hardest during economic recessions.

Now that you have read a sociological description of social class return to the question that began this exercise.

What is your social class?

Did your answer change?

For more information about social class see the PBS Web site accompanying the series *People Like Us* (http://www.pbs.org/peoplelikeus/). Play the games or read the stories about people and their social class.

References

Allport, Gordon W. 1954. *The nature of prejudice*. Reading, MA: Addison-Wesley Publishing Company. Amnesty International.

Aspinwall, Lisa G., and Shelley E. Taylor. 1997. A stitch in time: Self-regulation and proactive coping. *Psychological Bulletin* 121 (3): 417–436.

Bem, Sandra. 1993. *The lenses of gender: Transforming the debate on sexual inequality*. New Haven, CT: Yale University Press.

Blumer, Herbert. 1958. Race prejudice as a sense of group position. *Pacific Sociological Review* 1: 3–7.

Bobo, Lawrence, James R. Kluegel, and Ryan A. Smith. 1997. Laissez-faire racism: The crystallization of a kinder, gentler, antiblack ideology. In *Racial attitudes in the 1990s*, ed. S. Tuch and J. Martin. Westport, CT: Praeger Publishers.

Brown, Rupert. 1995. *Prejudice: Its social psychology*. Oxford: Blackwell Publishers Inc.

Crocker, J., B. Major, and C. Steele. 1998. Social stigma. In *Handbook of social psychology*. 4th ed. D. Gilbert, S. Fiske, and G. Lindzey. Boston, MA: McGraw Hill.

D'Augelli, A. R., and S. Herschberger. 1993. African American undergraduates on a predominantly white campus: Academic factors, social networks, and campus elite. *Journal of Negro Education* 62: 67–81.

DeMott, Benjamin. 1990. *The imperial middle class: Why Americans can't think straight about class*. New York: Morrow.

Devine, Patricia. 1989. Stereotypes and prejudice: Their automatic and controlled components. *Journal of Personality & Social Psychology* 56 (1): 5–18.

Ellis, Angele, and Marilyn Llweellyn. 1997. *Dealing with differences: Taking action on class, race, gender and disability*. Thousand Oaks, CA: Corwin Press, Inc.

Feagin, John R. 1991. The continuing significance of race: Antiblack discrimination in public places. *American Sociological Review* 56: 101–116.

Feagin, John, and M. Sikes. 1994. *Living with racism: The black middle class experience*. Boston, MA: Beacon Press.

Griffin, John Howard. 1961. *Black like me*. Boston, MA: Houghton Mifflin Publishers.

Hacker, Andrew. 1995. *Two nations: Black and white, separate, hostile, unequal*. New York: Ballentine Books.

Hochschild, Arlie. 1979. Emotion work, feeling rule and social structure. *American Journal of Sociology* 85: 551–575.

———. 1983. *The managed heart: Commercialization of human feelings*. Berkley, CA: University of California Press.

Hughes, Michael. 1997. Symbolic racism, old-fashioned racism, and whites' opposition to affirmative action. In *Racial Attitudes in the 1990s*, ed. S. Tuch and J. Martin, 45–75. Westport CT: Praeger Publishers.

Jones, Linda. 2002. *Social psychology of prejudice*. Upper Saddle River, NJ: Prentice Hall.

Landrine, H., and E. Klonoff. 1996. The schedule of racist events: A measure of racial discrimination and a study of its negative physical and mental health consequences. *Journal of Black Psychology* 22: 144–168.

Lippman, Walter. 1922. *Public opinion*. New York: MacMillan.

Marger, Martin N. 2000. *Race and ethnic relations: American and global perspectives*. 5th ed. New York: Wadsworth.

McIntosh, Peggy. 1989. White privilege: Unpacking the invisible knapsack. *Peace and Freedom* July/August: 10–12.

Monteith, Margo J., Julia R. Zuwerink, and Patricia G. Devine. 1994. Prejudice and prejudice reduction: Classic challenges, contemporary approaches. In *Social cognition: Impact on social psychology*, ed. P. G. Devine, D. L. Hamilton, and T. M. Ostrom, 323–346. San Diego, CA: Academic Press, Inc.

Moore, Timothy E., Karen Griffiths, and Barbara Payne. 1987. Gender, attitudes towards women, and the appreciation of sexist humor. *Sex Roles* 16: 521–531.

Nackenoff, Carol. 1994. *The fictional republic: Horatio Alger and American political discourse*. New York: Oxford University Press.

National Center for Criminal Justice. 2000. Taking America's pulse II. http://www.nccj.org/.

National Opinion Research Center. 1983–1987. General Social Survey. http://webapp.icpsr. umich.edu/GSS/.

———. 1988–1991. General Social Survey. http://webapp.icpsr.umich.edu/GSS/.

Olson, Steve. 2002. *Mapping human history: Gene, race and our common origins*. Boston, MA: Houghton Mifflin Company.

Ryan, Kathryn, and Jeanne Kanjorski. 1998 . The enjoyment of sexist humor, rape attitudes, and relationship aggression in college students. *Sex Roles* 38: 743–756.

Schuman, H., C. Steeh, and L. Bobo. 1985. *Racial attitudes in American: Trends and interpretations*. Cambridge, MA: Harvard University Press.

Sigelman, Lee, and Susan Welch. 1991. *Black Americans' views of racial inequality*. Cambridge, MA: Cambridge University Press.

Swim, Janet, Laurie Cohen, and Lauri Hyers. 1998. Experiencing everyday prejudice and discrimination. In *Prejudice: The target's perspective*, ed. J. Swim and C. Stangor, 37–60. San Diego, CA: Academic Press.

Swim, Janet K., and Charles Stangor. 1998. *Prejudice: The target's perspective*. San Diego, CA: Academic Press.

Theriault, Stephen, and Dianne Holmberg. 1998. The new old-fashioned girl: Effects of gender and social desirability on reported gender-role ideology. *Sex Roles* 39 (1–2): 97–112.

Vanneman, Reeve, and Lynn Weber Cannon. 1987. *The American perception of class*. Philadelphia, PA: Temple University Press.

C H A P T E R

Prejudice and Attitudes

2

In this chapter, prejudice will be defined as a type of attitude. The process of attitude formation will be described and a brief overview of attitude research will be presented.

Whenever my extended family gets together for a weekend or a holiday, talk of politics and social controversy is as much a part of the gathering as food, drink, and the latest photographs of the children. My father can always be counted on for politically conservative perspectives. My daughter will give the environmentalist view. My brother-in-law usually articulates the corporate perspective, and my sister explains her views as a stay-at-home mother. Only rarely does everyone agree. However, in our conversation, we do not expect to agree—the conversation serves a much more important purpose. We are each articulating our understanding of current issues from our differing social positions. We share with each other how we have come to understand the world. The attitudes people express are formed partly by the roles and social positions that they occupy. For example, because I am a working wife and mother, I have formed strong attitudes about women's rights and equal employment opportunity. Though my sister shares many of those attitudes, her role as a full-time homemaker has made her wary of according women respect only when they have paid occupational roles. Our attitudes about gender have been shaped by experiences we've had and the social roles we've performed. Being a male or female or being a stay-at-home parent or a working parent affects how we understand the world and the attitudes we form about it.

The same is true for attitudes about social class and race. People will use the values and experiences they have acquired from their social-class background to interpret the society around them. African Americans, Latinos, Chinese Americans, and Arab Americans use their subcultural vantage points to interpret the wider society. Because we occupy different positions in society, it should not be surprising that attitudes differ not only between individuals but also among social groups.

WHAT IS AN ATTITUDE?

Before we study attitude variation across groups, it's important to learn what social scientists mean by attitude. The study of attitudes and attitude change has been one of the most important concepts in social psychology. Unfortunately, for the student who wants a clear definition, there have been decades of debate on exactly what attitudes are, how to measure them, and what relationship they have to behaviors. Whereas some social psychologists have defined attitudes as simply as our "likes and dislikes" (Bem 1970), others have argued that as a scientific concept *attitude* is convoluted and logically flawed (Blummer 1955). One of the problems with understanding the concept is that the term is commonly used to refer to a number of different kinds of reactions. It can refer to a manner, disposition, feeling, or even a physical position as when someone displays a relaxed attitude. Symbolic interactionist Joel Charon (1989:19) uses a definition of attitude that combines three distinct components: an ***attitude*** is a "set of beliefs and feelings toward an object that predisposes the person to act in a certain manner when confronted by that object (or class of objects)." Social psychologists have identified these three components as cognitive (beliefs), affective (feelings), and behavioral (actions) (Breckler 1984).

Cognitive attitudes are ideas and beliefs a person has about an object, person, group, or behavior. Cognitive attitudes are part of a larger reasoning process, the goal of which is to create a definition of the situation that makes sense of what is going on around us. Our beliefs about an object are part of that process. There are several steps in this process. First, we recall information from our memory of experiences that seems relevant to the ongoing situation. For example, early one morning as I was coming to work, I encountered in the hallway a person that I had never met before. Because I work in a small building that houses faculty offices, it was unusual to encounter a stranger, especially so early in the morning. I needed to "make sense" of the stranger. I was about to ask him if I could be of help when he went into the restroom. I went on to my office but continued to wonder about the stranger. As I thought about the stranger, I used what little information about the man to construct possible explanations. I noticed he was a male and was wearing dark-blue workmen's clothing. I reasoned that he could be a member of the maintenance staff. I also noticed his race, but because our campus employs a diverse group of maintenance workers, it didn't further my attempt to "make sense" of the stranger's presence in my office building. As the day continued, I asked several others in the building if they had seen the man or knew of any maintenance being done on the building. My coworkers offered several possible explanations for a stranger in the building before eight o'clock in the morning. Someone suggested we call maintenance and find out if workmen were assigned to the building that day. The suggestions gave us a way of defining the situation and directed our subsequent actions.

In the second step of the reasoning, people combine their memories of similar experiences with the ongoing experiences and respond to the particular situation. Continuing with the example of the stranger, after finding out that no maintenance crew had been dispatched to the building, we needed to create another explanation to account for the stranger. My colleagues and I recalled similar experiences from our memories as we began voicing worries and fears. Yet another part of the reasoning process was also happening. We were engaged in a process of social inference, or reasoning. Our responses defined what was going on, allowing us to give meaning to an ambiguous situation and take action based on that definition. We had experienced several petty thefts from offices in the past few months, so we combined the information we had about the sex, age, class, and race of the person I had observed with our recent experiences. A strange man, well beyond the age of most college students, dressed in workmen's clothes, and a member of a minority race was in the building before normal business hours, and we had recently had an experience with petty theft. Our reasoning was obviously influenced by our prejudices. The stranger did not have the characteristics we expected of a student or colleague. When our initial supposition that he was a maintenance worker could not be confirmed, we constructed another explanation based partially on experience and partially on gender, class, and racial prejudices. We suspected that he might be a thief or vagrant.

In this case, prejudiced attitudes affected the ideas about the stranger who appeared at an unusual time in our small office building and the assessment of possible danger. My colleagues and I never did find out who the man was. The accuracy of the ideas and information is not the crucial factor. What mattered was not whether we were right about the stranger but that we defined the situation and were able to "make sense" of it. There were multiple prejudices that affected the process of making sense of the stranger. Although most Americans first think of race when discussing prejudices, there were also gender, class, and age prejudices that affected my interpretation of the stranger. I focused on these characteristics because they were immediately visible and I had no further interaction or information to help me give meaning to the encounter. Had the gender, age, or symbols of social class been different, I would have undoubtedly constructed different scenarios to explain the stranger. For example, had the man been wearing business clothes, I might have assumed he was a textbook representative; had he been younger, I might have assumed he was a student; had the person been female, fear may not have been a factor and the need to make sense of the situation may have been less pressing.

One of my colleagues in the building offered a strikingly similar experience. She encountered an unknown man in the same hallway about 9:30 one evening, long after the doors should have been locked. His age, clothing, and deferential attitude led her to assume he was a student, and thus she reasoned that he posed no threat to her. However, she was honest enough to wonder aloud whether she would have reached a different conclusion had he been African American.

I used this example in class and had still another response. When I asked students to "make sense" of the evening intruder my colleague had encountered, one woman said she would have been immediately suspicious that the young man was "up to no good." When asked to elaborate, she said that when a man—particularly a white man—acts deferential to a woman, he either wants something or is covering up something. Her interpretation was one I had not, until that moment, considered. In my own process of making sense of the encounter, I, like my colleague, had exempted the college-aged white man from suspicion. My student, who was an African American woman, did not exempt white men from suspicion. Thus, the cognitive aspect of prejudice includes both negative and positive prejudices and the activation of prejudices may be related to group membership and respective group position within our stratification system (cf. Blummer 1958).

When a cognitive attitude involves prejudice, the information is, by definition, flawed. We use hearsay, stereotypes, and accounts from others that we may know are biased. If we stop to examine our prejudices, we may even reject them as ignorance. The important distinction is that cognitive attitudes are ideas, information, and knowledge that we use as if it were true, to help us understand and give meaning to what is going on around us.

Affective attitudes are the feelings or emotional responses a person has toward an object, person, group, or behavior. The feelings associated with attitudes are perhaps the most familiar, and at times disturbing, component of attitudes. Sometimes we have clear-cut *gut* feelings about a person or group. A gut reaction is a familiar and seemingly simple reaction, but if one stops to consider these reactions, they are seldom clear-cut and simple.

Affective attitudes can be confusing because people can have both positive and negative emotions toward a single group. For example, I love and enjoy being with young children, but I also find them difficult and at times irritating. As a group children evoke conflicting emotional responses. It is difficult to say one simply likes or does not like children because emotional reactions toward children (or any group) depend on the social context. The relationship between the target group and one's own group influences the affective response. For example, the laughter of the children playing in the schoolyard across from my office window triggers a smile and nostalgia for my own childhood. However, if I were responsible for overseeing the behavior of the same group of children, or if they were to pay an impromptu visit to my office building, no doubt my affective attitude would be altered.

Mark Zanna (1994) describes a study that asked college students to describe their feelings toward several different groups and analyzed the content of the students' responses. He found that the emotions toward different groups varied in tone. Attitudes toward homosexuals were the most negative. They included confusion, discomfort, and disgust. Responses to other groups, such as French-Canadians, exhibited a wider range of response from pride to resentment. The response to different groups was more complex than simply liking or disliking an out-group. The relationship between one's own group and the target group is part of the affective component of prejudice. For example, a heterosexual man might view homosexual men as threatening and pushy. A heterosexual woman may view homosexual men as less threatening than heterosexual men. Affective responses to social groups and to the relationships between groups are part of the affective component of prejudice toward a social group and are perhaps the most complex and dynamic components of prejudice.

Behavioral attitudes are tendencies toward action connected to an object, person, group, or behavior. The behavioral component is perhaps the most contentious part of the study of attitudes. The link between attitudes and behavior is complex and difficult to predict. Behavioral attitudes may be as subtle as an incipient tightening of muscles or as overt as refusing service to a member of a racial minority. Besides the difficulties posed by the wide range of behavioral attitudes, situational constraints on behavior often override behavioral tendencies. In other words, what one thinks one will do when confronted with a hypothetical situation may be far different from one's behavior in an actual situation because behavior is determined by more than attitudes.

La Piere's 1934 classic study demonstrated how attitudes and behaviors can seem inconsistent. During the 1920s and 1930s there was substantial anti-immigrant prejudice in the United States. In the western United States, anti-Chinese sentiments were especially common. La Piere and a Chinese couple attempted to secure lodgings and to be served at restaurants in numerous cities and towns. Although they visited sixty-six places offering lodging and 184 eating establishments, they were refused service only once. About two months after the visits, La Piere sent mailed questionnaires to each establishment that had been visited and to a control group of establishments that were not visited. The questionnaire asked whether they would serve members of the Chinese race as guests in their establishment (La Piere 1934:232). More than 92 percent of the hotels and restaurants said they would not serve Chinese patrons.

Other studies have demonstrated a similar discrepancy between verbal accounts of prejudice and actual behaviors (cf. Saenger and Gilbert 1950; Kutner et al. 1952; Minard 1952). Long before the Civil Rights Acts was passed, Kutner, Wilkins, and Yarrow (1952) designed a field experiment similar to La Piere's. They sent two white female assistants to obtain a table for three at eleven restaurants in the New York area. Shortly after the two white patrons were seated, they were joined by a young black woman. In no case was the party refused service. Later each restaurant was sent a letter seeking reservations for a mixed race party. None of the proprietors responded to the letters, and when follow-up calls were made, all of them made excuses to avoid making the reservations.

How do social psychologists explain this discrepancy? Kutner and colleagues (1952) explained that it is more difficult to discriminate in face-to-face situations. Gordon Allport, one of the most influential early scholars studying prejudice, contended that discrimination and prejudice are practiced in covert, indirect ways to avoid embarrassment (1966). In other words, we may sincerely hold prejudiced behavioral propensities, but the social constraints of a face-to-face interaction may inhibit our actions. This has been called a *social-adjustive* function. The social-adjustive function operates to inhibit prejudice in some situations and facilitate it in others (Sampson 1999). For example, almost everyone can recall an incident at some family gathering when a member of the family expressed a prejudiced attitude. How you react to the prejudice depends on several variations in group dynamics such as the size of the group, the perception of support for the attitude among others in the group, and the relative statuses of the persons within the group. Hypothetically, if your grandfather expressed a prejudice at an extended family gathering it is less likely that you would voice a dissenting attitude than if a younger sister or brother expressed a similar attitude among two or three of your cousins.

In large groups responsibility to speak against prejudice may be diffused in the same way that the helping responses are weakened when the number of persons observing another person in need of assistance (cf. Darley and Latane 1968; Darley and Batson 1973). Even those objecting to a blatantly expressed prejudice may wait to see the response of others in the group before committing themselves to action.

The perception of group support for a prejudice can also weaken the link between attitude and behavior. If no one else in the group immediately objects to an expression of prejudice, this may be interpreted as tacit support for the attitude. The more support an individual perceives for the prejudice, the less likely they are to object to it. Group pressure, whether perceived or real, can alter behavior.

The classic experiments by Solomon Asch (1952) clearly demonstrate the effects of group pressure on individual judgment and behavior. Asch found that even in the simple task of comparing three lines of different lengths, a substantial minority of individuals altered their judgment to conform to "incorrect" answer given by others. The larger and more unanimous the group, the more likely research subjects were to conform to the group judgment (1952). The same can be applied to the expression of prejudice. Hesitation to speak against prejudice can create the illusion of group support for prejudice. Here again, it is the perception of group support for the prejudice that is important, not whether there is actual support.

Both internal (within a group) and external (the roles and positions outside of the group) status can affect the link between attitude and behavior. Kirchler and Davis (1986) designed an experiment to demonstrate the effect of status on changing decisions. In this experiment, subjects took a test that purported to measure decision-making ability. Then the subjects worked individually on several different problems. One task was intellectual and had a correct answer, whereas another was judgmental and was more a matter of opinion. After the subjects completed their tasks individually, they were assigned to three-person groups and instructed to make group decisions about each problem. Before the group work began, scores on the decision-making ability test were announced to the group. Some subjects were told they had low scores and others were told their scores were moderate or high. In actuality the scores that were announced were fictional; all the scores were randomly assigned. The groups were then asked to discuss the problems and come to some collective decisions. The experimenters wanted to see if the status assigned by virtue of the fictional decision-making ability score would influence which persons changed their individual decisions during the process of coming to a group decision. They found that in problems that had a correct answer (intellectual tasks), having the correct answer rather than status predicted who changed their decisions. However, in the judgmental task, status had an effect on who was more likely to change. In groups with equal status, members of the majority opinion won out, but in groups in which one member had a higher status than the others, the high-status member influenced the group decision. In prejudice, as in the judgmental task in the aforementioned experiment, status plays a role in acquiescence. High-status persons can influence the judgment of groups and affect their attitudes.

Behavioral attitudes (tendencies toward action) are a difficult component of attitudes to predict and understand. What we think we will do is often different from what we actually do because face-to-face interaction is more complex and potentially more constraining than expressing an opinion or predicting what one would do in an imagined hypothetical scenario. Group dynamics such as group size, perceived group support for prejudice, and the social status of people within the group can either inhibit or facilitate prejudice and discrimination.

FUNCTIONS OF ATTITUDES

Jack Levin (1975) argued that prejudices help serve functions both at the individual level in our interactions with and understanding of others and at the societal level by supporting and justifying the social structure. Social psychologists have further categorized the functions that prejudice serves into three levels: the *micro*, or individual, level, the *mezzo,* or group, level, and the *macro,* or societal, level.

Micro-Level Functions

Social psychologists have identified many purposes that prejudice serves for individuals as they interact and try to make sense of what is going on around them. Because prejudices are dynamic components of interaction, trying to create an exhaustive list of the purposes prejudices serve would be both unending and futile. Nonetheless, there has been substantial research into four commonly identified individual-level functions of prejudice: cognitive formation, value expression, ego defense, and utilitarian functions.

The *cognitive formation function* helps us simplify and integrate complex, rapidly changing information. Put simply, prejudices are employed as a mental shortcut. If you stop to think about it, human beings continuously process an immense amount of information. To figure out how to respond to this onslaught of stimuli, people categorize their experiences. People categorize new experiences by either their similarity or their contrast with other experiences or previously categorized information. This information-sorting process depends on making broad generalizations. Consider one of the most basic human categorizations: whether a person is female or male. If you were to describe traits common to women, you might mention nurturing, whereas men might be described as aggressive. Although we surely have all had experiences that run counter to these generalizations, we nonetheless use generalizations to help us anticipate or predict the behavior of others. Widely held beliefs and expectations about people based on social categorizations are called *stereotypes.* Stereotypes are composed of simplified and overgeneralized characteristics attributed to people based on group membership. And because they are *over* generalized, they are inaccurate. Even though some members of the group may exhibit the stereotyped characteristic, it may not accurately be applied to all or even most members of the group.

If on at least some level people are aware that stereotypes are inaccurate, why do they use them? Symbolic interaction theory explains that people interpret and anticipate the behavior of others both through their own direct experience with others and by a process known as the *generalized other.* When we are introduced to a new social environment, either during infancy/early childhood or later when entering into a new adult role, we have to learn what to expect from other people. Initially we carefully watch how other people respond in the unfamiliar environment. We may even consider a more experienced person as a *significant other.* We have many significant others throughout our lives. A significant other is a real person, such as a parent, a close friend, a teacher, or a mentor, whose responses to the social world influence our own understanding and the meanings we give to the world around us. In other words, we pay close attention to the behaviors and responses of the significant other and use them in our own attempts to *make sense* of the new environment. As we accumulate experiences in the new social environment we begin to build a set of expectations, based on our own experiences and the expectations we have culled from interactions with significant others. Gradually these expectations form the bases of the *generalized other.* A generalized other is not a real person. Rather, we compile our accumulated experiences and expectations and use them to anticipate and understand the behavior of others.

Stereotypes are incorporated into the generalized other at two levels: individually and culturally. *Individual stereotypes* are beliefs and expectations about a group that derive from experience with members of that group. For example, from my own experience working at colleges and universities, I have developed an individual stereotype about the characteristics of professors. My individual stereotype for professors includes traits such as detail oriented, contemplative, and argumentative. This description does not entirely match the cultural stereotype of the brainy, absentminded, slightly dowdy, and usually male professor.

Cultural stereotypes are widely shared beliefs about groups that emerge not from direct experience but from popular knowledge or what we sometimes refer to as *common sense*. Cultural stereotypes are especially interesting to social psychologists because they emerge from and reflect the structures that organize social life. We adopt cultural stereotypes that have already been formed though individual stereotypes emerge from our experience with a group. Nonetheless, cultural stereotypes affect how experience with the stereotyped group is interpreted. If you hold stereotypes about a group, you will use the stereotype to understand and make sense of their behavior. Thus, it seems as if the stereotype is confirmed by experience because we impose the stereotype on our experience to help make sense of ongoing situations.

The cognitive function of stereotypes is part of the schema we use to categorize, organize, and interpret people and events in our ongoing social world. Because of the complex and dynamic nature of human society, these schemas are at best oversimplified and overgeneralized. We not only develop individual stereotypes based on our own experiences, but impose cultural stereotypes to interpret other groups. These cultural stereotypes become self-confirming because they influence what we notice, how we interpret, and what we remember about the group.

The *value expression function* allows people to express important components of personality. *Values* are standards that people use to decide what goals and outcomes are desirable (Hewitt 1988). Prejudices may be used to display or indicate other underlying social values. For example, many middle-class people in the United States have learned to value meritocracy, or what has been called the *Protestant Ethic.* That is, they believe that working hard and developing one's talents (i.e., merit) will lead to success and rewards. This belief can also be used to explain why some people remain at the bottom of the social and economic hierarchy. Therefore, disdain for and prejudice against the homeless or poor is an expression of an underlying belief in a stratification system based on merit.

Value expressive attitudes can be used in strategies to reduce prejudice. Milton Rokeach developed a strategy called the *value confrontation model of change* (Rokeach 1979; Rokeach and Ball-Rokeach 1989). Through Rokeach's research and that of others (cf. Schwartz and Bilsky 1987; Snyder 1987; Katz and Hass 1988; Sidanius 1988) two central values were identified that were related to antiblack racial prejudice: freedom and equality.

Freedom is related to the concept of meritocracy and the Protestant Ethic. Sociologist Max Weber (1930) argued that the capitalist economic system required the support of a religious ideology to spread. Capitalism found its ideology in Protestant insecurity about salvation. According to Protestant theologies, spiritual salvation is granted by the grace of God, but only God knows which persons are destined for salvation. Not knowing who will be saved or damned creates anxiety, so people look for evidence of God's grace in the achievements and possessions a person accumulated. Those who are successful are no doubt in God's grace; those who are failures are obviously displeasing to

God. According to this belief, prosperity is not the cause of salvation; rather it is the consequence of God's pleasure. Thus, God's will is reflected materially and hard work is a virtue. People should be allowed the individual liberty—or freedom—necessary to reveal God's grace. They have the freedom to work hard—or not—to shape their own destiny and to accept the consequences of their own efforts.

The value for freedom and meritocracy conflicts with another core value—the value for equality. People who value equality emphasize social responsibility toward others and a society of equal rights and equal treatment for everyone. People who valued individual freedom were more likely to agree with antiblack prejudice, while people who valued equality were less likely to agree with antiblack prejudice (Katz and Hass 1988). Rokeach reasoned that if people could be persuaded to value equality over freedom, prejudice against blacks and other minorities could be reduced.

The strategy Rokeach developed was designed to force a confrontation between these two core values. First, participants were asked to rank order a list of values from least important to most important. Then they were exposed to a brief lecture about how their rankings were compared with other participants. They were informed that those who rank freedom higher than equality were interested in more freedom for themselves, not for others. The last step involved completing an attitude questionnaire containing questions about different social issues, including race relations and racial prejudice.

This strategy has been tested numerous times (Grube et al. 1994). A review of these studies indicated that the value confrontation techniques changed people's value rankings, decreased racial prejudice, and reduced prejudice behavior. Not only did value confrontation have immediate effects, it continued to affect people's attitudes and behaviors in follow-up studies done almost two years later.

The value expression function is important because it allows people to communicate key values that are part of how they define themselves and because it has been effective in persuading people to change their attitudes.

The *ego defense function* refers to using prejudices to bolster self-esteem. People, especially those who feel threatened, sometimes project negative attributes onto others to protect themselves from their own negative attributes and impulses. However, these people may not be aware that they are shifting the anger over their own insecurities onto the target group. Thus, for these people education and prejudice reduction strategies, such as the value confrontation approach, do not work because they rely upon the subjects' awareness of prejudice and their motivation to reduce it. Anger and hatred directed at an out-group helps persons define themselves and allows them to raise their self-esteem by comparison. Such people literally define themselves through their hatred. In a sense, their personalities are held together by hatred. The target group provides a contrast against which the person can construct boundaries and differences between themselves and the out-group. Rather than constructing a social identity proactively, a person using prejudice as an ego defense constructs their social identity negatively, in reaction to the target group.

Although the ego defense function has been identified as a component in the authoritarian personality, one need not have authoritarian tendencies to use prejudice as an ego defense. Fein and Spencer (1997) created experimental conditions that induced people to use prejudices against out-groups as a way of maintaining positive self-image. Experimental subjects were given an intelligence test and were given false-negative feedback. They were then asked to complete a judgmental task about a struggling

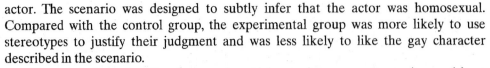

actor. The scenario was designed to subtly infer that the actor was homosexual. Compared with the control group, the experimental group was more likely to use stereotypes to justify their judgment and was less likely to like the gay character described in the scenario.

The ego defense function is a way in which people can use comparisons with an out-group to define themselves and bolster their own self-esteem. But because it is a reactive rather than proactive construction of the self, it is both a precarious and an irrational strategy. Prejudices adopted for ego defense are resistant to rational argument and anti-prejudice education.

Utilitarian functions of prejudice refer to using prejudices to obtain rewards or avoid sanctions. According to social exchange theory, people engage in interactions to obtain benefits from the process. Interactions and relationships that are rewarding persist, and those that are not are short-lived. Prejudiced attitudes can be linked to ideas, interactions, and events associated with reward or sanction. For example, people who have been rewarded with implicit praise or peer status when they have expressed prejudice are likely to continue to express prejudice. The prejudice continues not only because of the past reward but because the person expressing the prejudice anticipates further rewards. Fortunately, the utilitarian function of prejudice also responds to sanctions or punishment. If prejudice is associated with negative interactional consequences, expression of the prejudice may be inhibited.

On the surface, the utilitarian function may be confused with ingratiation, "political correctness," or "brown nosing." However, the process of attitude formation and change is considerably more complex. The dynamic nature of interaction and the process of making sense of interaction occur continually and with great speed. We often form attitudes in response to the emerging interactional situation. That means that we don't have the leisure to reflect on the implications or consistency of the attitudes we express. However, the reaction of the person we are interacting with provides feedback, which helps us to give meaning to the interaction and define the situation. If expressions of prejudice are met with approval, the interaction is not disrupted. The person expressing the prejudice has received the interactional reward and need not reflect further on the meaning or consequences of the prejudice. However, if the prejudice is met with disapproval, the interaction may be disrupted, which causes further reflection on the prejudice. Swim and Hyers (1999) illustrate the interactional dilemma involved in challenging prejudice. They undertook two studies that demonstrated the tension between challenging sexist remarks and the interactional costs of publicly responding to sexism. Although 45 percent of the women subjects objected to the man who made a sexist remark, only 15 percent did so directly. The results from their research indicated that social pressure to be polite, fear of possible retaliation, and diffusion of responsibility inhibited subjects' confrontation.

Social psychologists have identified many micro-level functions of prejudice (e.g., Katz 1960; Levin 1975; Ruscher 2001). Four widely identified micro-functions include cognitive formation, value expression, ego defense, and utilitarian functions. Researchers identifying these components don't always agree on the interpretation of these functions because they use a variety of different theoretical perspectives coming from two academic disciplines: sociology and psychology. While the terms used to identify them and the theoretical understanding of their purpose may differ slightly, the four micro-functions discussed in this section have proved useful concepts in understanding the dynamics of prejudice.

Mezzo-Level Functions

The mezzo level of analysis connects individuals to others in groups. This level of analysis bridges the gap between the micro-/individual level and the macro-/or structural level of analysis. Two often identified mezzo- or group-level functions of prejudice are the social functions and the group justification function.

Social functions refer to using prejudices to identify with and gain acceptance to social groups. Sharing prejudices with a group of like-minded people helps create boundaries between the in-group and the out-group. Derogating or putting down the out-group creates in-group solidarity and fosters loyalty among members of the in-group (e.g., Sherif et al. 1961; Hogg and Abrams 1988). Solidarity among group members varies greatly depending on the size, type, and purpose of the group. In a ***primary group*** such as a family, closeness and a sense of belonging are forged through the intimacy and relative permanence of the group. In larger ***secondary groups,*** membership is more formal, more impersonal, and less permanent. The feeling of belonging, or "we-ness," is harder to establish and members may have a weaker group identity. One way for groups to create stronger group identity is to pit members of the in-group against an out-group. Out-group derogation creates unity, but it also fosters group conflict, anger, and hatred.

Noel, Wann, and Branscombe (1995:127) conducted two experiments demonstrating that out-group derogation can enhance the effect of an insecure status within an in-group. In the first study, in-group membership was manipulated experimentally. In the second study, members and pledges to campus fraternities and sororities were used to represent secure and insecure group members, respectively. Both experiments found that people with insecure group status were more likely to publicly make negative out-group statements. Pledges were more likely to publicly derogate out-group members than active members of the fraternities and sororities.

Expressing prejudice and derogating other groups creates boundaries between in-groups and out-groups. It also allows peripheral members to gain acceptance and demonstrate loyalty to the in-group.

Group justification functions help foster collective self-esteem. The group justification function operates in two ways. First, it acts to bolster our collective social identity by exaggerating the differences between the in-group and out-groups. If we feel good about the groups we belong to, our self-esteem is positively affected. Positive prejudices and stereotypes about the in-group coupled with negative prejudices against the out-group enhance our collective group esteem and justify the exploitation and oppression of out-groups.

The second way in which the group justification functions is more subtle and complex. Membership in a targeted group can damage the self-esteem of group members. Symbolic interaction theory explains that the responses of others serve as a looking glass in which we see ourselves reflected (Mead 1934; Cooley 1970). According to the concept of the ***looking glass self,*** when others respond to us we incorporate those reactions into how we understand and define ourselves. Thus, positive responses should elevate self-esteem, whereas negative responses should lower it.

Extending this micro-level theory to the mezzo-level adds complications. Members of devalued groups recognize the negative responses from the members of groups with higher status. Thus, these responses should become internalized, producing lower self-esteem. Indeed early research on self-esteem among African American children (Clark and Clark 1947) became one of the pivotal arguments in a Supreme Court case that outlawed segregation (*Brown v. Topeka* 1954). However, more recent research focusing on the experience of groups targeted by prejudice has indicated that this is not always the case. The group justification function of prejudice can actually enhance collective social identity.

Social identity theory contends that part of our sense of self derives from group memberships (Taijfel 1982; Taijfel et al. 2004). However, self-esteem among minority group members is not always lower than dominant group members, and in some cases it is actually higher (e.g., Crocker and Major 1989). Opposition from out-groups can operate to protect group identity. Branscombe, Schmitt, and Harvey (1999) found that the negative consequences of being a target of prejudice can be neutralized by a social identity as a minority group member. In other words, the effects of prejudice can be counterbalanced by attributing prejudice to an external cause. If the negative reaction is attributed to being a member of a minority group, instead of stemming from a justified difference in behavior, self-esteem is not negatively affected.

The mezzo-level functions of prejudice explain how individual attitudes and behavior are related to group dynamics. The social function of prejudice serves to create and maintain group boundaries and produce loyalty to the in-group. The group justification function fosters collective group esteem and justifies prejudice and discrimination toward other groups. Mezzo-level functions also provide a bridge between micro-level analysis of individuals and macro-level explanation of social structures.

Macro-Level Functions

The macro- or societal level of analysis is perhaps the most important level at which prejudice should be understood. Macro-level functions of prejudice perpetuate ideologies such as racism and sexism that maintain the status quo. Whereas micro-level analysis explores why particular people are prejudiced, macro-analysis is concerned with how social systems and structures are created, maintained, and changed. From this perspective, prejudices do not arise from individual propensities, rather they emerge from, maintain, and help to justify existing social structures. Thus, at the macro-level prejudice serves a *system justification function*.

Prejudice as a belief system or ideology justifies *structural inequality*. Structural inequality occurs when the unequal treatment of people based on the groups to which they belong has become embedded in the social structure. Not only do members of the *dominant group* (the group with the most political, social, and economic power) profess the self-serving ideology, members of *minority groups* (groups with less power and access to resources) also come to believe and perpetuate prejudices against their own group. Karl Marx and Friedrich Engels (1848/1990) were the first social critics to write about this phenomenon. Their work has become the genesis for contemporary *conflict theory*. According to conflict theory, control of ideology is a pivotal tactic in suppressing social-class conflict. Keeping the working classes (*proletariat*) oppressed by force expends far too many resources. It is in the interest of the dominant social class to convince the workers that the latter's needs are met by the existing capitalist class system. If the workers accept capitalist ideology, then they will support rather than struggle against the interests of the big business (*bourgeoisie*). Powerful and wealthy, the controllers of multinational corporations have access to the means to promote ideologies that justify the exploitation of many groups. Capitalist ideology is so powerful that even those harmed by it come to accept it. Marx and Engels refer to this phenomenon as *false consciousness.* When false consciousness is successful, even the people that are harmed by the ideology embrace it.

Not only does conflict theory explain the spread of classist ideology, it also pertains to the oppression of other groups such as racial and gender oppression. This means that people in the minority or subordinate group actually hold prejudices against their own group. Both blacks and women have been shown to hold antiblack and antiwomen prejudices, respectively (Bayton et al. 1959; Banaji and Greenwald 1995; Kilianski and Rudman 1998).

Cecilia Ridgeway (2001) notes three ways in which legitimizing ideologies support structural inequality. First, legitimizing ideologies appear consensual: that is, people in all groups or categories accept the legitimacy of the dominant group. Second, though the ideology ascribes more positive attributes to the dominant group, it also attributes less valued, but nonetheless positive, traits to disadvantaged groups. Thus, whereas the disadvantaged group must accept that they are less competent in some areas, they also are better in other—albeit less valued—ways (2001:258). This ploy increases the likelihood that the ideology will be accepted by the disadvantaged. Third, there is a link between legitimizing ideologies and group stereotypes. Although group stereotypes differ greatly from group to group, they have a common reference. Women, racial and ethnic minorities, the working and poor classes are judged against the white, male, professional standard of competence. The resulting status hierarchy between groups is predicated on the implied superiority of the dominant group. Thus, what little status each group has is based on accepting the ideology justifying their oppression.

Prejudice is part of and stems from inequality embedded in our social structure. Specifically prejudice is part of racist, sexist, and classist ideologies that justify unequal treatment based on group membership. The system justification function is perhaps the most insidious component of prejudice because reducing or eliminating prejudice at this level requires a structural rather than individual change. At the micro- and mezzo-level of analysis change can be affected by confrontation, education, or altering the dynamics of intergroup relationships. The macro-level functions of prejudice are enmeshed in the organizations, policies, and social systems that form the structure of society. Prejudice reflects the racist, classist, and sexist structure of society, justifies it, and reinforces it. Although change at the structural level is certainly possible, it is much harder to affect. To affect change at the macro-level, legislative and organizational change is required. Because prejudice plays a role in system justification, it cannot be eliminated or reduced unless the system itself changes. In Chapters 6 and 9 we will return to the issue of structural change and examine some to the legislative changes that have been implemented to reduce discrimination and prejudice.

ATTITUDES AND INTERACTION: THE ATTITUDE–BEHAVIOR LINK

So far we've learned that prejudices are attitudes and that they are part of an ideology that both emerge from and support the social structure. Now we must explore the link between attitudes and behavior. How are attitudes related to what people do? Do our prejudices help predict or explain our behavior? If they don't, why study them at all?

Since the early work of Bogardus (1925), Thurstone (1929), and Allport (1935) there has been disagreement and debate over the measurement of attitudes, their relationship to behavior, and the very usefulness of the concept (Blummer 1955). Initially attitude research showed bright promise because it was assumed that what people said they thought and what they subsequently did were somehow related. Remember La Piere's (1934) field study in which a Chinese couple sought accommodations at inns and restaurants. Although the couple was refused service at only one of the 250 establishments they visited, the managers that were contacted several months later indicated they would refuse service to Chinese Americans. La Piere's work threw the attitude–behavior link into question.

There have been several attempts to access the usefulness of the attitude–behavior relationship. Wicker's review of attitude–behavior studies concluded that only rarely did an attitude account for over 10 percent of the variance in behavior (1969:65). Later assessments (Wiendieck 1975; Schuman and Johnson 1976; Ajzen and Fishbein 1977; Hill 1980) identified four problems that contribute to the weak link between attitudes and behaviors: (1) the effects of situational differences, (2) the problem of a one-to-one relationship between specific attitudes and behaviors, (3) the problem of whether attitudes cause behaviors or the vice versa, and (4) the question of validity in attitude measurement.

Our attitudes change as we go from one situation to another. What we think or feel about a group or social issues changes depending on the situational and interactional context we experience. Very general attitude measures, as are common in survey or laboratory research, cannot take into account the complex social environment of everyday life. Hill (1980) suggests that taking attitude research out of the laboratory and into the field might be one way to strengthen the attitude–behavior link. In my research, I have found that coupling survey research with in-depth interviews yields a richer and more useful understanding of both attitudes and their relationship to behavior (Bakanic 1995). By increasing the attention to the interactive context and how the specific situation affects attitudes and behavior, the attitude–behavior relationship becomes discernible.

One of the biggest problems in attitude research is the lack of a one-to-one relationship between a particular attitude and a specific behavior. We may hypothesize that an antiblack prejudice should affect discrimination, but what component of the prejudiced attitude and which specific discriminating behavior? Maass and her colleagues (2000) argue that the degree to which the prejudiced attitude may be intentionally controlled must be considered along with the social behaviors one would like to predict. This approach locates measures of prejudice along a continuum from explicit measures to implicit measures. Explicit measures include self-report measures of both old-fashioned and modern racism and sexism. Old-fashioned prejudices are overt and obvious. Modern prejudices are more subtle and are often blended with other social values such as meritocracy. Implicit measures of prejudice include spontaneous, difficult-to-control responses such as automatic responses of our cognitive system and physiological reactions (Maass et al. 2000:97). Explicit measures of prejudice are not very useful in predicting subtle biases, whereas implicit measures of prejudice are almost useless in predicting overt discrimination. Thus, matching the type of measurement to the level of behavior may diminish the gap between attitudes and behaviors.

Another problem concerns the causal direction between attitudes and behaviors. Attitudes and behaviors are an interactive process. The effects of behavior on attitudes are also an indirect consequence on the impact of attitudes on behavior. One strategy to disentangle the causal exchange between attitudes and behavior has been the incorporation of feedback loops using behavioral intentions rather than actual behavior as an in-between step in the process (Fishbein and Ajzen 1974). However, the link between behavioral intentions and behavior is also a problem. Behavioral intention is mitigated by social norms and situational constraints. For example, let us hypothesize that a person with antiblack attitudes might intend to discriminate against black people, but system-level norms such as employment policies may keep the person from acting on their intention.

Finally, the validity of attitude measurement must be considered. Self-report measures of prejudice have been indicating a decline in prejudice among people in the United States for decades (Schuman, Steeh, and Bobo 1985). Yet discrimination is common. This has called into question the validity of self-report measures. Three strategies have been designed to increase the validity of self-reported prejudice attitudes: (1) techniques to reduce deception, (2) analysis of verbal behavior and speech, and (3) use of multiple methods and indicators.

Two techniques intended to thwart attempts by research subjects to appear less prejudiced are the bogus pipeline technique and the lie detector expectation techniques. The bogus pipeline technique decreases attempts by research subjects to hide their prejudices by connecting the subjects to a bogus device. The subjects are told that the device registers their physiological response, thereby allowing the researcher to discover any attempt to deceive (Jones and Sigall 1971). Although the device does not measure physiological responses, the suggestion that it does significantly increases self-reporting of prejudice. A similar strategy, the lie detector expectation technique, simply informs subjects that a lie detector will be used in the next session of the interview to confirm their responses. The mere expectation that they will be subjected to the lie detector induces subjects to report more prejudice (Reiss et al. 1981).

Other techniques that are designed to increase the validity of self-reported prejudice include the analysis of verbal behavior and speech, which involves comparing the verbal behavior of people interacting with minority group members with those interacting with dominant group members. The signals the researchers look for include speech interruptions, speech errors, over-simplification of speech, and the relative abstractness of speech — that is, when participants use concrete expressions rather than abstract expressions (Maass et al. 2000:102). Analysis of these speech-based signals can be used with any interview technique in either laboratory or field settings. Neither do they require special equipment nor do they require the researcher to deceive the research participants (Maass et al. 2000:103).

Finally, use of multiple indicators of prejudice and triangulation of research methods have also been suggested as a means of circumventing subjects who try to appear less prejudice. Modern scales of racism and sexism have relatively good validity (McConahay 1983). These scales include multiple items that do not necessarily evoke socially acceptable responses. Because they include multiple indicators and are more difficult for respondents to second-guess, they are among the best self-report predictors of discriminatory behavior. Triangulation — using multiple methods to measure the same phenomenon — has also been effective at increasing the validity of prejudice measurement. By combining self-report close-ended survey questions with an in-depth analysis of responses to open-ended questions about prejudice, research subjects are less able to sustain their attempts to manage their public presentation of self.

The question of an attitude–behavior link has not been completely resolved by social psychologists. The social context and situations within which attitudes are learned and behavior is shaped defy research attempts to simplify and isolate the factors contributing to the process. Researchers grappling with the problem of predicting and disentangling the relationship between specific attitudes and behaviors have seen some progress. Measures of prejudice must be congruent with the type of behavior to be predicted. That is, measures of explicit prejudice such as old fashioned and modern racism scales are good predictors of overt discrimination whereas subtle measures of prejudice such as slight physiological reactions are not (see Dovidio et al. 1997). The puzzle of whether attitudes cause behavior or vice versa has led to the recognition of the reciprocal relationship between attitudes and behavior. Instead of simplifying the explanation, this reciprocal relationship has led to complex and difficult-to-predict feedback models. Finally, the question of the validity of attitude measurement remains tenuous. Using indices and scales rather than single items, the measures have improved validity, but respondents' attempts to publicly manage a less-prejudiced image continue to perplex researchers. Though it is good that blatantly prejudiced attitudes are no longer socially acceptable, it has created a more challenging situation for researchers investigating prejudices. There is no easy research solution to the normative denial of prejudice.

HOW ARE ATTITUDES STUDIED?

In studying attitudes, the methods used by social psychologists with a sociological background are different from the methods used by social psychologists with psychological approach. Sociologists are more likely to use self-report methods administered through survey methods such as interviews, questionnaires, and polls. Psychologists are more likely to use experimental methods. Social psychologists from both disciplines use observational methods, but the types of observational study are different. Sociologists are more likely to employ field observation in natural settings, whereas psychologists are more likely to study in controlled setting. Although there are distinct discipline preferences, social psychologists often cross discipline boundaries. Ultimately, the choice of method and measurement are more influenced by the research question and the theoretical perspective rather than the researcher's home discipline.

Survey Research

Many students think survey research is synonymous with questionnaires. *Survey research* is a research design that selects and analyzes information from a defined *sample* of a larger population. Information from the sample is generalized to the larger population. Although usually we survey people, a survey can use a number of different sampling units. A *sampling unit* is the element used to select cases from a larger population. Individual people, telephone numbers, households, residential blocks, car registration, local schools, and even units as large as cities and countries are examples of sampling units.

The survey method is used when a researcher is interested in collecting information about a sample that can be inferred to a larger population. Suppose a researcher is interested in describing the prevalence of prejudice in the United States. There are over 300,000,000 people in the United States. Asking each person about their prejudices would take too much time and too many resources. The survey method is a more efficient way to gather a manageable amount of information that can be generalized to the entire population.

But how does the researcher know that the sample is a good representation of the population? One way is to use *random selection.* Random selection is a systematic method of selecting samples from a population. Although there are different types of random selection, they are all based on probability. The odds of any member of the population being included in the population must be calculable. In other words, the researcher can give the precise odds of any unit from the population being included in the sample.

So, a survey is not merely a questionnaire. It's an inferential method that collects information from or about a sample that is generalized to a larger population. A questionnaire is only one of several tools that may be used to gather survey data.

When social psychologists use the survey method to sample opinions and attitudes, they often employ *self-report* measures. Self-report is the most direct and simplest way to measure attitudes. It includes all procedures by which a person is asked to report their own attitudes. Self-report measures may be either oral responses such as interviews or written responses such as questionnaires, journal entries, or diaries. Self-report measures assume that people are aware of their prejudices, are able to articulate them, and will be honest and open about revealing them.

Self-report measurements include both close- and open-ended formats. A *close-ended* format lists a limited number of responses from which the research participants must choose. It has the advantage of being easily quantified and therefore amenable to statistical analysis. An *open-ended* format allows the participants to respond in their own words. It allows research participants to express themselves in detail without the constraint of a limited number of imposed response categories. Researchers using this method get in-depth information, but it is more difficult and time-consuming to analyze the diverse responses that open-ended formats generate.

Sometimes survey researchers use a single item to measure attitudes. Single-item measures have the advantage of being simple and clear, but the concept the researcher is attempting to measure may have many components. For more complex issues, indices and scales may be preferable. An *index* is a composite measure that adds together multiple indicators of a concept. Your score on a multiple-choice test is an index of your grasp of the material you are being tested on. A *scale* is slightly more sophisticated composite measure of a theoretical concept. Several items are constructed to measure different aspects of the concept. The items that make up the scale must not only measure distinct aspects of the concept but also be interrelated with the other components used to construct the scale. That is, it's more than just adding up the items. A scale takes into account the patterns of responses to the items: for instance, does answering one way to item one relate to the way items two and three are answered?

Another strategy survey researchers use is to ask participants to report on the attitudes and prejudices of others. This method can be used in two ways. First, when people whose attitudes you are investigating are unable to provide accurate information, you can use reports of other people. For example, parents are often asked to report the attitudes of their children. Second, you can use these reports when the researcher wants information about how others behaved in a specific situation. This strategy rests on important assumptions: first, that the reporter is unbiased and will provide accurate and truthful information; second, that the reporter has knowledge of the attitudes of the people being studied and has had the opportunity to observe their behavior.

Experimental Research

Whereas survey research is designed to gather information from a sample and generalize it to a broader population, experimental research is designed to demonstrate causality. Experiments provide the strongest evidence of a causal relationship between variables. An experiment involves setting up controlled conditions in which the people being studied must react to a stimuli or treatment. The experimental treatment is called an *independent variable* and the reaction is called the *dependent variable.* The amount of control that an experimenter has over the conditions of the experiment affects how certain the experimenter can be about what caused the reaction of the experimental subjects. Though there are many types of experimental designs, true experiments have the strongest causality. A *true experiment* must meet four conditions. (1) It must have both control and experimental groups. (2) Subjects must be randomly assigned to control and experimental conditions. (3) There must be a pretest measurement of the dependent variable. (4) There must be a posttest measurement of the dependent variable. (Figure 2-1 shows the diagram of a classic true experimental design.)

An *experimental group* is the group subjected to the stimuli or treatment. A *control group* is a group that is not subjected to the experimental treatment. A control group is important because the experimenter is sure that any change observed is due to the treatment and not other unknown causes. If the change occurred in the experimental group and not the control group, we can be reasonably certain the treatment caused the change.

Random assignment is a procedure that controls assignment bias. Random procedures are used to place people either in experimental or in control group. Techniques include flipping a coin, pulling numbers out of a hat, or using a computer to randomly assign subjects, so that the subjects have an equal chance of being placed into one of the two groups. Randomization ensures that there will not be any systematic difference in individuals placed in groups.

Pretest and posttest measures allow the experimenter to gather information about the subjects before and after treatment so that comparisons can be made. Both independent and dependent variables are measured. The dependent variable must be measured to gauge any change that may happen because of the treatment. Though the treatment itself is an independent variable, there are other independent variables that are measured in the pretest. Sometimes characteristics of the research subjects, such as their age, gender, or even their attitudes, can have effects on the dependent variable. Often a questionnaire is used to gather pretest and posttest information. Attitude measures such as those used in survey research are also used in experimental research. By having pretest and posttest measures of factors that might affect the dependent variable, the experimenter

FIGURE 2-1	Diagram of a Classic True Experimental Design		
	Pretest	Treatment	Posttest
Experimental group	O	X	O
Control group	O		O

can construct a more precise accounting of any change produced by the experimental treatment.

Sometimes it is not possible or practical to satisfy all the conditions required for a true experiment. For example, a researcher may be interested in the reaction of people to a natural disaster or other naturally occurring event. Because the event could not be anticipated, it is not possible to have pretest measurement. This is sometimes called a *natural experiment.* In other experimental designs researchers may want to compare matched groups. If the control and experimental groups must be matched on selected characteristics, random assignment cannot be used. Designs that lack one or more of the components of a true experiment are called *quasi experiments.* Although the strength of causality is somewhat compromised in a quasi experiment, they are often a more valid representation of the phenomenon under study.

Observational Research

Observational research can be done in a laboratory or in a natural setting. *Field research* refers to the observational research conducted in a particular setting or environment outside of the laboratory. Observational research focuses on description. It addresses what the most important beliefs, behaviors, and attitudes of the people in a particular social environment are. If you are about to rent an apartment in an apartment complex, you might look at an apartment, speak to residents, and ask questions about what it's like to live there. In a sense, you are engaged in informal *participant observation*—a kind of research in which the observer joins in the setting that is being observed. There are advantages and drawbacks to becoming part of a social setting. Being part of the interaction allows the researcher to obtain a fuller understanding of the situation, people, and culture being studied. However, the participant also affects—or contaminates—the interaction being studied.

Laboratory or *controlled observation research* allows the researcher to control extraneous factors that might affect the phenomenon being studied. The laboratory is by design a neutral setting without diversions that might divert the attention of research subjects. The laboratory also has the advantage of using equipment that would be too intrusive in a field setting. For example, some studies of prejudice measure physiological responses and incipient movements as indicators of behavioral attitudes. Attaching electrodes to people in the field is clearly not an option.

MEASURING ATTITUDES

The choice of measurement depends on the research question, the method of research, and the theoretical perspective. Although it is not possible to describe every type of measurement used to study prejudiced attitudes, this section will describe several ways to measure prejudice amenable to each of the three methods (survey, experimental, and observational) that have been introduced in this chapter.

Self-Report Measures

The scaling methods discussed in this section are appropriate for questionnaires and interview schedules used in both survey research and experimental research. The three most-frequently used scaling methods are *Likert, semantic differential,* and *Thurstone* scales.

Likert Scaling

The most common way to measure prejudiced attitudes in survey research is using Likert-scaled items. In Likert scaling, a respondent is asked to decide on the degree of agreement (i.e. whether he or she agrees or disagrees and how strongly) with an item. Several different statements about the same issue and using the same response categories may be arranged in a matrix.

Five categories are normally employed, but sometimes the middle category is omitted to force respondents to take a position. Researchers have found that neutral items do not work well in Likert scales that measure controversial attitudes (Blanco and Alvarado 2005). It is also advisable to use an equal number of negatively and positively worded items. The correlation between each item's scores and the total score provides a measure of the interrelationship among the items used to construct the scale. (Figure 2-2 shows a typical Likert matrix.)

Semantic Differential Scaling

The semantic differential scale is intended to investigate the meaning of a concept. Typically, a seven-point scale is employed between two antonyms. Respondents are asked to indicate where on the scale their attitude belongs, by putting a check mark in one of the spaces between the polar opposites.

This technique was developed by Osgood and his colleagues (1957). They identified three recurring factors measured by semantic differential scales: evaluation (good–bad), potency (strong–weak), and activity (ambitious–lazy). The respondents' total score for all the paired opposites is the measure of the attitude. (For a typical semantic differential scaling, see Figure 2-3.)

Thurstone Scaling

One of the oldest and most reliable methods of measuring attitudes is Thurstone scaling. To create a Thurstone scale one must first collect a large number of statements that represents an extreme range of attitudes toward the subject in question (e.g., social class, gender, or race). Next, a large group of judges are recruited (approximately fifty). Each judge is asked to sort the statements into an odd number of piles (seven, nine, or eleven), the middle pile being neutral. Then the judges are asked to place each item along a continuum from one extreme to another, not letting their opinion about the

FIGURE 2-2 Likert Matrix

	Strongly Agree	Agree	Uncertain	Strongly Disagree	Disagree
Men are better leaders than women					
Women with children are less reliable workers					
Men have more financial responsibilities than women					
Women are more emotional than men					

FIGURE 2-3 Semantic Differential Scale

African Americans							
Good	------	------	------	------	------	------	Bad
Strong	------	------	------	------	------	------	Weak
Honest	------	------	------	------	------	------	Dishonest
Attractive	------	------	------	------	------	------	Unattractive
Ambitious	------	------	------	------	------	------	Lazy

subject influence the placements. After all the judges have ranked the items, a median (the position from where half the placements were lower and half were higher) is calculated for each individual item by using the pile numbers to which it was assigned. Items that had a wide range of placements or were ambiguous to the judges are discarded. The researcher then selects from the remaining items those that are most equally spaced along the entire range of the continuum. The selected items are then included in a questionnaire. The order of the statements is deliberately mixed so respondents will not notice the continuum. Respondents are asked to check all the items with which they agree. This scale reflects both the attitude of the respondents and those of the judges. This actually increases the validity of scale because the scale emerges from the responses of a large number of people. Thus the researcher constructs a consensus about the social meaning of the statements used in the scale.

Behavioral Measures of Prejudice

Behavioral measures are used in both laboratory and field settings. The types of behaviors measured by social psychologists range from deliberate actions of which people are aware to spontaneous actions that people do not reflect upon and of which they are unaware. Behaviors such as body language and seating distance can also be assessed in natural social settings, whereas behaviors such as muscle contractions and incipient movement can only be measured in a laboratory setting. According to Maass and her colleagues (2000:101), behavioral measures fall into two groups: social behaviors such as assistance, aggression, and punishment and nonverbal behaviors such as body language, seating distance, eye contact, and even blinking.

Social psychology has a rich history of studies that experimentally manipulate social behavior. The methods used range from ***ethnomethodology*** to measurement of physiological responses. Ethnomethodology is the study of "the body of common sense knowledge and the range of procedures and considerations [the methods] by means of which the ordinary members of society make sense of, find their way about in, and act on the circumstances in which they find themselves" (Heritage 1984:4). Early in the development of the method, ethnomethodologists used breeching experiments to demonstrate social reality. In ***breeching experiments,*** everyday ordinary social rules are violated to understand how people construct social reality. For example, Lynch (1991) alters the rules in a simple game of tic-tac-toe by placing the mark on the line between the squares in a tic-tac-toe grid. Ethnomethodologists study not only the initial reaction to the breech but also the ways in which people attempt to reconstruct order after the breech.

Contemporary ethnomethodologists employ conversational analysis as a behavioral measure, but instead of focusing on the relationships between interactants, they are concerned with the ways in which conversation is organized. Ethnomethodologists are concerned with how people accomplish social reality. They refer to this process as *doing* a social role (e.g., *doing gender*). Although there has been considerable work on how gender is accomplished in the organization of speech, there has been relatively little attention among ethnomethodologists on how race and class are accomplished in everyday interaction (see West and Fenstermaker 1995).

Laboratory studies of nonverbal behavior have concentrated on subtle behaviors people are aware of, but seldom focus more than passing attention. The most often examined behaviors are seating distance from out-group members, eye contact, blinking, body attitude (posture and orientation), and hand movements (Maass 2000). These studies have often noted the contradiction between verbal indicators of prejudice and nonverbal indicators. Though participants in behavioral studies displayed open and friendly verbal behaviors in interaction with out-group members, they sat further away, had less eye contact, and inclined their bodies away from out-group members (Hendricks and Bootzin 1976).

Cognitive Measures

Cognitive measures of prejudice are designed to measure the automatic responses of our thought processes. In other words, they reveal the ways that prejudices are part of the way we categorize and organize information. Not surprisingly, visible traits such as sex and race are one of the primary ways that people mentally organize information (Stangor et al. 1992). Categories based on visible attributes are used to activate stereotypes and make judgments.

There are many creative techniques designed to reflect cognitive bias (cf. Fazio et al. 1995; Blair and Banaji 1996; Greenwald et al. 1998). *Implicit Association Tests* (IAT) and *Response Time Bias* (RTB) measurements access the automatic application of stereotypes. These measures record the amount of time it takes for research subjects to make pairings between attributes and groups. Computer programs are used to administer and record the tests. The research participants are presented with sequences of positive and negative attributes that are to be paired with different groups of people. The participants are first asked to pair positive attributes with one group and negative attributes with the other. Then the association is to be reversed, that is, the group previously paired with the positive attributes is paired with negative ones. As words and images flash on the computer screen, participants' reaction times and errors in pairing are measured. These measures record the subtle cognitive process and prejudices of which the participants may be unaware.

Summary

Prejudices are attitudes. But knowing this doesn't simplify the study of prejudice. There has been a long debate about what attitudes are, how to measure them, and how useful they are in predicting behavior, which will no doubt continue. However, social psychologists from both sociology and psychology and from the often divergent theoretical perspectives encompassed by the two disciplines agree that attitudes are an important phenomenon in and of themselves regardless of whether they reliably predict specific behaviors. We use attitudes to understand others and to rationalize our own behavior.

Thus understanding attitudes is part of understanding human interaction and the nature of prejudice.

Attitudes encompass three components: affective, behavioral, and cognitive. Affective attitudes include emotional responses; behavioral attitudes include propensities toward action; and cognitive attitudes are the ideas and beliefs we hold. Our prejudices are an amalgamation or mixture of these different components that we use to construct and make sense of what goes on in the world around us.

Prejudices serve a number of purposes or functions. One way to help understand the functions of prejudice is to examine it on different levels. Micro-level analysis deals with how individuals use prejudice to define themselves, their ideas, and their relationships to others. The mezzo-level includes the role of prejudice in establishing membership in and boundaries between groups as well as the relationships between groups. Mezzo-level functions help people identify with and differentiate between groups. The macro-level functions examine how prejudices are used to justify social systems and may be used either to facilitate or to impede social change.

The link between our attitudes and our behavior is neither simple nor direct. Different social contexts and situations make it difficult to isolate the factors contributing to how people behave. Researchers have learned that measurement of prejudice must be appropriate to the type of behavior being predicted.

Attitudes are studied with a number of methods and types of measurement. Although self-report measures are most common, there is an increasing trend for people to deny their prejudice. In response to this trend, researchers have devised many creative ways to study prejudice. In survey methodology, open-ended questions have offered one way obtaining an in-depth, thus harder-to-conceal, picture of prejudice. Experimental designs offer a format to test ideas about attitude change and prejudice reduction as well as ways to measure subtle and implicit indicators of prejudice. Observational studies can be done in the field or in a laboratory setting. They range from participant observation in natural social settings to controlled observation or even the most subtle behaviors such as eye contact and blinking.

On the one hand, people increasingly recognize prejudiced attitudes as destructive and do not wish to appear prejudice. On the other hand, this recognition made it more challenging to study prejudice. In response, social psychologists continue to come up with inventive ways to measure attitudes and to explore the relationship between prejudices and the ways in which they affect behavior.

Key Terms

- Affective attitudes
- Attitudes
- Behavioral attitudes
- Bourgeoisie
- Cognitive attitudes
- Cognitive formation function
- Conflict theory
- Cultural stereotype
- Dependent variable
- Dominant group
- Ego defense function
- Ethnomethodology
- Experimental research
- False consciousness
- Generalized other
- Group justification functions
- Implicit Association Tests (IAT)
- Independent variable
- Individual stereotype
- Looking glass self
- Macro-level
- Mezzo-level
- Micro-level
- Minority group
- Observational research
- Primary group
- Proletariat
- Protestant ethic
- Random assignment
- Random selection
- Secondary group
- Significant other
- Social identity theory
- Stereotype
- Structural inequality
- Survey research
- System justification function
- Utilitarian function
- Value confrontation model
- Value expression function

Taking It Further — Class Exercises and Interesting Web Sites

Explore your hidden biases

Take an Implicit Association Test (IAT) at the Harvard Project Implicit Web site (https://implicit.harvard.edu/implicit/). Find out if you have any bias toward groups based on race, sex, sexual orientation, or even political affiliation.

References

Ajzen, Icek, and Fishbien Martin. 1977. Attitude-behavior relations: A theoretical analysis and review of empirical research. *Psychological Bulletin* 84 (5): 888–918.

Allport, Gordon. 1935. Attitudes. In *A handbook of social psychology*, ed. C. Murchison, 789–844. Worcester, MA: Clark University Press.

———. 1954. *The nature of prejudice.* Reading, MA: Addison-Wesley.

———.1966. *The nature of prejudice.* Cambridge, MA, Addison-Wesley Pub. Co., 1966 printing, c.1954.

Asch, Solomon. 1952. *Social psychology.* New York: Oxford University Press, 1987, c.1952.

Bakanic, Von. 1995. I'm not prejudiced, but . . . : a deeper look at racial attitudes. *Sociological Inquiry* 65: 67–86.

Banaji, Mahzarin R., and Anthony G. Greenwald. 1995. Implicit social cognition: Attitudes, self-esteem, and stereotypes. *Psychological Review* 102 (1): 4–27.

Bayton, J., L. McAlister, and K. Hamer. 1959. Race-class stereotypes. *Journal of Negro Education* 25: 75–78.

Bem, D. J. 1970. *Beliefs attitudes and human affairs.* Belmont, CA: Brooks/Cole.

Blair, Irene V., and Mahzarin R. Banaji. 1996. Automatic and controlled processes in stereotype priming. *Journal of Personality and Social Psychology* 70 (6): 1142–1163.

Blanco, Neligia, and Maria E. Alvarado. 2005. An attitudinal *scale* in relation to the scientific-social research process. *Revista de Ciencias Sociales* 11(3): 537-544.

Blummer, Herbert. 1955. Attitudes and the social act. *Social Problems* 3 (2): 59–65.

———. 1958. Race prejudice as a sense of group position. *Pacific Sociological Review* 1: 3–7.

———. 1969. *Symbolic interactionism: Perspective and method.* Englewood Cliffs, NJ: Prentice Hall.

Bogardus, E. 1925. Measuring social distances. *Journal of Applied Sociology* 9: 299–308.

Branscombe, Nyla, Michael Schmitt, and Richard Harvey. 1999. Perceiving pervasive discrimination among African Americans: Implications for group identification and well-being. *Journal of Personality and Social Psychology* 77: 135–149.

Breckler, S. J. 1984. Empirical validation of affect, behavior and cognition as distinct components of attitude. *Journal of Personality and Social Psychology* 47: 1191–1205.

Brown v. Board of Education of Topeka, 347 U.S. 483 (1954) http://www.law.cornell.edu/supct/html/historics/USSC_CR_0347_0483_ZS.html.

Charon, Joel. 1989. *Symbolic interaction: An introduction, an interpretation, an integration.* Englewood Cliffs, NJ: Prentice Hall.

Clark, Kenneth, and M. Clark. 1947. Racial identification and racial preferences in Negro children. In *Readings in social psychology*, ed. T. M. Newcomb and E. L. Hartley, 169–178. New York: Holt, Rinehart & Winston.

Cooley, Charles Horton. 1970. *Human nature and social order.* New York: Schocken Books.

Crocker, J., and B. Major. 1989. Social stigma and self-esteem: The self protective properties of stigma. *Psychological Review* 96: 608–630.

Darley, John, and C. Daniel Batson. 1973. From Jerusalem to Jericho: A study of situational and dispositional variables in helping behavior. *Journal of Personality and Social Psychology* 27: 100–108.

Darley, John, and Bibb Latane. 1968. Bystander intervention in emergencies: Diffusion of responsibility. *Journal of Personality and Social Psychology* 8: 377–383.

Dovidio, John F., Kerry Kawakami, and Craig Johnson. 1997. On the nature of prejudice: Automatic and controlled processes. *Journal of Experimental Social Psychology* 33 (5): 510–540.

Fazio, Russell H., R. Jackson Joni, and C. Dunton Bridget. 1995. Variability in automatic activation as an unobtrusive measure of racial attitudes: A bona fide pipeline? *Journal of Personality and Social Psychology* 69 (6): 1013–1027.

Fein, Steven, and Steven Spencer. 1997. Prejudice as a self image maintenance: Affirming the self through derogating others. *Journal of Personality and Social Psychology* 21: 333–340.

Fishbein, M., and I. Ajzen. 1974. Attitudes towards objects as predictors of single and multiple behavioral criteria. *Psychological Review* 81: 59–74.

Graham, Sandra. 1994. Motivation in African Americans. *Review of Educational Research* 64: 33–117.

Greenwald, Anthony G., Debbie E. McGhee, and Jordan L.K. Schwartz. 1998. Measuring individual differences in implicit cognition: The implicit association test. *Journal of Personality and Social Psychology* 74 (6): 1464–1480.

Grube, J. W., D. Mayton, and S. Ball-Rokeach. 1994. Indicating change in values, attitudes and behaviors: Belief systems theory and the method of value confrontations. *Journal of Social Issues* 50: 153–173.

Hendricks, M., and R. Bootzin. 1976. Race and sex as stimuli for negative affect and physical avoidance. *Journal of Social Psychology* 98: 11–120.

Heritage, John. 1984. *Garfinkel and eth-nomethodology*. Cambridge: Polity Press.

Hewitt, J. P. 1988. *Self and society: A symbolic interactionist social psychology*. Boston, MA: Allyn and Bacon.

Hill, R. J. 1980. Attitude and behavior. In *Social psychology: Sociological perspectives*, ed. M. Rosenburg and R. H. Turner, 347–377. New York: Basic Books.

Hogg, M., and D. Abrams. 1988. *Social identifications: A social psychology of intergroup relations and group processes*. London: Routledge.

Jones, Edward E., and Harold Sigall. 1971. The Bogus pipeline: A new paradigm for measuring affect and attitude. *Psychological Bulletin* 76: 349–364.

Katz, D. 1960. The functional approach to the study of attitudes. *Public Opinion Quarterly* 24: 163–204.

Katz, I., and R. G. Hass. 1988. Racial ambivalence and American value conflict: Correlational and priming studies of dual cognitive structures. *Journal of Personality and Social Psychology* 55: 893–905.

Kilianski, Stephen E., and Laurie A. Rudman. 1998. Wanting it both ways: Do women approve of benevolent sexism? *Sex Roles* 39 (5–6): 333–352.

Kirchler, E., and James H. Davis. 1986. The influence of member status differences and task type on group consensus and member position change. *Journal of Personality and Social Psychology* 51 (1): 83–91.

Kutner, B., C. Wilkins, and P.R. Yarrow. 1952. Verbal attitudes and overt behavior involving racial prejudice. *Journal of Abnormal and Social Psychology* 47: 649–652.

La Piere, R. T. 1934 Attitudes vs. actions. *Social forces* 13: 230–237.

Levin, Jack. 1975. *The functions of prejudice*. New York: Harper & Row.

Lynch, Michael. 1991. Pictures of nothing? Visual construals in social theory. *Sociological Theory* 9 (1): 1–21.

Maass, Anne, Luigi Castelli, and Luciano Arcuri. 2000. Measuring prejudice: Implicit versus explicit techniques. In *Social identity processes: Trends in theory and research*, ed. D. Capozza and R. Brown, 96–116. London: Sage Publications.

Marx, Carl, and Friedrich Engles. 1848/1990. *Manifesto of the Communist Party*. New York: International Publishers.

McConahay, J. B. 1983. Modern racism, ambivalence and the modern racism scale. In *Prejudice, discrimination and racism*, ed. J. F. Dovidio and S. L. Gaertner, 91–125. New York: Academic Press.

Mead, George Herbert. 1934. *Mind self and society*. Chicago, IL: University of Chicago Press.

Minard, R. D. 1952. Race relations in the Pocohontas coal field. *Journal of Social Issues* 8: 29–44.

Noel, Jeffery, Daniel Wann, and Nyla Branscombe. 1995. Peripheral ingroup membership status and public negativity toward outgroups. *Journal of Personality and Social Psychology* 68: 127–137.

Osgood, C. E., G. Suci, and P. Tannenbaum. 1957. *The measurement of meaning.* Urbana, IL: University of Illinois Press.

Reiss, M., R. J. Kalle, and J. T. Tedeschi. 1981. Bogus pipeline attitude assessment, impression management and misattribution in induced compliance settings. *Journal of Social Psychology* 115: 247–258.

Ridgeway, Cecilia L. 2001. Gender, status, and leadership. *Journal of Social Issues* 57 (4): 637–655.

Rokeach, Milton. 1979. *Understanding human values.* New York: Free Press.

Rokeach, Milton, and S. Ball-Rokeach. 1989. Stability and change in American value priorities 1968–1981. *American Psychologist* 44: 775–784.

Ruscher, Janet B. 2001. *Prejudiced communication: A social psychological perspective.* New York: Guilford Press.

Saenger, G., and C. Gilbert. 1950. Customer reactions to the integration of negro sales personnel. *International Journal of Opinion and Attitude Research* 4: 57–76.

Sampson, Edward E. 1999. *Dealing with differences: An introduction to the social psychology of prejudice.* Fort Worth, TX: Harcourt Brace.

Schuman, Howard, Charlotte Steeh, Lawrence Bobo, and Maria Krysan. 1985. *Racial attitudes in America rends and interpretations.* Cambridge, MA: Harvard University Press.

Schuman, Howard, and Michael P. Johnson. 1976. Attitudes and behavior. *Annual Review of Sociology* 2: 161–207.

Schwartz, S. H., and William Bilsky. 1987. Toward a psychological structure of human values. *Journal of Personality and Social Psychology* 53: 550–562.

Sherif, Musaf, O. J. Harvey, B. J. White, W. R. Hood, and Carolyn W. Sherif. 1961. *Intergroup cooperation and conflict: The robbers cave experiment.* Middletown, CT: Wesleyan University Press.

Sidanius, J. 1988. Political sophistication and political deviance: A structural equation examination of context theory. *Journal of Personality and Social Psychology* 55: 37–51.

Snyder, M. 1987. *Public appearances, private realities: The psychology of self-monitoring.* New York: Freeman.

Stangor, Charles, and David McMillan. 1992. Memory for expectancy-congruent and expectancy-incongruent information: A review of the social and social developmental literatures. *Psychological Bulletin* 111 (1): 42–61.

Swim, Janet K., and L. L. Hyers. 1999. Excuse me — What did you say?! Women's public and private responses to sexist remarks. *Journal of Experimental Social Psychology* 35 (1): 68–88.

Taijfel, Henri. 1982. Social psychology of intergroup relations. *Annual Review of Psychology* 33: 1–39.

Taijfel, Henri, John C. Turner, John T. Jost, and Jim Sidanius. 2004. The social identity theory of intergroup behavior. In *Political psychology: Key readings,* ed. John T. Jost and Jim Sidanius, 276–293. New York: Psychology Press.

Thurstone, L. L. 1929. A theory of attitude measurement. *Psychological Review* 36: 222–241.

West, Candance, and Sarah Fenstermaker. 1995. Doing difference. *Gender and Society* 9: 8–37.

Wicker, A. W. 1969. Attitudes versus actions: The relationship of verbal and overt behavioral responses to attitude objects. *Journal of Social Issues* 25 (4): 41–78.

Wiendieck, Gerd. 1975. The behavioral relevance of ethnic attitude studies. *Social Dynamics* 1 (2): 125–145.

Zanna, Mark P. 1994. On the nature of prejudice. *Canadian Psychology* 35 (1): 11–23.

CHAPTER

Theories of Prejudice

In this chapter, I will review theories of prejudice from sociology and psychology.

- Early Concepts of Prejudice
  Gordon Allport
  Otto Klineberg
  Pierre Van den Berghe
  Erving Goffman
  W. E. B. Du Bois
- Contemporary Theories of Prejudice
  Sociological Perspectives
  Psychological Perspectives
- Summary
- Key Terms
- Key People
- Taking It Further—Class Exercises and Interesting Web Sites
- References

A few years ago some friends and I were talking about our work experiences over a bottle of wine. During our rather light-hearted discussion, I amused them with an admittedly extemporaneous theory I concocted: earrings can be disruptive to people benefiting from patriarchal structures. A ***theory*** is a set of ideas that helps us explain and predict what happens in our world. The first step in building a theory is to identify the phenomenon you want to explain. In the case of my theory, I wanted to explain reactions toward earrings in the workplace. My earring theory was sparked by an incident with a senior colleague when I was a young assistant professor. One day I was wearing a pair of large, brightly colored earrings that jingled when I moved my head. My colleague flipped one of the earrings and said, "Are you going to a protest rally or something?" He seemed irritated and contended they were unprofessional. During our discussion, I discovered that he thought small studs were appropriate in the workplace, but large conspicuous earrings were not. I asked what if the studs were worn by a young male colleague of ours, and his reaction was even more irate. In his opinion, earrings on men were never appropriate. Obviously, earrings symbolized something threatening to him.

The next step in theory building is defining concepts. ***Theoretical concepts*** denote phenomena. That is, they define, distinguish, and clarify ideas. The first concept I created was the "symbolic value of earrings." From my colleague's reaction, I understood that we were talking about issues far beyond aesthetic preferences. For him earrings were a gendered symbol. That is, they convey ideas about appropriate masculine and feminine roles. So another concept in my theory is **patriarchy.** Patriarchy is a form of social organization that occurs in many social institutions. It literally means a hierarchy ruled by men. Although the twentieth century saw and the twenty-first century still finds women participating in greater variety of social roles than in previous centuries, the forms of organization and bureaucracy still sustain some advantages for men. In a patriarchy men as a group have greater access to resources and power than do women. However, in a patriarchy, as in any hierarchy, there are more people in the bottom ranks than at the top, so not all men are equally powerful. In fact, patriarchy is a system that limits the ways in which women and men participate in the social structure. Less-powerful men and those who dare to violate gender norms are also disadvantaged by a patriarchal structure.

Theories use **variables** to represent concepts. Variables are empirically identified concepts that can measure phenomena that differ in degree. So to be a variable a phenomenon must vary and it must be measurable. The variables that I might use to measure the symbolic value of earrings include the size, shape, and color of earrings; the number of earrings worn on an ear; if they are not worn on both ears, in which ear are they worn; and the sex of the person wearing the earrings.

Measuring patriarchy is more difficult than constructing variables for earrings, for patriarchy is a much more abstract concept. Nonetheless, one indicator of patriarchy could be the formality of the organizational setting. Some organizations are more patriarchal than others. Consider the setting of my initial earring epiphany: I was working at a university. A university is a formal, patriarchal bureaucracy. There are numerous formal and informal rules that apply to the appearance of people performing different roles at the university. Some employees must wear uniforms, whereas others have formal dress codes. Others, such as professors, have few formal dress codes but are still subject to informal norms of professional appearance. So one could measure patriarchy indirectly by noting the social context (i.e., setting and roles) in which the earrings were worn. For example, wearing flashy earrings while teaching might evoke a different response than wearing the same earrings while shopping at the mall.

Thus far, the variables we have mentioned are all **independent variables** — they are intended to explain variation in a dependent variable. The **dependent variable** measures the concept to be explained by the theory. In the earring theory, the dependent variable measures reaction to earrings. One could measure reactions in several ways. One might measure responses either by wearing earrings themselves or by observing others' reactions to the people wearing earrings, as an indication of how disruptive the earrings are to interaction.

Concepts, by themselves, are nothing more than definitions. The next step in theory building is to relate the concepts to each other. **Theoretical statements** specify how concepts are related to each other. Further, they must be systematically organized. That is, the interrelationship between the statements must be clear and consistent because without consistent order the statements cannot be tested. Theoretical statements can be organized using many **theoretical formats** (Turner 1978:6). The most common in social theory is an inductive, causal format. "[T]he causal process format presents a set of causal statements describing the effect of one variable on another without establishing a strict hierarchal ordering of the statements" (8). It is like a flowchart that maps the effects of variables on each other. So if we were to chart my earring theory using a causal format it might look something like Figure 3-1.

FIGURE 3-1   Flow Chart of the Causal Format for the Earring Theory

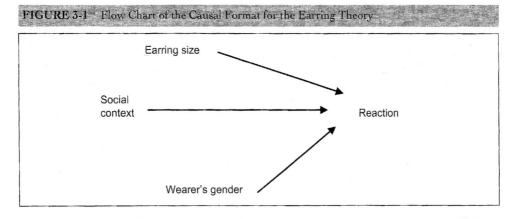

By tracing the causal connections between the variables, the goal is to account for as much variation in the dependent variable as possible.

Another common theoretical format is a deductive or ***axiomatic format.*** The axiomatic format is hierarchal. It begins with axioms. ***Axioms*** are highly abstract and untested assertions. Propositions and specific hypotheses are derived from the axioms that predict how an event should occur if the axioms are indeed true. This format is used more often with experimental research, whereas causal modeling is employed in inductive methods, such as survey research.

Even though explaining reactions to earrings is a rather frivolous, amusing example, the principles of theory building are the same for serious social issues. In the following section, we will examine examples of early theories of prejudice. The development of those early ideas will be traced to the contemporary theories of prejudice that dominate the field today.

EARLY CONCEPTS OF PREJUDICE

It is difficult to decide where to begin a discussion of the early works in the study of prejudice. This is because the roots of social psychology are entwined in many academic disciplines. Both sociological and psychological social psychologists study prejudice. The main theories within sociological social psychology are symbolic interaction and the social structure and personality perspective. Theories of prejudice from sociology are concerned with prejudice stemming from participation in social groups, how prejudice is used in interactions, the effects of the cultural environment on prejudice, and the relationship between prejudice and social structure. Psychological social psychology focuses on social influence at the individual level. Many theories address prejudice from psychological social psychology and include frustration aggression theory, authoritarian personality theory, the cognitive perspective, and social identity theory.

During its early development (1908–1924), social psychology drew ideas from social thinkers in a variety of emerging academic disciplines. At the turn of the twentieth century when social psychology began to evolve as a field of study, the boundaries between academic disciplines had not yet solidified. The first text in social psychology was written by William McDougall (1908). McDougall argued that human behavior was based on innate dispositions and instincts (Baron et al. 1988). Floyd Allport's (1924) text on social psychology is more similar to contemporary ideas about human behavior. Allport abandoned the biological determinism of McDougall's work in favor of the view that social behavior is affected by the presence and behavior of other people. In other words, our responses to other people and the situations in which we find ourselves explain more of our behavior than do our biological predispositions.

Social psychology underwent a period of rapid growth following the publication of Allport's book. It emerged as a hybrid of scholarship with contributions from philosophy, sociology, psychology, and even economics. For example, George Herbert Mead, whose ideas became the foundation for symbolic interaction (a major sociological theory), was influenced by the psychology of William James. He was also influenced by American pragmatism espoused by educator John Dewey and philosopher Charles Sanders Peirce. Gordon Allport, one of the first to directly address the topic of prejudice, was a psychologist. However, he also published widely in sociology journals and even sat on the editorial review board for the *American Journal of Sociology*. Gordon Allport acknowledged his own bent toward psychology while he applauded "the present tendency for specialists to cross discipline boundaries and borrow the methods and insights from neighboring disciplines in the interests of a more adequate understanding of a concrete social problem" (1954:206–207). Thus, separating the early work on prejudice into sociological and psychological perspectives is somewhat arbitrary. Much later in its history, social psychology branched into its more contemporary divisions, even prompting debates about whether there were two or three distinct social psychologies and the problems associated in each of these branches (cf. House 1977; Boutilier et al. 1980). More recently, a similar point is made about the early influence of Gordon Allport on the social psychology of prejudice and less-attended early work of W. E. B. Du Bois, the first African American sociologist and one of the founders of the National Association for the Advancement of Colored People (NAACP) (Gaines and Reed 1994).

Gordon Allport

Gordon Allport's work on prejudice (1954) was published in the same year that the Supreme Court issued its historic decision in *Brown v. Board of Education of Topeka*. Allport developed the concept of prejudiced personalities. Although he considered the role of social influence and the historical context affecting prejudices, his focus was primarily on the role of prejudice in the formation of the personality. He pioneered work on the authoritarian personality, demagogy, religious prejudice, and the tolerant personality. But his work on personality was situated in a very eclectic perspective that encompassed six major approaches: *historical, sociocultural, situational, personality, phenomenological,* and *stimulus object components* (Figure 3-2). Allport begins by noting the broad *historical context* in which prejudice takes place. He pointed out the important effects of slavery on antiblack prejudice and the backlash against Bismark's liberalism that fueled the anti-Semitism of Nazi-era Europe (1954:210). However, he doubted that prejudice could be fully explained by history. He suggested blending a historical emphasis with *Sociocultural factors,* such as group conflict and competition, to form what he called a *community pattern of prejudice* wherein individuals adopt the

Historical Approach	Socio-cultural Approach	Situational Approach	Personality Dynamics Approach	Phenomenological Approach	Stimulus/ Object Approach
Historical context	Competition	Contact between groups	Deprivation–frustration	Immediate causation	Group reputation
	Conflict	Intergroup competition	Socialization	Underlying dynamics of personality	Stereotypes
	Community patterns of prejudice	Relative density of populations	Development of prejudiced character		Scapegoating

FIGURE 3-2   Theoretical and Methodological Approaches to the Study of the Causes of Prejudice

prejudgments of their forebearers, viewing each competing groups through the lens of traditional prejudices (1954:212–213).

Situational factors bring prejudice from the macro-level closer to the individual, or micro-, level. They stress the type of contact between groups, competition between groups, and the relative density of the groups. The situation under which contact occurs is pivotal, for contact can either increase or decrease prejudice. For example, superficial, casual contact re-enforces stereotypes and increases prejudice between groups, whereas true acquaintance lessens prejudice. Situational factors are especially important because they form the social setting in which prejudice is enacted.

Allport's biggest contribution to a comprehensive theory of prejudice was his emphasis on *psychodynamic personality development.* He contended that deprivation and frustration lead to hostile impulses and the need to scapegoat less powerful groups. He argued that certain types of people develop prejudice as part of their character structure. According to him, early socialization plays an important role in creating the prejudiced personality. People with prejudiced personalities lack secure relationships in early childhood. To compensate for this fundamental insecurity, they prefer a definitive, black and white world. They yearn for authority so that they can control as much of their social world as possible. They both exclude and fear people with whom they are less familiar (Allport 1954:216).

The *phenomenological* emphasis concerns how individuals define their social world. Allport notes that a person's response to an ongoing interaction is part of this definition and that conduct proceeds from their view of the world. According to Allport, the phenomenological level is the immediate causation for the prejudice, but it must be considered along with the underlying dynamics of the personality as well as the situational, cultural, and historical contexts (1954:216–217).

The final stage of Allport's theory concerns the response to the *stimulus object* (i.e., the target of the prejudice). Hostile attitudes toward groups are determined partly by the reputation of the group and partly by situations beyond the control of the group such as traditional prejudice, stereotypes, and scapegoating. Allport combined all six levels in his approach to prejudice. He contended that no single level is sufficient to explain prejudice.

Otto Klineberg

Otto Klineberg's interest in prejudice began with his critical exploration of racial differences (1935). At a time when the eugenics movement had wide support in both the United States and Europe, Klineberg systematically considered the evidence of biological, psychological, and cultural differences between races and found them lacking.[1] Long before the controversial *Bell Curve* (Hernstein and Murray 1994) was published, Klineberg concluded: "there is no scientific proof of racial differences in mentality" (1935:345). He contended that the invention of racial differences was a rationalization for unequal treatment. He next turned his attention to racial and national stereotypes, particularly how these images are taught to children. He was interested in the role schools play in perpetuating prejudiced attitudes and their as-yet-untapped potential to change prejudiced attitudes (349).

Klineberg defined prejudice as a "feeling or response to persons or things which is before and therefore not based upon, actual experience. It may be either positive or negative, and it may be directed to any one of a large variety of objects" (Lindzey 1954). His work was primarily an exploration of prejudice as it is incorporated into childhood cognitive development and socialization. Developing children must learn the major social categories in their society, the criteria used to classify members into categories, and the appropriate attitudes and behaviors toward the categories of people. Perhaps his most important work was a comprehensive comparative study about the development of prejudice and stereotyped thinking of children that he did with Wallace Lambert. Lambert and Klineberg (1967) studied children of eleven nationalities. They found that the manner in which children are taught and learn a national identity has important, lasting consequences for adult prejudices. The process of creating a group identity produces a distorted and embellished view of one's own group. Thus, the process of stereotyping and forming prejudices begins with one's own group. Once this stereotyped identity of one's own group is formed, it is contrasted with out-groups of people "not like us." These contrasts leave the impression that out-group members are foreign, strange, and unfriendly (Lambert and Klineberg 1967:223–225).

Klineberg's work in cognitive development of prejudice was important for several reasons. First, while the process of contrasting in-group and out-groups appears to be part of a cognitive categorization schema taught to children in many different cultures, the attitudes that children form about out-groups vary. That is, the result of out-group contrast is not inevitably negative. Second, how children learn to react to socially distinctive peoples is carried over from one comparison to another. Once a child learns that one group is hateworthy, the rationalization and generalizations justify that hate can be carried over to other groups. Finally, early development of in-group–out-group contrast affects a child's self-concept. The self-concepts of children reflect the culturally

---

[1]The Eugenics Movement was a widespread movement to better the human population by selective breeding. The movement had its roots in Social Darwinism and reached its zenith during the Nazi era. The Nuremberg racial laws of 1935 prohibited marriages and any sexual contact between Germans and members of proscribed groups. These policies were supposedly based on biology and directed against groups of human beings inferior.

significant criteria used in training them to make distinctions between their own group and others (Lambert and Klineberg 1967:225). In other words, they value in themselves the criteria used to distinguish their group.

Pierre Van den Berghe

Pierre Van den Berghe contributed a more sociological perspective to the study of prejudice. He was a student of psychologist Gordon Allport and sociologist Talcott Parsons. His perspective considered the social conditions that caused racial prejudices to be rewarded or inhibited. Although he acknowledges the contributions of his mentor Gordon Allport, he considered both the frustration aggression and personality theories of prejudice incomplete. Instead, he focused on the circumstances under which prejudice at the personal level was affected by social structure. In other words, Van den Berghe professed a macro-perspective. According to the macro-perspective, prejudice does not emanate from individuals; rather, the inequalities in the social system are reflected in individuals' attitudes and behaviors. Like both Allport and Klineberg, Van den Berghe recognized social categorizations, such as race, as subjective. That is, they are not based on scientifically justifiable objective criteria. He argued that because race (or class or even gender) has no reality apart from its social context, it must be studied in the context of the whole society. He considered societies to be irreducible units. Attitude questionnaires and surveys, he argued, were psychological reductionism. Such studies were "the process of feeding social reality through gargantuan fact-digesting computers [that] often melt down priceless jewels into crude ingots" (Berghe 1967:149). Instead, he advocated the cross-cultural and cross-temporal approach that he called historico-comparative macro-sociology (148–149).

Stereotypes and prejudices against subjugated groups change as intergroup relations change. For example, Van den Berghe notes similarities in the development of multiracial cultures. Initially a paternalistic system develops to exploit the labor and resources of the subjugated groups. During this period, stereotypes of the subordinate groups include inferiority, simplicity, childishness, and irresponsibility. However, paternalistic systems are accompanied by assimilation and acculturation strategies. That is, the culture of the subjugated group is discouraged, and policies require the adoption of the language and culture of the dominant group. Assimilation was (and still is) sometimes brutally forced, destroying the cultures of the subjugated group (e.g., the cultural destruction of many Native American civilizations). However, paternalistic systems also sowed the seeds of their own destruction. Assimilation produced an elite within the subjugated group. Those who most successfully adopted the culture of the oppressor were rewarded, obtaining status and resources. Assimilation also creates a progressive minority within the dominant group. Van den Berghe believed that this created an ideological dialectic between the conflicting racial groups (Berghe 1967:126). This eventually broke down the façade of a benevolent patron relationship and replaced it with competition for scarce resources. At this point, stereotypes change from depicting the minority as simple and childlike to depicting them as dangerous, sly, and treacherous. Likewise, attitudes change from patronizing and condescending to wary and punitive.

According to Van den Berghe, prejudice and stereotypes arise from and change with changes in the social structure. Thus, they cannot be understood without their historical and sociocultural context. Any attempt to understand prejudice solely on the individual level is therefore fragmented and incomplete.

Erving Goffman

Erving Goffman was also a sociologist, but his work comes from a micro-perspective. Goffman's work on social stigma added an important dimension to the study of prejudice. *Stigma* refers to any "attribute that is deeply discrediting" (1963:3). Any person or group that possesses characteristics that are devalued can become stigmatized. This definition includes minority group members as well individuals with other attributes that are considered deviant. The elderly, the obese, the handicapped, ex-convicts, alcoholics, and the mentally ill are examples of stigmatized identities. Notice that the stigmatized attribute does not have to be physical. A person can be stigmatized because of some aspect of their behavior or because of some ascribed attribute such as family, nationality, or race. When the stigmatized attribute is not immediately observable, individuals may be forced to wear emblems signifying the discredited identity. Whether it's a scarlet letter, a yellow Star of David, or a dunce cap, the effect is to broadcast the deviant status.

Goffman (1963:4) identifies three different types of stigma: abominations of the body (physical deformities), blemishes of individual character (weak will, unnatural passions, rigid beliefs), and tribal stigmas (race, religion, nationality). An individual bearing a stigmatized trait is identified by that trait. Other attributes the individual possesses are irrelevant. The stigma becomes the master status—a status so powerful that the person is defined in terms of that attribute. So a student from New England attending a small southern college becomes "the Yankee"; a woman physician becomes "the lady doctor"; a person once hospitalized for mental illness becomes known as "the nutcase." The stigma spoils the social identity by fixing attention on only one aspect of the person.

Stigmatized people are treated differently. Ironically, it is the reactions of others rather than the stigmatized attribute that creates the deviant identity. Once a person is labeled deviant, we come to expect evidence of the deviant status. We look for confirmation of the stigma and use it to color our interpretation of interactions with the deviant. In a sense, we reward people for conforming to our expectations and ignore contradictory evidence. The stigmatized identity becomes a panacea. It can be used to account for any and all deviations from the expected. For example, my husband's family has been in the low country of South Carolina for almost three hundred years. I was born in Pennsylvania. While attending a family funeral, I overheard one of my in-laws explaining that I was to be excused for some behavior they found unusual because I was a Yankee. My daughter told me of similar experiences being a Southerner in the north. When she was about nine years old, we were preparing to move from Illinois to Mississippi. Her teachers and classmates began to warn her about problems she might encounter with Southerners. They also predicted she would have no trouble in school because the students would not be as advanced as those in her Illinois classes. They seemed unaware that she was a Southerner and that their prejudices and stereotypical beliefs might be offensive.

In summary, stigmatized individuals and groups are devalued and labeled deviant. They then become the targets of stereotyping, prejudice, and discrimination. The reactions of others reinforce the stigmatized attribute. Eventually the stigma becomes part of the self-concept, creating a deviant or—as Goffman put it—a "spoiled" identity.

W. E. B. Du Bois

Until recently, the work of *W. E. B.* Du Bois was not included in texts covering modern social theory. Ironically, racism—the very subject Du Bois sought to explain—limited his access to an academic audience. Stanley Gaines and Edward Reed (1994:8) contend that modern social psychology has all but "shunned" the work of Du Bois. Although Du Bois is credited with many firsts (e.g., he was the first African American to receive a Ph.D. from Harvard and a founder of the NAACP), his academic contributions were ignored by most of his white contemporaries. He was one of the first American scholars to use a Marxist class analysis, but this contribution was overlooked for most of the twentieth century. Perhaps his most important contribution to the social psychology of prejudice is the concept of double consciousness. **Double consciousness** refers to a dilemma experienced by people with conflicting social-class and racial group interests. Du Bois claimed that as black people became more affluent, their class interests and racial interest were likely to be at odds. On the one hand, they could identify with the economic interests of the middle class; on the other hand, they were still members of a racial minority group. This confusion makes identifying social and political interests more difficult and thus makes those in minority races more vulnerable to false consciousness (i.e., identifying with their oppressors).

According to Du Bois (1903) the most significant problem of the twentieth century was overcoming the color line:

> Herein lie buried many things which if read with patience may show the strange meaning of being black here in the dawning of the Twentieth Century. This meaning is not without interest to you, Gentle Reader; for the problem of the Twentieth Century is the problem of the color-line.

He was the first to write about racial prejudice from the target's perspective. Unfortunately, a century later, nearly all the research and theory on prejudice focuses on people who hold prejudiced beliefs (Swim and Sangor 1998). This is hardly surprising because most of the researchers belong to groups that have traditionally been perpetrators of prejudice rather than its targets. That Du Bois' early focus on the targets of prejudice was ignored illustrates how racism silences its victims.

Du Bois describes what it feels like to "be a problem" in a society and how this warps the sense of self. Rather than being understood as victims of an unjust system, blacks are cast by the white-dominated society as the source of social ills. He describes being made strange by seeing himself through the eye of the white world. He explains that when one sees oneself through the eyes of others there is no true self-consciousness. The self of black people, he claimed, is framed by contempt and pity reflected in the eyes of others. "One ever feels his two-ness—an American, a Negro; two souls, two thoughts, two unreconciled strivings; two warring ideals in one dark body—whose dogged strength alone keeps it from being torn asunder" (Du Bois 1903:1). Du Bois described the persistent and fundamental contributions of Blacks to American society although their voices have been silenced and their contributions co-opted.

The ideas of these five early contributors to theory and research on prejudice include micro- and macro-approaches from psychology and sociology. Allport situated his ideas about prejudiced personalities within a holistic framework that included historical, sociocultural, situational, psychodynamic, phenomenological contexts, and the immediate stimulus object of the prejudice. Klineberg focused on the cognitive development of prejudice during childhood socialization. Van den Berghe contributed a macro-sociological perspective that cast prejudice as arising from and reflecting the inequality embedded in social structure. Goffman, a micro-sociologist, contributed the idea of social stigma and its effects on social identity. Du Bois focused on the consequences of prejudice on the self concept and political consciousness of it's targets. Next, we shall see how these ideas developed into contemporary theories of prejudice in sociology and psychology.

CONTEMPORARY THEORIES OF PREJUDICE

Research on prejudice does not fall neatly into competing camps. In addition to the mix of sociological and psychological approaches, there is research on racism, sexism, ageism, homophobia, and other specific kinds of prejudice. Initially most researchers have followed Allport's lead by focusing on the perpetrator, but recently the perspective of the targets has generated some exciting new avenues of inquiry (e.g., Swim and Stangor 1998). Although the crossover between these areas of research indicates the usefulness and productivity of multidisciplinary collaborations, it also blurs their boundaries. Primarily to help students of prejudice understand the sometimes-subtle differences in ideas and the traditions they emerge from, I will continue to use the sociological and psychological divisions in social psychology to organize the presentation of contemporary theories of prejudice.

Sociological Perspectives

Micro-level Perspectives: Symbolic Interaction and Labeling Theory
Perhaps the oldest and most developed social psychological theory in sociology is **symbolic interaction.** Herbert Blumer (1937) applied this term to the theory some time after it began to emerge. Symbolic interaction rests on a foundation of ideas developed by George Herbert Mead, W. I. Thomas, Charles Horton Cooley, and other early-twentieth-century scholars. Blumer coined this term because of the prominence of symbolic communication within the theory. The basic premise of symbolic interaction is that people create and negotiate the meanings they apply to objects, events, and people through a process of interaction. Meaning is not fixed. It is not an inherent property of objects, actions, or words. It is generated in the responses of people to things, events, actions, and the words they and others use. People use a variety of symbol systems to communicate. These symbol systems include languages, gestures, postures, and a host of notation systems such as written language or musical scores.

Existence of human society would not have been possible if people could not come to some shared meaning. Still, people can never know absolutely that the meaning they intend to convey is the meaning that others perceive. So people engage in a dynamic and continual process of constructing subjective meanings trying to convey those meanings to others. By this process of symbolic interaction, people negotiate consensus or agreement about what is meant. According to symbolic interaction theory, human society is not a structure that imposes order upon people but a process by which people create structure and order.

Symbolic interaction perspective focuses on why and how people use prejudice in everyday interaction. But, instead of identifying a list of functions that prejudice fulfills, symbolic interactionists attend directly to how prejudice affects communication. Bob Blauner (1993) explains that people from different groups often "talk past" each other. That is, their experiences and the understanding are so different that although they may be using the same language, they are not sharing meaning. Blauner explains that black people and white people experience race relations from different social positions and interpret racism very differently. For example, white people who as individuals hold few or no negative attitudes about black people may not consider themselves racists because they don't *feel* racial hatred. Black people experience racism as more than personal animosity. They are more likely than whites to understand racism as an oppressive system, rather than an individual attitude (Wellman 1977).

Goffman's work on stigma is part of the symbolic interactionist tradition. His ideas are often used in conjunction with **labeling theory** (also known as **societal reaction theory**). Labeling theory has been used to explain how people come to have deviant identities. In each stage of the labeling process, individuals see themselves differently and are seen differently by others. When individuals accept the deviant attribute as part of their self, they have established a deviant identity. A deviant identity is not just based on reactions to behaviors—Goffman noted ascribed characteristics like race and sex can be considered deviant. So just being outside the dominant race, class, gender, or age groups can be considered deviant.

Prejudice is a reaction to a deviant status. It helps define the relationship with an individual and between groups. It can be used to define or label a person as deviant, to form expectations about how the person is likely to behave, and to interpret ongoing interaction. Ironically, this process works regardless of whether there is any actual deviant behavior. For example, suppose you are walking along a city street well after dark. You see several young men wearing baggy clothes loitering near an alley. If the young men were also members of a different race, no deviant behavior is necessary for the labels to be applied and expectations generated. Regardless of the behaviors or intentions of the young men, prejudices enter the process of giving meaning to the situation.

Symbolic interaction is a micro-perspective that focuses on how people generate meaning in everyday interaction. It helps explain why people from different groups come to have different understanding of their everyday world. It can also be used to explain how we use our prejudices to anticipate the behavior of others and interpret ongoing interaction.

Mezzo-level Perspectives and Personality Perspective: Social Structure and Personality, Contact Hypothesis, and Social Distance

Mezzo-level theories are often called bridging theories because they look at the effects of social structure within the context of individuals in interaction. They bridge the gap between individual motivations and social forces. The three mezzo-level perspectives discussed in this section explain how situational and structural context can affect the type and degree of prejudice that people express.

Research using the social structure and personality perspective emphasizes the components of social structure, such as social roles, statuses, and networks. According to James House (1992) there are three key principles that help us understand the effects of social structure upon the individual: components of social structure, the proximity principle, and the psychology effect. Connections between prejudiced attitudes and discriminatory behaviors and these components are identified and understood by their proximity. In other words, one can exhibit a prejudice while performing a particular role but show no signs of that negative attitude when in another role. To understand prejudice, one must investigate which aspects of the social structure are affecting the prejudiced person and how. According to this perspective, prejudice cannot be understood apart from the social environment in which it takes place.

According to the proximity principle, people experience the effects of social structure through interpersonal interactions with others (House 1992). The informal rules or **norms** that govern interaction compel people to act in proscribe ways. Proximal experiences become part of the personality when individuals internalize norms. Whether a person chooses to follow the rules or not, they are acutely aware of them. You may remember feeling awkward or uncomfortable if you have ever broken a social norm by behaving inappropriately in a social situation. Those feelings of embarrassment indicate the effects of a social force. Individuals can choose to follow or disregard a social norm, but if people disregard social norms, there are consequences. If a person does not behave in the expected normative manner, interaction with others is disrupted. Others can no longer anticipate the actions and reactions of the nonconformist. Thus they can't make sense of the interaction.

Have you ever noticed that when you really get to know a person, you no longer identify them as a member of a particular group? You no longer pay attention to the race or ethnicity of your friend; a woman friend is just one of the guys; or perhaps the age disparity you found so noticeable in the beginning of a friendship no longer seems like such a difference. When people become friends, they cease to be a representative of a group; instead, we see them as individuals with unique characteristics. This simple observation is the major premise of ***contact theory.*** Getting to know people in other groups helps reduce prejudice. Intergroup contact can break down stereotyped notions and reduce prejudices against other groups (Myrdal 1944; Williams 1947). Contact theory contends that physical and social separation, which reduces contact between groups, promotes ignorance. Ignorance increases reliance on stereotypes, negative beliefs, and hostility between groups. Encouraging contact between groups dispels inaccurate ideas and reduces hostility between groups.

Can it really be as simple as that? Unfortunately, not all contacts lead to a reduction in prejudice and intergroup hostility. Contact theory has been amended over the years by many studies specifying the nature of intergroup contact (see Pettigrew 1971). There are five conditions under which contact reduces prejudice. First, brief or sporadic contact has little or no effect on prejudice. To reduce prejudice, the contact must be sustained over time (Brewer 1996). Second, the contact must involve cooperation. Prejudice is reduced only when the contact is not competitive (Sherif et al. 1956/1988). Third, mere acquaintance with people from other groups does not significantly reduce prejudice. Contact must be personal and informal for prejudice reduction. Fourth, the contact between groups should have the sanction and support of legitimate authority. That is, both individuals in positions of authority and the policies of institutions and organizations should facilitate contact and advocate prejudice reduction. Finally, the setting in which contact occurs should bestow equal status on both groups. This is possibly the most important and difficult condition to meet because people existing in a system of

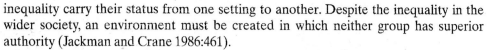

inequality carry their status from one setting to another. Despite the inequality in the wider society, an environment must be created in which neither group has superior authority (Jackman and Crane 1986:461).

Contact theory has been criticized by macro-sociologists because it ignores structural and institutional causes of prejudice and reduces prejudice to individual ignorance. This allows governments and policy makers to sidestep responsibility for inequality generated by policies, practices, and organizational structure. This has led some researchers to deem contact theory irrelevant, despite its long record of empirical support (e.g., Jackman and Crane 1986). Other researchers contend that it is premature to dismiss contact theory even though it has been used to reduce intergroup conflict to a micro-level problem (Connolly 2000). Contact theory is a mezzo-level theory, despite the individualistic conclusions that have been drawn from contact research. That is, the theory can potentially bridge the gap between individual behavior and the broader social structure. Several studies have focused more on the group experience than on individualistic experience. Gaertner and colleagues argue that in addition to group identities, a superordinate identity that encompasses all the groups in contact can lead to a greater reduction of prejudices (1996). Another example of the mezzo-level implications drawn from contact research suggests that groups that retain their group identities while engaging in a cooperative task with another group have a more positive contact experience (Deschamps and Brown 1983; Hewstone and Brown 1986).

Although contact theory has a long and reliable record of empirical support, it seems that contact reduces prejudice only under specific, and sometimes highly artificial, circumstances. On the one hand, there is consistent evidence that under specific conditions, increased contact between groups leads to a reduction of stereotypes and prejudice. On the other hand, some of these circumstances, especially equal status for participating groups, are hardly likely to occur outside of a controlled experimental environment. Another criticism of the theory is the political use to which the theory has been put. The results of contact experiments have been used to shift attention and responsibility away from institutional or structural causes of inequality and its attendant prejudices.

Social distance theory examines the conditions under which people avoid contact with people from other groups. The concept of social distance isn't new, but it continues to be important because it has been one of the most reliable indicators of intergroup prejudices and stereotypes. Park and Burgess (1921) defined social distance as the tendency to approach or withdraw from another group. Emory Bogardus converted the concept into a scale that measures social distance. The Bogardus scale asks people how willing they would be to interact with members of various groups in specific situations. Some kinds of contact (e.g., dating or marrying outside of your own group) are more likely to be avoided than others (e.g., shopping or working in the same office). Generally the more intimate the contact, the more it is resisted (Bogardus 1971). The Bogardus scale has been used to track changes in the degree of social distance between groups over time (Owen et al. 1981). The tendency has been a gradual reduction of social distance over the twentieth century. This reduction has been accompanied by a decline in overt expressions of prejudice. The decline of overt expression of prejudice and the denial of prejudice has led to several new theories that explain more covert forms of prejudice (see Chapter 8). These theories initially sought to explain covert forms of racism (benevolent racism, modern racism, and symbolic racism) but have been applied to other forms of inequality as well (e.g., symbolic sexism and homophobia).

Sociological social psychology is distinguished by its focus on (1) interactions between people, (2) participation in groups, and (3) the effects of the surrounding culture and underlying social structure on interaction. In other words, sociologists concentrate on the social circumstances surrounding the individual rather than on the personal characteristics of individuals.

Macro-level Perspectives: Order and Conflict

Macro-level perspectives focus on collectivities of people rather than individuals. They are called macro-level theories because they investigate the interaction between groups and the parts of social systems rather than that between individuals. The debate between two competing macro-theories—functionalism and conflict theory—has shaped sociological studies of prejudice. The **functionalist perspective** is also called an *order,* or *consensus, theory* because one of its basic premises is that social order arises out of consensus. Functionalism is built on the theoretical foundations of Auguste Comte, Emile Durkheim, and Talcott Parsons. It dominated sociological theory for much of the twentieth century. According to this theory, patterns of social behavior are created and perpetuated because they perform functions for society. In other words, they meet some social need. Society is made of many interdependent parts, so that a change in any part of society affects every other part. Each part of society performs functions within the social system. If the society is functioning properly, balance and stability are maintained. If, however, the system is changing rapidly, social order breaks down. The system becomes dysfunctional thereby preventing it from meeting the needs of society. Thus, order and stability are desirable, whereas rapid change threatens society.

According to functionalism, people and groups in a society depend on each other to meet basic needs. Cooperation is necessary if the needs of society are to be met. Consensus on basic social values is necessary for cooperation. Thus, social values are the glue that holds a society together and prejudices are part of that value system.

How are prejudices part of our value system? A **value** is a standard judgment by which people decide on desirable goals and outcomes (Hewitt 1988). Values are the criteria by which we judge other people, issues, and events. They justify the rules by which we live and how we think people should behave. One important distinction is that values express how we *should* behave and how our system *ought* to work. However, values are *not* an accurate description of how things actually work. This explains why people's behavior is not always consistent with their values. Prejudices are prejudgments of people, issues, events, or things. Values are the criteria we use to make judgments. People often make judgments about others either before they've had relevant experiences with them or that ignore experiences that are contrary to their prejudices. Those judgments often stem from beliefs about how things *ought* to be—in other words, they stem from our values.

Consider, for example, the family values that became the focus of political attention over the last two decades. Lack of proper family values was cited as the catalyst for all sorts of social problems: illegitimacy, welfare mothers, drug use, delinquency, and crime, to name but a few. But what exactly are those family values? Did they mean the only acceptable family was a traditional, father-headed, single-wage-earner family that included a legally wedded husband and wife and their biological offspring? Did they mean there should be no divorce or remarriage? Did they mean the only alternative to out-of-wedlock pregnancy was marriage? Did they mean that households with an employed wife and mother were less acceptable? If we compare our families with this rather narrow view of family values, most of our families would not be in complete compliance. But, how our individual families measure up isn't really the purpose. Remember, people don't have to behave consistently with their values to hold them. Family values represent what ought to be, an ideal to which we aspire. The family value concept, narrow or not, expresses a standard by which we judge ourselves and others. However people interpret family values, it reminded people that families should be a priority.

The family values issue had another important use: it preserved other social hierarchies. *Family values* became a buzzword that encompassed a profusion of prejudices including homophobia (e.g., the exclusion of homosexuals from marriage), sexism (e.g., the stigma attached to unwed mothers and mothers with careers), and even racism (e.g., the stereotypes of minority welfare mothers). So homosexuals, women, and minorities were judged as falling further from the ideal family.

The vagueness of the family values concept is not a hindrance because its very ambiguity hides potential value conflicts and creates an illusion of consensus. Nearly everyone agrees that family is important, but there is much less agreement about what constitutes family. So is it family we valued or is it protecting and preserving a particular form of family? From the functionalist perspective both amount to the same thing. Value consensus—or the illusion of consensus—promotes social stability and inhibits change. By making family values a political issue, attention was focused on recent changes in family, calling them into question. That is why functionalism is a theory often favored by political conservatives. It seeks to conserve the system as it exists, by resisting and impeding further change.

Although functionalism was the dominant social theory for most of the twentieth century and is still viable, the second half of the century gave rise to more critical theories. Functionalism was criticized for accepting and justifying existing social arrangements without exploring how they benefit the powerful groups while exploiting other groups. Chief among the critical theories is **conflict theory.** Whereas functionalism contends that social order stems from consensus and cooperation, conflict theory contends that social order arises from conflict. Conflict theory is built on the foundation laid by Karl Marx and Friedrich Engels (Tucker 1978). Marx and Engels' ideas were almost exclusively concerned with economics. Modern conflict theory is much broader. It's not one single theory but a set of related theories that have been applied to subjects as diverse as gender inequality, race relations, and collective behavior. These theories agree that society is composed of competing groups with conflicting interests. Social order arises from the process and the resolution of these conflicts. Competing groups have different sources and amounts of power. For instance, one group may have greater access to wealth, whereas another may have greater numbers and better group solidarity. Groups use whatever power they can generate to protect their interests. When in conflict, one group usually becomes dominant. The dominant group uses its power to change the way the social structure operates, so that the structure serves its interests. Once the dominant group succeeds in rewriting the rules, it can control a disproportionate share of society's resources.

It is in the interests of the dominant group to suppress opposition. When I explained system justification in Chapter 2, I pointed out that control of ideology is a pivotal tactic in suppressing challengers. Ideas can be suppressed directly by coercion.

But this is likely to be a costly and unstable strategy. The direct suppression of ideas is often met with backlash and subversive resistance. An indirect yet effective strategy is *false consciousness.* False consciousness occurs when disadvantaged groups accept ideas that are not in their interests. When false consciousness is successful, even people harmed by the ideology embrace it. So the appearance of consensus, which is touted as the basis of social order and stability by the functionalists, is artificial and unstable according to conflict theory. The illusion of consensus is either directly enforced by coercion and repression or indirectly accomplished through false consciousness.

Prejudices are part of ideologies used to justify and perpetuate the oppression of disadvantaged groups. It's easy to understand how prejudices held by members of the dominant group about oppressed groups are used to justify the advantages of the dominant group. However, it's not unusual for people in disadvantaged groups to hold prejudices against other disadvantaged groups and even their own group. By appealing to the prejudices of each group toward the other, attention is deflected from the dominant group. Accepting the dominant group's prejudices and stereotypes about other disadvantage groups offers some small measure of status within a system of inequality. For example, consider the racial tension between African Americans and Latinos. Both minority groups struggle with poverty and unemployment; yet instead of joining forces to combat racial and ethnic prejudices and discrimination, they are often locked into conflict against each other. Ironically, this makes it easier for the dominant group to maintain its advantage over both groups and provides justification for these advantages. Members of the dominant group might ask, why should they censure their prejudices if the minority groups exhibit the same prejudices against each other?

Prejudice toward lower-status members of one's own race mirrors and reinforces racial stratification between different racial and ethnic groups. Consider the phenomenon of *colorism.* Colorism refers to discrimination against darker-skinned people by lighter-skinned members of the same group. Lighter-skinned people claim a higher status, but the price of that status is high. Colorism creates a mirror image of racial inequality within the racial group, thus legitimizing the ideology that justifies racial oppression in the wider society.

Another form of false consciousness is *double consciousness.* As mentioned earlier, the term was first coined by W. E. B. Du Bois (Du Bois 1969; Dennis 1996; Rawls 2000). Conflicts between two social identities contribute to double consciousness. As African Americans enter the middle-class, their class interests and racial interest were likely to be at odds. This dual social identity causes confusion and makes racial minorities more vulnerable to false consciousness (i.e., identifying with their oppressors). Double consciousness can also be applied to explain similar dilemmas faced by women as they rise through the occupational ranks.

Sometimes people distance themselves from the negative attributes of their groups by contrasting their personal attributes with stereotyped attributes of their group. In feminist theory this is called being *male identified.* For example, some women may claim to enjoy being with male friends more because they contend that most women talk of trivial, uninteresting matters. This tactic may distance an individual woman from the negative attribute, but at the same time, it affirms the stereotypes and perpetuates the devaluation of women as a group. Even though individuals or groups may use these tactics to boost their status by contrast with the devalued group, they have actually perpetuated their group's disadvantage and ultimately their own.

Realistic conflict theory is an interesting contemporary hybrid of the conflict perspective and psychological research on intergroup relations. According to this theory, groups can have incompatible goals and be in competition for scarce resources. This extends the uses of prejudice beyond the tactics of false consciousness. The conflict is "real" in the sense that the groups have distinctive interests that generate conflict between them. This contrasts with the more psychological argument that prejudice is used by groups to generate intergroup conflict and animosity. Intergroup conflict creates solidarity within each group and may be used as a solution for factions within a group. Thus, it is used to solve intragroup dynamics (Jackman 1994:38–39). According to realistic conflict theory, animosity between the groups can also be generated by real conflicts. These conflicts are caused by a real difference in each group's self-interest, or they can be manipulated by a dominant group that pits minority groups against each other.

The functional and conflict perspectives are competing theories. Functionalism contends that society is organized in ways that serve people's basic needs. Social order and stability emerge from value consensus. Conflict theorists believe that a powerful dominating group arranges the social systems in ways that serves the interests of the powerful few at the expense of the rest of society. For conflict theorists, value consensus is an illusion perpetuated by the powerful to quell conflict.

Psychological Perspectives

Although there is much cross over between sociological and psychological theories of prejudice, psychological theories attempt to "explain how the thoughts, feelings, and behaviors of individuals are influenced by the actual, imagined, or implied presence of others" (Allport 1968). The theories described in this section concentrate on the attributes of prejudiced individuals or the processes that incorporate prejudices into social identity.

Frustration Aggression and Relative Deprivation

Shortly after the terrorist attacks in September 2001, there was a rash of attacks on people thought to be Arabs. One of these incidents occurred in Arizona, where a convenience store clerk was murdered because he was wearing a turban. Given that the clerk was a Sikh from India, not an Arab or a Moslem, we see that actual conflict between groups is not necessary for prejudice to have dire consequences. Sometimes people blame troubling events on out-group members who have nothing to do with the events. Allport referred to this phenomenon as *scapegoating* (1954:244). The term comes from a Hebrew religious ritual in which a goat was used to symbolically assume the sins of the people. The goat was then released into wilderness, symbolically carrying with it their transgressions (Leviticus 16:20–22). Psychological scapegoating involves two distinct psychological processes: projection and displacement. *Projection* refers to seeing our own inadequacies in other people. It allows people to externalize distressing thoughts and behaviors, so that misfortune is a result of others' behaviors or faults rather than one's own fault. *Displacement* refers to targeting anger toward a convenient or vulnerable target rather than targeting the responsible party. Both processes are part of the *Frustration Aggression* theory of prejudice. This theory contends that troubling or stressful events trigger aggressive impulses, which are directed at convenient and vulnerable out-group members, regardless of whether the person or their group is responsible for the troubling events. It follows that in times of economic, political, social, or personal stress, prejudice and discrimination should increase.

Evidence for the frustration aggression hypothesis is mixed. Although there seems to be a relationship between economic downturns and increased prejudice, it is neither strong nor consistent (cf. Hovland and Sears 1940; Hepworth and West 1988; Green et al. 1998). Studies conducted by the U.S. military during and after World War II further specified the frustration–aggression link by adding the concept of *relative deprivation* (Stouffer et al. 1949–1950). Relative rather than absolute deprivation is more likely to trigger frustration and aggression. That is, if one feels disadvantaged relative to their reference group, they are more likely to become discontent and frustrated. So discontent and frustration do not necessarily arise from real obstacles; they can also emerge from the perception of disadvantage relative to others.

Another offshoot of the frustration aggression theory is *cognitive neoassociationist view* (Berkowitz 1984). This perspective suggests that exposure to aversive events generates negative feelings. Negative feelings can trigger aggression in some and flight or withdrawal in others. This extends the frustration aggression idea in two ways. First, the theory acknowledges that frustration is not the only stimulus that triggers prejudice and aggression. Prejudice can also be triggered by external conditions. Second, aggression is not the only response to frustration. Withdrawal and avoidance are also responses to aversive events and negative feelings. So frustration stemming from real obstacles or from feeling of deprivation in comparison with others can lead to aggression and prejudice, but the same circumstances can also lead to withdrawal and avoidance of the target group. What accounts for the variation in response? The next theory we consider asks if there is something about an individual's personality that can explain differing reactions.

The Authoritarian Personality

Social theories are more or less logical, but often people's behavior is more rationalizing than rational. Everyone can recall someone whose prejudices seemed to be an irrational hodgepodge of conflicting biases. Research about the authoritarian personality describes how prejudice can be used to connect seemingly unrelated elements of political, economic, and social views.

One of the reasons I personally became interested in the subject of prejudice was the vehemence with which people confound their logic with their prejudices. Some time ago I was interviewed by a reporter from the Associated Press on the unlikely topic of soap operas. A television rating service had identified the college town where I then taught and lived as the place with the largest proportion of residents watching daytime dramas (soap operas). The reporter wanted some insight from a social psychologist to explain this phenomenon. I told the reporter that because it was a fairly small city, soap operas might provide some vicarious excitement. My comment seemed pretty innocuous to me, but the responses I got were venomous. I've never given an opinion to the press that generated as much passionate hate mail as this seemingly mild statement. What was fascinating about the responses was the leap in association that people made. First, every letter-writer assumed I was criticizing soap opera viewers. This was followed in more than one letter by the charge that I was an elitist snob. One man even questioned my loyalty to the United States. All these deductions were made from a two-line quote in a generally positive story about the popularity of soap operas in a small southern college town.

I found the letters fascinating, but disturbing, so I decided to analyze the letters. First, all the people who wrote happened to be male. This struck me as peculiar because the majority of the viewing audience for daytime drama is female. Second, every letter mentioned either a religious or military affiliation. Finally, my gender was mentioned critically by every letter-writer—either they used my gender to discredit my opinion or they suspected my sexual orientation was not heterosexual. The results of my informal analysis of the hate mail I received were surprisingly consistent with the research that has been done on prejudiced personalities.

Psychological social psychologists first began investigating the idea of a prejudiced personality in the 1950s. Adorno and his colleagues (1950) found that the political, economic, and social opinions often formed a coherent pattern indicating a deep-lying personality trend they called the *authoritarian personality*. According to Adorno's research, people with an authoritarian personality are usually reared in a very traditional, rigid, patriarchal family. In this type of family, a powerful father figure controls almost every aspect of the family's life. Physical punishment and fear are the primary means used to control family members. One response of children raised in this kind of environment is strict adherence to authority combined with a very deep resentment of authority. Because this anger cannot be directed at the powerful father figure, it is displaced on targets that occupy powerless positions in the wider social order. The displacement of anger allows a vent for the anger and at the same time reinforces the authority structure that produced the rage. The targets chosen by the authoritarian person occupy a position similar to the powerless position of a child in a patriarchal family. So the authoritarian submits to authority, but acts aggressively to those below him in the social order. In effect, he mirrors the authority that he hates.

Although I have used the male pronoun, women can also exhibit authoritarian traits. However, in our patriarchal culture, males are more likely than females to have authoritarian personalities. The authoritarian personality also projects concerns about sex and sexuality onto others. Sexual control is central to the maintenance of patriarchal authority. Repression of sexuality leads people with authoritarian personalities to project their own repressed desires onto others. They see evidence of wanton sexuality everywhere, which they need to control in others as much as they need to repress and control themselves. This manifests itself both as homophobia and in prejudices against women.

The authoritarian personality both submits to and is enraged by authority, but the very authority structure that caused the paradox provides the illusion of control vital to the authoritarian. The authoritarian can only manage the inner conflict by living within a very strict and concrete system of rules and sanctions. This allows the authoritarian to control both himself and others. The external rules and laws such as those provided by military institutions and some religions meet this need.

Adorno and his colleagues (1950) found that people with authoritarian personalities were highly prejudiced. They tended to be anti-Semitic, antiblack, anti-homosexual and held very traditional and limited ideas about gender roles. As you might image, this research was extremely controversial especially given the political climate in the early 1950s.[2] It was criticized by conservatives who felt it was politically biased. However,

---

[2] During the early 1950s the House Committee on Un-American Activities led by Joseph McCarthy conducted a political witch hunt for people suspected of ties to the Communist Party.

more recent work on authoritarianism confirms the link between the right-wing political ideology and authoritarianism (Altmeyer 1981, 1994).

Cognitive Theories of Prejudice

Work on the authoritarian personality overlapped with and produced some insights into the cognitive dimensions of prejudice, particularly the intolerance for ambiguity. The need to be able to make clear-cut distinctions is by no means limited to authoritarians. People categorize things as a means of processing information. If the categories are fuzzy, it becomes more difficult to make decisions. Cognitive theories of prejudice contend that prejudice is a by-product of categorizing. Because the social world we live in is exceedingly complex, people must simplify it to make it more manageable. Categorization is a fundamental process of differentiation. We categorize people in much the same way that we categorize objects and events. Not only does categorization differentiate between us and them, it also magnifies similarities among members of out-groups. Whereas people recognize diversity and unique individual attributes of members of their group, they overestimate the similarity of out-group members. This allows people to make the differences between us and them more starkly.

The cognitive perspective contends that prejudices and stereotypes can be understood as products of the cognitive processes we use to process information (Anderson and Klatsky 1987). This involves how memory operates, how reasoning occurs, and how information is integrated during complex social interaction. Because interaction is so dynamic, people often use shortcuts so that they can process information quickly. These shortcuts are called *cognitive strategies*. Although not infallible, they provide quick and simple ways to deal with fast-moving interaction. They allow people to make sense of ongoing interaction and for the most part they work. That is, despite inaccuracies, people use cognitive strategies to quickly size up a situation and form a response without disrupting the flow of interaction.

People typically categorize objects, events, and other people based on similarity or perceived similarity of attributes. Of course, visible attributes make for the easiest and fastest categorization. So we find highly visible attributes, such as sex, age, and race are used universally to make categorizations. As soon as people are separated into groups, stereotypes and prejudices begin to emerge. Tajfel (1978) demonstrated this process in his work on the "minimal group paradigm." In his experiment, subjects were divided into groups based on fictional test scores. Subjects who had no prior contact with each other were told that their group assignment was based on whether they overestimated or underestimated the number of dots presented on flash cards. Even without any real basis of shared attributes or conflict between groups, subjects demonstrated in group favoritism and negative stereotyping of the out-group.

Thus, people use categorization to make sense of the complex and fast pace of social interaction. Once people are sorted into groups, regardless of the validity of the differences used to make the categorization, stereotyping and prejudice emerge. Therefore, the cognitive process of categorization is at the heart of prejudice and stereotyping.

Stereotypes are exaggerated beliefs associated with a group or category of people. We use them as cognitive shortcuts. Although for the most part the shortcuts work, there are some drawbacks. Some cognitive strategies lead to greater reliance on prejudices and stereotypes. Numerous cognitive strategies have been identified. Below I describe strategies that have important connections with prejudice and stereotyping.

One cognitive strategy that exacerbates or exaggerates prejudice is the tendency to use more-recent events or associations that come easily to mind to categorize: that is, to use what comes first to mind. This is called the ***availability heuristic.*** For example, have you ever noticed a new word that you recently learned seems to frequently be popping up in conversations and your reading? Because you recently attended to the word, it becomes more noticeable. It is the same cognitive process that allows recent experiences come to mind easier than prior experiences. For example, most people are aware of the dangers of travel by automobile and the relative safety of air travel. However, the highly publicized air disasters of September 11, 2001, made people reluctant to fly and crippled the airline industry. People ignored the statistics and the improbability of a recurrence because the images of the disaster were so readily available.

Stereotypes, by definition, are overgeneralizations. There is usually a kernel of truth behind the stereotype, but that kernel gets exaggerated and overapplied. People sometimes use stereotypes as if they were reliable standards. They make judgments based on the resemblance of a person, object, or event to stereotypical cases. This strategy is called the ***representativeness heuristic*** (Tversky and Kahnman 1982). Let's say you see a relatively young man wearing blue jeans, work boots, and a protective hard hat. Chances are he's a construction worker. The representativeness heuristic involves making a guess based on how closely the person resembles the stereotype. Male nurses are assumed to be physicians; African Americans are assumed to be employees rather than customers; and female professors are taken for secretaries—all examples of errors based on the representativeness heuristic. Once our department administrative assistant had made an appointment with me for two publishing representatives. I had never met or spoken with either representative. When they arrived for their appointment, the administrative assistant was temporarily out of the office. I walked into the office immediately after the representatives arrived. They said they had an appointment with Dr. Bakanic. I stuck my hand out and said I was Dr. Bakanic. One of the book representatives hesitated and said, "Are you sure?" We all laughed. Obviously, I did not match the professor stereotype.

A third cognitive strategy that contributes to prejudice and stereotyping is the ***illusory correlation.*** This refers to seeing patterns or links between things that are not really present. The link is an illusion. There are two phenomena that contribute to the illusory correlation. First, people tend to focus on and remember distinctive and negative events. For example, a lone man at a meeting of women stands out. We also tend to remember obstacles and take for granted a clear path. So if a distinctive person takes part in a negative event, we associate the attributes that make the person distinctive with the negative event (Baumeister et al. 2001). Another factor contributing to the illusory correlation is the confirmation bias. That is, people tend to notice and recall things that support their beliefs. We see what *we* want or expect to see.

Theory perseverance is another cognitive bias. Sometimes it's hard to let go of an idea. But, holding on to old beliefs and ideas results in prejudices that continue long after they've been debunked. The endurance of false beliefs creates an *incorrigible proposition*—a belief that people maintain despite overwhelming evidence to the contrary. We hold on to many of our prejudiced beliefs with a tenacity that would put mules to shame. Even social scientists hold to some incorrigible propositions. In a content analysis of obituaries of eminent psychologists, Radtke and her colleagues (2000:213) found that despite women becoming the numerical majority in the field of psychology "the predominant image of the successful psychologist remain the male scientist."

False consensus is another example of overgeneralizing, but this time what is overgeneralized is the similarity of our conclusions to others. People sometimes overestimate how many other people would make the same judgment as they did (Nickerson 1999). Overimputation of one's beliefs to others contributes the illusion of *common sense.* Remember, in Chapter 1, I contended that common sense is neither common nor simple. People understand common sense as simple ideas and meanings that everyone knows and accepts, although it is a false consensus resulting from another cognitive shortcut.

The cognitive perspective contends that prejudice and stereotyping are a consequence of categorization. Categorization is the basic cognitive process that people use to make complex social situations and information manageable. For the most part, categorization and cognitive shortcuts work well: they allow people to make rapid categorizations, interpret ongoing situations, and make decisions without disrupting the flow of interaction. However, the process is not always accurate. Cognitive shortcuts, such as availability, representativeness, illusory correlation, perseverance of beliefs, and false consensus, make the reduction of prejudice and stereotyping a persistent and perplexing challenge.

Social Identity Theory

Research on in-group favoritism lead to the development of social identity theory (Taijfel and Turner 1985). According to this theory, people need to feel good about both themselves and the groups they belong to. Part of how we think about ourselves comes from the groups with which we identify (i.e., in-groups). Comparing the in-group with outgroups helps create and maintain a positive social identity.

Of course, people have multiple ways of identifying themselves. We identify ourselves by our personal attributes (e.g., musical ability or having a good sense of humor) and by the groups we affiliate with (e.g., Baptists, Asian Americans, and Dallas Cowboys fans). The latter is called a ***social identification.*** Once a person has come to identify with a group, they make comparisons between their group and other groups. For example, people who identify themselves as Southerners might make comparisons with Yankees. These comparisons serve two purposes: they help people differentiate between groups and they help elevate the perception of their group. By making favorable comparisons to their group, they enhance their self-esteem and their group's status.

Let me illustrate with a fairly common and seemingly minor social identity. My husband is a die-hard Dallas Cowboys fan. I'm from Pittsburgh, so I pull for the Steelers. Come football season, we don our football identities and compare our teams with the others. We sing the praises of our teams' players and coaches and derogate the members of competing teams. We wear jackets with our team's colors and logo, and we feel affiliation with other fans of our respective teams. When our teams win, we vicariously claim victory. We feel good about ourselves even though we personally had nothing to do with the victory. Although this may seem like a trivial identification, there is

plenty of evidence to the contrary. Professional football is a multibillion-dollar industry, which relies heavily on fans' affiliation with the teams. In addition to the serious
economic component of this particular social identity, consider the intensity of emotions fans invest in the sport. Fans shout jubilantly, hug strangers, and occasionally even
become violent in response to the game. Nyla Branscombe and Daniel Wann (1992)
studied social identification with sports teams. They found that the more highly fans
identified with their team, the more likely they were to derogate other sports teams.
Out-group derogation was even more likely following a defeat. Platow and colleagues
(1999) found that social identification with sports teams also effects pro-social behavior. Charitable contributions were sought before and after six games. Charitable workers identified with the in-group team collected more contributions than those not
identified with the team. In addition, donations solicited after the games were higher
for those charitable workers identified with the winning team.

The extent to which people identify with an in-group is related to the likelihood of
intergroup prejudices. Strong identification with one group leads to greater derogation
of other groups (Wann and Branscombe 1992), discrimination toward out-groups
(Perreault and Bourhis 1999), and the need to maintain clear boundaries between
groups (Blascovich et al. 1997).

Like the mezzo-level theories in sociology, social identity theory bridges the gap
between the individual and society. It contends that part of our identity as individuals
comes from the groups we belong to. How we feel about ourselves depends in part on
how the groups we belong to compare with other similar groups. Out-group derogation
is one way to bolster in-group esteem. Prejudices can be a form of out-group derogation.

Summary

In this chapter, we have described the components of social theory, reviewed the work
of early theorists working on explaining prejudice, and reviewed some of the sociological and psychological theoretical contributions to the social psychology of prejudice.

The work of Gordon Allport was particularly influential in the psychological theories of prejudice. His work laid the foundations for frustration aggression theory and
the authoritarian personality. Some of the insights he contributed in his work on prejudiced personalities were influential in the development of the cognitive perspective on
prejudice and stereotyping.

Klineberg's work influenced the development of the cognitive perspective. His
work on effects of stereotyping in the cognitive development of children lead the
way to understanding how the categorization process contributes to prejudice and
stereotyping.

Van den Berghe brought the concept of social structure to the study of prejudice.
He saw prejudice as emerging from inequities built into the structure of society rather
than emanating from individuals. Goffman contributed the concept of social stigma.
His work had a profound impact on the development of symbolic interaction and labeling theory. None of the theories reviewed in this chapter offers a complete understanding of prejudice. But each offers a slightly different, and sometimes overlapping,
perspective that contributes to a better understanding of an extremely complex social
process.

Key Terms

- Authoritarian personality
- Availability heuristic
- Axiomatic format
- Causal format
- Cognitive neoassociationist view
- Conflict theory
- Contact theory
- Double consciousness

- Frustration aggression hypothesis
- Functionalism
- Illusory correlation
- Labeling theory
- Realistic conflict theory
- Relative deprivation
- Representativeness heuristic

- Social distance
- Social identification
- Stigma
- Symbolic interaction
- Theoretical concept
- Theory
- Values
- Variables

Key People

Erving Goffman
Gordon Allport
Otto Klineberg

Van den Berghe
W. E. B. Du Bois

Taking It Further — Class Exercises and Interesting Web Sites

Stigma Vs Freedom of Speech?

Go the National Mental Health Association's Stigma Watch Web site (http://www1.nmha.org/ newsroom/stigma/index.cfm). Click on the "ABC Crumbs sitcom" link.

How much harm is done by portraying mentally ill characters in a comic or boorish manner? Compare the comic treatment of gender or race in other contemporary sitcoms to the portrayal of a stigmatized trait. In what ways are the social effects the same and in what ways are stigmatized traits different.

References

Adorno, T. W., E. Frenkel-Brunswik, D. J. Levinson, and R. N. Sanford. 1950. *The authoritarian personality*. New York: Wiley Science Editions.

Allport, Floyd. 1924. *Social psychology*. New York: Johnson Reprint Corporation (1967).

Allport, Gordon W. 1954. *The nature of prejudice*. Reading, MA: Addison-Wesley Publishing Company.

———. 1968. The historical background of modern social psychology. In *Handbook of social psychology,* ed. G. Lindzey and E. Aronson, 1–80. Reading, MA: Addison-Wesley.

Altmeyer, Bob 1981. *Right wing authoritarianism.* Winnipeg: University of Manitoba Press.

———. 1994. Reducing prejudice in right wing authoritarians. In *The psychology of prejudice the Ontario Symposium,* Vol. 7, ed. P. Mark

Zanna and M. James Olson. Hillsdale, NJ: L. Erlbaum Associates.

Anderson, S. M., and R. L. Klatsky. 1987. Traits and social stereotypes: Levels of categorization in person perception. *Journal of Personality and Social Psychology* 53: 235–246.

Baron, Robert A., Donn Byrne, and Jerry Suls. 1988. *Exploring social psychology.* 3rd ed. Boston, MA: Allyn & Bacon.

Baumeister, Roy F., Ellen Bratslavsky, Catrin Finkenauer, and Kathleen D. Vohs. 2001. Bad is stronger than good. *Review of General Psychology* 5 (4): 323–370.

Berkowitz, Leonard. 1984. Some effects of thoughts on the anti- and prosocial influences of media events: A cognitive neoassociationistic analysis. *Psychological Bulletin* 95: 410–427.

Blascovich, Jim, N. A. Wyer, L. A. Swart, and J. L. Kibler. 1997. Racism and racial categorization. *Journal of Personality and Social Psychology* 72: 1364–1372.

Blauner, Robert. 1993. Language of race: Talking past one another. *Current* 349: 4–11.

Blumer, Herbert. 1937. Symbolic interaction. In *Man and society: A substantive introduction to the social sciences.* ed. E.P. Schmidt. New York: Prentice Hall.

Bogardus, Emory. 1971. *Immigration and race attitudes.* New York: J.S. Ozer.

Boutilier, Robert G., J. Christian Roed, and Ann C. Svendsen. 1980. Crisis in the two social psychologies: A critical comparison. *Social Psychology Quarterly* 43: 5–17.

Branscombe, Nyla, and Daniel Wann. 1992. Role of identification with group arousal, categorization processes, and self esteem in sports spectator aggression. *Human Relations* 45: 1013–1033.

Brewer, M. B. 1996. When contact is not enough: Social identity and intergroup cooperation. *International Journal of Intercultural Relations* 20: 291–303.

Brown v. Board of Education of Topeka, KS. 1954. 347 U.S. 483.

Capozza, D., and R. Brown. 2000. *Social identity processes: Trends in theory and research.* London: Sage Publications.

Connolly, Paul. 2000. What now for the contact hypothesis? Towards a new research agenda. *Race and Ethnicity Education* 3: 169–193.

Dennis, Rutledge M. 1996. Du Bois's concept of double consciousness: Myth and reality. *Research in Race and Ethnic Relations* 9: 69–90.

Deschamps, J. C., and R. J. Brown. 1983. Superordinate goals and intergroup conflict. *British Journal of Social Psychology* 22: 189–195.

Du Bois, W. E. B. 1903. *The souls of black folks: Essays and sketches.* Chicago, IL: A.C. McClurg & Co.

———.1969. *An ABC of color.* New York: International Publishers.

Gaines, Stanley O., Jr., and Edward S. Reed. 1994. Two social psychologies of prejudice: Gordon W. Allport, W.E.B. Du Bois, and the legacy of Booker T. Washington. *Journal of Black Psychology* 20: 8–28.

Gaertner, Samuel L., John F. Dovidio, and Betty A. Bachman. 1996. Revisiting the contact hypothesis: The induction of a common ingroup identity. *International Journal of Intercultural Relations* 20 (3–4): 271–290.

Goffman, Erving. 1963. *Stigma: Notes on the management of spoiled identity.* Englewood Cliffs, NJ: Prentice Hall.

Green, Donald P., Dara Strolovitch, and Janelle S. Wong. 1998. Defended neighborhoods, integration, and racially motivated crime. *American Journal of Sociology* 104 (2): 372–403.

Hepworth, Joseph T., and Stephen G. West. 1988. Lynchings and the economy: A time-series reanalysis of Hovland and Sears (1940). *Journal of Personality and Social Psychology* 55 (2): 239–247.

Herrnstien, Richard J., and Charles Murray. 1994. *The bell curve: Intelligence and class structure in American life.* New York: The Free Press.

Hewitt, J. P. 1988. *Self and society.* Boston, MA: Allyn & Bacon.

Hewstone, M., and R. Brown. 1986. Contact is not enough: An intergroup perspective on the "contact hypothesis." In *Contact and conflict in intergroup encounters,* ed. M. Hewston and R. Brown, 1–44. Oxford: Basil Blackwell.

House, James S. 1977. The three faces of social psychology. *Sociometry* 40: 161–177.

———. 1992. Social structure and personality. In *Social psychology: Sociological perspectives,* ed. M. Rosenberg and R. Turner. New Brunswick, NJ: Transaction Publishers.

Hovland, C. I., and R. R. Sears. 1940. Minor studies in aggression, VI: Correlation of lynchings with economic indices. *Journal of Psychology* 9: 301–310.

Jackman, Mary R. 1994. *The velvet glove: Paternalism and conflict in gender, class and race relations.* Berkeley, CA: University of California Press.

Jackman, Mary R., and Marie Crane. 1986. Some of my best friends are black. . . . *Public Opinion Quarterly* 50: 467–486.

Klineberg, Otto. 1935. *Race differences.* New York: Harper & Brothers Publishers.

Lambert, Wallace E., and Otto Klineberg. 1967. *Children's views of foreign peoples.* New York: Appleton Century Crofts.

Lindzey, Gardner. 1954. *Handbook of social psychology.* Cambridge, MA: Addison-Wesley.

McDougall, William. 1908. *An introduction to social psychology.* Boston, MA: J.W. Luce & Company.

Myrdal, Gunnar. 1944. *An American dilemma: The negro problem and modern democracy.* New York: Harper and Brothers.

Nickerson, Raymond. 1999. How we know—and sometimes misjudge—what others know: Imputing one's knowledge to others. *Psychological Bulletin* 125 (6): 737–759.

Owen, Carolyn, Howard Eisner, and Thomas McFaul. 1981. A half century of social distance research: National replication of the Bogardus studies. *Sociology and Social Research* 66: 80–98.

Park, Robert, and Ernest Burgess. 1921. *Introduction to the science of sociology.* Chicago, IL: University of Chicago Press.

Perreault, Steephane, and Richard Y. Bourhis. 1999. Ethnocentrism, social identification, and discrimination. *Personality and Social Psychology Bulletin* 25 (1): 92–103.

Pettigrew, T. F. 1971. *Racially separate of together.* New York: McGraw-Hill.

Platow, Michael J., Maria Durante, Naeidra Williams, Matthew Garrett, Jarrod Wlashe, Steven Cincotta, George Lianos, and Ayla Barutchu. 1999. The contribution of sport fan social identity to the production of prosocial behavior. *Group Dynamics: Theory, Research and Practice* 3 (2): 161–169.

Radtke, Lorraine, Madelene Hunter, and Henderikus Stam. 2000. In memoriam as in life: Gender and psychology in the obituaries of eminent psychologists. *Canadian Psychology* 41 (4): 213–229.

Rawls, Anne W. 2000. A "race" as an interaction order phenomenon: W.E.B. Du Bois's "double consciousness" thesis revisited. *Sociological Theory* 19: 241–274.

Sherif, Muzafer, O. J. Harvey, B. J. White, W. R. Hood, and C. W. Sherif. 1956/1988. *Robber's cave experiment.* Middletown, CT: Wesleyan University Press.

Stouffer, Samuel A. 1949–1950. *Studies in social psychology in World War II . . . prepared and edited under the auspices of a special committee of the Social Science Research Council.* Princeton, NJ: Princeton University Press.

Swim, Janet, and Charles Stangor. 1998. *Prejudice: The target's perspective.* San Diego, CA: Academic Press.

Tajfel, H. 1978. *Differentiation between social groups: Studies in the social psychology of intergroup relations.* London: Academic Press.

Tajfel, H., and J. C. Turner. 1986. The social identity theory of intergroup behavior. In *Psychology of intergroup relations,* ed. S. Worchel and L. W. Austin, 7–24. Chicago, IL: Nelson.

Tucker, Robert C. 1978. *The Marx Engels reader.* New York: W. W. Norton & Company, Inc.

Turner, Jonathan H. 1978. *The structure of sociological theory.* Homewood, IL: Dorsey Press.

Tversky, A., and D. Kahneman. 1982. Judgement under uncertainty: Heuristics and biases. In *Judgment under uncertainty,* ed. D. Kahneman, P. Slovic, and A. Tversky, 3–22. New York: Cambridge University Press.

Van den Berghe, Pierre L. 1967. *Race and racism.* New York: John Wiley & Sons, Inc.

Wellman, David. 1977. *Portrait of white racism.* Cambridge, MA: University of Cambridge Press.

Williams, Robin. 1947. *Reduction of intergroup tension.* New York: Social Science Research Council.

CHAPTER

The Role of Stereotypes in Prejudice

In this chapter, I will identify common stereotypes and explore how they emerge, whether they have any empirical basis and under what conditions people are likely to express them.

When I teach about prejudice, I ask students to help me identify and describe stereotypes. On anonymous forms, I have them list up to twenty attributes for categories of people. Sometimes I ask about racial groups; at other times I ask about age or gender categories. At first, the students are embarrassed and reluctant to list any attributes. I have to remind them that the lists they hand in are anonymous and that I do want them to identify stereotypes, both good and bad. Once they get over their reluctance, I get remarkably consistent lists from students even though they compile their lists independently: they identify the same attributes for the same groups. My students know what stereotypes are and can describe them accurately, but why the

73

initial awkwardness and embarrassment? The reason is the same every time. They don't want me to think they, as individuals, believe the stereotypes. They don't want me to think they use the stereotypes to make prejudiced judgments. Many of my students suspect that being aware of the stereotypes is somehow an implicit endorsement of them.

I encourage students to express and elaborate their opinions in class. Usually, it's not a problem to get students to take a stand and defend it. However, during our discussion of stereotypes students are uncharacteristically cautious, and they preface their remarks with a lot of extraneous disclaimers. I get comments that begin like these: "I don't believe this myself, but . . .," "It's really an exaggeration, but . . .," "Well, not everyone is like this, but . . .," "You don't fit the stereotype at all, but grandmothers are . . ." What my students and I come away from the discussion with is: (1) we all know what the stereotypes are, (2) we all know they are at some level inaccurate, and (3) we sometimes use them anyway.

WHAT IS A STEREOTYPE?

In Chapter 1, we learned that stereotypes are exaggerated beliefs or overgeneralizations associated with a group or category of people. Stereotypes are not all negative. For example, contemporary stereotypes include that African Americans are good athletes and Asians are good at math. Stereotypes are not always inaccurate either. For example, many gender stereotypes are reasonably accurate (see Swim 1994). Women may indeed be more nurturing than men, whereas men are more aggressive than women. However, whether the stereotype is positive or negative and despite its accuracy for particular individuals, stereotyped traits are attributed to a group in comparison with other groups (Judd and Park 1993). That is, the trait does not have to occur in every or even most individuals in the group; it need only be more prevalent in one group compared with another.

The word *stereotype* was borrowed from journalism. Originally, the term referred to a process of making printing plates so that pictures could be reproduced in newspapers or books. Journalist-turned sociologist Walter Lippman applied the term to help understand a common cognitive process. He described stereotypes as "pictures in our head" that allow us to quickly categorize people and make sense of them (1922:3). The mental stereotype was like the stereotype printing plate in that it could reproduce an entire set of ideas and expectations instantly. Cognitively, people use stereotypes to categorize our experiences and make comparisons between experiences and between groups. But where do the stereotypes come from, and how do we form these "pictures in our heads"?

WHERE DO STEREOTYPES COME FROM?

Many processes contribute to the creation of stereotypes. The formation of stereotypes is linked to the way the human mind processes information. Stereotypes can be used as cognitive shortcuts we use when interacting with others. They are embedded in our culture and are both directly and indirectly transmitted to individuals through the socialization process.

Cognitive psychologists regard stereotyping as a by-product of an innate cognitive process (Fiske and Taylor 1991). By a system of comparing and sorting, we organize the information we perceive. We attempt to identify patterns in what we see and experience so that we can make the world more predictable. This allows a person to benefit from experiences, avoid pitfalls, and make projections about what might happen and plans for possible future activities. In a sense, human beings impose order on events as they unfold in the chaotic world.

Consider for a moment how overwhelming this process can be. First, bear in mind the amount of sensory and social input a person processes in an ordinary events. For example, let's examine the cognitive complexity involved in a mundane event such as crossing a street. One must be attentive to the sounds of traffic, to the distractions of other people coming and going in multiple directions, to traffic lights, to cars, trucks, bicycles, skateboarders, and even to weather conditions. Fortunately, one can safely disregard much of this input most of the time. In the absence of such harbingers as squealing tires, we merely look for oncoming vehicles and cross when the road is clear. In other words, we selectively disregard most of what is going on around us. We make assumptions about what information is important and what we expect based on past similar experiences of ours and what others have communicated to us about similar experiences they have had. We do this instantly without really thinking about the process. Although crossing the street may be ordinary, the cognitive processes employed in negotiating it are extraordinary.

Now, imagine the complexity of a far more subtle business of interacting with people. When encountering a new person, what kinds of cues do people look for to help them decide how to react? In other words, how do we know what to expect, what we should attend to, and what we can safely ignore? Many times—especially if we have limited experience with a group of people—we rely on stereotypes to help us make these decisions. For example, one of the first things noticed about a new person is gender. Knowing a person's gender allows us to make a number of assumptions about how they are likely to behave and guides possible responses to them. In fact, gender stereotypes and gendered patterns of interaction are so deeply embedded in our culture and in our selves that it would be difficult to even talk about a person if you did not know their gender. For instance, how would you negotiate use of gendered pronouns and other gendered terms in such a conversation? Gender stereotypes help guide interaction in much the same way as categorizing people according to race, age, or social class allows people to tap into a wealth of assumptions, expectations, and stereotypes.

The interactive process of sensing and making sense of the world is dynamic. It occurs continuously and instantaneously. Because people are incessantly processing a barrage of incoming information, we find ways to make shortcuts. One of these mental shortcuts involves interpreting ongoing events through the lens of stereotypes. When we encounter people, we categorize them and make generalizations about them based on these categorizations. These generalizations often concern trait attributions. The traits we attribute to people based on how we have categorized them are for the most part *unjustified* by our observations. In actual ongoing interaction, not all the attributions we make can be based on direct experience because of the number of attributions we make and the speed with which we make them. So stereotypes are really more about our expectations of how a person or a group of people are likely to behave rather than our experiences with the person or group.

The stereotypes and expectations we have about others are learned both directly and indirectly through the socialization process. We directly pass on stereotypes when we uncritically instill them in children as knowledge. With a moment's reflection, you can probably recall a stereotype you were taught as a child. What we may initially and nesciently accept as fact, we may latter learn is stereotype. By then, it has become embedded in our consciousness and can be activated even though we have better, more justified information about the person or group.

We also learn stereotypes indirectly from our culture when we watch television, read popular books and magazines, and listen to the lyrics of popular songs, or through any of a myriad cultural activities. Some of the most popular sitcoms use stereotypes and stereotyped characters to generate humor. The popular cartoon show *The Simpsons* is a good example of the humorous use of a number of stereotypes. Homer's insensitivity is a gross exaggeration of male stereotypes. Grandpa's character depicts a number of age stereotypes. Social class, race and ethnicity, and even sexual orientation are lampooned by exaggerating the stereotypes. But making fun of stereotypes also becomes a vehicle for transmitting them. Young children watching such shows are not yet able to appreciate the subtlety of satire, but they are able to remember and apply the trait attributions they learn while watching.

Stereotyping is both an activity we learn and part of the way humans process information. The process of stereotyping goes on both inside the mind of an individual and in interaction with others. We use stereotypes as a template to help us rapidly make sense of what is going on in our social environment. However, stereotypes are not a reflection of the way the world is organized; they are a tool we use to organize the world. In other words, stereotypes don't arise from our observations of the world; we impose the stereotypes to give order to our observations.

HOW ARE STEREOTYPES DIFFERENT FROM OTHER GENERALIZATIONS?

Everyone categorizes and generalizes — even social scientists do. But, how is stereotyping different than the scientific generalizations you learn in social science courses? When social scientists generalize, they adhere to strict methodological criteria. First, social scientists do not make sweeping generalizations. They can make scientific generalization only when data from a representative sample is applied to a specified population. Second, they know that even a most careful generalization cannot apply to every individual or person in a category. Third, they systematically control for biases that might affect the generalizability of their data.

Let me tell a story about how important controlling bias can be for scientifically valid generalization. While I was a graduate student, I took a part-time job as market researcher. One assignment I was given involved asking the shoppers at an urban mall to sniff air freshener samples and give their preferences. I had a quota of completed applications to fill, but no instructions for how to select the subjects whose olfactory preferences I solicited. During my lunch break, I went through my completed forms and noticed a pattern. The first sheet provided basic information about each person who took part in the research. It recorded demographic information like sex, approximate age, and race. First, I noticed that I had all female subjects. That made me wonder about other selection biases I might have inadvertently incorporated. Second, the form had five age categories: all my subjects were in the first two categories. Next, I noticed all my subjects were white. My data had several obvious biases. Faced with the intimidating task of soliciting strangers for marketing research, I chose people that I felt comfortable approaching—people just like me, young, female, and white. There were probably even more biases in my selection process. Because I did not have a procedure to systematically select my subjects, any generalization from my data would be invalid. The data was scientifically worthless because the market for air fresheners was not limited to young, white women. Although I spent the remainder of the day deliberately soliciting people from other groups, I had no way of knowing what other biases might be affecting my selection. The data, though less obviously biased, was still not generalizable because my sample was not systematically drawn from a specified population.

When we use stereotypes we don't control for our biases, we don't consider representativeness of our observations for the entire category and we don't check to see if our stereotypes square with data collected by social scientists. Stereotypes are not valid representations of any category or group. They are a set of unverified beliefs about the attributes of a group or category of people supported by anecdotal evidence, common sense, and folk wisdom. Yet, as inaccurate as they may be, everyone can think of instances when they or others behaved in ways that are consistent with stereotypes. For example, some of the stereotypes about professors include wearing glasses and reading a lot. I must plead guilty to both attributes. Does this mean that stereotypes are based on a *kernel of truth*? Is there some underlying observational basis for the stereotypes we hold?

A Kernel of Truth?

A woman I go to church with told me a story about her experiences with Mexicans at the hospital where she works. The story was about one man who was hospitalized for injuries received in a fight. The man did not have medical insurance, was not regularly employed, spoke little English, and was not a U.S. citizen. The hospital social worker was trying to help the man with the paperwork to become a legal U.S. resident and eventually a citizen. The man wanted to know if he would have to pay U.S. taxes if he were to become a citizen. When he was told that he would, the man said he'd rather not become a citizen. The woman telling me the story used this anecdote to justify stereotypes about Latinos. She concluded he was out to get a free ride. He wanted all the benefits of living in the United States, but did not want to contribute either by paying taxes or by holding a full-time job.

It appears, in this example, there was some truth about the stereotypes. People who fit the stereotypes can easily be found in any group. The flaw in stereotypic reasoning is in overgeneralizing from anecdotal evidence and in not looking beyond the stereotypes when coming to conclusions. Of course, not all Latinos are illegal immigrants; the majority of Latinos living in the United States are citizens, legal residents, or have work visas. The rate at which contemporary immigrants learn English is much faster than that of European immigrants who migrated in the early twentieth century. Unemployment and being without medical insurance are widespread throughout the population and not conditions unique to Latinos. Although these overgeneralizations are easily pointed out, the kernel of truth, however exaggerated, could not be denied. But, what of the conclusions reached about the Latino?

I dug a little deeper into the story of the hospitalized Mexican immigrant and found he had a major misconception. He thought as long as he worked day labor for cash, he owed no U.S. taxes. He was unaware that he was violating the law by "working under the table." His day labor barely allowed him to pay his living expense and still send money home to his family. He reasoned that if he became a citizen, he would be accepting an obligation to pay U.S. taxes and if he paid the taxes, he would no longer be able to support his family. In his way of reckoning, it would be dishonest and selfish to accept citizenship if he could not fulfill his obligation to pay taxes and still support his family. Regardless of the extent to which the stereotypes are overgeneralized, the most serious flaw in stereotypic reasoning is in extrapolating conclusions.

There are some stereotypes about group attributes that are relatively accurate. Janet Swim (1994) confirms that stereotypes about women and men are consistent with tests devised to measure gender traits. Although overestimation of traits does occur, Swim found that the tendency was to be accurate or to underestimate differences between women and men (Janet Swim 1994:34). But, although some stereotypes may be reasonably accurate, the kernel of truth is not uniformly sown throughout the field of stereotypes.

Judd and Park (1993) contend that there are three ways in which stereotypes may be inaccurate: stereotypic inaccuracy, valence inaccuracy, and dispersion inaccuracy. *Stereotypic inaccuracy* results because of the prevalence of the attributes in the target group compared with other groups. If the stereotyped attribute is seen as more prevalent than it actually is, then stereotypic inaccuracy has occurred (Judd and Park 1993:110). *Valence inaccuracy* refers to how one judges the central tendencies of a group compared with other groups. This is related to ethnocentrism—the tendency to see in-groups more positively than out-groups (112). The in-group is believed to have more favorable and less unfavorable attributes than the comparison group. For example, I may assume the average IQ of professors to be higher than construction workers, and the average use of profanity by professors to be lower than that of construction workers. *Dispersion inaccuracy* refers to how widely or narrowly the trait is dispersed throughout the group in comparison with other groups (112). This is commonly called *overgeneralization*. For example, the stereotype that Asians are good at math underestimates the dispersion or range of mathematical ability, or lack thereof, among Asians.

To summarize, stereotypes are not always inaccurate. They are not completely devoid of an underlying kernel of truth. The point is that people do not know the accuracy or inaccuracy of the stereotypes they employ. They are also unaware of the ways in which the stereotypes are inaccurate. So even though it appears that there is a kernel of truth behind the stereotype, how that truth is stretched and twisted by the stereotype is unknown. This makes the accuracy of stereotypes questionable. So if stereotypes are by definition suspect, of what use are they?

WHAT USE ARE STEREOTYPES?

People use stereotypes every day, often not aware that the stereotypes are being employed. There are four common uses for stereotypes in everyday interaction: (1) to group people by shared attributes, (2) to enhance an illusion of similarity among people within a group, (3) to interpret differences or distinctive attributes, and (4) to help rationalize our prejudices and justify our advantages.

Stereotypes are useful because they allow us to treat incredibly diverse groups and the unique individuals within them as if they were the same simply because we have grouped them together based on some attribute(s) we assume they share. As was mentioned elsewhere in this text, stereotypes are, in part, a by-product of cognitive processes linked to categorizing people. When human beings categorize, they must decide on the criteria that define the categories. So we look for common characteristics that members of the group or category supposedly share. But, herein lies a problem. Human beings are wonderfully diverse. People, even within very homogeneous groups, exhibit a wide range of attributes. Even characteristics that appear common are not present in all members of a group.

A second use of stereotypes involves creating and enhancing an illusion of similarity among group members. We use stereotypes so that the individual differences that make each person unique can be marginalized. Stereotypes create an illusion of **homogeneity.** Homogeneity literally means same (*homo*) kind (*genos*). We regard people in the stereotyped group as more alike than the individuals we know in our groups. Because we don't consider the unique attributes or the variations between individuals within the stereotyped category, making decisions regarding members of the stereotyped group becomes easier.

This tendency to see members of other groups as more alike is in contrast to how we view members of our group. Because we are most familiar with members of our group, we are aware of the diversity and unique attributes of people within our in-group. Thus, people have a tendency to see out-groups as homogeneous, at the same time noting the individuality and diversity within our in-groups. This is called the ***out-group homogeneity effect.*** For example, it's difficult for many white Americans to recognize the differences between Navaho, Paiute, Hopi, Cheyenne, Apache, or Cherokee people. Important cultural and even physical distinctions between these groups are overlooked. They are lumped together under the title "Native American" though each of these groups sees themselves as distinctive peoples.

Out-group homogeneity is so effective that people have trouble telling out-group members apart. Tara Anthony and her colleagues (1992) have demonstrated that people are less accurate in distinguishing faces of racial groups other than their own and that this tendency is even more pronounced among members of the dominant group. In a study involving 1,750 white and black research subjects, they found that people could more easily distinguish between the faces of people within their own racial group and that white subjects had slightly more difficulty identifying the faces of black people than black people identifying the faces of white people. Members of the out-group were perceived as looking alike, especially to members of the dominant group.

Another factor influencing categorization is distinctiveness. Stereotypes help people make sense of the differences and distinctiveness they notice between groups. People notice characteristics that are atypical or distinctive from their own. Distinctiveness need not refer to truly unusual characteristics; it has only to be unique in the social situation. Thus, we notice the only African American in the classroom more quickly than we attend to the white people, or we notice the fellow wearing blue jeans while everyone else is dressed in business attire (Taylor 1981; Jones 2002). When people notice distinctive traits or unusual behavior among minority group members, they often overestimate the association between the distinctive trait or behavior and being a member of the minority group. This perceived association is called an ***illusory correlation*** (Hamilton and Gifford 1976; Taylor 1981). For example, imagine you are stuck in slow-moving traffic. You notice that a particularly slow-moving vehicle seems to be the source of the jam. When you finally pass the slow-moving vehicle, you notice the driver is an older woman. Based on this observation you associate slow-driving with elderly women. Although there may be some association between gender, age, and driving speed, we may perceive the relationship to be much stronger than it is. This is particularly the case if the behavior being observed is in any way deviant or undesirable and the person doing the behavior is distinctive. You are more likely to make an association between an annoying behavior done by an out-group member than the same behavior done by a member of your group. This is because you have attended to the incident in two ways. First, you noticed aberrant behavior (driving too slowly). Second, you noticed that the person committing the behavior is distinctive (an out-group or minority group member).

A fourth reason that stereotypes are useful is because they allow people to rationalize their prejudices and justify their advantages. Some researchers have suggested that stereotyping is the cognitive component of prejudice (Harding et al. 1969). We categorize to simplify our complex social environment; the attributes that distinguish the categories we create become the basis of our prejudices. If we accept the stereotype, we can rationalize that it is the attributes of the group that guide our treatment of them rather than personal biases and prejudices. For example, if we accept the stereotype that welfare mothers are just too lazy or ignorant to support themselves, then the cause of their poverty is in their own lack of initiative. We are thus absolved from any responsibility or blame for the social conditions that have created the growing number of women and children living in poverty.

We also use stereotypes to justify advantages. In any system where social inequality exists, people have differing access to resources depending on their social position. Some people are more disadvantaged by their position relative to others, whereas others are relatively advantaged. Race, gender, and social class are three of the most influential dimensions of social inequality. People have no control over their race and gender and little over their social class. Yet these characteristics influence nearly every aspect of life. The privileges afforded members of the more powerful groups are numerous but are so taken for granted that they are invisible to the recipients (cf. McIntosh 1988). Of course, anyone can see that some people are rich, whereas others are poor, but few people seriously examine whether their access to resources is because of their efforts or the privileges of rank. Most people assume that their hard work, wise choices, or superior abilities are responsible for any advantages they may have attained (Smith 1985). Americans are uncomfortable with unearned rank because an important part of American values rests on the idea of equal opportunity and faith in the American dream. When faced with glaring social inequality, people often use stereotypes to explain and justify it. For example, men make more money than women. Stereotypical male traits include being aggressive and ambitious. These traits can be applied to explain and justify the gender wage gap. If the disparity in wages is attributed to individual traits like drive and ambition, then those with greater access to resources feel they deserve their advantage.

In sum, stereotypes are used in several ways. First, they are part of the process of categorization, which people use to simplify the complex social world. Second, we use them to create an illusion of homogeneity that makes decisions regarding the way we should treat people easier. Third, we use them to make sense of differences and link distinctive behavior to particular groups. Finally, stereotypes help us rationalize our prejudices so that we can avoid taking responsibility or blame for social problems and to justify our advantages.

ARE STEREOTYPES INEVITABLE?

Because stereotypes are learned early, appear frequently in the media, and are uncritically applied to explain everyday situations, they affect everyone. Does this mean they are inevitable? The answer is both yes and no. Yes, stereotypes affect everyone, but it does not mean that people are powerless to control the effects of stereotypical thinking.

Many social psychologists have suggested that stereotyping is the inevitable outcome of categorization and that prejudice is the inevitable outcome of stereotyping (Allport 1954; Tajfel 1981; Billig 1985). Howard Erlich (1973) argued that stereotypes are part of our social heritage. No one can avoid learning them or being influenced by them. We begin learning stereotypes at an early age, well before we develop our personal belief systems (Allport 1954; Lambert and Klineberg 1967; Higgins and King 1981). Because we learn stereotypes so early and have made the stereotyped association in our minds many times, they can become automatic. That is, unless we deliberately monitor our thoughts for the influence of stereotypes, they may influence our judgments and actions even though we may have developed personal beliefs that are at odds with the stereotypes. Stereotypes may become part of an automatic or habitual response. In fact, stereotypes are so much a part of our taken-for-granted "knowledge" that we are sometimes unaware that we have employed them.

Social cognition research has focused on the difference between the intentional application of stereotypes and automatic activation of stereotypes. Although the terms that are used to refer to this difference vary (e.g., conscious–unconscious, intended–unintended), the distinction is fundamentally between **explicit** and **implicit** stereotyping (Greenwald and Banaji 1995). **Explicit stereotyping** occurs when a person is aware of the stereotype and their decision to employ it. That is, they have attended to and recognize the influence of the stereotype on their interpretations and reactions. **Implicit stereotyping** occurs when a person is not aware that a stereotype is influencing their interpretations and reactions.

As you might imagine, researchers encounter special difficulties studying implicit stereotypes because if the research subject is made aware of the stereotype, it is no longer implicit. To circumvent this difficulty, researchers employ **priming methodologies.** These methods involve exposing subjects to a prior stimulus, without allowing time for the subject to reflect upon it. For example, Dovidio, Evans, and Tyler (1986) presented white research subjects with the priming words "black" or "white." They had the subjects respond as rapidly as possible to link words describing traits (e.g., ambitious, lazy) with the priming words. They found that white subjects responded more rapidly when positive traits were linked with the priming word "white" and negative words were linked to the priming word "black."

In their early research, Dovidio and his colleagues (1986) allowed the priming words to remain on the screen for two seconds. Later tests decreased the time the priming word was displayed to a flash and increased the speed with which the link between the priming word and trait were made (Dovidio et al. 1997). Priming methods for measuring implicit biases have culminated in a method for detecting hidden biases called an *Implicit Association Test* (IAT). IATs use words, pictures, or ethnically distinctive names as primes. The amount of time it takes to make the link between the priming word or picture and the positive and negative trait indicates the strength and direction of the bias (Greenwald, McGhee, and Schwartz 1998; Greenwald et al. 2002). Evidence gathered from IATs has consistently shown that even though people may report that they hold little or no prejudice, they still have considerable bias against blacks (Fazio et al. 1995), Hispanics (Ottaway et al. 2001), women (Rudman and Kilianski 2000), homosexuals (Steffens et al. 2003), and obesity (Teachman et al. 2003). (For an online example of this method, see http://www.tolerance.org/hidden_bias/index.html.)

WHEN ARE PEOPLE MOST LIKELY TO RELY ON STEREOTYPES?

The research on implicit stereotypes has demonstrated that whether people are aware of the impact of stereotypes, stereotypes have an affect on how we perceive others. So at what point and under what conditions are people most likely to use stereotypes?

According to *compunction theory*, there is a distinction between stereotypic knowledge and personal beliefs (Devine 1989). Because we live in a racist, sexist, homophobic, ageist, and classist society (to mention but a few), everyone is aware of the stereotypes concerning disadvantaged groups. The stereotypes come to mind regardless of whether we act upon them. The more frequently one is exposed to stereotypes, the more easily they are activated. Even people who are committed to nonprejudiced beliefs have trouble blocking stereotypic responses. Suppressing stereotypes is especially difficult when people must respond quickly. It is also difficult in a context that is constrained by others who either support the stereotypes or are perceived as supporting the stereotypes. Exposure to stereotypes and a social context in which stereotypic responses are supported can compel people to use stereotypes. For people with low or antiprejudiced personal beliefs, this causes a compunction, or feeling of uneasiness and guilt, for behaving in ways that are inconsistent with their personal beliefs.

To understand compunction, it is helpful to differentiate between stereotype activation and stereotype application (Gilbert and Hixon 1991). *Stereotype activation* is precipitated by association with a group or category of people (Fiske 1998). In other words, just noticing attributes such as a person's age, race, or gender can trigger the stereotypes. *Stereotype application* occurs when the stereotypes affect our thinking or behavior. But, whereas stereotype activation may be virtually automatic, application of stereotypes is not inevitable. Research indicates that it may be possible to avoid applying stereotypes (Devine et al. 1991; Devine and Monteith 1993; Dovidio et al. 1997). However, research concerning whether it is possible to reduce stereotype activation has been controversial (Dovidio et al. 2002). Even people who reject prejudices have been shown to exhibit implicit or automatic biases (Devine 2001). Debate has arisen over whether the effects of implicit stereotyping can be suppressed or reduced. How can we suppress stereotypes that come unbidden to our minds?

WHEN ARE PEOPLE MOTIVATED TO SUPPRESS STEREOTYPES?

Anyone who has ever been on a diet or tried to stop smoking can attest to what happens when you are explicitly trying to avoid thinking about the banned substance. The more you try to avoid thinking about it, the more it invades your thoughts. Daniel Wegner and his colleagues (1987) studied what happened when research subjects were instructed not to think of white bears. Ironically, the more subjects tried to suppress the thoughts, the more preoccupied they were with white bears. When people are instructed to avoid a thought, they actively monitor their thoughts for the banned subject. Paradoxically, monitoring for the banned subject causes it to be recalled even more easily. When the explicit instruction to avoid the thought is removed, the attention called to the topic remains, but the constraint has been removed. This increased attention to a topic following a task in which it was suppressed is called a ***rebound effect***.

Suppression has the same effect on stereotypes as it has on food for the dieter or cigarettes for those trying to quit smoking. Neil Macrae and his colleagues (1994) found that stereotype suppressors responded more negatively to the stereotype target than people who had not been instructed to suppress stereotypes. Research subjects randomly assigned to the experimental and control conditions were shown a picture of a male skinhead and were instructed to write a brief description of a typical day in the life of the depicted skinhead. Those in the experimental group were told that prior research had shown that the impressions we have of others are biased by stereotypes. The subjects were instructed to actively avoid the use of stereotypes while writing their description of the skinhead's day. Next, a second picture of another skinhead was presented to the research subjects. This time there was no mention of restricting the use of stereotypes. Although the use of stereotypes did decrease when subjects were directly instructed to avoid the stereotypes, it increased when the restrictions were removed. By comparing the written descriptions of a typical day in the life of the second skinhead with that of the first skinhead, Macrae and his colleagues were able to show that the use of stereotypes was higher among the group that had previously suppressed stereotypes (1994:810). They did two other variations of the skinhead stereotype suppression experiment and showed that stereotype suppression increases avoidance of the target group and the speed with which words associated with the stereotype are identified (811–813).

If our attempts to suppress stereotypes only exacerbate them, then it would seem that stereotypes are indeed inevitable. However, there is evidence of an interaction between the level of prejudice a person holds and the impact of stereotypes. Compunction theorists (Devine 1989) contend that there is an important distinction between knowing what the stereotypes are and accepting them. Devine has shown that both prejudiced and nonprejudiced people are aware of stereotypes. She tested three models to determine under what conditions stereotypes were likely to affect judgment. Subjects were asked to complete the modern racism scale that measured their personal beliefs about black people. Depending on their responses, they were identified as holding either high- or low-prejudiced attitudes. In the first stage of her research, Devine found that both high- and low-prejudiced people are equally knowledgeable about cultural stereotypes (Devine 1989:7). Next, she examined an automatic stereotype priming effect for both high- and low-prejudiced subjects. Subjects were given tasks that required quick decision-making so that they could not regulate the effect of stereotypes. In this model, she found that when the ability to consciously monitor prejudice is impeded, both high- and low-prejudiced people use stereotypes. In the third model, she found that in tasks in which the subjects were made conscious of the link between stereotypes and the task at hand, low-prejudiced people actively suppressed stereotypes. Both high- and low-prejudiced people have learned stereotypes equally well and can suppress the effects of stereotypes when instructed to do so. Low-prejudiced people, however, are also successful at suppressing stereotypes when they feel personally motivated to do so.

THREE LEVELS OF EXPLANATION: MICRO, MEZZO, AND MACRO

Some people explicitly and voluntarily try to control stereotypical thinking, whereas others exploit and advocate stereotypes. There are individual attributes (micro-level), group dynamics (mezzo-level), and social forces (macro-level) that have been found to be associated with the suppression or facilitation of stereotypes. The individual attributes that help explain how likely a person is to use stereotypes include both demographic characteristics, such as age, gender, race, income, and education, and variations in attitudes and values. Intergroup dynamics also affect whether and how stereotypes are used. The position a person occupies within a group and the position of groups within the social hierarchy are related to the motivation to use or suppress stereotypes. Research supporting the contact theory (see Chapter 3) suggests that contact with and between other groups decreases the use of stereotypes, but only under certain conditions. Finally, macro-level explanations emphasis the role of stereotypes and prejudices in ideologies that justify and maintain systems of social inequality.

The Micro-Level: Individual Attributes and Motivations

Micro-level explanations focus on individual attributes to explain why some people are more or less likely to suppress stereotypes. Individual attributes associated with stereotype suppression also help discern people who are less prejudiced. Prejudice and stereotypes are not synonymous, however. Remember, prejudices are negative prejudgments based on the perceived group membership of the target of the prejudice. Stereotypes are exaggerated beliefs or overgeneralizations associated with a group or category of people. People who report lower levels of prejudice are less likely to rely upon stereotypes when making judgments about others and more likely to actively suppress stereotypes. This does not mean that they are somehow immune to stereotypes. Both low- and high-prejudiced people are aware of stereotypes, and the automatic activation process affects both low- and high-prejudiced people in much the same way. However, low-prejudiced individuals are motivated to suppress the effect of stereotypes on their judgments.

Patricia Devine (1989) has argued that reducing prejudice is a process. First, a person must decide that responding in a biased way is inappropriate. Then they must form and adopt nonprejudiced beliefs. These beliefs must then be incorporated into their self-concept. Finally, implicit or automatic responses must conform with their nonprejudiced values (Devine et al. 2002:835–836). In other words, egalitarian standards toward others must become part of how the person defines and assesses their self. For a person who has incorporated nonprejudiced ideals, responding in stereotypical ways would be a violation of personal standards and have negative effects on self-esteem. Suppressing stereotypes is not easy even when personally motived to do so. Even people who report low levels of prejudice show biases when subjected to implicit measures of bias (Greenwald and Banaji 1995; Greenwald et al. 1998). Despite the difficulty of establishing and maintaining low levels of prejudice and controlling implicit biases, low-prejudiced people have been shown to be more successful at stereotype suppression (Devine et al. 2002).

Social Dominance Theory

If we know that low-prejudiced people are more successful at suppressing stereotypes, who is more likely to be low prejudiced? Studies have shown the women (Sidanius 1993), political liberals (Shapiro and Mahajan 1986), highly educated people, and those with higher incomes (Sidanius, Pratto, and Bobo 1994) express lower levels of prejudice. Of these, the most-consistent indicator of lower prejudice is gender. Sidanius and his colleagues (2002) contend that women are less likely to have a high **Social Dominance Orientation** (SDO). Social psychologists have found that men and women differ in their orientations toward intergroup relations and their willingness to use violence against other groups (Sidanius et al. 2002:998).

Social dominance orientation is an orientation toward antiegalitarian values, competitiveness between groups, preference for hierarchies, and a desire for in-group dominance over out-groups (999). Comparing women's and men's SDO scores across age groups, political preferences, religions, income levels, educational levels, and ethnicity, Sidanius and his colleagues found that women invariably had lower average SDO scores. In addition, they found that men in older age groups have higher average SDO scores, whereas the opposite is true for women. That is, as men age they become more likely to support domination of others, whereas women become more likely to support an egalitarian orientation.

Ego-Defense Function

People who use stereotypes to bolster and protect their self-esteem are more likely to express stereotyped attitudes and to rely upon stereotypes to form their opinions. This is called the **ego-defense function** of stereotyping. Some people criticize others as a way of feeling better about themselves. This strategy relies on focusing on negative stereotypes to feel better by comparison. It also suggests that when people feel threatened, they will be more inclined to espouse negative stereotypes. Fein and Spencer (1997) found that when subjects were told that they had done poorly on an intelligence test, they were more likely to rely on negative stereotypes about homosexuals when evaluating a scenario about a struggling actor. Negative views of homosexuals helped subjects recover some of their self-esteem. Using out-group animosity to maintain self-esteem is a risky strategy at best. A personality held together by hatred needs an ever-increasing supply of targets to maintain a precarious self-worth.

Social Identity Theory

Social Identity Theory (SIT) contends that stereotypes help people fit in and identify with groups (Tajfel 1981). According to this theory stereotypes protect more than an individual's ego—they also bolster and protect our collective self-esteem (Jones 2002:79). SIT explains that we create part of our sense of self from the groups with which we identify. People can bolster self-esteem by holding positive stereotypes about the groups to which they belong and negative stereotypes about out-groups. Differences between the in-group and other out-groups are exaggerated by stereotypes. This helps create a distinctive and positive social identity. Note the difference between the ego-defense function and SIT. The ego-defense function concentrates almost exclusively on negative stereotypes. Self-esteem is bolstered by derogating others. SIT incorporates both positive and negative stereotypes and can be applied to both individual and collective self-esteem. Whereas the ego-defense function applies to pathological personality development, SIT can be used to explain both ego enhancement and less self-enervating uses of stereotypes. Stereotypes (both positive and negative) are used to exaggerate differences between groups rather than to merely denigrate out-groups.

In summary, individuals are motivated to suppress stereotypes when they have incorporated low-prejudiced, egalitarian values into their self-concept. Patricia Devine (1989) contends that when individuals are motivated to suppress stereotypes, they can effectively monitor and control them. Social dominance theory contends that the desire for dominance over other groups explains why some people are more prejudiced and more prone to use and express stereotypes. Women, liberals, highly educated, and higher-income people are more likely to have a low social dominance orientation and are therefore more likely to suppress stereotypes. The ego-defense function of stereotypes helps maintain positive self-esteem by exaggerating the negative stereotypes about other groups and focusing on them while allowing people to lay claim to positive stereotypes about their own groups. Social identity theory furthers this idea by suggesting that part of our identity is based on the groups to which we belong. Stereotypes not only allow individuals to maintain a positive self-esteem but also create collective self-esteem within groups.

Mezzo-Level: Group Roles and Contact between Groups

There are several aspects of intergroup relations that are associated with a greater motivation to suppress stereotypes. First, the relative position and role of an individual within a group is related to the amount of out-group prejudices and stereotypes they report. Second, the relative positions of groups within a hierarchy determine the amount of out-group hostility expressed. Those expressing less hostility are more likely to avoid stereotypes. Finally, the amount and quality of the contact between groups is related to the acceptance of and motivation to suppress stereotypes.

The roles that individuals occupy within a group or category of people affect their orientations toward out-groups (cf. Benne and Sheats 1948). Paul Moxnes (1999) contends that there are three basic roles within any group, which are a product of the same cognitive processes that lead people to categorize as they make sense of their social world. The simplest form of categorization is a duality. Moxnes claims that group roles are affected by three dualities: a gendered duality (male vs. female), an evaluative duality (good vs. bad), and a hierarchical duality (superordinate vs. subordinate).

Gendered Roles

The gendered duality results in males performing instrumental roles and females performing expressive roles. Other social psychologists have also noted gendered roles within groups. Carlson (1971) also uses the terms "expressive" versus "instrumental," whereas Moely and her colleagues (1979) contrast female cooperation with male competition. Eisler and Loye (1983) explain the gender differences in out-group orientations as *ranking* versus *linking.* They explain that ranking is an orientation based on male dominance, hierarchical social organization, and violence; linking is based on co-operation, creative solutions, and a commitment to peaceful resolutions. Other researchers have expressed gendered differences in intergroup relations using different terms but expressing similar ideas. Women occupy facilitator roles within groups. People performing these roles find compromises and are more likely to take the role of peacemaker. Whereas men are more likely to play roles involving intergroup competition and conflict, women are in roles that elicit cooperation and minimize differences. Thus, women are less likely to rely on stereotypes. The linking role they perform as peacemakers is not helped by reliance on stereotypes. But, stereotypes do help polarize the differences between "us" and "them." Competition rather than cooperation is facilitated by this adversarial juxtaposition. So in addition to the tendency of women as a group tending to less prejudiced, the roles they are likely to perform within groups are not facilitated by stereotyping.

Evaluative Roles

Paul Moxnes (1999) identified two other dualities that affect group roles: an evaluative role and a hierarchical role. The evaluative role involves the sorting of objects, experiences, and people into good or bad. Although individuals make evaluative decisions—sometimes before a person is even aware they are making a judgment—the evaluative role within the group helps define the boundaries of the group and sets standards for evaluative judgments (Bargh et al. 1996). The boundaries delineate acceptable or normative behavior and help distinguish between "us" and "them." People performing an evaluative role within the group employ stereotypes to make the differences between the in-group and out-groups more distinguishable.

Hierarchal Roles

The hierarchical imperative within a group calls for a ranking of members according to domination and submission. Not only does a status hierarchy emerge within a group, out-groups are ranked in relation to the in-group. Here, again, stereotypes are useful. Stereotypes are, by definition, overgeneralizations that obscure the diversity of the targeted group or the multifaceted nature of an individual targeted within the group. This greatly simplifies the situation, making it easier to rank individuals or groups. Ho and his colleagues (2002) have shown that the perceived hierarchical status of a group affects the stereotypes of that group and other groups. This suggests that stories in the popular media about the success of individuals in one minority group can have an adverse effect on stereotypes about other groups.

The use of stereotypes is not limited to those who benefit from comparisons with other groups. Stereotypes are so pervasive that they are even employed by people in the groups disparaged by them. So ironic as it may be, it is *not* those on the top of the social hierarchy that are most likely to express agreement with stereotypes. There is a well-established relationship between agreement with stereotypes, education, and social status (Schuman et al. 1997; Ho, Sanbonmatsu, and Akimoto 2002). People with higher levels of education, higher household incomes, and higher social status are less likely to agree with explicit stereotypes. Self-reported levels of prejudice and agreement with stereotypes also decrease as education, income, and status increase. This does not mean that the educated and affluent have overcome or evolved past prejudice and stereotypes. It is more likely people have learned that prejudices and stereotypes are not politically or socially correct (Bakanic 1995).

Contact between Groups

Contact theory is one of the earliest theories that explain the variation in prejudice and stereotypes (cf. Allport 1954). In Chapter 3, it was noted that when people from different groups become friends, they cease to be seen as a representative of a group. Getting to know people in other groups helps reduce reliance upon stereotypes. The contact, however, must be more than simple co-presence. As we learned in Chapter 3, there are five conditions under which contact reduces prejudices and reliance upon stereotypes. First, brief or sporadic contact does little to dispel stereotypes and it may even exacerbate them. To reduce reliance on stereotypes, the contact must be sustained. Second, the contact must involve cooperation. Competitive contact pits groups against each other making the use of stereotypes more, rather than less, probable. Third, simply co-existing with people from other groups does not significantly reduce reliance on stereotypes. It takes more than standing in a check-out line at Walmart with a diversity of people. To reduce reliance on stereotypes the contact must be personal and interactive. Fourth, the contact between groups should have the support of legitimate authority. Both individuals in positions of authority and the policies of institutions and organizations should facilitate contact and dispel stereotypes. Finally, the setting in which contact occurs should be conducive to equal treatment for everyone. Stereotypes are often used to justify inequality. For example, gender stereotypes are used to present women's lower earning potential and greater burden in childcare as "natural."

The mezzo-level explanations for the persistence and use of stereotypes focus on roles within groups and on contact between groups. Moxnes (1999) contends that there are three divisions in social groups that correspond to cognitive dualities: gendered roles, evaluative roles, and hierarchical roles. These dualities create inequality within groups. Stereotypes are used to justify status differences and to create social distance between "us" and "them." Contact theory explains the likelihood of using stereotypes as a product of the extent and quality of contact between groups.

Macro-Level: Stratification of Groups within the Social Hierarchy

As you may recall from Chapter 3, macro-level explanations focus on structural or society-wide dynamics. In a system of social inequality, groups and individuals are ranked in a hierarchy. Although the term "majority group" seems the obvious contrast to minority groups, sociologists prefer to use the term "dominant group." A *dominant group* is a group controlling most of the power and resources within a society. Often the dominant group is also either the majority or a plurality (largest group) within the population, but it need not be. For example, whites in South Africa were the dominant group during apartheid, but they were a not the numerical majority or even a plurality in the population. A *minority group* is any group with considerably less access to power and resources in the society. Using the same definitions, we can say that although women are more than half the population in the United States, they are a minority group rather than the dominant group.

Stereotypes and prejudices are part of the ideology used to maintain the hierarchical structure in a system of social inequality. Characteristics we hold in high esteem are attributed to the dominant group, whereas less-valued characteristics are attributed to the minority group. For example, gender stereotypes cast women as gentle, nurturing, and subservient, while men are perceived as aggressive, ambitious, and dominant, thus confirming the "natural"gender hierarchy. The stereotypes need not be explicitly negative (although they sometimes are negative); they must merely be of slightly less value. So even though there is clearly value in nurturing, we see its relatively lower value reflected in the amount of pay earned by people in nurturing occupations such as day-care workers, teachers, and social workers.

Racial and ethnic stereotypes are used to justify a multitiered racial stratification system. Stereotypes not only justify the superordinate position of the dominant group (e.g., white people of European decent), they also help create and maintain the varying and unequal statuses of many different races and ethnic groups within society. One of the most important tactics for creating this multilayered racial and ethnic hierarchy is the use of positive stereotypes.

Model Minorities

Positive images of minority groups have been used in the media and by politicians who present the groups as **model minorities.** This concept first appeared in a magazine article by a sociologist about the successful assimilation of Japanese Americans (Chin 2001). William Peterson (1966, 1971) contended that a strong work ethic and conservative family values enabled the Japanese Americans to overcome intense discrimination. He contrasted the success of Japanese Americans as model minorities against "problem minorities" (Negroes) Although Peterson's article was intended as a tribute to Japanese Americans, the contrast of "problem" vs. "model" minorities had detrimental effects both on Asian Americans and on other minorities for several reasons. First, it overgeneralized the success of a small portion of the Japanese American community to the entire Asian American community, thereby masking serious problems such as discrimination, anti-Asian violence, and continuing prejudice. Second, by juxtaposing the successful minority group with problem minority groups, it pitted minority groups against one another, causing an increase in racial tension between the groups. The "model vs. problem" contrast made inter-ethnic cooperation less likely and distracted public attention from the dominant racial and ethnic group whose governmental, economic, and social policies fostered racism toward all the minority groups. Third, the model minority concept was soon picked up by politicians to discredit the civil rights movement. By attributing Asian Americans' success to hard work and conservative values, the model minority was touted as proof that the American opportunity structure could work for all groups. Finally, the model minority concept was not, and still is not recognized as a stereotype by most people. Because it is positive, the damage it does eludes many people. Although the "model minority" is purportedly intended as praise, it is still a stereotype and thus, by definition, it is inaccurate. The damage it has done to Asian Americans and to the fight against racism is perhaps greater than the demeaning negative stereotypes easily recognized by most Americans.

Conflict Theory and False Consciousness

Stereotypes are part of an ideology used to create and maintain systems of social inequality. Hegel (1807/1967) and later Marx (Tucker 1978) emphasized the importance of ideology for both facilitating and impeding social change. The ideas of these two theorists have become the bases for conflict theory. Perhaps the most important tenet of conflict theory is that conflict between groups competing for scarce resources is the basis for social order. Social order arises from conflict or—perhaps more precisely—from how people manipulate conflicts.

Hegel explained ideological change through what he called *the dialectic*. According to this theory, an idea, or thesis, would come into conflict with a competing idea, or antithesis. During the conflict, both sides would use whatever resources they had to prevail, but what actually emerged from the conflict would be synthesis or blending of ideas from both ideological camps (Ritzer 1996:156).

Marx applied the dialectic to economic changes creating an argument called *the material dialectic*. He contended that history was a record of the struggles between two great camps: the *bourgeoisie*—those who owned the means of production—and the *proletariat*—those who sold their labor (Marx and Engels 1948). The bourgeoisie has considerable economic and political resources to maintain power, but the proletariat has far greater numbers. The all-out class warfare Marx predicted never emerged. Modern conflict theorists explain the importance of political ideology and false consciousness for maintaining our capitalist system.

False Consciousness is the illusion of the oppressed that they are not oppressed. It's an incorrect assessment of how capitalism works and how it is related to class interests. False consciousness affects both the proletariat and the bourgeoisie, the difference being that the proletariat has some hope of eventually understanding their role, whereas the bourgeoisie has little motivation to understand its own culpability for the development of capitalism (Ritzer 1996:177). For the bourgeoisie, it is far more expedient and less costly to convince workers that what benefits big business also benefits them than it would be to fight labor unions and striking workers. If the battle between the haves and have-nots can be won on the ideological field, it is not necessary to sacrifice profits to class warfare. The trick is to convince the masses that what is good for those in power is also good for the common person. Marx contrasted false consciousness with class consciousness (Ritzer 1996:177). ***Class consciousness*** is an awareness of common economic and political interests among a group of people (Tucker 1978:158). That is, they benefit from similar economic or political policies. If large corporations can convince workers that they share the same economic and political interests, they can quell class conflict before it emerges.

So how do stereotypes fit into false consciousness and the ideological battle between the haves and the have-nots? Modern conflict theorists have expanded Marx's ideas beyond the economy. Power to control the economy, not simply ownership, is the most important element for contemporary conflict theorists. They have also acknowledged that the battle for control of resources is far more complex and multidimensional than the great two camps Marx envisioned. Maintaining power in a postindustrial multinational economy requires a coalition of many groups and perhaps even more important, dissension rather than unity among minority groups.

Appeals to fear and prejudice are nothing new in the arsenal of political persuasion. A recent review about the psychology of economic and political conservatives has linked conservatism with resistance to change, a tolerance for inequality, and the use of fear and aggression (Jost et al. 2003). Just as the model minority concept was used to resist the civil rights movement and create dissension between racial minority groups, stereotypes have been used to sustain systems of inequality by creating fear and fostering bigotry. Perhaps the most notorious twentieth-century example of this was the Nazis' use of anti-Semitism, racism, and heterosexism to create political support for their party. Negative stereotypes of Jews and homosexuals were used to distance the German people from minority groups in their midst. A new master race, the Aryans, embodied all the nationalist virtues to which the German people aspired. This master race was defined primarily by its contrast to negative stereotypes of Jews, gypsies, and homosexuals. The racial purity of the German people polarized the population into superior Aryans verses all other inferior races and peoples. Fear of being grouped with the inferior peoples and subjected harsh discrimination led many Germans to support a political regime that led them into world war and genocide.

One need not go as far back as World War II for examples of this strategy. Using stereotypes to generate animosity is a well-known political tactic. A notorious example of this tactic is exemplified by news stories concerning Willie Horton, published during the 1988 Presidential campaign. Horton was a prison trustee on furlough from a Massachusetts correctional facility. While on furlough, he committed an armed robbery and murder. His crime was used to discredit a Democratic Presidential candidate, Michael Dukakis, who was then the governor of Massachusetts. Booking photographs of the prisoner, who was African American, were widely published. Fear of crime was blended with racism in a successful ploy to defeat the candidate. More recently ethnic animosity against the French was used to create national solidarity during the second Gulf War. Although this campaign produced much silliness such as renaming French fries, as "freedom" fries, it also generated vitriolic, hatred-laced letters to the editors at newspapers around the country. Perhaps the best examples of appeal to prejudice, fear, and stereotypes can be found among political talk radio shows. Talk radio shows hawking extreme political positions have been dubbed "hate radio" by the media. Even among institutions known for their benevolence, such as religious denominations and the Boy Scouts, homophobia and stereotypes about homosexuality have been used as a derisive political tactics.

Macro-approaches focus on the role of stereotypes as a tactic to justify and maintain systems of inequality. Stereotypes are used to distance groups from each other, to generate fear, and to cast blame for social, economic, and political problems on other groups. From this perspective, stereotypes and prejudice do not emerge from individual personalities; rather they arise from the social structures they are designed to perpetuate.

WHAT ARE THE CONSEQUENCES OF STEREOTYPING?

Thus far in this chapter we've learned that stereotypes are inaccurate but do contain some bits of truth. We've found that stereotypes have many uses. They are used as a cognitive shortcut, a way of delineating the differences between groups, a method for maintaining group boundaries, and as part of a rationale for justifying inequality. Although stereotypes are deeply embedded in us, they are not necessarily inevitable. People with high motivation to suppress stereotype application can do so effectively. But what would happen if stereotypes went unchecked? What are the consequences of stereotyping?

One thing stereotypes do is simplify our social world. Cognitively, they are mental shortcuts that allow us to quickly categorize people and make attributions to them based on perceived group traits. Even though most of us know that stereotypes are flawed and inaccurate, we act as if they were reliable. We get by with this strategy super-ficially; but when stereotypes are used to simplify and cut down complex information, they also limit both how we perceive others and how we perceive ourselves. When we meet new people and know little about them we may use stereotypes to infer attributes. For instance, if you were introduced to a very tall person you might assume they play basketball. If someone were introduced to you as an environmentalist, you may make assumptions that they hold liberal political views. In other words, people infer behav-iors and attitudes based on group membership. Stereotypes aren't always applied after a person has been categorized; sometimes displaying stereotyped attributes can be used to place a person in a category or group. For example, if you know that a person is an outspoken advocate of free-market economics and a critic of social welfare pro-grams, you might assume that he belongs to the Republican Party and holds other conservative political opinions. It might surprise you that I was referring to former president Clinton in this last example.

Not only can stereotyping lead to some very sloppy categorizations, it can also become a self-fulfilling prophecy. A *self-fulfilling prophecy* occurs when expectations about how someone will behave cause the anticipated behavior. This concept is part of labeling theory (see Scheff 1966). According to this theory, stereotypes play an impor-tant role in building a deviant self-concept and establishing a career of deviant behavior.

According to labeling theory, most people break social norms with regularity and with few social consequences. Consider, for example, how many times you have jay-walked, gone faster than the posted speed limit, or opened mail addressed to a family member. All these activities are in violation of laws (codified social norms). This kind of minor rule-breaking is unlikely to lead to a criminal career because it is of little signifi-cance and transitory. However, if the rule-breaking is consistent with stereotyped expectations, it may lead to labeling.

When rule-breaking behaviors become annoying or disruptive to others, they (the others) may seek to discourage the behavior. For example, if someone is playing loud music in the dorm late at night, suite mates might glare, complain, or ask the hall's resident advisor to intervene. If the problem persists, those who are disturbed by the loud music might seek explanations for the rude behavior. Should an applicable stereo-type include similar disturbing behavior, it becomes a convenient way to explain the problem. Once the stereotype has been applied, other behaviors associated with the stereotypes are anticipated. In some ways, the labeled person is actually rewarded for displaying the stereotyped role. To extend the music example, the person playing the music may be labeled the dorm floor's "wild child" or "party animal." Bored students may actually seek out the party animal when they want to cut loose. Should our hypo-thetical party animal attempt to return to a more conventional or studious role, people who have come to expect the stereotyped deviant behavior are once again disturbed and may even exert social pressure for him to return to the initially annoying behavior. Being able to predict and explain the rule-breaking behavior makes the behavior less disturbing. In this instance, being unpredictable can be more disruptive than raucous music. If the rule-breaker accepts the label, predictability restores a sense of order. The rule-breaking has become a part of the person's social identity. It becomes part of how others define the deviant and how the deviant defines themselves. The behavior may continue or even increase, but it is more tolerable because it has become part of an expected pattern. Ironically, the stereotype has been incorporated into the rule-breaker's sense of self and the resulting behavior confirms the legitimacy of the stereotype. This classic circular reaffirmation has become a self-fulfilling prophecy.

Numerous studies attest to the power of self-fulfilling prophecies (Rosenthal 1995). Rosenthal and Jacobson (1968) demonstrated this power in a well-known field experiment. Schoolchildren were given a test designed to measure their intelligence and achievement. Their teachers were told that the test also measured the potential to succeed or "bloom" academically in the near future. In reality, there was no such measure. A randomly chosen set of students were selected for an experimental treatment. Teachers were told that the students in this group had scored high on the test and were expected to blossom intellectually within the next school year. At the end of the school year, the children were tested again. Although no other information was provided to the teachers about any of the children, the ones who had been identified as intellectual bloomers had significant gains in their intelligence and achievement compared with the other children. The researchers planted the expectation of greater academic achievement in the minds of the teachers and the teacher's expectations were fulfilled. Although Rosenthal's experiment planted a positive expectation, the phenomenon works just as well for negative expectations.

NEGOTIATING REALITY: "TALKING PAST" ONE ANOTHER

Stereotyped expectations can affect not only how we understand stand others but how they come to understand themselves. In other words, stereotypes affect both the target and the perpetrator. The stereotype becomes part of the currency used in negotiating an understanding of what's going on. Interpreting social interaction is a fluid process rather than concretely definitive. You can never be certain that your interpretation of the situation matches the understanding of others. To explain further, people use their experiences to help make sense of ongoing interaction. However, no two people have exactly the same set of experiences and reactions. Because we all bring different experiences to our interpretations, we don't define situations exactly the same way. Although we have much overlap in our experiences because we are exposed to national media networks, we are taught from standardized curriculum in schools, we speak a common language, and we have been socialized to recognize stereotypes; there are, nonetheless, significant variations in the ways people in different social groups experience the world. The less we have in common with the experiences of others, the more disparate our understanding of the situation will be. For example, most middle-aged, middle-class white people have positive evaluations of community police. This is not the experience among lower-class African Americans. Ronald Weitzer (1999) conducted in-depth interviews with 169 people residing in three neighborhoods in the Washington, DC, area. He found that race, social class, and neighborhood context shape people's perceptions of police conduct. Both white and black residents of middle-class neighborhoods had more positive perceptions of police than residents in a predominantly black lower-class neighborhood.

Because people bring different experiences to their understanding of social reality, even those experiencing the same event can have very different interpretations. Even if they are using the same words to describe an event, their understandings may not coincide. Bob Blauner (1993, 1999) calls this "talking past one another." Blauner contends that blacks and whites in the United States have distinctly different understandings of social reality. Even though we might use the same language to talk about our experiences, how we understand what is being related is fundamentally different. Under these conditions, interracial dialogue becomes a frustrating miscommunication for both sides. Talking past is by no means confined to differences in race. It takes only a moment's reflection to come up with examples of the same phenomenon occurring between genders, across social classes, cross nationally, and even across geographical regions. Students in my classes come up with wonderful anecdotes of Southerners and "Yankees" talking past each other. Although most of those examples are amusing, not all such miscommunication is harmless.

Stereotypes contribute to the phenomenon of "talking past." Earlier in this chapter we discussed how stereotypes contributed to the illusion of homogeneity. That is, stereotyping leads people to overestimate the similarity of people in the stereotyped group. Imagine communicating with someone who understands you through the lens of a stereotype. Add to that the stereotyped images about the other person's groups that you bring into the conversation. Getting past the stereotypes requires that both parties in the interaction become aware of the stereotypes that are influencing their perceptions and be motivated to suppress the effects of the stereotypes. This is an investment few people are able or willing to expend on casual or chance interactions.

One reason that people engaged in ongoing interaction are unlikely to suppress the effects of stereotyping is that ordinarily people don't reflect upon and analyze the complex and varied cultural influences from which stereotypes emerge. When people interact, they focus on the others we are interacting with, determining the meaning of their words and behaviors, and formulating their own responses. Even a casual interaction with another person is a complex and dynamic process. Simultaneously screening thoughts for stereotypes and trying to mitigate their influence adds additional layers of complexity. Although most people recognize stereotypes, they may not have thought about where the stereotypes come from or how they affect their perceptions. In the next section we will examine one well-known stereotype and its impact on how people perceive social class.

FOCUS ON CLASS: THE REDNECK STEREOTYPE

One of the most pervasive social-class stereotypes in the United States is the "redneck." Although the term originated in Northern England during the seventeenth century (Bultman 1996), it has been applied broadly to rural, Southern, or working-class people throughout the United States. The term was used in the United States during the 1830s to refer to working-class white settlers who worked in the hot North Carolina sunshine (Eisiminger 1984). The farmer with a sun-reddened neck evoked both the image of hard but honest labor and the protestant ethic characteristic of the rural working class. During the twentieth century the term "redneck" was used to refer to poor white Southerners. This may have been because poor people living in rural areas suffered from a niacin deficiency, which caused the neck and chest to redden (Eisiminger 1984).

The term "redneck" was also used to refer to union organizers and supporters in the coal-mining industry (Huber 1994). Miners often wore kerchiefs around their necks to keep dirt and coal dust from seeping under their collars and down their backs. Members of the United Mine Workers of America began wearing red kerchiefs as a symbol of their labor union. The red neck kerchief became a symbol of working-class identity and labor-union allegiance (1994).

By the late twentieth century, "redneck" referred to poor or working-class whites in general, regardless of the region of the country in which they lived. Two overlapping social movements contributed to the spread of the redneck stereotype: the reaction among whites to the civil rights movements and the rise in popularity of country music. The two-tiered wage system prevalent among many factory and mills before and during the civil rights movement pitted working-class whites against African American workers. White workers expected to make more than their African American counterparts. When the civil rights movement put pressure on employers to pay equal wages, many working-class whites believed that they lost an economic advantage and suffered a status decline because of the success of the civil rights movement. "Redneck" was used as a way to express both racial and class identity. It provided a new American identity to the by-now-assimilated children and grandchildren of European immigrants. Being a redneck was more than a working-class identity—it represented white American ethnicity.

During the late 1960s and 1970s the term "redneck" began appearing in many popular country music songs. Songs such as "Redneck in a Rock and Roll Bar" and "A Few More Rednecks" blended class, gender, and political images. The lyrics of songs like these present a working-class man who is honest, hardworking, patriotic, and masculine (Jarosz 2002). Fox (2004) argues that country music emerged as the voice of working-class culture in America. Country music transformed "redneck" from a working-class identity into a means of political solidarity.

Politicians did not take long to recognize the importance of country music as a portal to working-class voters. President Nixon, who was a country music fan, successfully used it to attract working-class voters. Music historians have argued that President Nixon cemented the relationship during his years in the White House (e.g., Malone 2002; Feder 2007). The "redneck" stereotype now transformed from its former association with labor unions to a conservative, political identity along with its racial and class components.

During the same time, the entertainment industry was spreading and embellishing the redneck image. Early depictions in shows such as *The Beverly Hillbillies, Petticoat Junction,* and *Green Acres* depicted rednecks as unsophisticated but loveable buffoons. Part of the reason this image attracted audiences is that beneath the crude exterior, the "redneck" represented solid values, hard work, and common sense.

In the 1990s Jeff Foxworthy created the very successful comedy show "You might be a redneck if . . ." According to Jarosz and Lawson (2002) Foxworthy's depiction of rednecks as intellectually challenged, sexist, alcoholics obscured working-class disadvantages with ridicule and laughter. Foxworthy's redneck created a distinction between middle- and working-class whites. It allowed middle-income whites to view rednecks as deserving of any disadvantages they might experience and to distance themselves from the possibility of a similar fate. The economic erosion of the middle- and working-classes was obscured by humorous stories about dilapidated houses, cars on blocks, numerous hound dogs, and unmanageable children.

The "redneck" stereotype is more than an overgeneralized snapshot that we use to help us categorize people and enable cognitive shortcuts. It is also a powerful class, racial, and political symbol. Ironically, it has been used to both organize labor and to convince

---

BOX 4-1

Working-Class Stereotypes Celebrated

Unlike racial stereotypes, working-class stereotypes are often lampooned and celebrated with little or no political fallout. Two famous working-class annual celebrations are the Redneck Games held in East Dublin, Georgia, and Baltimore's Hon Fest.

According to the official Web site the Redneck Games began in 1996. The games were originally called the Bubba-Olympics. They were intended as a parody of the Olympic Games held in Atlanta that year. They feature contests like bobbing for pig's feet, seed-spitting, dumpster diving, hubcap hurling, spitball bug zap, and mud pit belly flop. There are also fashion and beauty contests like the big hair contest and plenty of opportunities for beer belly and butt crack displays. The games attract over 10,000 people each year.

Baltimore, Maryland, has been celebrating its working-class heritage with the Hon Fest since 1994. A "hon" is a working-class waitress. The term is short for "honey" and is used in friendly greeting such as "Hi ya hon what can I get for ya?" The festival features contests in working-class accent and elocution, with contestants in beehive hairdos and spandex outfits. According to their Web site, over 30,000 people visited the 2006 festival.

SOURCE: For more information, you can visit the Redneck Games and Hon Fest at the following websites, respectively: http://www.eccentricamerica.com/redneck.htm and http://www.honfest.net/about.htm.

---

working-class voters to support pro-business politicians. It has been used both to create a white ethnic identity and to justify racism. It has raised consciousness among the working class and obscured the common class interests of the middle and working classes. "You might be a redneck if . . ." assumes that we all know and recognize what a redneck is, but not which meaning we bring to our interpretations of others. (Box 4-1)

HOW CAN WE CHANGE OR REDUCE RELIANCE UPON STEREOTYPES?

From the focus on the redneck stereotype, it became apparent that stereotypes are deeply embedded in our selves and our society; so if we can't eliminate them, can we at least reduce our reliance upon them? There are two levels at which strategies for change can be formulated: an individual level and a societal level. On an individual level, reducing personal reliance on stereotypes requires a strong personal motivation. Even when motivated, suppressing stereotypic thoughts requires constant vigilance and may lead to the rebound effect discussed earlier in this chapter (see Bodenhausen and Macrae 1996). Supposing that those with both the motivation and the diligence to monitor and suppress their own reliance on stereotypes did so, it is unlikely that there is a measurable impact on the use of stereotypes among the general population. Remember, research has shown that efforts at stereotype suppression are successful only among people who already have egalitarian values and report low levels of prejudice (Devine et al. 1991).

There has been some research that indicates that even highly prejudiced people will adhere to social norms against the stereotyping of others. Monteith, Spicer, and Tooman (1998) measured the use of stereotyped attitudes toward gays among college students. Both low- and high-prejudiced subjects showed no rebound effect in stereotype application when made sensitive to social norms censuring stereotype use. This suggests that much maligned "political correctness" may have some useful purpose impeding the application of stereotypes. If expressing stereotypes becomes passé, rude, or otherwise socially unacceptable, their use may diminish. Of course, to establish social norms against the use of stereotypes would require challenging the stereotypes. This would be a marked departure from our current practice of embedding stereotypes in our entertainment and socialization.

On a societal level, stereotypes function to support a system of inequality. Reducing stereotypes on this level requires changing our social structure. Because racial stereotypes maintain and justify racism, racism must be diminished or dismantled before the use of stereotypes will decline. Because gender stereotypes and homophobic stereotypes support a sexist social structure, patriarchy and heterosexism must be abandoned, so that the gender stereotypes will diminish. Eliminating racism and sexism are not small undertakings. Although social change occurs continually because of ongoing human interactions, society is far too complex to easily engineer a particular result.

The first obstacle in orchestrating societal change is the recognition of structural inequality. ***Structural inequality*** occurs when policies, practices, and/or social organization create unequal access to resources and opportunities. For example, in the United States there is structural inequality built into the housing market. For most Americans, their home represents their largest source of personal wealth. Home ownership provides not only a place to live but also equity that can be used to finance an education or as collateral for other property. However, the value of property is measured by the both the physical aspects of the property and the value of surrounding property. If the property is located in a good neighborhood, the value of the home may increase over time. If the neighborhood declines, so does the property value. Banks and other lenders calculate this value when deciding whether to make home loans and at what interest rate. When members of a racial minority move into a predominantly white neighborhood, property values may decline. For a member of a racial minority, the very act of moving into a desirable neighborhood may lead to a decline in the value of the property in that neighborhood. This kind of structural racism occurs regardless of the personal feelings of people living in the neighborhood. Americans are not accustomed to thinking of racism or sexism as consequences of social structure; yet prejudices and stereotypes they are more familiar with provide the support that maintains structural inequality. Becoming aware of structural inequities is an important first step in eliminating the racist, sexist, and classist ideology that keeps them in place.

Summary

Stereotypes are widely shared, often exaggerated, beliefs. They contain both good and bad traits associated with groups. Sometimes, as in many gender stereotypes, they are reasonably accurate, but more often they are gross overgeneralizations. Although almost everyone can identify stereotypes, and most people know their accuracy is questionable, people use them anyway. Cognitive psychologists explain our reliance on stereotypes as a product of how humans organize and process information. People make comparisons and look for patterns in the behavior of others. Stereotypes are useful because they allow people to make cognitive shortcuts. Even though we know that not everyone in the group exhibits the stereotypes attributed to the group, we use them to help us understand and anticipate the behaviors of others.

Stereotypes also create an illusion of similarity among group members. Even though we recognize a wide range of individual differences between members of the groups to which we belong, we judge people in other groups to be more similar to each other. This allows people to contrast groups, making it easier to rationalize treating them differently. We simplify complex social situations by using stereotypes to differentiate groups and justify unequal treatment. The association between the stereotype and the group is further reinforced when we notice a person from the group exhibiting the stereotype.

Stereotypes are not just part of how we think; they are also embedded in language and culture. We acquire stereotypes during socialization, use them in a variety of ways to interpret interaction, and pass them on through language, music, and popular culture. Although they may be an inevitable part of social life, people can control when and how they are used. Research on stereotype suppression indicates that people both recognize and can control their use of stereotypes. Although people who are individually motivated to suppress stereotypes are most successful, even highly prejudiced people can reduce their reliance upon stereotypes when norms discouraging stereotyping are supported. Stereotypes are a human invention and people are capable of deciding whether and when to use them.

Key Terms

- Class consciousness
- Compunction theory
- Contact theory
- Dispersion inaccuracy
- Evaluative roles
- Explicit stereotyping
- False consciousness
- Hierarchical roles
- Homogeneity
- Illusory correlation

- Implicit Association Test (IAT)
- Implicit stereotyping
- Model minorities
- Out-group homogeneity effect
- Priming methodologies
- Rebound effect
- Self-fulfilling prophecy
- Social dominance orientation (SDO)

- Social identity theory (SIT)
- Stereotype
- Stereotype activation
- Stereotype application
- Stereotypic inaccuracy
- Structural inequality
- Talking past
- Valence inaccuracy

Taking It Further — Class Exercises and Interesting Web Sites

Stereotypes of Indigenous People

Consider how stereotypes of Indians have affected what you think you know about Indians.

What do Indians look like? Does this question bring to mind images of the Indian maiden on Land o' Lakes products, the image on U.S. nickels, Disney's Pocahontas? Americans use Indigenous People as mascots for many sports teams and as product logos. We use words and names from their languages as slang and for derogatory nicknames. We use gestures such as the tomahawk chop to symbolize the supposed violence in Indigenous cultures. How does this distort the image we have of indigenous tribal peoples?

Make a list of Indian words and images. Use the Internet to find out what the words mean and where the images originated.

To compare the Pocahontas legend to the actual account of Pocahontas' life see the Web site of Association for the Preservation of Virginia Antiquities www.apva.org/history/pocahont.html And the of Powhatan (http://www.powhatan.org/pocc.html). How have stereotypes affected the Pocahontas' story?

Gender Stereotypes

Where did the dumb-blond stereotype come from? We've all heard dumb-blonde jokes and watched buxom actresses depict the stereotypically beautiful, but shallow and naive dummy. In class, discuss the role of Hollywood in the creation and perpetuation of the dumb-blonde stereotype. Begin by asking for examples of famous blondes. You might prod the memory of students by mentioning Mae West, Jean Harlow, Gracie Allen, or Marilyn Monroe. Ask them to identify more contemporary dumb-blonde roles such as Lisa Kudrow and Jennifer Anistan's roles on *Friends*. Next, ask the students to identify what physical attributes and character traits these roles have in common. In what way do these traits distinguish them from other nonblonde women? What purposes might be served by polarizing women into blonde and nonblonde categories? Finally discuss how the dumb-blonde stereotype objectifies women. You might discuss the blond bombshell as a sex object, or how the stereotype encourages women to objectify and distance themselves from other women. You can find an interesting pop history of the stereotype at *The Maven's Word of the Day* at http://www.randomhouse.com/wotd/index.pperl? date=20010205.

References

Allport, Gordon W. 1954. *The nature of prejudice*. Reading, MA: Addison-Wesley Publishing Company.

Anthony, Tara, C. Cooper, and B. Mullen. 1992. Cross-racial facial identification: A social cognitive integration. *Social Psychology Bulletin* 18: 296–301.

Bakanic, Von. 1995. I'm not prejudice, but. . . . A deeper look at racial attitudes. *Sociological Inquiry* 65: 67–86.

Bargh, John A., Shelly Chaiken, Paula Raymond, and Charles Hymes. 1996. The automatic evaluation effect: Unconditional automatic attitude activation with a pronunciation task. *Journal of Experimental Social Psychology* 32: 104–128.

Benne, Kenneth D., and P. Sheats. 1948. Functional roles of group members. *Journal of Social Issues* 4: 41–49.

Billig, M. 1985. Prejudice, categorizations and particularization: From a perceptual to a rhetorical approach. *European Journal of Social Psychology* 15: 79–104.

Blauner, Bob. 1993. Language of race: Talking past one another. *Current* 349: 4–10.

———. 1999. Talking past each other: Black and white languages of race. In *Race and ethnic conflict: Contending views of prejudice, discrimination and ethnoviolence*. 2nd ed. Fred Pincus and Howard Ehrlich, 30–40. Boulder, CO: Westview.

Bodenhausen, G. V., and C. N. Macrae. 1996. The self-regulation of intergroups perception: Mechanisms and consequences of stereotype suppression. In *Stereotypes and stereotyping*, ed. C. N. Macrae, C. Stangor, and M. Hewston, 227–253. New York: Guilford.

Bultman, Bethany. 1996. *Redneck haven: Portrait of a vanishing culture*. New York: Bantam Books.

Carlson, Richard. 1971. Sex differences in ego function: Exploratory studies of agency and communication. *Journal of Consulting and Clinical Psychology* 37: 267–277.

Chin, Andrew. 2001. A brief history of the model minority stereotype. http://Modelminority.com/modules.php?name=News&file=articles&sid=72.

Devine, Patricia. 1989. Stereotypes and prejudice: Their automatic and controlled components. *Journal of Personality and Social Psychology* 56 (1): 5–18.

———. 2001. Implicit prejudice and stereotyping: How automatic are they? *Journal of Personality and Social Psychology* 81 (5): 757–759.

Devine, Patricia, and M. I. Monteith. 1993. The role of discrepancy associated affect in prejudice reduction. In *Affect, cognition, and stereotyping: Interactive processes in-group perception*, ed. D. M. Mackie and D. L. Hamilton, 317–344. New York: Academic Press.

Devine, Patricia, M. I. Monteith, J. R. Zuwerink, and A. J. Elliot. 1991. Prejudice without compunction. *Journal of Personality and Social Psychology* 60: 817–830.

Devine, Patricia, E. A. Plant, D. M. Amodia, E. Harmon-Jones, and S. L. Vance. 2002. The regulation of explicit and implicit race bias: The role of motivations to respond without prejudice. *Journal of Personality and Social Psychology* 82: 835–848.

Dovidio, John F., N. Evans, and R. B. Tyler. 1986. Racial stereotypes: The contents of their cognitive representations. *Journal of Experimental Social Psychology* 22: 22–37.

Dovidio, John F., Kerry Kawakami, C. Johnson, B. Johnson, and A. Howard. 1997. On the nature of prejudice: Automatic and controlled processes. *Journal of Experimental Social Psychology* 33: 510–540.

Dovidio, John F., Kerry Kawakami, and Samuel L. Gaertner. 2002. Implicit and explicit prejudice and interracial interaction. *Journal of Personality and Social Psychology* 82 (1): 62–68.

Eisler, Riane, and David Loye. 1983. The failure of liberalism: A reassessment of ideology from a new feminine–masculine perspective. *Political Psychology* 4: 469–475.

Erlich, Howard. 1973. *The social psychology of prejudice: A systematic theoretical review and propositional inventory of the American social psychological study of prejudice*. New York: Wiley.

Eisiminger, Sterling. 1984. Redneck. *American Speech* 59: 284.

Fazio, R. H., J. R. Jackson, B. C. Dunton, and C. J. Williams. 1995. Variability in automatic activation as an unobtrusive measure of racial attitudes: A bona fide pipeline? *Journal of Personality and Social Psychology* 69 (6): 1013–1027.

Feder, Lester. 2007. When country went right. The American Prospect. http://www.prospect.org/web/printfriendly-view.ww?id=12473.

Fein, Steven, and Steven Spencer. 1997. Prejudice as self-image maintenance: Affirming the self through derogating others. *Journal of Personality and Social Psychology* 73: 31–44.

Fiske, Susan T. 1993. Controlling other people: The impact of power on stereotyping. *American Psychologist* 48: 621–628.

Fiske, Susan T. 1998. Stereotyping prejudice and discrimination. In *The handbook of social psychology*, ed. D. T. Gilbert, Susan T. Fiske, and Lindzey, Gardner, 357–411. New York: McGraw-Hill.

Fiske, Susan T., and S. E. Taylor. 1991. *Social cognition*. 2nd ed. New York: McGraw Hill.

Fox, Arron A. 2004. Real country: Music and language in working class culture. Durham, NC: Duke University Press.

Gilbert, Daniel T., and J. Gregory Hixon. 1991. The trouble of thinking: Activation and application of stereotypic beliefs. *Journal of Personality and Social Psychology* 60: 509–517.

Greenwald, Anthony G., and R. Mahzarin Banaji. 1995. Implicit social cognition: Attitudes, self-esteem and stereotypes. *Psychological Review* 102: 4–27.

Greenwald, Anthony G., R. Mahzarin Banaji, Laurie Rudman, Shelly Farnham, Brian Nosek, and Deborah Mellott. 2002. A unified theory of implicit attitudes, stereotypes and self-concept. *Psychological Review* 109 (1): 3–25.

Greenwald, Anthony G., D. McGhee, and J. Schwartz. 1998. Measuring individual differences in implicit cognition: The implicit association test. *Journal of Personality and Social Psychology* 74: 1464–1480.

Hamilton, D. L., and R. K. Gifford. 1976. Illusory correlation in interpersonal perception: A cognitive basis of stereotypical judgment.

Journal of Experimental Social Psychology 12: 392–407.

Harding, John, Proshansky Harold, Kutner Bernard, and Chein Isador. 1969. Prejudice and Ethnic Relations. In *The handbook of social psychology*. Vol. 5, 2nd ed. Gardner, Lindzet and Anderson, Elliot. Menlo Park, NJ: Addison Wesley Publishing Co.

Hegel, G. W. F. 1807/1967. *The phenomenology of the mind*. New York: Harper Colophon.

Higgins, E. T., and G. King. 1981. Accessibility of social constructs: Information processing consequences of individual and contextual variability. In *Personality and social interaction*, ed. N. Cantor and J. F. Kihlstrom. Hillsdale, NJ: Erlbaum.

Ho, Edward A., D. M. Sanbonmatsu, and Sharon Akimoto. 2002. The effects of comparative status on social stereotypes: How the perceived success of some persons affects the stereotypes of others. *Social Cognition* 20: 36–57.

Huber, Patrick. 1994. Redneck: A short note from American labor history. *American Speech* 69: 106–110.

Jarosz, Lucy, and Victoria Lawson. 2002. Sophisticated people versus rednecks: Economic restructuring and class differences in America's West. *Antipode* 34: 8–20.

Jones, Melinda. 2002. *The social psychology of prejudice*. Upper Saddle River, NJ: Prentice Hall.

Jost, John T., Jack Glaser, Arie Kruglanski, and Frank Sulloway. 2003. Political conservatism as motivated social cognition. *Psychological Bulletin* 129: 339–375.

Judd, Charles, and Bernadette Park. 1993. Definition and assessment of accuracy in social stereotypes. *Psychological Review* 100: 109–128.

Lambert, Wallace E., and Otto Klineberg. 1967. *Children's views of foreign peoples*. New York: Appleton Century Crofts.

Lippman, Walter. 1922. *Public opinion*. New York: Macmillan.

Macrae, C. N., G. V. Bodenhausen, A. B. Milne, and J. Jetten. 1994. Out of mind but back in sight: Stereotypes on the rebound. *Journal of Personality and Social Psychology* 67: 808–817.

Malone, Bill C. 2002. *Don't get above your Raisin: Country music and the southern working class*. Urbana, IL: University of Illinois Press.

Marx, Karl, and Frederick Engels. 1948. *The communist manifesto*. New York: International Publishers.

McIntosh, Peggy. 1988. *White privilege: Unpacking the invisible knapsack*. Wellesley, MA: Wellesley College Center for Research on Women.

Moely, Barbara, Kurt Skarin, and Sandra Weil. 1979. Sex differences in competition and cooperative behavior of children at two age levels. *Sex Roles* 5: 329–342.

Monteith, M. J., C. V. Spicer, and J. D. Tooman. 1998. Consequences of stereotype suppression: Stereotypes on and not on the rebound. *Journal of Experimental Social Psychology* 34: 355–377.

Moxnes, Paul. 1999. Understanding roles: "Psychodynamic model for role differentiation in groups." *Group Dynamics* 3: 99–113.

Ottaway, Scott, C. Davis Hayden, and A. Mark Oakes. 2001. Implicit attitudes and racism: Effects of familiarity and frequency in the implicit association test. *Social Cognition* 19 (2): 97–144.

Peterson, William. 1966. Success story: Japanese American style. *New York Times Magazine* January 9, 1966, 11.

———. 1971. *Japanese Americans*. New York: Random House.

Ritzer, George. 1996. *Classical sociological theory*. 2nd ed. New York: McGraw Hill.

Rosenthal, Robert. 1995. Critiquing Pygmalion: A 25 year perspective. *Current Direction in Psychological Science* 4: 171–172.

Rosenthal, Robert, and L. Jacobson. 1968. *Pygmalion in the classroom*. New York: Holt Rhinehart and Winston.

Rudman, Laurie A., and S. E. Kilianski. 2000. Implicit and explicit attitudes toward female authority. *Personality and Social psychology Bulletin* 26: 1315–1328.

Sampson, Edward E. 1999. *Dealing with differences: An introduction to the social psychology of prejudice*. New York: Harcourt Brace.

Scheff, Thomas J. 1966. *Being mentally ill*. Chicago, IL: Aldine.

Schuman, Howard, L. Steeh, L. Bobo, and M. Krysan. 1997. *Racial attitudes in American: Trends and interpretations*. Revised ed. 352 Cambridge, MA: Harvard University Press.

Shapiro, Robert, and Harpreet Mahajan. 1986. Gender differences in policy preferences: A summary of trends from the 1960s to the 1980s. *Public Opinion Quarterly* 50 (1): 42–61.

Sidanius, Jim F. 1993. The psychology of group conflict and the dynamics of oppression: A social dominance perspective. In *Exploration in Political Psychology*, ed. S. Iyengar and W. McGuire, 183–219. Durham, NC: Duke University Press.

Sidanius, Jim, and Bo Ekehammer. 1983. Sex, political party preference, and higher-order dimensions of sociopolitical ideology. *Journal of Psychology: Interdisciplinary and Applied* 115: 233–239.

Sidanius, Jim, Felicia Pratto, and Lawrence Bobo. 1994. Social dominance orientation and the political psychology of gender: A case of invariance? *Journal of Personality and Social Psychology* 67 (6): 998–1011.

Sidanius, Jim F., Shana Levin, and M. Christopher Federico. 2002. Social dominance orientation and intergroup bias: The legitimation of favoritism for high-status groups. *Personality and Social Psychology Bulletin* 28 (2): 144–157.

Smith, Kevin B. 1985. I made it because of me. *Sociological Spectrum* 5: 255–267.

Steffens, Melanie C., and Axel Buchner. 2003. Implicit associations test: Separating transsituationally stable and variable components of attitudes toward gay men. *Experimental Psychology* 50 (1): 33–48.

Swim, Janet K. 1994. Perceived verses meta-analytic effect sizes: An assessment of the accuracy of gender stereotypes. *Journal of Personality and Social Psychology* 66: 21–36.

Tajfel, Henri. 1981. Social stereotypes and social groups. In *Intergroup behavior*, ed. J.C. Turner and H. Giles. Chicago, IL: University of Chicago Press.

Taylor, S. E. 1981. A categorization approach to stereotyping. In *Cognitive processes in stereotyping and intergroup behavior*, ed. D. L. Hamilton, 83–114. New York: Erlbaum.

Teachman, Bethany A., D. Katherine Gapinski, and D. Kelly Brownell. 2003. Demonstrations of implicit anti-fat bias: The impact of providing causal information and evoking empathy. *Health Psychology* 22 (1): 68–78.

Tucker, Robert C. 1978. *The Marx-Engels reader*. 2nd ed. New York: W.W. Norton and Company.

Wegner, D. M., D. J. Schneider, S. Carter, and L. White. 1987. Paradoxical effects of thought suppression. *Journal of Personality and Social Psychology* 53: 5–13.

Weitzer, Ronald. 1999. Citizens' perceptions of police misconduct: race and neighborhood context. *Justice Quarterly* 16 (4): 819–846.

CHAPTER 5

Prejudice and Discrimination

In this chapter I will define prejudice as an attitude and discrimination as a behavior. The link between attitudes and behavior will be addressed as well as the difficulties of trying to predict behaviors with attitudes. Finally, strategies for the reduction of discrimination will be reviewed.

- What Is Discrimination?
- The Missing Link: Attitudes and Behavior
- Why Are Behaviors So Hard to Predict?
- Problems in Measuring Discrimination
    Aggregate Measures
    Power
    Causal Order
- What Best Predicts Discrimination?
    Group Size
    Competition
    Power
    Social Distance
    Status Consciousness
    Behavioral Attitudes
    Direct Experience
- Discrimination and the Law
    When Is Discrimination a Violation of Civil Law?
- Focus on Gender: Gender Discrimination or Gendered Choices?
- Reducing Discrimination in Everyday Life
- Summary
- Key Terms
- Taking It Further—Class Exercises and Interesting Web Sites
- References

Prejudice and discrimination are two tools in an arsenal of machinations that maintain a system of dominance and inequality. That sounds harsh, so let's step back and examine what that means and what role these components play in creating and maintaining a stratified social order. At the beginning of the twenty-first century, people living in the United States, Canada, and the European Union are living in the uppermost stratum of the most complex and widest ranging social order that has ever existed. The economic, political, cultural, and geographical boundaries that once delineated our societies have been pushed back by the expansion of economy and technology.

Computer and communications technology makes doing business with a company in India as convenient as doing business with a company in the same city in the United States. With the expansion of multinational business, a global and highly stratified social structure has emerged.

Any analysis of society that does not consider the impact of this emerging global stratification system is incomplete, yet people living in postindustrial capitalist economies, such as the United States and Canada, don't understand the vast system of inequality from which they benefit. Occasionally, we hear horror stories of sweatshop labor in third-world countries, but the connections between inhumane labor conditions and advertisements about falling prices at retailers like Wal-Mart are remote at best. Ordinary people are glad to buy goods at reasonable prices. Where and under what conditions the goods were made is not as important as being able to buy what is needed and wanted. However, most people do feel the economic pinch of stagnant wages, declining job security, and little, if any, financial cushion. No matter whether people have hourly waged jobs or salaried professions, they worry about being able to maintain their position.

Anxiety about maintaining social position leads people to view others as competitors for scarce resources. Negative attitudes about other groups are reinforced by stereotypes and used to justify discrimination. For example, job insecurity may lead a blue-collar worker to view Mexican Americans as job competitors who are willing to work for lower wages. Racial stereotypes about Mexican Americans ("They are all illiterate" or "They're illegal aliens") may be used to construct a rationale for discriminating against the potential job usurpers ("They slow down a job because you can't communicate with them" or "You can't depend on them because they are hiding from immigration"). Discrimination occurs when actions are carried out by members of the dominant group that have a harmful impact on members of a minority group (Feagin 1989). Although this example is an oversimplification, it demonstrates how prejudice and discrimination are used to control and eliminate competition from unwanted groups.

In this chapter, we will explore the relationship between prejudice and discrimination. Discrimination will be examined both as a cause and a consequence of prejudice and as a distinct and independent phenomenon. The particular problems of sorting out the link between prejudiced attitudes and discriminating behaviors will be investigated. Finally, some of the legal and social strategies for regulating discrimination will be reviewed and analyzed.

WHAT IS DISCRIMINATION?

Virtually everyone can remember an incident from their past in which they believe they were treated unfairly. Perhaps you were denied a privilege afforded a brother or sister because you were younger or a different gender. You may have consistently been picked last when sports teams were formed at school or passed over for a promotion or honor you felt you deserved. Though these slights can generate hurt feelings and fuel rivalries, most are not a consequence of prejudice nor where they generated by an intent to hurt or harm. Every day, people make decisions and distinctions that have inequitable impact on others. What distinguishes discrimination from the inevitable slights and oversights we experience is the scope and patterns of inequitable treatment. Discrimination becomes a social issue when a *pattern of unequal treatment* systematically affects large numbers of people.

Many of the early theorists studying prejudice saw discrimination as the acting out of prejudice (Myrdal 1944; Allport 1954) or as a form of "applied prejudice" (Kinloch 1974). The idea was that discrimination was a consequence of prejudice. In everyday discourse, prejudice and discrimination are so closely linked that the terms are sometimes used interchangeably. Although discrimination is sometimes a result of prejudice, the two phenomena are not synonymous. *Prejudice* is an attitude. *Discrimination* is a behavior. Prejudices are literally prejudgments. They are usually negative and are often based on stereotypic attributes rather than actual experience. Discrimination is unequal treatment. It includes the denial of opportunities, the inequitable application of laws, differences in access to resources and services, or simply condescending, disrespectful treatment.

The impetus or cause for discrimination is as varied as the forms it takes. Discrimination can be a result of a personal decision based on individual prejudices. It can also be an unintended but corollary result of preferences for another group. That is, discrimination may be a result of predilections (favorable inclinations) rather than antipathy or hostility. Discrimination may come as a result of an intent to harm someone or members of a particular group, or it may be motivated by a desire to maintain advantages. Finally, it may not be the result of personal preferences or prejudices at all: it may be an impersonal result of the policies of an institution. Social policies and practices can perpetuate inequality because they were designed to meet the needs of one group, but now serve a larger or more diverse population. Although the policymakers did not intend to discriminate, the policies perpetuate an advantage for people in the dominant group.

Joe Feagin (1989) identifies four types of discrimination: isolate, small-group, direct institutional, and indirect institutional. *Isolate discrimination* means intentionally harmful actions carried out by an individual of a dominant group against one or more persons in a minority group. It's called *isolate* because it occurs without the imminent support of a large group or organization. Some examples of isolate discrimination are a store clerk waiting upon African American shoppers last; a police officer asking teenagers sitting in a public park to move on while allowing older adults to remain; or a teacher giving more time and attention to the boys in the class than the girls. Isolate discrimination may be only a minor inconvenience—unfair and irritating but not necessarily worthy of a public outcry. However, it is the most frequent form of discrimination and serves as a constant aggravation and reminder of inferior status to those in minority groups.

Small-group discrimination refers to deliberately malevolent actions taken by a small group of individuals from the dominant group who act collectively against members of a minority group. Hate groups, vigilante groups, and terrorists engage in this type of discrimination when they boycott, vandalize, attack, and threaten members of a minority group. Although small-group discrimination is less frequent than isolate discrimination, a growing number of hate groups, hate Web pages, and hate crimes attest to the seriousness caused by this type of discrimination and the potential for social disruption.

Institutional discrimination refers to discrimination as a product of policies, practices, or organizational procedures rather than individual action. There are two types of institutional discrimination: direct and indirect. *Direct institutional discrimination* refers to prescribed, intentional actions that have become institutionalized. That is, discrimination has become part of patterned, predictable, taken-for-granted behavior.

Private schools with restricted memberships, exclusive gated communities, and private clubs are examples of direct institutional discrimination. Discrimination against the lower classes provides myriad examples because it is a legitimate and perfectly legal part of our capitalist society. Exclusive groups can engage in and even boast about their discriminatory policies. Even the term "exclusive," which means "to exclude," has a positive connotation. In fact, many people wouldn't consider this a form of discrimination because exclusivity denotes high status rather than injustice to others.

Discrimination against homosexuals is also widely condoned and institutionally supported. The U.S. military's "don't ask, don't tell" policy was an ineffectual attempt to sidestep the issue of institutional discrimination against gay and lesbian military personnel. Recently the Boy Scouts, the Episcopalian Church, and many other organizations have waged derisive battles about antigay policies.

Indirect institutional discrimination refers to policies, practices, or organizational procedures that are not a product of prejudices or intended to harm or handicap anyone; yet they have unequal and deleterious impact on some groups. For example, employment seniority systems were created to protect the jobs of older workers, but the "last hired, first fired" rules disproportionately and adversely affect women and minorities who may have only recently overcome hiring discrimination. Another example comes from the institution of higher education. The most common pedagogies used in school curricula rely primarily on visual and auditory learning skills. Students with learning disabilities often face teachers with little or no training in alternative ways of learning and teaching because such methods have not yet been fully integrated into the curricula used in teacher-education programs. So, children with learning disabilities are confronted with indirect institutional discrimination, even though their teachers hold no animosity toward those who have learning disabilities.

Another type of discrimination that has made headlines and fueled prejudices in recent years is *reverse discrimination.* This type of discrimination has negative consequences for the dominant group rather than minority groups. This occurs when members of the dominant group are excluded, or rejected, for positions in favor of women and other minorities. Reverse discrimination is sometimes compared and contrasted with primary discrimination. *Primary discrimination* refers to discrimination against traditional minorities and women. The rate of primary discrimination against women and minorities is usually measured with aggregate indicators. *Aggregate data* is information gathered from a large number of subjects showing a common characteristic. Rates of discrimination are measured aggregately so that patterns of inequality can be discerned. In this way, comparisons between the amount of discrimination affecting different groups can be made.

When primary discrimination is compared with reverse discrimination, clear gaps in education, income, and wealth become apparent. Measured on the aggregate level, there is no widespread effect of reverse discrimination on white people or men. Although whites and men can give many examples of isolated discrimination in anecdotal accounts, there is no measurable aggregate affect of reverse discrimination on whites or males. So, social scientists refer to reverse discrimination as a "myth." This does not mean that reverse discrimination does not happen: however, it does not happen often enough to have measurable effects on the population as a whole. In other words, although isolated reverse discrimination may have profound consequences for an individual, it is not a widespread social problem.

THE MISSING LINK: ATTITUDES AND BEHAVIOR

What is the link between prejudice (an attitude) and discrimination (a behavior)? If prejudiced people are more likely to discriminate, it should be fairly easy to document. But, early efforts to document this link were omens of a long and puzzling research problem. In Chapter 2, I mentioned a 1934 study that first documented the gap between attitudes and behaviors. Richard La Piere (1934) investigated the link between anti-Chinese prejudice and discrimination against the Chinese. La Piere visited 66 hotels and 184 restaurants while traveling around the United States with a Chinese couple. They were refused service only once during their three-month sojourn. Several months after the trip ended, a letter asking if they would serve Chinese customers was sent to each establishment they visited. Only half of the businesses replied; of those, 92 percent claimed they would not serve Chinese guests. In other words, when asked what they thought they'd do, most expressed a prejudiced response, but actually discrimination was very rare.

Other studies have demonstrated the same phenomenon with other ethnic and racial groups (cf. Saenger and Gilbert 1950; Kutner et al. 1952; Minard 1952). Wicker (1969) reviewed forty-two studies that examined the link between attitudes and behaviors and claimed that there was no evidence that attitudes guided behavior. This generated a debate about the usefulness and validity of attitude research and precipitated a crisis in the confidence of the field of social psychology in general (cf. Elms 1975; Fishbein and Ajzen 1975). What emerged from the debate was a more complex and cautious approach to attitude research (Hill 1981). Fishbein and Ajzen (1975) argued that part of the problem was measurement and oversimplification of the link between attitudes and behaviors. They argued that there is a difference between beliefs, attitudes, and intentions. Separating beliefs from attitudes requires clarification and specification. Beliefs are much more general; attitudes involve some evaluation of an object. Using general attitudes to predict specific behaviors does not work nearly as well as using specific attitudes to predict specific behaviors. Fishbein and Ajzen (1975) also argued that behavioral intentions are an intervening step between attitudes and behavior.

WHY ARE BEHAVIORS SO HARD TO PREDICT?

The relationship between attitudes and behavior is not a simple one-way causal link. It is a complex interactive process, with contextual and situational changes intervening to alter both attitudes and behavior (Hill 1981). Let's consider La Piere's study further. What might account for the attitude behavior discrepancy he found?

First, La Piere's study does not take into account situational constraints. In many situations, our behavior is a product of the expectations of others. For example, if your friend asked you if you like her new outfit, you are expected to be complimentary. In La Piere's experiment, it may have been too socially awkward to tell potential customers face-to-face that they were not welcome. La Piere's presence as a male and as a member of the dominant racial group may have constrained discrimination. Other factors such as slow sales and low occupancy may have also intervened.

A second reason for the discrepancy is oversimplification. Behaviors are seldom determined by a single cause. People often do things that seem at odds with their beliefs because some other goal, belief, or motivation prompts the seemingly inconsistent behavior. For example, I neither like nor approve of firearms, yet I have purchased and am a registered owner of two guns. Both were purchased as gifts for my husband, who is a hunter. So my attitude toward guns is inconsistent with my behavior, but perfectly reasonable when considering other factors.

A third explanation for the discrepancy is methodological. Perhaps the anti-Chinese prejudice was not adequately assessed. As we learned in Chapter 2, attitudes can be measured with several methods and scales. La Piere measured anti-Chinese prejudice by asking whether the establishments would deny service to Chinese patrons. He did not ask for an evaluation of Chinese people or whether they were liked. The questions asked can have a tremendous impact on the answer. For example, if asked whether you preferred dining at Mexican or Italian restaurants, you may readily answer Italian, but then go to McDonald's for dinner. Attitudes toward eateries are not adequately addressed by a single dichotomous (yes/no) question.

Not only must the attitude be adequately measured, so must the behavior. The attitude and behavior must be measured at the same level of precision because if the attitude is measured broadly, it is unlikely to predict a specific behavior. For example, if someone asks you, "Do you like *Star Trek*?" your answer would probably not predict what television program you decided to watch tonight. The behavior is much more specific than the attitude.

Another reason for the attitude–behavior discrepancy concerns time. If attitudes and behaviors are not measured closely in time, any number of intervening events can affect the relationship. In the Chinese couple example, there was a substantial time gap between the behavior and the attitude, and the behavior was measured before the attitude. To understand the importance of time on attitude change, recall how quickly public perception of politicians changes. Political polls months before an election are not nearly as predictive of election outcomes as those taken a week before the election. The time lapse of La Piere's experiment was over six months. In that period staff, management, and policies at the establishments could have changed.

Finally, although La Piere asked about attitudes toward Chinese patrons after he and his Chinese confederates visited the establishments, the attitudes he elicited were not necessarily formed on the basis of behavioral experience. The people who served the Chinese customers may not have been the same people who responded to his follow-up questionnaire. Indeed, some of the people responding to the questionnaire may have had little or no experience interacting with Chinese people. Attitudes based on experience are much more predictive of future behaviors than are those based on hypothetical speculation. For example, attitudes about premarital sex change substantially after a person becomes sexually active; your attitudes about college have undergone significant revision since your high-school days. Behaviors change attitudes more reliably than attitudes change behavior!

PROBLEMS IN MEASURING DISCRIMINATION

Aggregate Measures

Just as there are problems measuring prejudice, there are several difficulties measuring discrimination. First, what constitutes discrimination? Discrimination is unequal treatment, but it's more complex than simply treating one person differently from another.

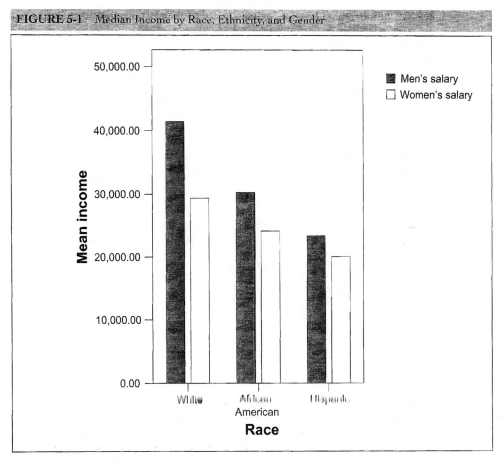

FIGURE 5-1   Median Income by Race, Ethnicity, and Gender

Source: U.S. Bureau of Census 2000 (pp. 60–209)

It involves a pattern of differential treatment that results in the denial of opportunities and civil rights to entire groups of people. Because discrimination involves disparities in how groups are treated, it is measured aggregately. For example, comparison of income averages for different groups is used to show the effects of employment discrimination. Figure 5-1 shows the wide gaps in income between women and men in the three largest racial/ethnic classifications in the United States.

Notice that white men earn more than twice the average income of Hispanic women. This indicates significant discrimination. But because discrimination is measured aggregately and prejudice is measured individually, there is a problem. How can the prejudices of individuals be linked to disparities in treatment that are measured by comparing groups?

Power

A second problem measuring discrimination involves power. While anyone can be prejudiced, not everyone has the power to discriminate. To discriminate against another person, one must have the power to make a decision affecting the other person. For example, as a professor I must determine grades for each of my students. Thus, while the students are enrolled in my course I have the power to discriminate against them. Once they have completed the course, I can no longer discriminate because I, as a professor, do not have the power to make decisions affecting them. An employer can discriminate against an employee, but an employee cannot discriminate against the boss. For most people, the ability to discriminate is limited by social statuses, such as occupation and the resources they control. So, low-wage construction laborers or minimum-wage cashiers have little opportunity to discriminate against anyone, regardless of the prejudices they hold. A loan officer at a bank or a personnel manager has more power to make decisions; thus their prejudices are more likely to have a discriminatory impact. Yet, the more educated a person is and the higher their income, the more likely they are to deny personal prejudices.

Richard Schermerhorn (1970) notes that power is related to numbers, cohesion, and resources. *Numbers* refers to size of the dominant group in relation to other groups. If a dominant group is also the numerical majority or even the *plurality* (i.e., the largest group but not more than half the population), then they can maintain at least a façade of democracy to legitimate their power. However, a numerical advantage is not a necessity. Elite groups maintain power via cohesion and resources.

Cohesion is collective solidarity. Cohesive groups display homogeneity among members. *Homogeneity* means that members have very similar characteristics/A group is *homogenous* if its members have very similar characteristics. For example, North Dakota is racially homogenous because almost 92 percent of the population considers themselves to be white. Hawaii, the most racially diverse state, is *heterogeneous* (members have different characteristics). Whites comprise only 24.9 percent of Hawaii's population. Asians are the plurality at 42 percent, but no group has a majority (Bureau of the Census. 2006). Racial homogeneity is only one characteristic; the more characteristics members have in common, the more cohesive the group. Sharing a common cultural heritage, a common language, and common values creates social cohesion.

Power is also a function of access to, and control of, resources. Legitimate resources include income, wealth, prestige, knowledge, competence, charisma, physical strength, social connections, traditions, legal authority, and political rights. Other resources may include characteristics outside of socially sanctioned means, such as deceit, fraud, secrecy, claims of supernatural or metaphysical power, and willingness to use violence. Both groups and individuals with power use these resources to establish and maintain domination over others. Groups that are most effective at discrimination can pass laws and establish rules that delineate those who have legitimate authority and access to resources. They can use these rules to maintain and legitimate their advantages. Once established, the rules, laws, and policies that protect the advantages of the dominant group become part of the social structure. Structural discrimination does not need to be fueled by individual prejudices. Individuals in the dominant group begin to take their advantages for granted, which they may not even recognize. Because the disadvantages faced by minority groups are not obstacles for those in the dominant group, the dominant group discounts the disadvantages. Many of those in the dominant group come to believe that their social status and access to resources is entirely a result of their personal characteristics and efforts.

The combination of structural discrimination and the belief that social position is owing to an individual's merit makes the link between prejudice and discrimination less apparent. In fact, fewer and fewer people will admit to having any prejudices at all, even in areas infamous for racially motivated crimes (Bakanic and Simon 1995).

Causal Order

Structural discrimination reveals yet another problem in documenting the link between prejudice and discrimination: the causal order of the link. Does prejudice cause discrimination, or do prejudices justify discrimination? The causality issue is particularly disturbing because even definitions of prejudice include the possibility of reciprocal causality. For example, sociologist Arnold Rose (1951:5) contended that prejudice "is a set of attitudes which causes, supports, or justifies discrimination." It is a chicken or egg dilemma of the first order. Let me illustrate the problem by recounting an incident with my five-year-old neighbor. While my young neighbor was playing with my grandchildren, a dispute arose. My youngest grandson came to me for arbitration. Before I could respond, my neighbor said empathically, "She's not the boss of this house!" I asked why he thought so. He replied, "Because girls can't be the boss of boys." At five he had incorporated gender prejudices that support a patriarchal structure, yet because of his age he did not have the power to discriminate. At that point in his development his gender prejudices were a reflection of the structure he experienced at home. That is, gender inequality caused his prejudice. Later in life, he may make discriminatory decisions based on his prejudices. If that happens his prejudices will have caused discrimination.

WHAT BEST PREDICTS DISCRIMINATION?

There are many variables that predict discriminatory behavior both at the aggregate and at the individual levels. Aggregate predictors include group size, economic competition, and power (Kitano 1991). Individual level variables that predict discrimination include social distance, status consciousness, behavioral attitudes, direct experiences with other groups, and the frequency and quality of those experiences.

Group Size

As the United States' population becomes more diverse, the effects of group size will become a more important factor in discrimination. The threat from growing minority groups—whether actual or conjectured—causes negative perceptions of the group and prompts the dominant group to protect and even extend their advantages. Small groups are usually less threatening. One or two families from a different group moving into a community is often accepted with little or no reaction. A group with small numbers of people can be considered interesting or exotic. Members of the dominant group may even consider the token minorities evidence of their tolerant, progressive attitudes. However, a large influx of minority group members into an area is more likely to be met with an increase in prejudice and attempts to deny housing and employment opportunities to the invading group. This phenomenon has been observed with gender groups as well as racial minorities. Barrie Thorne (1993) observed schoolchildren engaged in gendered play. She observed elementary students at two public schools, one in California and the other in Michigan. At first, she saw few patterns in the chaotic pushing, grabbing, and poking that went on between the genders. Eventually, she began to see that the children were engaged in "border work." That is, the distinctions between boys and girls were sharpened. Chasing, playground territories, and competitions between girls and boys all served to make clear boundaries between them. Thorne was particularly interested in observing children who crossed gender lines and the impact such a crossing had on gender boundaries. When a single individual crossed gender lines, the reaction of both girls and boys was fairly tolerant and the gender lines remained intact. However, when a group sought to cross gender lines, they were met with more resistance (Thorne 1993:133). So, with gender—as with race and ethnicity—when the size of the minority group increases, the opposition and resistance (i.e., discrimination) they face from the dominant group also increases.

Competition

Competition arises when two or more individuals or groups are pursuing the same scarce resources. *Scarce resources* can include basics such as jobs, housing, access to good schools, and public facilities. They can also extend to any valuable commodity including such intangibles as political clout. If jobs are scarce, the successful application of one candidate for a job means other applicants failed to get the job. So job applicants try to use whatever resources they have to obtain the scarce positions. Discrimination is one way of limiting competition. The likelihood of discrimination increases as competition increases. The number of competing groups, the power of the competitors, and the availability of alternatives all affect the likelihood of discrimination.

An example of the link between competition and discrimination has been occurring in many states across the southern United States. Like other southern states, the state I live in had a significant increase in Mexican American immigrants during the past decade. According to Census statistics, between 2000 and 2005 the percentage of Hispanics in South Carolina grew by 42 percent (Bureau of the Census 2006). Mexican laborers worked long hours for low wages. They worked temporary jobs and seasonal work with no benefits or job security. Lawn services, janitorial services, and restaurants and construction jobs had a plentiful supply of cheap labor. Many of these Mexican immigrants lived cheaply by sharing living quarters. As long as the economy was growing, there were few complaints. However, when the economy experienced a prolonged downturn, both white and black workers complained that Mexican immigrants were a threat to jobs and income. Suddenly, Mexican laborers, who had been praised for their hard work, became unfair competitors who undercut wages and displaced black and white workers.[1]

Racial tensions increased and charges of discrimination and reverse discrimination appeared on the editorial pages of local papers. Violence between African Americans and Latinos increased, as did the need for public services among the Latino community. Bilingual workers were needed in schools, police departments, and social service positions. Because most of these positions were for those with college degrees, the competition for jobs crept into the domain of the middle class. Although the number of Latinos competing for middle-class positions is small, those in administrative and management positions have significantly more power to discriminate. Thus, because they have more power, even a small amount of perceived job competition among middle-class professionals can affect discrimination.

---

[1]The terms blacks and whites refer to racial groups, while the terms African American or Mexican American refer to ethnic groups. Although most of the black people in South Carolina are African American there are also many people whose ethnicity is Carribean. I have used "black" in this case because it is more inclusive.

Power

When members of the dominant group perceive that minority groups are increasing in political and social power, discrimination increases. Notice, it is the *perception or threat* of using power that is important. Fear of increasing power, irrespective of actual increases in power, can fuel discrimination. For example, the racial violence experienced across the Deep South in 1964 and 1965 was a reaction to the Voting Rights Act and an anticipated increase in political power for African Americans.

The summer of 1964 was dubbed ***Freedom Summer*** because a coalition of civil rights groups organized volunteers recruited from college campuses to come to Mississippi to help register African Americans to vote. Although approximately 45 percent of the state's population at that time was black, only 5 percent of the voting-age African American population was registered to vote. Few African Americans were registered to vote because the Mississippi's state constitution required voter applicants to read and interpret a section of the state constitution. White voter registrars would decide if the passage was correctly interpreted. Few African Americans passed, even those with advanced college degrees. Few whites failed, even those who were marginally literate. All-white Citizen's Council groups emerged to discourage voter registration and foster other forms of discrimination and resistance. On June 21, 1964, only the day after 200 college volunteers left Freedom Summer training held at Western College for Women in Oxford, Ohio, three Freedom Summer workers were shot and buried in an earthen dam just outside of Philadelphia, Mississippi (Bakanic and Simon 1995). Although Freedom Summer succeeded in drawing national attention to gross violation of civil rights, the impact on voter registration and the balance of political power in the state was negligible. Forty years after Freedom Summer, there are over twenty four million African Americans of voting age in the United States, but less than fifteen million are registered to vote. Less than half of these registered voters turned out for the 2000 presidential election (McDonald et al. 2000). Clearly, it was the threat of a change in the power for whites that fueled the reactionary violence and discrimination in Mississippi rather than any actual increase in power.

Social Distance

Social distance is the tendency to approach or withdraw from a group (Park and Burgess 1921). Because minority groups are often perceived and treated as if they were inferior, members of groups with more status attempt to maintain a social distance. This is done in part to insulate themselves from the association with the devalued group and to protect themselves from similar discrimination. Social distance can be maintained in many ways. People may avoid renting or buying homes in integrated neighborhoods. They may seek to send their children to schools with a low percentage of minority students or avoid sending them to public school altogether. Ability tracking within a school that also separates students by race or gender is another way to maintain social distance within a school while complying with federal integration and antidiscrimination policies. At the micro-level, avoiding intergroup friendships and disapproval of intergroup dating are examples of how social distance is maintained.

The distastefulness of associating with members of a disparaged group is illustrated by an incident that occurred while I was teaching at a university in the deep South some years ago. I offered extra credit to students in one of my classes if they attended a university-sponsored lecture by the noted civil rights activist Julian Bond. I noticed that one of the students had not attended the lecture and asked her why. She raised her hand to her mouth as if to prevent others from hearing and said sotto voce, "That was a black people's thing. I couldn't go there." Her desire to maintain social distance was more important than her grade in my course.

Emory Bogardus (1930) created a scale to empirically measure social distance that has become known as a *Bogardus scale.* Bogardus asked research subjects whether they would permit a variety of contacts with people from different racial and ethnic groups and to rate each contact from 1 to 7. The responses were used to create a scale measuring social intimacy. At one extreme of the scale, subjects were asked about inter-group marriage. At the other extreme, they were asked whether the racial or ethnic group members should be excluded from the country. Figure 5-2 lists seven items used to construct a Bogardus scale. A score of 1 indicates no social distance, whereas a score of 7 would indicate complete separation. The Bogardus scale has been used to show a consistent pattern in the distance that people from different social classes with different levels of education and even from different countries wish to maintain between themselves and other groups. Although the pattern revealed by Bogardus and other researchers is discouraging, it is hardly surprising. However, there is evidence that the patterns may be shifting. Although a Bogardus scale is constructed from individual-level responses, these responses can be aggregated so that average social distance scores can be compared. Studies conducted over time have indicated declining social distance between groups both in the United States and elsewhere (Schaefer 2000). Bogardus (1968) compared social distance scores from a study with that from a similar 1966 study. He found that both the average social distance score and the spread between the scores decreased. More recent studies indicate that the trend is continuing (Song 1991).

Status Consciousness

Social status refers to the relative positions of persons in a social hierarchy. It is often measured as occupational prestige. Social status can also be measured by combining measures of the average income and educational level of those in the occupation with prestige rankings established for occupations. Besides these, other positions can also

FIGURE 5-2   Bogardus Scale

How willing would you be to interact with (racial or ethnic group) in the following social situations:	
To close kinship by marriage	(1.00)
To my club as personal chums	(2.00)
To my street as neighbors	(3.00)
To employment in my occupation	(4.00)
To citizenship in my country	(5.00)
As visitors my country	(6.00)
Would exclude from my country	(7.00)
A score of 1 indicates no social distance.	

offer social status: for example, the standing and reputation of one's family can establish status, as can wealth or holding advanced degrees. Status-conscious people avoid lower-status individuals and seek alliances with those above their position. Status consciousness is one of the most subtle and pervasive form of discrimination (Blalock 1967). Because minority groups and women occupy lower statuses, they are often avoided, excluded, or dismissed as unimportant.

Because status can be associated with a number of positions, a person's status may vary depending on which social position is applicable in a particular social situation. Status inconsistency refers to discrepancy among various dimensions of social status. For example, I hold a Ph.D. that has high educational status, but professors do not make a lot of money; so although my occupational prestige and educational prestige are high, my income is relatively low.

Status inconsistency can lead to confusion, tension, and conflicts. Women and minority group members—lower in status by virtue of their group affiliations—who achieve status through education, occupation, marriage, or recent acquisition of wealth, are more likely to experience status inconsistency. For example, a common faux pas at colleges and universities is to refer to women professors by the honorariums Mrs. or Ms., while conferring Dr. or Prof. upon male instructors regardless of their rank. African Americans often experience similar confusion generated by status inconsistency. African American professionals are mistakenly assumed to be maintenance staff. Women administrators are mistaken for secretaries; and male nurses are confused for physicians. Students are sometimes confused by the inconsistency in gender and occupational prestige. These are just a few examples of confusion generated by status inconsistency.

The authority and competence of dominant group members is taken for granted but is not automatically conferred on subordinate group members. The burden of constantly demonstrating competence and the right to authority is more than an annoyance. It takes time and energy away from more productive efforts; it makes minorities and women defensive and sensitive to condescension from dominant group peers; and it can turn cooperative efforts into competitions. Still, even with all these undercurrents of status occurring, the dominant group member may be unaware of the dilemma caused by status inconsistency because it is not an obstacle to them. Their competence and authority are taken for granted and unquestioned, and therefore the problem remains invisible to them. However, contact between equal-status members of dominant and subordinate groups can be confusing and threatening for both. The understandings and interpretations of what is actually happening may vary widely. To the dominant group members, peers from subordinate groups may seem overly aggressive and defensive; to the subordinate group members, the dominant group appears arrogant, rude, and clueless.

Because status consciousness is seldom explicitly discussed, the conflict is masked behind social machinations, office politics, and "games." For example, a woman manager may avoid close contact with secretaries, or a Latino law associate may join a predominately white country club and take golf lessons. While status-conscious minorities are seeking to avoid lower-status contacts and facilitating contact with members of the group to which they aspire, dominant group members take for granted the advantages of their status. A casual invitation to join the boss for a game of handball at his club may lead to a work related discussion afterward. The advantages of business discussed in locker rooms and on golf courses exclude women and minorities. This subtle, but very powerful, form of discrimination is pervasive. Because it bridges the business and social worlds, status consciousness falls through the cracks in antidiscrimination policies.

Although not all discriminatory behavior is motivated by status consciousness, scales measuring the awareness and importance of status are consistent predictors of discrimination (Jones 1991).

Behavioral Attitudes

When the study of prejudice began, prejudiced attitudes were seen as one of the determinants of discriminatory behavior. If prejudiced attitudes caused discriminatory behavior, then prejudice would be the independent variable and discrimination would be the dependent variable. However, if our experiences in life help develop, clarify, and change our attitudes, then attitudes become dependent variables affected by our behaviors. This realization allowed social psychologists to consider more complex ties between behaviors and attitudes. Instead of merely viewing the relationship between the two variables as causal, social psychologists began to locate attitudes and behaviors in a causal process with multiple steps and the possibility of feedback loops that allows for mutual causation among the components. By considering possible intervening steps in a process linking attitudes and behaviors, social psychologists have improved the predictive ability of their models. Instead of measuring attitudes as a single phenomenon, beliefs, evaluations, and intentions are measured as different components in a dynamic process. Fishbein and Ajzen (1978) proposed a general model depicting the iterative or repetitive cycle in the relationship between attitudes and behavior. In this model, beliefs and attitudes have a reciprocal relationship: that is, our beliefs about a group influence our prejudices, and our prejudices reinforce our beliefs. A belief is a judgment that links the group to some attribute, whereas an attitude is an evaluative judgment about the group (Fishbein and Ajzen 1978:378). Attitudes also affect our behavioral intentions concerning the group. An intention is a judgment about the probability of a course of action; it is what a person believes they would do in a specified situation. Behavioral intentions affect actual behaviors. In the final step of the model, behaviors are linked by a feedback loop to beliefs (Figure 5-3).

By breaking down prejudices into beliefs, attitudes, and behavioral intentions, the prediction of actual behavior improves. However, it's important to note that beliefs and attitudes predict behavioral intentions, not the behaviors themselves. The ability to predict behavior rests on the strength of the link between intentions and actual behavior. The more specific the behavioral intention and the shorter the interval between intention and actual behavior, the better the prediction.

FIGURE 5-3   Fishbein–Ajzen Model

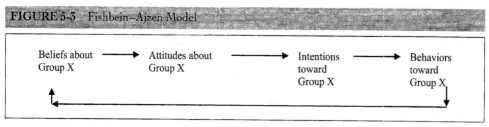

Source: Fishbein and Ajzen 1975

Direct Experience

Discrimination is the behavioral component of prejudice. However, as we have seen, although the two concepts are interrelated, they are qualitatively distinct phenomena. Because prejudices are attitudes—even when they are measured as behavioral tendencies—they are only moderately predictive. Perhaps the best predictor of future behavior is past behaviors. Asking individuals whether they have engaged in discriminatory actions in the past not only helps predict further discrimination but also helps predict and explain prejudices. Thus, to fully understand the relationship between prejudice and discrimination, one must understand that prejudice is the cause, the support system justifying, and the consequence of discriminatory actions.

Although the relationship between attitudes and behavior is a complex interactive process, it is possible to use prejudices and many other social and situational factors to help predict discriminatory behavior. Aggregate predictors, such as group size, economic competition, and power, help explain variation in the rates of discrimination and allow for comparisons across countries, states, communities, and time periods. Individual-level variables that predict discrimination, such as social distance, status consciousness, behavioral attitudes, and direct experiences, help explain variation in the behavior of individuals. In the next section, we will examine some attempts to reduce discrimination. Specifically, we will consider the effects of antidiscrimination legislation.

DISCRIMINATION AND THE LAW

The role of the law in discrimination is convoluted at best. In conflict theory the law is seen as the instrument of the dominant group. Laws are written to reflect and legitimate the interests of the powerful. Because those in power make the laws, the task of eliminating discrimination would be at odds with the self-interests of the powerful. The dominant group that benefits the most from discrimination is the same group that must legislate change. It's rather like asking perpetrators to police themselves. Nonetheless, there are numerous laws and government policies aimed at limiting discrimination. The legislative strategy for controlling intergroup conflict and decreasing discrimination has been fought primarily in the civil courts, but occasionally extends to criminal jurisdictions (e.g., hate crimes). In this section, we will explore when, where, and what kind of discrimination is illegal.

When Is Discrimination a Violation of Civil Law?

Before we can assess the role of law in either causing or preventing discrimination, a brief review of the laws pertaining to discrimination is necessary. In the United States most of the laws prohibiting discrimination are based on civil rights guaranteed in the 13th, 14th, and 15th amendments to the Constitution and the 1964 Civil Rights Act. The 13th amendment prohibits slavery and has been interpreted by the courts as prohibiting public or private racial discrimination in the disposal of property, employment, and in the making or enforcing of contracts. The 14th amendment specifies that all persons born or naturalized in the United States are citizens and that no state can make or enforce any laws that abridge the rights of citizens. It also guarantees every citizen equal protection under the law. The 15th amendment specifies that the right to vote cannot be denied or abridged "on account of race, color, or previous condition of servitude." These three amendments were passed in the years following the Civil War during Reconstruction. Together they form the basis of subsequent civil rights legislation and have been broadly interpreted by the courts as a bulwark protecting the civil liberties of all citizens.

Perhaps the single most important piece of antidiscrimination legislation enacted during the twentieth century was the Civil Rights Act of 1964 (Figure 5-4). Through this legislation, discrimination on the basis of race, creed, color, national origin, and sex was prohibited. Although this act encompasses public policies and facilities at both the federal and the state level, it does not entirely forbid discrimination in the private sector. Private clubs, private schools, private resorts, private eating establishments, and many other organizations can legally discriminate as long as they do not accept public funds or do not have a connection to interstate commerce. This means, for example, that a privately owned and operated school can restrict its enrollment to whites only or Catholics only. A private country golf club can limit its membership to men only. The Boy Scouts can extend membership to God-fearing heterosexual males while excluding homosexuals and atheists. The Civil Rights Act pertains to public institutions and organizations, institutions receiving public funds, and establishments engaging in interstate commerce. This can be confusing because many private institutions participate in programs funded by the government. For example, Harvard University is a private school, but it accepts grants, loans, and subsidies from the federal government; so it must abide by nondiscrimination statutes like the Civil Rights Act and Affirmative Action.

Civil rights legislation does not protect people from individuals who make racist, sexist, anti-Semitic, or other offensive comments unless that person is acting under the authority of government. This means, a private citizen can shout racist slurs without violating anyone's civil rights, but a police officer, public schoolteacher, elected official, or anyone acting under the "color of law"—anyone acting under the authority of the state—is prohibited from discriminating while they are acting in their official capacity. So, although all individuals have the right of free speech in their capacity as private citizens, their self-expression can be legally curtailed when they are acting under the authority of the state in their official capacity.

The Civil Rights Act of 1964 was an extension of the legislation passed in the Civil Rights Acts of 1957 and 1960. It contains eleven titles. A *title* is the legal evidence, justifications, and specifications used to establish a legal right. Subsequent antidiscrimination policies have been written under the authority of one or more of these titles. For example, Title VII outlaws employment discrimination. The Equal Employment Opportunity Commission (EEOC) was also established under Title VII. Since the passage of the Civil Rights Act of 1964, other pieces of legislation have extended protection

---

FIGURE 5-4   The Civil Rights Act of 1964

"Neither the United States nor any State shall discriminate on the basis of race, color, creed, national origin or sex."

Source: For the full text of the Civil Rights Act of 1964 go to http://www.usinfo.state.gov/usa/infousa/majorlaw/civilr19.htm

against discrimination to other groups or under certain conditions. The Age Discrimination in Employment Act, the Americans with Disabilities Act, and the Civil Rights Act of 1991 are all important components of the legal protection against discrimination, but no other single piece of legislation has had the encompassing impact of the 1964 Civil Rights Act.

Affirmative Action

The Affirmative Action policies in use today were established under Title VII of the 1964 Civil Rights Act. Title VII establishes equal employment opportunities for all citizens. **Affirmative Action** refers to policies requiring that constructive or proactive steps be taken by employers to ensure equal employment opportunities. Unfortunately, it is one of the most misunderstood government policies. The history of Affirmative Action pre-dates the Civil Rights Act of 1964 by more than two decades. In 1941, because of the lobbying efforts of A. Phillip Randolph and the National Association for the Advancement of Colored People (NAACP), President Franklin D. Roosevelt signed Executive Order 8802 (McLemore 1991:188). This order established the "full participation in defense programs of all people regardless of race, creed, color, or national origin" (Roosevelt 1967:400). It also created the Fair Employment Practices Committee to investigate discrimination claims. Presidents Truman and Eisenhower extended Affirmative Action policy to all government contractors and subcontractors.

Under pressure from these policies, overt discrimination declined, but still minorities were grossly under-represented (McLemore 1991:188–189). Years of employment discrimination meant that few minority candidates could compete with the experience and seniority of white workers. Ending overt discrimination didn't go far enough; something needed to be done to redress past discrimination. In Executive Order 10925 President Kennedy mandated that positive assistance or "affirmative action" be assured for minority workers employed by the federal government and its contractors and subcontractors (1991:189).

Under Title VII of the 1964 Civil Rights Act, Affirmative Action was extended beyond federal contractors to private-sector employers and labor unions. It also directed the U.S. Attorney General's Office to sue the violators if there was evidence of employment discrimination. Another important addition supplied by Title VII was the inclusion of sex as a protected category. On February 8, 1964, "sex" was added in a one-word amendment to Title VII of the Civil Rights Act by Rep. Howard Smith of Virginia (Freeman 1991). Smith was part of a southern bloc of congressmen who staunchly opposed the bill. Although many considered the inclusion of "sex" to be a fluke, Jo Freeman argues that the inclusion of women in antidiscrimination law was the result of persistent lobbying and fortunate opportunism (Freeman 1991:164).

By including women as a protected category in employment discrimination, protective legislation limiting the hours, types, and conditions of women's work came in conflict with federal law. Gay rights activists have lobbied to include sexual orientation as a subcategory of "sex." Lobbyists and activists for gay and lesbian groups have been successful in many of their legal battles. They have successfully challenged the laws that criminalized many behaviors associated with homosexual sex. They have convinced the courts that violence against homosexuals is a category of hate crime. They continue fighting to extend marriage or domestic partnership rights to homosexuals in many states. However, the federal courts have consistently refused to recognize sexual orientation under Title VII of the Civil Rights Act. Thus far, the term "sex" is limited to being a male or female, not to one's sexuality.

Affirmative Action policies are also required by colleges and universities. In 1972, Congress amended Title VII to cover educational institutions. Soon after, Allen Bakke brought suit against the University of California at Davis [see *Regents of the University of California v. Bakke*, 438 U.S. 265 (1978)]. He was a white, male student who was denied admission to the medical school. He argued that he had been discriminated against because the University of California at Davis preferred less-qualified minority candidates. His grades were higher than some of the minority candidates who were admitted. The suit challenged Affirmative Action policies that specified a number of positions that were "set aside" for the top minority candidates. Bakke's case successfully argued that these "set aside" goals were in fact quotas. The use of a quota system is specifically prohibited under Federal Affirmative Action guidelines. Affirmative Action policies can set goals, but they cannot set quotas. A quota is established by hiring, promoting, or accepting a specified number of people in each protected group, even if the candidates in the protected group have lower standards of merit than other candidates. A goal is a targeted percentage of minorities or women needed for the group to reach parity (i.e., to be proportionately represented). Goals may be set and good faith plans to achieve those goals implemented so long as no other group is discriminated against as a result of trying to achieve the goals. For example, if a job requires only a high-school education and 20 percent of the people in a geographic area who have high-school diplomas are African American, then a business might set a goal of hiring at least 20 percent of their workforce from the African American population. The firm must show evidence of a positive effort to include minority candidates, but it cannot set quotas or set aside a number of positions specifically for minorities. The minority candidate can only be preferred when they meet the requirements set for the job and their group is under-represented in the company's workforce (or in the case of schools, the student body). If a better-qualified candidate from a dominant group applies for the position, the firm cannot prefer an unqualified minority candidate (Bureau of National Affairs 1979).

Not all businesses and schools are required to implement Affirmative Action policies. If a business or educational institution accepts government contracts, grants, or loans, or has more than a specified number of employees, it is required to have an affirmative action policy that is consistent with federal guide lines.[2] Because more people are employed at small businesses, most people are not working at places required to have Affirmative Action policies. Some businesses and schools that are not required to implement Affirmative Action voluntarily comply. Far more people are protected by Affirmative Action policies when they apply to and attend colleges and universities.

Part of the confusion about Affirmative Action comes from the many and vastly different policies that fall under the program. The government does not dictate the Affirmative Action policy; rather, each institution creates its own policy with the aid of federal guidelines. Although the attorney general is empowered to bring class action suits against violators of affirmative action even if no private suit has been filed, the federal government does not actively police affirmative action. The government relies

---

[2]Because most commerce is regulated by states, the number of employees a business can have before they are required to develop an Affirmative Action policy varies from as few as fifteen to as many as fifty.

upon individuals to bring suit in civil court when they believe a company's or institution's policy or practices are in violation of Title VII.

When a person believes they have been discriminated against at work (or school) because of race, color, ethnicity, religion, or sex, they can file a civil suit against their employers based on Title VII and Affirmative Action. To be successful, the lawsuit must demonstrate to the court that there is pattern of discrimination against the protected group and the individual because they are a member of the group. To demonstrate a pattern of discrimination, the institution's records of hiring, firing, and promotions (or admissions in the case of colleges and university) are subpoenaed and analyzed. The EEOC requires that all applicable business and institutions keep standardized records on applications, hiring, firing, and promotion. Simple statistical tests are applied to determine if there is a disparate impact on the group. Once a pattern of discrimination has been documented, the plaintiff must show that the negative consequences they have experienced are a result of discrimination and not because of job or academic performance. Any person can sue based on Title VII, even members of the dominant group. In fact, white males have very successfully used Affirmative Action to protect themselves against discrimination (e.g., *Bakke v. University of California Regents* 1978). Not only has Affirmative Action been used to protect white males from so-called reverse discrimination, it has also helped minorities and women move up in the workforce and protect themselves from both primary and reverse discrimination (U.S. Labor Department 1995).

Environmental Justice

Environmental justice refers to the equitable distribution of environmental benefits and harms. The environmental justice movement primarily involves protecting the poor and minority groups from a disproportionate exposure to environmental hazards. Communities inhabited primarily by woman-headed households, people of color, and the poor receive less environmental protection and intervention than affluent communities inhabited mostly by whites. Like Affirmative Action, the environmental justice movement bases its legal redress on the 1964 Civil Rights Act. Title VI prohibits discrimination by government agencies that receive federal funds. Although Title VI of the Civil Rights Act was not intended as an environmental statute, it has been interpreted by the federal courts as prohibiting actions that have a discriminatory effect (Rechtschaffen and Gauna 2002). In other words, discrimination is prohibited regardless of whether an agency or individual intends discrimination.

The environmental decisions made by the heads of corporations, municipalities, and other governmental agencies are influenced by science, technology, politics, economics, and special interest groups. Hazardous environments and toxic wastes are often intentionally located in areas where the inhabitants do not have the resources to block them. Even though no one wants an environmental hazard located in their neighborhood, poor people and people of color live in the most polluted neighborhoods, work in more dangerous jobs, and send their children to schools and playgrounds rife with environmental dangers. Industrial polluters, seeking the path of least resistance, choose to locate in lower socioeconomic areas. The government agencies entrusted to protect the public from pollution devote fewer resources to areas inhabited by the poor and people of color. In an analysis of the Environmental Protection Agency's (EPA's) records, Lavelle and Coyle (1992) found that penalties leveled for pollution in primarily "white" areas were 500 percent higher than penalties for polluting in minority areas. The unequal impact of environmental threats and unequal protection afforded by the EPA and other government agencies has resulted in a callous disregard for the health and safety of the poor—who are disproportionately women and children—and people of color. The prejudices implicit in targeting areas populated by people unlikely to resist and the discrimination embedded in agencies charged with protecting all of the people have made environmental justice one of the most critical arenas in the civil rights struggle.

In this section we focused on how governments, businesses, and economic policies contribute to institutional discrimination. However, there are some types of discrimination that bridge the span between macro-level social forces embedded in social structures and institutions and the micro-level choices people make in their everyday lives. In the next section we move from the macro-level to the mezzo-level by looking at how gender differences are embedded in the toy industry, the toy preferences of children, and, subsequently, the socialization of girls and boys.

FOCUS ON GENDER: GENDER DISCRIMINATION OR GENDERED CHOICES?

Sometimes it is difficult to decide whether the social structures we create cause people to be treated differently or whether people choose to be different. Next time you are at a store such as Target, Kmart, or Toys R Us, visit the toy section. Notice how toys are marketed by gender. The girls' section is immediately identifiable by the predominance of pink. The number-one toy for little girls is still the doll. There are baby dolls that crawl, talk, drink, and wet. Toy manufacturers also offer clothes, diapers, bottles, strollers, diaper bags, and even car seats for these plastic progeny. Of course, baby dolls are only one genre. There are fashion dolls like Barbie and Bratz. There are doll families complete with daddy and mommy dolls and even doll pets. There are doll ponies with long, multi-colored, brushable manes. Of course, to properly play dolls, little girls need an entire play household. So the stores sell toy dishes, pots and pans, pretend food, toy stoves, refrigerators, and even the kitchen sink. You can buy miniature furniture to fit both the child and her dolls. If all the dolls' possessions create a messy pretend household, then you can purchase toy vacuum cleaners, brooms, and cleaning products. The world of girls' toys is a fantasyland of anticipatory maternity and domestic materialism.

The toys in the boys' section are a bit different. Little boys don't play with dolls; they play with "action figures." Of course, like the dolls, they have a vast array of outfits that may be purchased so that G.I. Joe can wear the proper fashions for desert warfare or competing in a karate tournament. But action figures aren't meant to be nurtured, they are meant for undertaking difficult missions and fighting bad guys. So the toy industry has provided a truly horrendous assortment of bad guys and monsters as adversaries. Of course both dolls—I mean action figures—and boys will need weapons with which to save the world. Toy makers have conveniently provided guns, swords, bows and arrows, knives, and cannons. To get your guys to where the action is, there are all kinds of cars, trucks, helicopters, planes, trains, and tanks. To prepare older boys for the real world of computerized weaponry, there's an endless supply of violent video games. The world of boys' toys is frightening.

The question is not about whether the toy industry treats its male and female customers differently; it's about whether it is catering to gendered choices or creating gender segregation. Many people believe that the differences between males and females are a natural product of our biological differences. According to this perspective, little girls are naturally nurturing so they prefer playing with dolls and dishes and little boys are naturally aggressive and would be bored with quiet domestic play. Because we begin the process of gender socialization at birth, we may never know how much of the differences in gender preferences are a part of our nature and how much are learned. But one does wonder if motherhood is so natural, why do we need to create a multitrillion-dollar industry to teach the maternal arts? An even more disturbing question is, if boys are naturally aggressive why are we spending an equal amount to teach boys the art of warfare?

REDUCING DISCRIMINATION IN EVERYDAY LIFE

Earlier in this chapter, we have reviewed legislation that has been employed to reduce discrimination at the institutional or structural level of social organization. According to sociologists, such structural changes are the most effective way of reducing discrimination and eventually the prejudices that justify inequality. However, discrimination can also be affected at the micro-level. In a recent study of the campus climate at my college, my research team asked if students, faculty, and staff ever felt discriminated against or harassed because of their race, ethnicity, gender, social class, religion, or sexual orientation. Almost a third (32.1 percent) said yes (Bakanic et al. 2007). However, when we asked what happened we found that most discrimination was in the form of being ignored (26.2 percent) or receiving an inappropriate comment (29 percent). Among students, the person responsible for the discrimination or harassment was most likely to be another student (74.8 percent). Likewise faculty most often attributed their incidents of discrimination to other faculty (45.2 percent) and staff to other staff (72.3 percent). Consequently very few respondents said they reported the discrimination (9.2 percent). Being ignored or receiving inappropriate comments from people in similar institutional roles is hardly the scenario for which discrimination laws and policies are designed. Yet these types of interactions are how most people experience everyday discrimination. The offenses may seem small, but they are anything but inconsequential. Feeling slighted, ignored, or disrespected affects how we understand and respond to the social situation around us. In our study, people who indicated that they had experienced discrimination were more likely to report feeling unwelcome at campus events, rated the campus environment as less comfortable, and felt less a part of the campus community. Although policies like affirmative action eventually change the composition and structure of the institutions to which they apply, they can't address everyday discrimination as it is being experienced by individuals. Individual intervention requires individual awareness of discrimination and commitment to reducing it.

Individual-level interventions include awareness, and suppression, of the affects of stereotyping, self-regulation of prejudiced responses and discriminatory actions, and commitment to actively recognize and resist discrimination wherever and whenever it occurs.

The first step toward reducing discrimination is becoming aware of the effects of stereotypes and self-censoring them on our behavior. This is perhaps the most introspective and the most difficult strategy for reducing discrimination because it involves becoming aware of, and acting against, the social forces that create and maintain systems of inequality. The individual must attempt to swim against the tides of racism, sexism, or classism.

Think for a moment about how difficult it is to banish unwanted thoughts or worries from your mind. The moment you give yourself the instruction to stop thinking about a subject, that very thought becomes the focus of all your attention. As soon as you give yourself the instruction to avoid an idea, you begin to monitor your thoughts for the unwanted idea, which of course brings it constantly to your attention (cf. Wegner et al. 1987). Although this strategy may seem as daunting as the Aegean stables, some studies have demonstrated that people committed to lowering prejudice and discrimination are effective in their attempts to resist the negative affects of stereotyping (Macrae et al. 1994; Monteith et al. 1998).

The next step in reducing discrimination in everyday life requires self-regulation of discriminatory responses. Patricia Devine (1989) and Patricia Devine and her colleagues (1991) provide evidence that people who strongly endorse egalitarian values can control the extent to which prejudices affect discriminatory responses. These people want to treat others fairly. When confronted with an inconsistency between discrimination and their egalitarian values, they experience guilt. Jones (2002) suggests that guilt can be put to constructive purposes for high-prejudiced people as well. People who embrace the value for equal opportunity might be more likely to refrain from discrimination if the inconsistency between equal opportunity and their discriminatory behavior was apparent.

Although monitoring one's own behavior for discrimination is a challenging task requiring vigilance and introspection, it is also important to react actively against discrimination committed by others. Becoming actively antiracist (or antisexist, anticlassist, antihomophobic, antiageist, etc.) requires us to overcome the sometimes paralyzing effects of social embarrassment. Almost everyone can recall an incident in which they witnessed someone being treated unfairly; yet they felt so constrained by the social situation that they did not intervene. Unfortunately a passive response to discrimination can be translated into tacit support for discrimination. Critical theorists contend that refraining from discrimination is not enough; one must actively fight against discrimination (cf. O'Brien 2001; Shanks-Meile 2001; Gillespie et al. 2002).

Summary

This chapter began by clarifying the distinction between prejudice (an attitude) and discrimination (a behavior). The terms are sometimes used as if they are synonymous because prejudice is assumed to be a prime motivator of discrimination. We learned that though discrimination can be a result of a personal decision based on individual prejudices, it can also be the result of preferences for another group or may be motivated by a desire to maintain advantages. We also learned that discrimination can occur without any personal prejudice or antipathy when it results from the policies of an institution.

The link between attitudes and behavior has vexed social scientists ever since La Piere demonstrated that even when prejudice was freely admitted, discrimination seldom followed. This led us to review why behaviors such as discrimination are so difficult to predict. We found that the complexity of behavior and situational constraints cannot simply be attributed to one cause. Even the causal ordering between prejudice and discrimination cannot be taken for granted because sometimes prejudices emerge as a post-hoc defense of discrimination.

The last part of the chapter investigated attempts to reduce discrimination. Not all instances of discrimination are considered social problems. For example, although discrimination based on sex is considered a problem and is specifically prohibited by the 1964 Civil Rights Act, discrimination based on sexual orientation is not prohibited. In addition to reviewing legislative attempts to reduce discrimination, we examined two areas of social policy stemming from the 1964 Civil Rights Act: Affirmative Action and environmental justice. Although civil rights legislation has helped reduce discrimination, the areas of life regulated by such laws fall far short of the reality of everyday discrimination. We learned that individuals motivated to reduce their own prejudices and discriminatory actions can overcome their biases. However, effectively reducing discrimination and prejudice on the micro-level requires one to work actively against them when they are encountered in everyday interaction. Individuals can learn to become aware of and suppress their prejudices and discriminatory responses, but grassroots social change requires that the unfair treatment of others be challenged.

Key Terms

- Affirmative Action
- Aggregate data
- Bogardus scale
- Civil Rights Act of 1964
- Cohesion
- Direct discrimination
- Discrimination
- Environmental injustice

- Freedom Summer
- Heterogeneous
- Homogeneity
- Indirect Institutional discrimination
- Institutional discrimination
- Isolated discrimination
- La Piere's study

- Plurality
- Power
- Primary discrimination
- Reverse discrimination
- Small-group discrimination
- Social status
- Title VII of the 1964 Civil Rights Act

Taking It Further — Class Exercises and Interesting Web Sites

Freedom Summer

The PBS series *Eyes on the Prize* chronicles the civil rights movement from 1954 to 1985. *Mississippi: Is This America?* describes Freedom Summer and the murders of three civil rights workers in Mississippi. Watch the film and discuss the different types of discrimination documented by the film. For more information about the *Eyes on the Prize* series see: http://www.pbs.org/wgbh/amex/eyesontheprize/index.html.

The Gendered World of MTV

Film maker Sut Jhally has produced three powerful films about how gender is portrayed in music video: *Dreamworlds: Desire, Sex, Power in Rock Video* (1991), *Dreamworlds 2: Desire, Sex, Power in Music Video* (1995) and *Dreamworlds 3* (2007). All three videos portray the impact that sex and violence in media have on society and culture in our everyday life. For more information see: http://www.mediaed.org/videos/MediaGenderAndDiversity/Dreamworlds2/studyguide/html and http://www.sutjhally.com

People Like Us

Americans have notoriously poor class consciousness, or do we? *People Like Us: Social Class in America* (2001) exposes both our consciousness of social class and our class prejudices. In this film, income, family background, education, attitudes, aspirations, and even appearance are explored as marks of our social class. The film discusses how social class plays a role in the lives of all Americans, whether they live in penthouses, trailer parks, or suburban gated communities. Watch the film and visit the PBS Web site for games, stories, and exercises to accompany the film: http://www.pbs.org/peoplelikeus/film/index.html

References

Allport, Gordon W. 1954. *The nature of prejudice.* Reading, MA: Addison-Wesley Publishing Company.

Bakanic, Von, Carolyn Morales, Karin Roof, and Janet Key. 2007. *A campus climate survey: Executive summary strategic diversity management council.* South Carolina: College of Charleston.

Bakanic, Von, and Rita J. Simon. 1995. A Mississippi learning: Racial attitudes twenty five years after freedom summer. *Studies in Communication* 5: 101–112.

Blalock, Hurbert M. 1967. *Toward a theory of minority group relations.* New York: John Wiley and Sons.

Bogardus, Emory. 1930. A social distance scale. *Sociology and Social Research* 17: 265–271.

———. 1968. A comparing social distances in Ethiopia, South African and the United States. *Sociology and Social Research* 52: 149–156.

Bureau of the Census. 2006. Factfinder: 2005 American community survey data profile highlights. http://factfinder.census.gov/servlet/ACSSAFFFacts?_event=Search&geo_id=&_geoContext=&_street=&_county=&_cityTown=&_state=04000US15&_zip=&_lang=en&_sse=on&pctxt=fph&pgsl=010 (accessed August 13, 2007).

Bureau of National Affairs. 1979. *Uniform guideline on employee selection procedures.* Washington, DC: United States Government Printing Office.

Devine, Patricia. 1989. Stereotypes and prejudice: Their automatic and controlled components. *Journal of Personality & Social Psychology* 56 (1): 5–18.

Devine, Patricia G., Monteith, Margo J., Zuwerink, Julia R., and Elliot, Andrew J. 1991. A prejudice with and without compunction. *Journal of Personality and Social Psychology* 60 (6) June: 817–830.

Elms, A. C. 1975. The crisis of confidence in social psychology. *American Psychologist* 30: 967–976.

Feagin, Joe. 1989. *Racial and ethnic relations.* Englewood Cliffs, NJ: Prentice Hall.

Fishbein, Martin. 1978. Attitudes and behavioral prediction: An overview. In *Major social issues: A multidisciplinary view,* ed. J. M. Yinger and S. J. Cutler, 377–398. New York: Free Press.

Fishbein, Martin, and I. Ajzen. 1975. *Belief, attitude, intention and behavior: An introduction to theory and research.* Reading, MA: Addison-Wesley.

Freeman, Jo. 1991. A how "sex" got into title VII: Persistent opportunism as a maker of public policy. *Law and Inequality: A Journal of Theory and Practice* 9: 163–184.

Gillespie, Diane, Leslie Ashbaugh, and JoAnn DeFlore. 2002. A white women teaching white women about white privilege, race cognizance and social action: Toward a pedogogical pragmatics. *Race, Ethnicity and Education* 5: 237–253.

Hill, Richard. 1981. Attitudes and behavior. In *Social Psychology: Sociological Perspectives,* ed. M. Rosenberg and R. H. Turner, 347–377. New York: Basic Books, Inc.

Jones, Evonne Parker. 1991. The impact of economic, political and social factors on recent overt black/white racial conflict in higher education in the United States. *Journal of Negro Education* 60: 524–537.

Jones, Melinda. 2002. *Social psychology of prejudice.* Upper Saddle River, NJ: Prentice Hall.

Kinloch, Graham. 1974. *The dynamics of race relations.* New York: McGraw Hill.

Kitano, Harry. 1991. *Race relations* (4th ed.). Englewood Cliffs, NJ: Prentice Hall.

Kutner, B., C. Wilkins, and P. R. Yarrow. 1952. Verbal attitudes and overt behavior involving racial prejudice. *Journal of Abnormal and Social Psychology* 47: 649–652.

La Piere, Richard T. 1934. Attitudes vs. behavior. *Social Forces* 13: 230–237.

Lavelle, M., and M. Coyle. 1992. Unequal protection. *National Law Journal* 21 September 1992: Section S1–S12.

Macrae, C. M., G. V. Bodenhausen, A. B. Milne, and J. Jetten. 1994. Out of mind but back in sight: Stereotypes on the rebound. *Journal of Personality and Social Psychology* 67: 808–817.

McDonald, Timothy, Albert E. Love, and Earl T. Shinhoster. 2000 *A voter's manual for African American ministers.* Washington, DC: People for the American Way Foundation.

McLemore, Dale S. 1991. *Race and ethnic relations in America* (3rd ed.). Boston, MA: Allyn and Bacon.

Minard, R. B. 1952. A race relations in the pocohontas coal field. *Journal of Social Issues* 8: 29–44.

Monteith, M. J., C. V. Spicer, and J. D. Tooman. (1998). Consequences of stereotype suppression: Stereotypes on and not on the rebound. *Journal of Experimental Social Psychology* 34: 355–377.

Myrdal, Gunnar. 1944. *An American dilemma.* New York: Harper and Brothers.

O'Brien, Eileen 2001. *Whites confront racism: Anti-racists and their paths to action.* Lanham, MD: Rowman & Littlefield.

Park, Robert E. and Ernest W. Burgess. 1921. *Introduction to the science of sociology.* Chicago, IL: University of Chicago Press.

Plous, S., ed. 1996. Ten Myths About Affirmative Action. In *Understanding prejudice and discrimination,* 206–212. New York: McGraw-Hill.

Rechtschaffen, Clifford and Eileen Gauna, eds. 2002. *Environmental justice: Law, policy and regulation.* Durham, NC: Carolina Academic Press.

Regents of the University of California v. Bakke, 438 U.S. 265 (1978) http://www.oyez.org/cases/1970_1979/1977/1977_76_811 (accessed August 13, 2007).

Roosevelt, Franklin D. 1967. A executive order 8802. In *The burden of race,* ed. Gilbert Osofsky, 400–401. New York: Harper Torchbooks.

Rose, Arnold. 1951. *The roots of prejudice.* Paris: UNESCO, pub. 85.

Saenger, G., and C. Gilbert. 1950. Customer reactions to the integration of Negro sales personnel. *International Journal of Opinion and Attitude Research* 4: 57–76.

Schaefer, Richard T. 2000. *Racial and ethnic groups* (8th ed.). Englewood Cliffs, NJ: Prentice Hall.

Schermerhorn, Richard. 1970. *Comparative ethnic relations: A framework for theory and research.* New York: Random House.

Shanks-Meile, Stephanie. 2001. The changing face of the white power movement and the anti-racist resistance. *Research in Political Sociology* 9: 191–195.

Song, Tae-Hyon. 1991. Social contact and ethnic distance between Koreans and the U.S. whites in the United States unpublished paper. Macomb, IL: Western Illinois University.

Thorne, Barrie. 1993. *Gender play: Girls and boys in school.* New Brunswick, NJ: Rutgers University Press.

United States Labor Department. 1995. *Reverse discrimination.* Washington, DC: United States Government Printing Office.

Wicker, A. W. 1969. Attitudes versus actions: The relationship of verbal and overt behavioral response to attitude objects. *Journal of Social Issues* 15: 41–78.

Wegner, D. M., D. J. Schneider, S. Carter, and L. White. 1987. Paradoxical effects of thought suppression. *Journal of Personality and Social Psychology* 53: 5–13.

CHAPTER 6

Racism, Sexism, and Classism: Triple Trouble

In this chapter I explore the similarities in the process used to create and maintain race, gender, and class prejudices and how they justify and reinforce inequality in society.

- What Is Social Structure?
- Racism, Sexism, and Classism
- The Structure of Advantage
  - *Racial Advantage*
  - *Social-Class Advantage*
  - *Gender Advantage*
  - *Heterosexism and Marriage*
- Building Prejudices into Social Structure
  - *Changing Values: Micro-Level Change*
  - *Social Change: Macro-Level Change*
  - *American Ideology*
- Intersection of Race, Gender, and Class
  - *Focus on Race: The Declining or Inclining Significance of Race?*
- Summary
- Key Terms
- Taking It Further—Class Exercises and Interesting Web Sites
- References

When I teach about prejudice or race and ethnicity I get questions about the difference between prejudice and racism. The questions are usually phrased something like this: "I've got a black friend that claims black people can't be racist. Is that true?" This question stems from a confusion between racism and racial prejudice. Although terms like "racist" and "sexist" are used to identify a person who espouses prejudices, they actually refer to a far broader, more entrenched—and therefore more enduring—social phenomenon. Racism, sexism, and classism refer to social structures that perpetuate inequality.

Getting back to the student's question, anyone can hold prejudices, but social structures like racism, sexism, and classism give advantages to the dominant group while creating obstacles for minority groups. Because prejudices are part of the ideological justification for racism, sexism, and classism, the prejudices of the dominant group have a greater impact than the prejudices of minority groups. So, in a way, the hypothetical black friend is right. Black people are harmed by racism in ways most white people neither experience nor even notice. Although some black people may respond to racism with antiwhite prejudice, these prejudices are not accompanied by an entire social system constructed (sometimes unknowingly) to perpetuate disadvantages for an entire category of people.

In this chapter, we will learn that prejudice and discrimination are both the producers and products of structural inequality. In Chapter 5, we learned that prejudices are attitudes and discrimination is a behavior. Although prejudice and discrimination are distinct phenomena and can occur independently, they are also bound together in reciprocal relationships. Discrimination may emerge out of prejudice, or prejudice may be used as a post hoc justification for discrimination. However, remember the explanation of institutional discrimination in Chapter 5: it is also possible that discrimination will occur without any prejudice at all. In this chapter, I will explain the components of social structure. We will explore how language reflects and helps perpetuate structural inequality and how systems of advantage become embedded in social structure. Finally, we will examine how prejudice becomes infused within the dominant ideology and contributes to the formation and maintenance of three social structures that perpetuate inequality: racism, sexism, and classism.

WHAT IS SOCIAL STRUCTURE?

According to sociologists, *social structures* are the basic framework or architecture of social order. They provide the social context in which interaction between individuals takes place. Among its many components, social structure includes social roles, statuses, norms, forms of organization, cultural beliefs, and values. Social structure frames and shapes human interactions giving people a sense of predictability. Although the actual predictability of human behavior may be tenuous, the sense that we understand what is going on and what is likely to happen next is an indispensable component of social order. For example, when you walked into the class the first day of the semester, you made assumptions about what was likely to go on. You probably took a seat in one of the desks, got out notepaper and pen, then waited for a professor to go to the front of the classroom. You made these assumptions based on what you already knew about the structure of educational institutions.

But, let's look closer at this seemingly simple event. When you walked into the classroom, you entered a space that was physically structured to facilitate a particular type of interaction. Chairs may have been arranged in rows or even bolted to the floor. A small writing desk may have been attached to the side of your chair. The chairs were probably facing a lectern, podium, or desk. There may have been a board, television, or computer screen at the front of the room. The lack of comfortable chairs and distracting decorations as well as the orientation of the chairs toward a single direction make it easier to focus on the professor. Taking up a position in one of the chairs or at the podium implies a social role: those occupying the desks are students and the person at the lectern is the professor. These roles are as much a part of the social structure as desks are part of the physical structure of the room. The roles of student and professor help you know what is expected of you and anticipate what others are likely to do. *Social roles* are a set of behavioral expectations attached to a social position. They often have statuses as well. *Social status* is a named social position that implies the relative prestige of that position. For example, the status of the instructor can be indicated by special honorariums such as "Dr." or "Professor."

The classroom you entered is part of a larger organization at your college or university. A *social organization* is a configuration, or network, of social roles and positions. Teachers are grouped according to their academic disciplines into departments and stratified by their rank (assistant, associate, or full professor) within the department. Departments are organized into schools or colleges headed by deans. Deans are subject to the authority of those still higher in the administration. Even the president or chancellor of your school is subject to some higher authority such as a board of trustees.

Your college or university is part of the institution of higher education and adheres to institutionalized norms. A *social institution* is a network of roles, statuses, groups, and organizations designed to accomplish a basic social goal. The goal of most colleges and universities is providing education. Examples of institutionalized norms include the expectation that it will take approximately four to five years of full-time enrollment to complete a bachelor's degree or that students must take a minimum number of hours to be considered full time. Although there are differences between particular schools, there are many more similarities.

Cultural beliefs are shared ideas that describe how our culture operates. Cultural beliefs can include information about social history, explanations for contemporary social issues, and predictions about our collective future. One of these widely held beliefs is that education is the means to achieving financial success and higher social position. Another belief—that people making 'A's are smarter and harder working—legitimates achieved inequality among students and alumni. The beliefs and values that support a social structure become further embedded through the language we use. The terms we create to describe the context of the educational structure gradually come to be used describing other events and circumstances. Some examples include, the ABCDF grading system (used as an evaluative language for many events and products outside of the classroom), referring to immature behavior as "sophomoric," or describing learning the basics of any task as "101." As the terms spread throughout the language, understanding of and support for the educational structure becomes infused throughout the entire social system. The ideas, beliefs, and values that support the educational structure are used to make sense of other situations and interactions. Thus, social structures not only influence our behaviors when we interact within the parameters of the structure but also help us interpret and anticipate the behavior of others in wider social context.

Whereas cultural beliefs describe how we interpret and understand our society, *values* are shared ideas about what is right and what is wrong. That is, cultural beliefs are about what *is,* and values are about what *should be.* Although people in a society share many of them, values are not consistently adhered to and seldom predict an individual's behavior. In Chapter 2, I explained why there is a weak link between attitudes and behavior; the same explanation holds for the link between values and behavior. Values are abstract notions about how things should be, but they don't take into account the effects of situational differences. For example, one may sincerely value the sanctity of human life but make a decision to remove a loved one from life sustaining machinery because of the tremendous strain and agony being suffered by family members.

Another reason for the weak relationship between values and behavior is lack of one-to-one relationship between a particular value and a specific behaviors. If a young woman says she holds strong traditional family values, does that mean we can predict that she will remain a virgin until marriage, never divorce, and acknowledge her husband as head of the family? Unfortunately, empirical studies have not provided much support for a specific cause–effect relationship between values and specific behaviors.

This leads to a third reason for the weak link between values and behavior: do values cause behaviors or behaviors affect values? Some experiences, indeed, lead people to reconsider their values. For instance, a near-death experience may cause you to reprioritize how and with whom you spend your time. This is clearly an example of experience affecting values, which in turn affects behavior. Reciprocal causation leads to the classic chicken-or-egg dilemma: which comes first, the value or the behavior?

Despite the intricacy of the relationship between values and behavior, the role values play in maintaining social order is clear. Values support, justify, and legitimate social order. They arise from social structures; as the structure changes, so do values. You may remember the political hyperbole about the decline in family values that was blamed for high divorce, increased delinquency rates, and myriad other social problems. Simply reinforcing traditional values is not likely to reverse the social trends that brought a growing percentage of women out of house and into the workforce. Nor will traditional values compensate for less parental supervision in both single-parent households and households in which both parents work. It is more likely that new values justifying changing family structures will emerge to support working parents. The traditional values that supported a working father, stay-at-home mother, and multiple children are a poor fit with today's varied family forms. Not only are more mothers working outside of the home, there are more single-parent households and more grandparents raising children. Even though social movement organizations, such as the Promise Keepers,[1] have expended great effort to return to traditional values, values alone cannot inhibit structural change.

Although I have addressed the components of social structure individually, they must be understood as an integrated system. Roles are accompanied by statuses, both of which have behavioral expectations (i.e., norms). The configuration of roles and statuses forms the basic skeleton of social organization, whereas cultural beliefs and values legitimate and justify social structure. The next section discusses three specific systems of structural inequality: racism, sexism, and classism.

RACISM, SEXISM, AND CLASSISM

Racism, sexism, and classism are social structures. ***Racism*** refers to the entire complex of roles, statuses, norms, organizations, and institutions that creates and perpetuates advantages for the dominant racial/ethnic group and disadvantages for other races and ethnic groups. Similarly, ***sexism*** and ***classism*** refer to comprehensive social structures perpetuating advantages for men and the upper classes, respectively. Advantages for the dominant group and disadvantages for subordinate groups become infused in every aspect of society. Even how we speak, and therefore how we think, reflects the inequality embedded in our social structure (cf. Haskell 1986; Asante 1998).

Remember the example presented earlier in this chapter about how the language of education spreads beyond the classroom. Just as the words and terms initially associated with education have been used to describe other aspects of our society, the language of racism, sexism, and classism is infused throughout the culture.

---

[1] The Promise Keepers is a national social movement whose goal is to restore traditional family values, encourage men to take back control of their family and encourage Christian fellowship.

The language of racism goes far beyond racial slurs used for name-calling. According to Asante (Asante 1998:87), racism is entangled in "the most intricate patterns of our conversation and language." Consistent with the theory of modern racism, the majority of Americans reject explicit or overt racism and racist language. Today's more subtle racism indirectly associates whiteness with status. Thus, by implication, people of color lack status. For example, when a white person is identified by a high-status position, that position is not prefaced by an adjective indicating race. However, when a person of color merits similar status, the status is commonly preceded by racial identifiers, such as "African American doctor" or "Latino professor."

Some of the more colorful uses of language appear in idioms. An idiom is an expression whose meaning is not derived from the words of the idiom themselves, but from a cultural reference. For example, "kick the bucket" means "to die," whereas "getting a kick out of something" means "to be amused." Because idioms can be understood only from their cultural context, they reflect the social inequities and prejudices of the culture. The idiom "keep your cotton pickin' hands off" has both racist and classist connotations. The historical context from which this idiom emerged was the use of African Americans as field hands. The idiom conveys both the low status of field workers and the suspicion of theft. The term "black" is often used in idioms as a euphemism for bad. For example, the "black sheep of the family" is one who brings disgrace to the family; someone who is "black hearted" has a cruel disposition; and being "blacklisted" is to be excluded. "White," on the other hand, is associated with positive or benign effects (e.g., "That's very white of you" or "a little white lie"). "Ghetto blaster" (a large portable radio, tape, or CD player) is an example of a contemporary racist idiom. Idioms such as "ghetto bootie" and "brown sugar" mix sexism with racism. Classism is also reflected in idioms such as "born with a silver spoon in his mouth" or being "poor as dirt." The latter idiom comes from the period of western expansion in U.S. history when settlers were too poor to install wood flooring in their cabins, leaving the floors as dirt. Anti-Semitic idioms ("Jewing down price"), sexist idioms ("Who wears the pants in the family?"), ageist idioms ("slower than grandma," which turns out to be sexist, too) are just a few of the forms of inequality that color our speech.

Racism has left its mark in how people use language, the idioms we create, and even in the rhymes children sing. In a recent civil case, two African American women sued Southwest Airlines in a U.S. district court over a paraphrased line from a rhyme with a racist history. Over the plane's loud speaker system, a flight attendant had said "Eenie, meenie minie moe; pick a seat we gotta go." The plaintiffs claimed that they were embarrassed and humiliated because the first part of the rhyme comes from a racist rhyme that contains a blatant racist slur. The flight attendant contended that she did not know about the earlier version of the rhyme, and an all-white jury found for the defendants (Associated Press, January 22, 2004). It's not surprising that the white flight attendant and the all-white jury did not see the racism embedded in the rhyme. Whites are seldom the targets of racial slurs and have little experience as targets of pervasive racism. No racial slur was actually uttered by the flight attendant, hence no discrimination. However, the association with older racist rhyme had an immediate impact on members of the minority group. Regardless of the intent of the flight attendant, the African American women felt the sting of the racist reference.

Sexism and homophobia are also infused in our language. Using "sissy" to mean weak or cowardly is a gendered insult because "sissy" is a slang word for sister. It takes only a few seconds to think of the many derogatory words in our language that refer to promiscuous women, whereas the list of negative terms for promiscuous men is much shorter and not nearly as insulting. For example, in a comparison of the negative impact of "stud" versus "slut," "stud" can be used to describe male virility, whereas the word "slut" denotes a woman of easy virtue.

Slang terms used to identify homosexuals and lesbians are closely related to gendered insults. The word "fag," used in reference to a homosexual, originated as a reference to the burning of homosexuals. They were used as faggots (small sticks) to light the fires used to execute the condemned in the sixteenth-century Europe. Slang words such as "gay," "pansy," "dyke," and "queer" have been so thoroughly linked with homosexuality that dictionaries started including the disparaging slang meanings among the uses for the words (see Eble 1996).

Our language also reflects the inequalities of social class. Consider the difference between the verb "exclude" and the adjective "exclusive." "Exclude" implies limiting, restricting, or rejecting, whereas "exclusive" implies prestige, excellence, and distinction. Words and phrases that are used to describe the working class and poor are frequently negative. "Redneck," "roughneck," "no-neck," or "working stiff" are terms used to invoke stereotypes of crude, violent, brutish working-class men. Working-class or poor women are sometimes described as trailer park trash, poor white trash, or honky tonk angels. Grammar mistakes and regional accents are also indicative of social class. Although few (if any) people speak flawlessly all the time, grammar errors coupled with a southern drawl bring to mind stereotypes of uneducated, slow-witted, working-class and poor people.

As we have seen, the language of inequality involves more than slang and slurs. Inequality becomes part of how we speak and therefore how we think. Even though we may not know the etymology of words and phrases or attend to the racist, classist, and sexist connotations of our speech, language conveys culture with all its complexities and inequities.

THE STRUCTURE OF ADVANTAGE

Thus far, I have focused on the disadvantages experienced by minorities; however, the most insidious aspect of racism, sexism, and classism is the invisibility of advantages. People seldom notice obstacles that are not in their path. If a system works well for many, or most, people, those who are well served assume that a failure by minority group members is a product of their individual characteristics rather than the system. It's easy to see poverty, low levels of education, and inadequate health care as social problems arising from disadvantage. It's much harder to see advantage and privilege as social problems.

The investigation of advantage and privilege was spurred by Peggy McIntosh's essay on white privilege (2001). While teaching courses in Women's Studies, she noticed the unwillingness of men to recognize their privilege in our patriarchal society. As she was pondering male privilege, she realized that as a white person, she had been taught that racism disadvantages people of color, but she had not been taught to recognize her privilege as a white person. So she decided to try identifying the privileges she enjoyed as a white person in a racist society. Although she had had many advantages, she reports having trouble remembering those privileges until she wrote them down (Box 6-1).

BOX 6-1

Peggy McIntosh's Original List of Privileges

1. I can, if I wish, arrange to be in the company of people of my race most of the time.

2. If I should need to move, I can be pretty sure of renting or purchasing housing in an area that I can afford and in which I would want to live.

3. I can be pretty sure that my neighbors in such a location will be neutral or pleasant to me.

4. I can go shopping alone most of the time, pretty well assured that I will not be followed or harassed.

5. I can turn on the television or open to the front page of the paper and see people of my race widely represented.

6. When I am told about our national heritage or about "civilization," I am shown that people of my color made it what it is.

7. I can be sure that my children will be given curricular materials that testify to the existence of their race.

8. If I want to, I can be pretty sure of finding a publisher for this piece on white privilege.

9. I can go into a music shop and count on finding the music of my race represented, into a supermarket and find the staple foods that fit with my cultural traditions, into a hairdresser's shop and find someone who can cut my hair.

10. Whether I use checks, credit cards, or cash, I can count on my skin color not to work against the appearance of my financial reliability.

11. I can arrange to protect my children most of the time from people who might not like them.

12. I can swear, or dress in second-hand clothes, or not answer letters, without having people attribute these choices to the bad morals, the poverty, or the illiteracy of my race.

13. I can speak in public to a powerful male group without putting my race on trial.

14. I can do well in a challenging situation without being called a credit to my race.

15. I am never asked to speak for all the people of my racial group.

16. I can remain oblivious of the language and customs of persons of color who constitute the world's majority without feeling in my culture any penalty for such oblivion.

17. I can criticize our government and talk about how much I fear its policies and behavior without being seen as a cultural outsider.

18. I can be pretty sure that if I ask to talk to "the person in charge," I will be facing a person of my race.

19. If a traffic cop pulls me over or if the IRS audits my tax return, I can be sure I haven't been singled out because of my race.

20. I can easily buy posters, post-cards, picture books, greeting cards, dolls, toys, and children's magazines featuring people of my race.

21. I can go home from most meetings of organizations I belong to feeling somewhat tied in, rather than isolated, out-of-place, outnumbered, unheard, held at a distance, or feared.

22. I can take a job with an affirmative action employer without having co-workers on the job suspect that I got it because of race.

23. I can choose public accommodation without fearing that people of my race cannot get in or will be mistreated in the place I have chosen.

24. I can be sure that if I need legal or medical help my race will not work against me.

25. If my day, week, or year is going badly, I need not ask of each negative episode or situation whether it has racial overtones.

26. I can choose blemish cover or bandages in "flesh" color and have them more or less match my skin.

SOURCE: —McIntosh, Peggy, 1988, "White privilege: Unpacking the invisible knapsack" (Copyright 1988 by Peggy McIntosh).

Like the men in her Women's Study classes, she had been carefully taught not to see her unearned advantages (McIntosh 2001:100).

Members of advantaged groups may assume that when they are the target of prejudice from minorities, they have suffered an equalizing injustice. The logic seems to be that one's own prejudices are vindicated because others are also prejudiced. To illustrate, I will tell you about the experience of a student who told me he had been sexually harassed. He went to a campus-cosponsored demonstration protesting violence against women. The event included a charity auction. One of the volunteers at the rally asked if he and his male friend wanted to volunteer to be auctioned as part of a "date package." The student complained that he and his companion were highly offended by the sexism implicit in being offered as a commodity. The student used this example to support his contention that he had experienced just as much sexual harassment and discrimination as women (Box 6-2).

Let's deconstruct this scenario. If we grant, for the sake of argument, that the request was an example of sexist prejudice, what are the consequences of that prejudice for the young men? The men were not employed by the groups sponsoring the event, so no threat, real or implied, was made to coerce them into participating. The men were not physically intimidated by the woman, nor was there a community history of violence against men by female perpetrators. Although the men might have been offended by the request, the prejudice they discerned was not accompanied by the weight of a sexist structure because neither the volunteer who made the suggestion nor the organizations sponsoring the event had any power to discriminate against the men. So, even though the request may be interpreted as a type of reverse gender prejudice, it does not have the same impact as anti-woman prejudices and gender discrimination that are backed up by a long history of oppression and violence.

BOX 6-2

Take Back the Night

Take Back the Night is an international social movement intended to protest rape and other forms of violence. The movement's name came from a memorial read by Anne Pride at an antiviolence rally in Pittsburgh in 1977 (see Anne Carson's 1997 entry on WMST-L discussion at http://research.umbc.edu/~korenman/wmst/takenite2.html). Since then annual rallies and marches have been conducted on many colleges and cities. Women and girls are often advised not to go out at night or to take special precautions. Although the movement originally was a way to protest violence against women when they were out at night, it has expanded and evolved to cover violence against all people regardless of where or when the violence takes place. Protesting domestic violence and sexual abuse within the home have been incorporated into the movement's agenda. There is no single date or time of year for a Take Back the Night march. Some are held in October to correspond with Domestic Violence Awareness Month, whereas others are held in March to celebrate Women's History Month or April for Child Abuse prevention month.

SOURCE: For more information visit the Take Back the Night Web site: http://www.takebackthenight.org/

Racial Advantage

How does the advantage of whites contribute to the disadvantage of racial minorities? It has been argued that as racial minorities enter the middle class, race becomes less significant (cf. Wilson 1978). If this is so, why can't racial minorities just emulate the behavior of hardworking, financially prudent white people? The answer is that the system does not work in the same way for minorities as it does for whites. Let's take, for example, the privilege of home ownership. Equity in a home accounts for most of the personal wealth acquired by white middle-class families. White men returning from World War II were able to use the GI Bill to purchase homes with little or no down payment at reasonable interest rates. Hundreds of thousands of returning soldiers took advantage of the federally guaranteed program. Their property steadily accrued in value, creating equity that could be used to secure car loans, college tuition loans, or even the acquisition of more property. So why couldn't people of color take advantage of these programs? Setting aside for the moment the problem of residential segregation, the fact is that the value of a house is determined by its perceived value. Although the condition and size of the house help determine part of its value, the surrounding neighborhood is also a factor. When banks assess the value of a property as part of a loan application, they also assess their risk in making the loan. When a black or Latino family moves into a predominately white neighborhood, the value of their newly purchased property and that of their neighbors are affected. Realtors of the 1960s and the 1970s were quick to capitalize on the fears of falling property values because of integration. They offered to buy the homes of white residents at deflated prices and then sold the properties to black families at inflated prices. This caused other white home owners to sell out as soon as racial minorities began purchasing homes in their neighborhoods. The mass exodus of whites became known as **white flight**. So the system that worked so well for white families did not work for minorities. Not only did minority-owned houses decrease in value, resentment and racial prejudices increased because white home owners lost equity when minorities moved into their neighborhoods (cf. Horton and Thomas 1998; Lipsitz 1998). Minority home owners face a catch-22. Not only do they pay higher prices for property and higher interest rates on mortgages, they were also more likely to have their loans called by banks when the value of their property falls below the amount of their mortgage. They are not as likely to accrue equity in homes because the moment they buy a home in a predominately white neighborhood, the value of the property declines.

The members of the dominant group are more likely to understand the disparity in home ownership from the individual perspective. That is, the housing gap is a matter of the personal choices and inadequacies of racial minorities. From their perspective, the social-class system is open and everyone has the capacity to rise in the social hierarchy (Willie 1989). So if racial minorities do not accrue wealth from home investment, it's because they don't keep their property repaired or they prefer to rent rather than buy. But, from the perspective of racial minorities, federal housing policies offered separate and unequal housing opportunities. Minorities were offered subsidized rent in urban housing projects, whereas whites were offered federally guaranteed loans so that they could purchase homes in the suburbs.

In this section, we have used the housing market to illustrate structural inequality. The value of housing is determined in part by the race of one's neighbors, giving whites a tremendous advantage in the housing market and in the acquisition of wealth. In the next section we will explore the hidden advantages of social class.

Social-Class Advantage

Class advantages are ironically the most likely to be displayed and yet the hardest for the privileged to see. Like Peggy McIntosh, members of the middle to upper classes have been carefully trained to overlook their unearned advantages. Because social-class advantage is legitimate and desirable in our economic and social system, members of the advantaged classes are proud of the symbols of success that come their way. Sending one's children to private schools is a sign of success both because parents can afford the tuition and because their children have been accepted into exclusive institutions. Class privilege distances members of the upper classes from experiences common to the working class and poor. For example, during his 1992 presidential campaign, President George Herbert Walker Bush was filmed marveling at the checkout scanners at a grocery checkout. What was clearly a novelty to the former president is an everyday part of the life to the middle class, working class, and poor.

The privileged are sheltered, both from knowledge of their position in the social structure and from the consequences of social class for people in other classes. Similar to people attributing the infamous quote "Let them eat cake" to Marie Antoinette, today's affluent classes are unaware of the harsh realities experienced by lower classes. Poor social-class consciousness not only leads the lower classes to misidentify their economic interests but also prevents the upper classes from recognizing that their experiences are qualitatively different from those of the lower classes.

Widespread confusion about what constitutes social class results in up to 50 percent of Americans describing themselves as "middle class" (Gilbert and Kahl 1982). Many people assume there are but three social classes: the poor, the wealthy, and the broad middle class in between (MacKenzie 1973:117). Whereas most social scientists rely on occupation as the best indicator of class, most laypeople use income groupings to define their class. Although both the academic and popular press have sounded alarms about the declining middle class and the polarization of the American class structure, most Americans continue to identify themselves as middle class (cf. Ehrenreich 1989, 2001; Rothman 1993).

Although the upper classes share the widespread cultural value for social equality, they react negatively whenever their advantage is challenged. Because the privileged believe that their experiences are or should be the norm, they respond to policies designed to ameliorate class differences as unfair. For example, a commonly heard complaint of college students is that their parents make too much money, so they are not eligible for need-based grants and loans. Yet the tremendous advantage of graduating from college without debt from loans is seldom recognized.

Perhaps the most obvious structural advantage enjoyed by the affluent is their disproportionate benefit from government programs. The vilification of welfare recipients during the 1980s and 1990s led both major political parties to decrease already-inadequate social welfare programs, while at the same time funding record bailouts for banks and business (e.g., the saving and loan bailout of the mid-1980s and the Enron scandal of 2001). Government programs aimed at subsidizing business and industry have been dubbed ***corporate welfare*** or more pejoratively ***wealthfare*** (cf. Nadar 2000; Whitfield 2001). In an analysis of who benefits and who pays for welfare versus wealthfare programs, Mimi Abramovitz (2001) concludes that social, fiscal, and corporate welfare continue to serve middle class and wealthy households and large corporations. Although stereotypes of welfare "Queens" have been used effectively by the popular media and politicians to convince the public that social welfare recipients were among the undeserving poor, corporate welfare has not resulted in a similar concept of the "undeserving rich" (Egan 2003). Even with visible upper class targets such as Martha Stewart during her trial for insider trading, the stereotypes and prejudices evoked by pundits and political cartoonists focused more on gender prejudices than social-class prejudices.

In this section we learned that most Americans are unaware of their class advantages and are often mistaken about to which social class they belong. The acquisition of wealth and social-class advantage distances the affluent from the lower classes resulting in greater reliance on stereotypes and prejudices. In the next section we will turn to gender advantages.

Gender Advantage

Gender advantages are as common as race and class advantages and just as hard to see. Advantages for males are common in the retail and service industries. The values of services are determined by the gender of the client, the gender of the service provider, or both. A trip to the dry cleaners will convince you that the idiom "being taken to the cleaners" has a special meaning for women. Women pay more for having their clothes cleaned than men do. The rate for cleaning women's clothing is as much as three times the price for cleaning similar men's items (Whittelsey 1998). Women pay more for all sorts of services and products. For example, products such as deodorants and shampoos are priced as high as 50 percent more per ounce when packaged for women. Men's consumer advantage extends beyond prepriced merchandise into markets that allow consumers to bargain over the price. In a study involving more than three hundred audits at new-car dealerships, dealers quoted significantly lower prices to white males than to black or female test buyers (Ayres and Siegelman 1995). All the test buyers used identically scripted bargaining strategies. Even the initial offer by the car dealers was significantly lower when the customer was a white male. The assumption that men have better bargaining skills leads the salesperson to make lower opening offers and created a self-fulfilling prophesy: the final price white men paid was significantly less. It is interesting to note that the salespersons at car dealerships occasionally used racist and sexist language during the bargaining process revealing that personal prejudices and stereotypes are used to justify discrimination (Ayres and Siegelman 1995:319).

The assumption of competence is another taken-for-granted advantage enjoyed by men. Studies of children indicate that gender role stereotyping and the generalized expectation of greater male competence begins as early as age four (Tryon 1980). Although men make greater use of the male competence stereotype, females also assume greater competence among men (McKillip, DiMiceli, and Luebke 1977; Butler and Geis 1990; Foschi 1992). Whereas men are assumed to be competent at most tasks, females must demonstrate competence. For example, my eldest daughter told me a story that happened during her job as an environmental field technician. She wanted to remove a bolt from the door of her work van. She asked the maintenance worker for a drill. The maintenance worker seemed hesitant even when she assured him that she had operated a drill before. He accompanied her to the van to supervise the removal of the bolt. He hovered over her shoulder, interfering with the job. Irritated, she told him again that she could operate the drill. In frustration, she told him that her father had owned a construction company and that he had taught her how to operate power tools. It took the mention of a male authority to convince the maintenance worker that she was competent to operate the drill.

Butler and Geis (1990) conducted an experiment in which research subjects observed a four-person discussion group comprised of confederates (persons employed by the experimenters to play a scripted role) in which a male or female confederate assumed a leadership role. While the research subjects watched through a one-way mirror, the confederates worked at solving a task given to them by the experimenter. Although the script used by the confederates participating in the discussion was identical, female leaders received more negative comments than positive comments, though the reverse was true for male leaders. The assumption of male competence is probably one of the most expansive advantages men enjoy. It has been exploited in venues as disparate as using male voice-overs in commercial advertising (Browne 1998; Whipple et al. 2002) to student evaluations of professors' teaching (Dukes and Gay 1989; Burns-Glober et al. 1995).

Heterosexism and Marriage

Heterosexism is part and product of sexism. It is based on the belief that heterosexual orientation is the only natural and acceptable sexual behavior. Because it is part of a social structure, it includes more than beliefs. *Heterosexism* is an entire complex of ideas, values, norms, policies, and organization that gives advantages to heterosexuals and withholds them from all other sexual orientations. It is a social structure embedded within the patriarchal structure. *Patriarchy* establishes a system of gendered behavior in which behaviors are proscribed, prohibited, and evaluated according to the sex of the individual. Boys must do boy things and girls must do girl things. Violations of gender roles can result in a variety of sanctions, from being the target of laughter to being the target of lethal violence. Prejudice against people who violate traditional gender roles is one of the sanctions used to support sexism. Homosexuals, lesbians, bisexuals, and transgender people are a threat to the patriarchal structure because they entail violation of gender norms (Box 6-3).

Gender insults and homophobic reactions are used to compel gender role conformity. *Gender insults* are comments intended to embarrass individuals into gender role compliance. They include intentionally misidentifying a person's sex in an attempt to ridicule the person. For example, addressing a group of boys or men engaged in a competition or training as "girls" or "ladies" is intended to shame them into performing better. Gender insults not only produce conformity to traditional gender roles but also reinforce the inferiority of women. Cleverly using the implied prejudice against women to produce conformity and support the patriarchy makes women the scapegoat for men's feeling of inadequacy, at the same time legitimizing male superiority. By tying gender prejudices against women to men's self-esteem, men are made to feel good about themselves by comparison to women. Even though women are not the direct target of this kind of gender insults, the prejudices against them are reinforced in the reactions of the person(s) being insulted and by the inferior and subordinate status attributed to women. Although women and girls are sometimes teased with terms like "tomboy," gender insults aimed at women and girls are not as affective because

---

BOX 6-3

Homophobia and Hate Crime

The Murder of Matthew Shepard

In many ways Matthew Shepard was a typical college student. He had recently transferred to the University of Wyoming and was a political science major. Like most students he enjoyed going out to bars to meet friends and enjoy music. But, in the wee hours of the morning on October 7, 1998, two men he met at a bar robbed him, savagely beat him, and left him for dead. Russell Henderson and Aaron McKinney began conversing with Shepard, pretending to be gay to gain his trust. Shortly after midnight Shepard asked them for a ride home. Instead of taking him home, Henderson and McKinney took him to a remote rural area, robbed him, pistol whipped him, and left him tied to a fence. Shepard suffered severe brain damage and never regained consciousness. He died as a result of his injuries on October 12, 1998.

During their trials Henderson and McKinney's lawyers used a gay panic defense. They argued that their clients were driven to attack Shepard because of his sexual advances toward them. However, the defendants' girl-friends—Chastity Pasley and Kristen Price—testified that the men had plotted to pick up and rob a gay man. Henderson pleaded guilty and agreed to testify against McKinney. Both men were convicted and are currently serving two consecutive life sentences.

At the time of the trial neither Wyoming state law nor the United States federal government had laws making crimes committed on the basis of sexual orientation prosecutable as hate crime. Shortly after the trials the Wyoming state legislature failed to pass legislation that would have defined attacks motivated by a victim's sexual identity as hate crime. Federal legislation to extend protection against hate crime to homosexuals, women, and people with disabilities also failed to become law.

On March 20, 2007, The Matthew Shepard Act (HR 1592) was introduced to the U.S. Congress. The bill passed the House of Representatives in May, but even if it passes the Senate, President Bush has indicated he will veto it.

SOURCE: For more information visit the Matthew Shepard Resource Site at the University of Wyoming: http://www.uwyo.edu/News/shepard.

---

applying male traits to a woman invokes a more powerful status. Girls are not ashamed at being called a tomboy because it implies they have the superior traits associated with being a male.

Gender insults aimed at women sometimes use a slightly different strategy. Traits that are seen as positive in men are depicted negatively when applied to women. A man may be described as forceful and ambitious, whereas the same traits in a woman would be described as overbearing and pushy. This strategy presents the woman with a dilemma: she can either choose to conform to the generally positive male attributes at the expense of her femininity or abandon the higher-status male attributes to conform with subordinate feminine traits. It has been argued that professional women are deviant regardless of the option they choose (Bernstein and Bohrnstedt 1972; Schur

1984; Katz 1987). For women to be successful in the professional realm, they must have attributes more commonly associated with men, and in doing so, they will be violating female gender norms. If women choose to follow the more traditional female gender norms, they will be in violation of the norms operating in the corporate environment. Either way women are deviant.

Homophobia is the fear and loathing of gay, lesbian, bisexuals, and transsexuals. Even though gender insults are intended to make the boundaries between acceptable male and female behavior distinct, homosexual, lesbian, bisexual, and transsexual people blur the distinctions between the sexes. The traditional role of dominant male and subordinate female doesn't apply in the same way to same-sex relationships or transsexual people. The social androgyny implicit in nonheterosexual orientations threatens the carefully constructed and maintained differences between the sexes and, thus, the "natural" superiority of the male. Regarding nonheterosexuals as deviant is therefore necessary to maintaining patriarchy. Any attempt to legitimize homosexuality directly threatens the patriarchal social structure. Attempts to extend marriage to same-sex couples expose the inequality central to the roles of husband and wife. Alternatives such as domestic partnerships are also problematic. If domestic partnerships were made available, heterosexual couples would also be able to select that option. Our marriage laws are derived from contracts in which women were ***chattel*** (personal property). Until recently (and in many countries still), a marriage contract was a sales agreement between a woman's father and her husband. Although modern marriages in Western culture have evolved into a contract between a man, a women, and the state, many heterosexual couples might choose domestic partnership as more egalitarian. Providing a legitimate alternative to marriage would further erode patriarchy not only in the institution of family but in other social institutions as well. In that sense, heterosexism is a bulwark sustaining and protecting patriarchy and sexism.

The advantages of race, social class, sex, and sexual orientation are a product of the social structure. Although it is possible to become aware of one's advantages, most of us are not. We like to think that our position is deserved because of the hard work and sustained effort it took. Admitting to ourselves and others that we attained our social status at least in part because of unearned advantage is humbling. The advantages I have enjoyed as a white, middle-class, heterosexual woman helped me to achieve my position. Even if I wanted to forfeit those advantages, I could not. This is because the advantage is in the social structure and not under my individual control.

BUILDING PREJUDICES INTO SOCIAL STRUCTURE

Prejudices become part of the social structure through the ideology that supports it. ***Ideology*** is a body of beliefs and values that guides individuals, groups, organizations, and social institutions. It shapes how people understand their society and how they as individuals fit into the social order. Ideology is the rationale that explains and justifies the social order. Prejudices become infused in ideology when there is a need to support and defend structural advantages. When we judge others as inferior, by implication we proclaim ourselves superior, thus deserving advantage. It's fairly easy to imagine why the elite would uncritically accept prejudices that support their privilege. The more interesting point is, why do the disadvantaged support the very system that oppresses them? The willing acceptance of the prevailing system of inequality by most members of a society is accomplished by accepting values that are part of the dominant ideology. Because values are ideas about what should be, rather than a description about the way the world actually works, the discrepancy between the haves and the have-nots can be attributed to a lack of the proper values on the part of individuals.

Changing Values: Micro-Level Change

Cultural beliefs and values are dynamic. They are changing all the time, but the changes are slow enough for most people to adjust without creating social instability. Social scientists have charted changing values by asking samples of people about their beliefs and values year after year. One such study is the annual freshmen survey that has measured value changes over forty years. Every year, freshmen entering many two- and four-year colleges across the United States are given the opportunity to take part in the freshmen survey. The questionnaire they answer includes many items asking how important certain values are to them. Over the last few decades the values of college students in the United States have shifted toward greater concern with being financially well-off (Astin et al. 1997). This shift has occurred in response to the increasing polarization of the U.S. economy and the shrinking of the middle class. Other values such as developing a meaningful philosophy of life have declined during the same period. As it becomes more difficult for the children of the middle class to maintain their social class as adults, the values supporting financial ambition become stronger. The intellectual value of education becomes less important because achieving financial stability is more doubtful. The values promoting financial and material goals emerge at times when economic competition is increasing.

When the economy slows down and jobs become scarce, values promoting equality become less important, especially for people in the dominant group. Survey data gathered each fall since 1966 by the Higher Education Research Institute indicates that as students focus more on material goals, they become less concerned with social problems (Astin 1991). As financial and material goals increase, support for improving race relations declines, but not at the same rate for all groups. The support among white students has declined more than it has for racial minorities. This has created a gap in values between whites and racial minorities. The same pattern occurs with support for women in the workforce, with males becoming increasingly more conservative in tough economic times. However, there is some evidence that the value gap between races is wider than the gap between women and men (Kluegel and Bobo 2001).

Two theories of racism explain why self-reported estimates of racial prejudice have declined, even though behavioral indicators of segregation and discrimination persist. Modern racism and symbolic racism contend that overt, old-fashioned racism has decreased. People are not comfortable with blatant expressions of racial bias. Old-fashioned racism has been replaced with a more subtle form of modern racism. *Modern racism* involves three assumptions. First, it contends that racism has diminished to the point that it is no longer a social problem. Second, minority group members are responsible for any disadvantage they may suffer. Finally, government programs designed to ameliorate racial inequality are unjustified and unnecessary.

Symbolic racism contends that contemporary racism is disguised by our values. Abstract values, such as the work ethic and meritocracy, have become thinly disguised symbols for the tacit racism. Symbolic racism is expressed indirectly through feelings of social awkwardness and discomfort rather than blatant expressions of prejudice. Symbolic racists are more likely to deny racial prejudice but to avoid minorities and discussion of race. The ideas behind both modern and symbolic racism have been applied to sexism as well. Blatant endorsement of social inequality based on race and sex are no longer socially acceptable. But though people deny prejudices in one breath, they elaborate support for inequality with the next.

Value changes at the individual or micro level are in response to changes in society, but the changes are most often gradual and not even across all social groups. At the micro-level, the focus is on individuals changing their personal values in response to societal conditions. As we shall see in the next section, the focus at the macro-level is on ideological changes.

Social Change: Macro-Level Change

Can ideology be manipulated to produce or resist social change? There are two competing perspectives that explain the role of ideology in social change: the conflict perspective and value consensus perspective. The conflict perspective asserts that social order arises from conflict between competing ideologies. German philosopher Georg Hegel (1770–1831) developed the theory of the *dialectic* to explain this process. According to Hegel, ideologies are born of a dynamic process in which an initial idea or set of ideas (the thesis) is challenged by another set of ideas (antithesis). Conflict between ideologies inevitably results in a blending of ideas (synthesis). Karl Marx applied the dialectic process to the study of economics. His material dialectic focused on the role of ideology in either facilitating or impeding social change. Marx contended that manipulating ideology was a much more efficient way for the bourgeoisie (the owners of the means of production) to control the proletariat (the workers). If the owners could convince the workers that what was good for business was also good for labor, there would be no resistance to the exploitation of workers. Marx called this ideological manipulation *false consciousness.* False consciousness is the illusion of the oppressed that they are not oppressed. If this tactic is successful, the members of the subordinate group will come to accept their exploitation as legitimate. *Ideological hegemony* (the dominance of one ideology over all others) occurs when an ideology explaining and justifying the power of an elite group is accepted even by the oppressed.

Prejudices come into the dialectic process in two ways. First, the elite may appeal to the prejudices of the masses, so that inequities between groups are seen as individual deficiencies rather than systemic inequality. For example, racial minorities might be depicted as lazy or ill-educated therefore deserving less pay. Stereotypes of lazy minorities are intentionally activated so that values supportive of the social structure (e.g., the work ethic) will deter change. Even members of the defamed minority will support the ideology, believing that if they exhibit the virtue of hard work and accept the dominant ideology, they will not be limited to the lowly position occupied by most of their race.

Another key factor in maintaining a dominant ideology is to induce conflict between subordinate groups. Let's say we have two groups of workers: one white and one black. When white workers ask for a raise or better working conditions, the management replies that there are many black workers doing the same jobs for less money and fewer benefits. This pits the white workers against the black workers and keeps the cost of labor down for the company. The white workers blame the black workers for undercutting their pay, while at the same time directing anger away from management. Black workers use prejudices voiced by white workers to explain their lower rate of pay. Racial prejudices on both sides keep the workers divided and unable to effect any changes. Although the example uses the worker-versus-owner conflict, these two strategies (appealing to prejudices and pitting groups against one other) are adaptable to other social institutions too. Politicians, pundits, televangelists, advertisers, and even educators have used these tactics to shape public opinion. Remember the Willie Horton story of Chapter 4. In the 1988 presidential campaign, the picture of Willie Horton, a black convict who committed a crime while on furlough from a Massachusetts prison, was used to discredit Massachusetts governor Michael Dukakis. The mug shot of Willie Horton appealed to racial prejudices and fears of violence harbored by white voters. Advertisers use variations of these strategies both explicitly and in cleverly veiled subliminal advertisements. This is most easily seen when prejudices against the obese are blended with gender norms used to sell beauty and diet products. One way the persuasiveness of these tactics can be measured is by the alarming number of young women with severe eating disorders.

American Ideology

An alternative to the conflict perspective relies on *value consensus* to explain the maintenance of the dominant ideology. Flagrant class, race, and gender inequality in the United States is accepted by the vast majority of its citizens. Even among the poor, there is little support for policies aimed at redistributing income (Ladd 1994). Although the gap between our values and the reality of social inequality is easily observable, a web of interrelated beliefs and values induces most of us to ignore the contradictions. According to Marger (2005:357), the most essential of these are "individualism, equality of opportunity, meritocracy, the work ethic, and liberal capitalism."

Individualism is the belief that a person is responsible for their own actions and the consequences of those actions. Personal effort and ability account for a person's position in the social hierarchy. More than any other value, individualism is at the core of the American ideology. Although ascribed characteristics such as race and gender have obvious impact on life chances, most people assume that with enough effort, they can even overcome these handicaps.

The means to overcoming any and all obstacles to upward social mobility is attributed to *equality of opportunity.* It does not bother Americans when their eyes tell them that not everyone is equal in society. Although outcomes are not equal, Americans firmly believe that opportunities are equal. Thus, social inequality comes from squandering opportunity. With enough effort and persistence, anyone can succeed.

Our persistent belief that all Americans have access to an open opportunity structure leads to the belief that those at the top of the social hierarchy must be the hardest working and most talented. The idea that those who demonstrate the most merit will rise to the top ranks of society is called *meritocracy.* The vast public education system in the United States is the key to both meritocracy and equal opportunity. Even though American tax payers are overwhelmingly opposed to social welfare programs, they do not oppose investing tax dollars on education.

The *work ethic* is the belief that hard work not only leads to success but is also a reward unto itself. The work ethic is more than a value; it is also a virtue. If, as most American's believe, the opportunity structure in American society is equal, then willingness to work is a key variable explaining success. Equal opportunity provides everyone with a ladder to social mobility, but work is how one climbs the social ladder.

Liberal capitalism is the blending of democracy and a capitalist economic system. Liberal philosophy, which reached its zenith in the eighteenth and nineteenth centuries, challenged inherited rights and privileges. Classical liberalism contends that individuals will pursue self-interest and should have the liberty to do so.[2] Following from this premise, government should interfere as little as possible with the pursuit of self-interest. The primary responsibility of government is to protect the rights of individuals, especially property rights (Marger 2005:366). According to classical liberalism, the government has no right to seize personal property and should not interfere with the operation of free markets. However, it is the responsibility of the government to protect free markets from interference and to provide equal access to free markets for its citizens. Under liberal capitalism, the rights of individuals are paramount. The government has to ensure equal opportunity to access free markets. It is then up to individuals to work hard and make efforts to pursue their interests to the best of their ability. Liberal capitalism consolidates individualism, equal opportunity, and the work ethic, forming the foundation for the American Dream.

The American ideology is a system of beliefs and values that legitimates and supports social inequality. We learn the values as a part of the socialization process. Schools, in particular, teach the values of meritocracy and the work ethic. These ideas are presented uncritically, as if they were the only viable alternatives. When other ideas are mentioned, they are used as negative examples to be contrasted with the correct American model. For example, socialism and communism are vilified rather than explained. The result is an ethnocentric and deeply rooted belief in the American way. We judge ourselves and others using these values as the standard. Those who have achieved material success are legitimated. Whatever power and privilege they have acquired is deserved. Those who do not succeed are responsible for their own plight and are owed no recourse.

The conflict and consensus perspectives differ in the attribution of the dominant ideology. Whereas conflict theorists contend that the elite manipulate the ideology to retard the emergence of class consciousness, the consensus perspective contends that we are socialized with common values that stabilize and legitimate the social structure to the benefit of all.

INTERSECTION OF RACE, GENDER, AND CLASS

The *intersection of race, gender, and class* refers to overlapping systems of structured inequality. *Structured inequality* means a patterned hierarchy of advantage that is supported by an ideology that legitimates and justifies subordination. The ordering of groups in the hierarchy is complex because one's place in the hierarchy is not determined by a single characteristic. Race, class, and gender are three important dimensions of inequality, but they are not the only components contributing to social inequality. Age, disabilities, sexual orientation, religion, and even physical attractiveness are but a few of the influences affecting placement in the stratification system. Unfortunately, we

---

[2] Classical liberalism should not be confused with contemporary liberalism. Liberalism today maintains that the government should provide equal access to social and economic opportunities. Today's conservative thought is more consistent with classical liberalism. For further information, see Marger (2005).

can't just add up subordinate and dominant group memberships to figure out a person's placement. Race, class, and gender intersect, so that the effect of each is mitigated by the other two traits. Being white, being male, or belonging to an affluent class opens the door of opportunity. All of these three exposes one to an interlocking, invisible system of advantage. Unfortunately, the reverse is also true. Being a racial or ethnic minority, being female, and belonging to the working or poor class results in multiple disadvantages that are often difficult to sort out.

Because there are multiple dimensions of inequality, it is sometimes difficult to determine which characteristic is eliciting prejudice. The target of prejudice might feel animosity from others, but not be able to discern what triggered the negative reaction. Indeed, it may not be any single attribute because our prejudices are not neatly compartmentalized. People hold multiple prejudices, which they apply according to circumstances. So its not surprising that the targets of the prejudice have difficulty discerning which characteristic activated prejudice. Several years ago I was asked to compile statistical data for a racial discrimination case. However, the test for a pattern of racial discrimination yielded nothing significant. Because I had the data set at my disposal, I checked for other patterns of discrimination. I found two: gender and age. The plaintiff felt she had been judged unfairly, but she misidentified the prejudices and predilections (positive prejudices, or preferences) underlying the discrimination.

Although the multidimensional aspects of social inequality and prejudices can be confusing, they are not without pattern. Remember, structured inequality is a patterned hierarchy. **Structural discrimination** is a corollary of structured inequality. It refers to the existence of institutionalized bias. Race and ethnicity, gender and sexual orientation, and social class discrimination are products of our stratification system. Support for institutionalized bias appears in prejudices and stereotypes that confirm the negative judgment. Because sources of bias are multidimensional, the prejudices that we use to justify and legitimate the bias are directed at multiple subordinate statuses. A women may be a target of prejudice simply because she is female or because she is an old women, a person of color, or a lesbian. Sometimes we even hold prejudices against groups to which the target does not belong. One of my favorite panprejudice designations is "man-hating, lesbian, bitch." This is usually applied to feminists. It implies that the insult is deserved because the target has challenged the legitimacy of patriarchy (man-hating), is a member of a subordinate sexual orientation (lesbian), and her gender places her in a social position on par with female dogs (bitch). Whether the person is a lesbian or a man-hater is irrelevant, the use of multiple prejudices expresses the degree of contempt aimed at the target.

Focus on Race: The Declining or Inclining Significance of Race?

When I speak to groups of African American women, I ask them about how they determine if they are the targets of race or gender prejudice and which they think occurs more often. These questions always spark lively discussion. Although there is usually some disagreement about what cues they have noticed to differentiate between sexism and racism, there is surprising consensus about the most common prejudice: race. One of my students explained her experiences this way: A woman can be shielded from the effects of social class and gender inequality by marrying a man who will share his status and resources with her, but racism can't be entirely mitigated by class or gender. An African American man is not protected from racism simply because he is male. Neither does an upper-class African American woman ever cease being a black just because she is educated and affluent.

Sociologist William Julius Wilson, in his 1978 book ***The Declining Significance of Race,*** argues that as African Americans entered the middle class, the effects of racism on their life chances would decline. Wilson's argument was a macrosociological explanation for race and class inequality. He describes how the economy and the government responded across three historical periods to produce different structures for racial group access to resources and status (Wilson 1978). Although he traces race relations through the preindustrial and industrial development, it is his explanation on contemporary race relations that sparked a decades-long debate about the relative significance of race and class (cf. Willie 1989).

Wilson argues that changes in the economy have shifted racial antagonism over work and economic competition to social, political, and community issues. This has produced a growing class divide among African Americans (1978). Affluent African Americans seek the same occupational and educational opportunities as their white counterparts and enjoy a similar lifestyle.

Charles Willie (1978) countered Wilson's theory by arguing that the significance of race is increasing. He points out that as school and residential segregation decreased, whites and blacks came into increasing social contact. This extended contact has increased the impact of race, especially for middle-class African Americans. Wilson sees the evidence of what W.E.B. Du Bois (1903) called dual consciousness. Not only are the barriers to economic opportunity still in place for most African Americans, but those who have made it to the middle class are estranged from their racial community. They have fled to the suburbs and to private schools taking their resources with them. Class division within the race eroded the solidarity of the African American community that is needed to dismantle racism. Racism in wider economic and social institutions continues unchecked as classism within the racial community pits affluent African Americans against the poor. African Americans are stymied by the cross-currents of racism and classism, while whites see dissension within the African American community as a confirmation of and justification for their continuing racial prejudice.

Summary

Racism, sexism, and classism are social structures that produce and maintain social inequality. Social structures include forms of organization, roles, statuses, norms, beliefs, and values. Prejudices help create, maintain, and legitimize structural inequality. They become infused in the language, thereby affecting how we think and act toward minorities, women, homosexuals, and people in the lower classes. Our prejudices justify inequality and solidify a structure of advantage. Because prejudices are embedded in our values and cultural beliefs, they become infused in the ideology when there is a need to support and defend structural advantages. The theories of modern and symbolic racism contend that overt expression of racial prejudice has been replaced by racism hidden within our value system.

Ideology and values are the repository of modern racist, sexist, and classist beliefs. The American ideology contains four interrelated values: individualism, equal opportunity, the work ethic, and liberal capitalism. The conflict perspective contends that ideology is manipulated by the elites to reduce resistance to policies that serve the interests of the elite at the expense of subordinate groups. The consensus perspective contends that the American ideology emerged from a broad consensus of values that stabilize and legitimate the social structure.

Racism, sexism, and classism converge to form an overlapping system of structured inequality. Their intersection creates a complex social hierarchy. Race, sex, and class are three of the most important dimensions of inequality. Individuals can be in the dominant group on one dimension, but in the subordinate group for the other. This makes it difficult to determine which characteristic elicits prejudice. The interconnection between the dimensions of inequality can amplify subordination when an individual is a member of several subordinate groups.

This chapter has focused on the role of prejudice in the legitimation and support of structural racism, sexism, and classism. In Chapter 7, we will explore the role of prejudice in creating group boundaries and intergroup dynamics.

Key Terms

- Advantage
- Beliefs
- Chattel
- Class advantage
- Dialectic
- Gender advantage
- Gender insults
- Heterosexism

- Homophobia
- Ideology
- Ideological hegemony
- Individualism
- Liberal capitalism
- Meritocracy
- Norms
- Patriarchy

- Race advantage
- Roles
- Social institution
- Social organization
- Social structures
- Statuses
- Structural discrimination
- Values

Taking It Further — Class Exercises and Interesting Web Sites

White Advantage, Gender Advantage, Class Advantage, National Advantage

In 1986 Peggy McIntosh, while teaching a women's studies course, was lecturing about male privilege. One of her students asked about the privileges she as a white woman enjoyed. This started Professor McIntosh thinking. Back at her office, she began generating a list of the privileges she enjoyed as a member of the dominant racial group. Although it was difficult at first, she soon generated a list of forty white privileges. In this exercise, students should generate their own lists of advantages. Most people in U.S. colleges fall into at least one advantaged position. For example, by virtue of being in the United States even those in the lower classes enjoy a level of affluence unmatched by most other countries. Students should identify a privileged status they hold and list advantages it brings them. Lists should include both micro and macro advantages. Most students will be able to identify micro advantages. For example, white people have no difficulty finding "flesh"-colored band-aids that approximate their skin color. However, the macro advantages may present more difficulty. A macro advantage for white would be the high probability that homes in neighborhoods where whites are the majority will increase in value over time. Students can generate lists of advantages either as individuals or in small groups. After students generate their lists, the teacher should lead a group discussion to compare lists and advantages enjoyed by different groups.

Gender Insults

Gender insults are used to encourage gender role conformity. Calling boys "sissies" or referring to them as females are common examples. In this exercise, students should make lists of gender insults they have heard. One list should contain insults directed at males, another targeting females, and a third leveled at both groups. The list can be generated either individually or in groups. After generating the lists, the teacher should lead a group discussion comparing the lists. Which gender is more often targeted by gender insults? When gender insults are used to target either males of females, does the insult invoke male or female gender symbols in the insult?

References

Abramovitz, Mimi. 2001. Everyone is still on welfare: The role of redistribusiton in social policy. *Social Work* 46 (4): 297–308.

Asante, Molefi Kete. 1998. Identifying racist language; linguistic acts and signs. In *Communicating prejudice,* ed. Hecht, Micheal, 877–878. Thousand Oaks, CA: Sage Publications.

Astin, Alexander. 1991. The changing American college student: implications for educational policy and practice. *Higher Education* 22 (2): 129–143.

Astin, Alexander, Sarah A. Parrott, William S. Korn, and Linda J. Sax. 1997. *The American freshman: Thirty year trends.* Los Angles, CA: Higher Education Research Institute.

Associated Press. 2004. Jurors find no discrimination in flight attendant's rhyme use. January 22, 2004.

Ayres, Ian, and Peter Siegelman. 1995. Race and gender discrimnation is bargaining for a new car. *The American Economic Review* 85 (3): 304–321.

Bernstein, Ilene H., and George W. Bohrnstedt. 1972. *Professional women as deviants.* New York: Russell Sage Foundation.

Browne, Beverly A. 1998. Gender stereotypes in advertising on children's television in the 1990s: A cross-national analysis. *Journal of Advertising* 27 (1): 83–96.

Burns-Glober, Aylson, and Dale J. Veith. 1995. Revisiting gender and teaching evaluations: Sex still makes a difference. *Journal of Social Behavior and Personality* 10 (6): 69–80.

Butler, Dore, and Florence Geis. 1990. Nonverbal affect responses to male and female leaders: Implications for leadership evaluations. *Journal of Personality and Social Psychology* 58 (1): 48–59.

Du Bois, W. E. B. 1903. Leadership education. In *The black American* (1976), ed. L. Fishel and B. Quarles, 226–228. Atlanta, GA: Scott, Foreman and Co.

Dukes, Richard and Victoria Gay. 1989. The effects of gender, status and effective teaching on the evaluation of college instruction. *Teaching Sociology* 17 (4): 447–457.

Eble, Connie. 1996. *Slang and sociability.* Chapel-Hill, NC: University of North Carolina Press.

Egan, Daniel. 2003. The undeserving rich: How the news media cover "corporate welfare." *Humanity and Society* 27 (2): 108–124.

Ehrenreich, Barbara. 1989. *Fear of falling: The inner life of the middle class.* New York: Pantheon Books.

———. 2001. *Nickel and Dimed: On (not) getting by in America.* New York: Metropolitan Books.

Foschi, M. 1992. Gender and the double standards for competence. In *Gender interaction and inequality,* ed. C.L. Ridgeway, 181–207. New York: Springer-Verlag.

Gilbert, Dennis, and Joesph A. Kahl. 1982. *The American class structure* (4th ed.). Belmont, CA: Wadsworth Publishing Co.

Haskell, Robert E. 1986. Social cognition, language and the non-continuous expression of racial ideology. *Imagination, Cognition and Personality* 6 (1): 75–97.

Horton, Hayward, and Melvin Thomas. 1998. Race, class and family structure: Differences in housing values for black and white homeowners. *Sociological Inquiry* 68 (1): 114–136.

Katz, David. 1987. Sex discrimination in hiring: The influence of organizational climate and need for approval on decision making behavior. *Psychology of Women Quarterly* 11 (1): 11–20.

Kluegel, James R., and Lawrence Bobo. 2001. Perceived group discrimination and policy attitudes: Sources and consequences of the race and gender gaps. In *Urban inequality: Evidence from four cities,* ed. Alice O'Connor, Chris Tilly, and Lawrence D. Bobo, 163–213. New York: Russell Sage.

Ladd, Everett C. 1994. *The American ideology: An exploration of the origins, meaning and role of American political ideas.* Storrs, CT: The Rope Center for Public Opinion Research.

Lipsitz, George. 1998. *The possessive investment in whiteness: How white people profit from identity politics.* Philadelphia: Temple University Press.

McIntosh, Peggy. 2001. Unpacking the invisible knapsack. In *Race, class, and gender in the United States,* ed. Paul Rothenberg, 163–168. New York: Worth Publishers.

MacKenzie, Gavin. 1973. *The aristocracy of labor.* New York: Cambridge University Press.

Marger, Martin. 2005. *Social inequality: Patterns and processes* (3rd ed.). New York: McGraw Hill.

McKillip, Jack, Anthony DiMiceli, and Jerry Luebke. 1977. Group salience and stereotyping. *Social Behavior and Personality* 5 (1): 81–85.

Nadar, Ralph. 2000. *Cutting corporate welfare.* New York: Seven Stories Press.

Rothman, Robert. 1993. *Inequality and stratification: Class, color and gender* (2nd ed.). Englewood Cliffs; NJ: Prentice Hall.

Schur, Edwin. 1984. *Labeling women deviant.* New York: McGraw Hill.

Tryon, Bette W. 1980. Beliefs about male and female competence held by kindergartners and second graders. *Sex Roles* 6 (1): 85–97.

Whipple, Thomas W., and Mary K. McManamon. 2002. Implications of using male and female voices in commercials: An exploratory study. *Journal of Advertising* 31 (2): 79–91.

Whitfield, Dexter. 2001. *Public services or corporate welfare: Rethinking the nation state in the global economy.* Sterling, VA: Pluto Press.

Whittelsey, Frances C., and Amanda Walmac. 1998. How women can stop paying more than men for the same thing. *Money* 25 (6): 47.

Willie, Charles. 1989. *Caste and class controversy on race and poverty: Round two of the Willie/Wilson debate* (2nd ed.). Dix Hills, NY: General Hall Inc.

Wilson, William J. 1978. *The declining significance of race.* Chicago, IL: University of Chicago Press.

CHAPTER
7
Groups, Intergroup Relations, and Prejudice

How do groups use prejudice to distinguish between themselves and other groups? First, group identity and boundary formation will be explained. Next, the role of prejudice in intergroup dynamics and interactions will be explored. Finally, the role of leadership in groups and the potential to manipulate prejudices to maintain leadership will be examined.

- Types of Groups
- Group Dynamics and Prejudice
- Intergroup Relations
- Individualism versus Collectivism
- Leadership
- Leadership and Sources of Authority
- Summary
- Key Terms
- Taking It Further—Class Exercises and Interesting Web Sites
- References

Have you ever noticed that people behave differently when they are in a group compared with when they are alone? Not only do you alter your behaviors and responses when you are part of a group, but the response of others to you is different when you are in a group. When you are part of a group, the group's identity affects your identity. That is, the group affects how you think about yourself and how others react to you. You have probably heard about this when your parents told you that the friends you choose and the company you keep affect your reputation. Even temporary groups can affect how one is perceived, as the following example indicates.

When my daughter was about twelve years old, she attended Space Camp at NASA's National Space Technologies Laboratory. On the final day of the camp, parents were invited to see what their budding astronauts had accomplished and to tour the facilities. All the parents who attended that day were mothers. I was very excited to be there and had questions, but I was surprised by how we were reacted to by the camp leaders. We were introduced to the people who had worked with our children by their professional honorariums. This didn't make me uncomfortable because I work at a university, where people are routinely addressed as doctors and professors. What surprised me was how I was addressed. Despite having a name tag, I was not called by my name, my professional title, or even the "Mrs." honorarium routinely given to married women. I was addressed all day long as "Mom." "The Moms" were addressed both as a group and as individuals with their familial role. This was a first for me. Although I was comfortable being addressed as Mom by my family, I didn't know how to react to adult men in lab coats and uniforms calling me "Mom." When I mentioned my discomfort to the other women in my group, they said they hadn't even noticed. I was puzzled by the difference in my reaction, so as a good social scientist, I decided to gather more information. As it turned out, all the other women were full-time homemakers. They routinely occupied public roles in which their family role designation was used. They were "room mothers," "den mothers," "mothers against drunk driving" and were used to being publicly addressed by adult, nonfamily members as "Mom." "Mother" was a core part of their social identity. ***Social identity*** refers to an identity as a member of a particular group or social category. This is in contrast to ***personal identity,*** which refers to your unique identity as an individual. Prejudice usually involves intergroup relations, so the social identity becomes important in understanding prejudices.

In this chapter, we will learn about how being associated with a group affects our prejudices and how prejudice affects groups. We will investigate how group dynamics can be used to encourage and discourage the expression of prejudices. But, first, we will review the different types of groups and the fundamentals of group dynamics.

TYPES OF GROUPS

A ***group*** refers to two or more people who interact with each other and are conscious of their identity as a group. This is in contrast to a social category. A ***social category*** is composed of people who share a common characteristic (such as race, national origin, gender, or age) but do not necessarily interact with each other. In fact, people in a social category can be widely dispersed throughout the population. Nonetheless, a social category may be the basis of a shared identity. Statuses related to categories such as race, ethnicity, gender, religion, or age can be an important part of a person's social identity even though they are not groups. Both groups and social categories are important to understand prejudice because people construct their social identity from the groups and categories with which they identify. There is a strong tendency for people to prefer others that they define as like themselves. Even when groups are temporary and formed arbitrarily, people demonstrate favoritism toward other members of their groups or their social categories (Messick and Mackie 1989). This has been demonstrated very effectively in recent reality shows. The shifting team alliances on the popular show *Survivor* are a wonderful example of how even temporary group membership affects attitudes.

A ***primary group*** consists of a small number of people who have direct, extensive, and extended contact with other members of their group. People in primary groups have considerable inside knowledge about each other. Interactions with primary group members extend beyond a single role or set of tasks. Family and close friends are best examples of a primary group. Charles Horten Cooley (1864–1929) was the first to use the term "primary group." He contended that family was primary because it is the first group people experience in life. Friendship groups are primary because they are of major importance to how we come to understand and evaluate our experiences. Although family plays an important role in the primary formation of personality and self-concept, both family and friends continue to play important roles in the continuing process of socialization. Because family and friends are a fundamental influence on our values and beliefs, they impact our reaction to others and the formation of prejudices against other groups.

A *secondary group* is a larger, less personal, and more formal group that is formed for a limited set of tasks or goals. Group members know less about each other and are less emotionally attached. The role of an individual in a secondary group is both more structured and more limited—more structured because the role of the individual is limited to the tasks or goals of the group. For example, family members (a primary group) are called upon to do an almost unlimited variety of tasks, from wiping noses to financial counseling, whereas members of a social psychology class (a secondary group) usually confine their activities to note-taking, discussion, and other educational pursuits. Secondary group members such as co-workers or classmates have less commitment to the group and a far narrower range of tasks. The relationships between secondary group members are less emotional and less personal.

Primary groups are more enduring than secondary groups. Although primary groups do add and delete members, losing or adding a member will have a far greater impact on the identity of a primary group. Consider the impact of one of your classmates dropping the class compared with losing a family member. Secondary groups change members more often and more easily. It's much harder to lose a sibling, a parent, or a grandparent than to lose a classmate.

A *reference group* is used as a standard for evaluating behaviors and attitudes. One does not have to be a member of a group to use the group as a referent. For example, children often use the friends of an older sibling or a popular clique at school in judging their own development, appearance, and character. Obviously, the reference can be either positive or negative. Most often, groups to which we belong (or aspire to belong) are positive references. Groups that we reject (or that reject us) are negative references. Negative reference groups can be used to make us feel better about ourselves by comparison. Using a comparison with another group to bolster one's ego is sometimes called an *ego-defense* function. The potential for using prejudices against a negative reference group is obvious. The more one disparages the out-group, the better one feels about both their own group and their self.

Formal task groups have established goals that define the group. The primary purpose of a formal task group is to accomplish a specific goal. Members of an organized athletic team or a committee are examples of being a member of a formal task group. The goal for the sports team is to win as many games as possible. The pursuit of the goal requires that the group members have interconnected roles and an easily discernable structure. In other words, each player on the sports team knows both the norms governing her or his position and the norms for other positions played by her or his teammates. Their roles are interdependent because behavior of any team position depends on the behaviors of the other players. For example, the behaviors of the baseball shortstop depend on what the batter, the outfielders, and the basemen do. The relationship between the interconnected positions creates the groups structure.

Informal groups are highly flexible. They are often temporary, and the roles of their members change according to the situation. Norms within the informal group are emergent and also subject to change with the situation. Goals for informal groups are short-lived and are not central or necessary for group formation. For example, a group of friends may get together with an express purpose such as throwing a surprise birthday party, but on another occasion they just hang out together with no particular goal. Group leaders emerge only when necessary and the person fulfilling the leadership role may change with the situation.

Aggregates are simply a category of people with no common bond, no goal, and little or no interaction. An aggregate may be a line of people waiting to buy tickets to a concert or the occupants of an elevator. They are in the same place at the same time, but have no common connection to each other. Aggregates can quickly transform into a group if some event necessitates group communication and coordinated effort. For example, the elevator may stop between floors, requiring its occupants to find a solution to their common problem. The occupants may have begun their ride as an aggregate but will transform quickly into an informal group. Should the situation call for a prolonged effort, they may decide to assess the abilities of group members, divide their labor, and become a formal task group.

Aggregates are important for another reason. Social scientists often present aggregated data to show the effects of discrimination. This is an important tool for discerning patterns of discrimination. *Aggregated data* refers to data that are grouped by a characteristic, such as state or country of residence, race, sex, or age. Summary statistics are calculated for the aggregated data so that the aggregate can be used as the unit of analysis. For example, SAT scores are often aggregated by state. An average SAT score is calculated for each state; then associations between other aggregate variables such as per capita income or average educational attainment can be compared by state.

People move in and out of groups daily. If you live with your family or a group of close friends, you probably start and end your day interacting with your primary group. When you attend classes or are at work, you will be interacting in secondary groups. You may have more than one reference group against which you compare your own behaviors, ideas, values, statuses, or material possessions. When you have a specific task to complete or a problem to solve, you may take part in a formal task group. For example, you may be given a group project to complete during a class or science lab. Chances are good that you have gotten together with friends or acquaintances in an informal group at lunch or for an evening of recreation. If you need to go shopping, do some banking, or do other errands, you will join aggregates of people engaging in the same pursuits at the same time and place. Each of these types of groups has an impact on your behavior and your understanding of the social situation. What transpires in groups can affect the prejudices people express and whether prejudices are reinforced or discouraged.

GROUP DYNAMICS AND PREJUDICE

Group dynamics refer to the social processes that affect the outcomes of interaction within and between groups. Prejudices can be either encouraged or suppressed according to the dynamics generated within groups (Kenworthy and Miller 2002; Crandall and Eshleman 2003). To understand the role of group dynamics in the expression of prejudices, it is necessary to explore some key group processes. We will investigate four factors that affect group interaction: group cohesion, polarization, ethnocentrism, and xenocentrism.

Group Cohesion refers to the level of bonding or attraction of group members to each other. The cohesiveness of the group is very important because it affects group stability and endurance. Primary groups have more cohesiveness than other types of groups because of the level of intimacy between members and the wide variety of behaviors and situations experienced with members of primary groups.

Communication is an essential element in group cohesion. For a group to endure, members of the group must develop a sense of solidarity and belonging. Primary groups have the highest levels of group cohesion because they have regular face-to-face communication. On the other hand, aggregates have little or no cohesiveness because they are merely a category of people with little, if any, interaction. Secondary groups (both formal and informal) fall in between primary groups and aggregates. Because informal groups are emergent and highly flexible, the level of group cohesiveness among members of informal groups waxes and wanes depending on many factors. The size of the informal group, the group's goals, the tasks that are under way, and many other situational factors affect the cohesion of informal groups.

Communication in more formal groups includes written communication. Written communication is a characteristic of formal groups, such as bureaucracies, because it allows the dissemination of information from a central authority. It increases consensus among group members, enables groups to coordinate behaviors, and creates tighter cohesion among group members. The power of written communication is being demonstrated by the rapid rise in communication through email and the Internet. Computer technologies have not only allowed the spread of information globally but also facilitated the spread of prejudices, bigotry, and hate groups (McVeigh 2004). Web sites, chat rooms, spam, blogging, and text messaging have created vast—yet remarkably efficient—networks. Because the technology is recent, social scientists are just beginning to study the role of the Internet in creating cohesive groups and virtual communities (e.g., Adamic and Adar 2003; Bennett 2003).

Group polarization refers to the tendency of groups to make more extreme or polarized decisions than individuals. After taking part in group discussion, group members shift to more extreme views (Brauer, Judd, and Gliner 1995; Brauer et al. 2004). Even though there have been several theories that attempt to explain group polarization, social comparison and persuasive argument approaches have been the best supported (Burnstein and Vinokur 1977). The *social comparison approach* contends that before group discussion, most individuals within a group assume that their views are as good as or better than that of other members of the group. However, one outcome of group discussion is learning that one's views may not be nearly as good or well thought-out as first imagined. Because most people want both themselves and others to evaluate them positively, they make favorable comparisons between their views and the views expressed by others in the group. This process of social comparison shifts the position of the group toward more consensus. Consensus reduces the range of opinion, resulting in a polarization of the group's attitude.

The *persuasive argument approach* contends that during a group discussion people present arguments that support their views. Some of these arguments are persuasive enough to alter the attitudes of other group members. As more members of the group are convinced by the persuasive arguments, the attitude of the group shifts toward that view, resulting in the polarization of attitudes (Vinokur and Bernstein 1974).

Both social comparison and persuasive arguments can play a role in understanding group polarization. Regardless of which dynamic creates polarization, the process can cause shifts toward extreme attitudes, including prejudices. A highly effective charismatic individual may persuade some members of a group, thereby affecting the comparisons made between members of the group. This drift toward extremes interferes with the ability of the group and the individuals in the group to make unbiased assessments and choices. At its worst, polarization can result in group think.

Group think is a process that severely alters the decision-making capacity of the group. There are three indicators of group think (Janis 1982). First, group members believe that the decision they make cannot possibly be wrong. They believe themselves to be infallible. Second, they discredit, ignore, or destroy information that is inconsistent with the group's position. Finally, members of the group are unwilling to contradict or question the group's position. As you might expect, group think can lead to catastrophic consequences, especially if the prejudices of group members influence their decision making. Despite its potential for disastrous decisions, group think is not unusual. History abounds with examples of occasions when unanimous support was valued over facts. The presidential advisory committee that urged President Kennedy to invade the Bay of Pigs in Cuba, the decisions of the Bush administration to invade Iraq because Saddam Hussein was thought to have weapons of mass destruction, the disastrous explosion of the space shuttle Challenger in 1986, and the equally catastrophic Columbia shuttle disaster in 2003 are examples of monumentally flawed decision making attributable to group think.

Ethnocentrism refers to an in-group's belief that its values, ideas, and norms are superior to those of out-groups. In other words, it is the belief that one's group is superior and all other groups are inferior. Ethnocentrism is a common tendency among humans worldwide. It is partially the result of being more comfortable with the ways of those most familiar to us and being suspicious of the unknown. The behavior of people in our own group is easier to predict and feels right to us. The behaviors of others outside of our group are less easily interpreted and harder to anticipate. This uncertainty about the behavior and responses of others makes a fertile environment for prejudices. For example, you may feel very comfortable interacting with new acquaintances on your college campus. Your classmates probably dress in similar clothing, listen to the same types of music, and come from similar family and cultural backgrounds. Their behavior seems normal and natural to you. However, if you are given an opportunity to study at a university in Japan, the behavior of students would seem abnormal, weird, and worrisome. Instead of the laid-back atmosphere found on many American campuses, the competitive and more intense academic culture in Japan may seem intimidating and hostile. Misunderstandings resulting from ethnocentrism fuel prejudices and harm both in-groups and out-groups.

The opposite of ethnocentrism is xenocentrism. **Xenocentrism** refers to belief in the superiority of people outside of one's group. It includes a preference for ideas and ways of behaving found among cultural communities or groups different from one's own. Sometimes called negative ethnocentrism, xenocentrism results from the undervaluing of one's group and the overvaluing of other groups. Being the target of prejudice can result in self-denigration and rejection of one's group.

Perhaps the most famous study pertaining to xenocentrism was a study of black children's racial preferences (Clark and Clark 1940, 1947). In 1939 Kenneth and Mamie Clark questioned 253 black children between the ages of three and seven. They conducted the interviews at two sites: one in Arkansas and the other in Massachusetts. The children were shown four dolls, two with brown skin and black hair and two with white skin and yellow hair. The researchers then asked questions designed to elicit the children's preferences and their awareness of racial differences. Whereas nearly all of the children could correctly identify the race of the dolls, the children's preferences provided the most startling results. The majority of black children preferred the white doll and rejected the black doll. Two-thirds of the children indicated that they liked the white doll best and would prefer playing with it. About 59 percent indicated that the black doll looked bad. The results of this study clearly demonstrated that being the target of prejudice can lead to devaluation of one's group and a preference for others.

You might argue that it's been a long time since Clark and Clark's original 1939 study. Did the civil rights movement, the "Black is beautiful" campaign, and the emphasis on a multicultural society decrease xenocentrism among African Americans? Subsequent studies have had mixed results. Some have replicated the Clark's findings. Asher and Allen (1969) found that black children's preferences for white dolls were still high. Other studies have attempted to analyze how changing historical or social conditions can affect racial identity and self-worth (e.g., Ward and Braun 1972; Brand et al. 1974). These findings have been contradictory. Even though early studies suggested that many racial minorities evidence some degree of racial self-hatred (Lewin 1941; Kardiner and Ovesey 1951), more recent studies that employ better measures of self-esteem and racial identity indicate self-esteem scores for racial minorities are higher than those for whites (Gray-Little and Hafdahl 2000). Some researchers have suggested that preferences for black or white dolls vary according to the strength of black pride and self-esteem (Hraba and Grant 1970). Still others have suggested that the age and developmental stage of children can explain xenocentric responses (Ponterotto and Pedersen 1993; Pederson et al. 1996).

Xenocentrism can also be understood in terms of reference group theory (Montera 1986) and social identity theory (Tajfel 1974). These theories hypothesize that people will be more likely to claim membership in a social group when that group is positively evaluated. When a group is not well regarded, members of that group may choose to distance themselves from the group. If they cannot, they may suffer from lower self-esteem. From this perspective, members of a minority group who choose an assimilationist strategy (i.e., blending into the dominant group) may suffer from lower self-esteem.

As our culture has increased in diversity and many communities have embraced multicultural strategies, simple, clear-cut results demonstrating ethnocentric attitudes among the dominant group and xenocentric attitudes among minority groups are being challenged. Yip and Cross (2004) found that ethnic identity was positively related to psychological well-being and community involvement among Chinese American youths. They analyzed diary entries of approximately one hundred American youths of Chinese American descent. They categorized the participants into four ethnic identity orientations (Chinese, American, bicultural, and other). Counter to what social identity theory predicted, they found that community involvement was more predictive of self-concept than ethnic identity.

Judd and his colleagues (1995) found that ethnocentrism varied between different racial groups. Whereas African American subjects exhibited positive self-esteem and attitudes consistent with ethnocentrism, white respondents did not display ethnocentrism or out-group stereotyping. The researchers suggest that the lack of ethnocentric attitudes among white participants may be due to race-blind socialization among whites. As the studies by Yip and Cross and by Judd and his colleagues indicate, the extent of ethnocentrism and xenocentrism found in ethnic and racial groups varies. The role of ethnic identity, racial pride, and acceptance of diversity has a complex effect on both social identity and intergroup relations.

In this section, we have learned that group dynamics affect the role of prejudices in interactions both within and between groups. Group cohesion affects the stability and endurance of groups. Prejudices against other groups can be used to create a sense of solidarity and superiority among group members. Being the target of prejudice also increases group cohesion. This is because shared injustice strengthens affinity and helps define group boundaries and makes groups more distinctive.

Theories about group polarization explain why groups make more extreme decisions than do individuals. Two competing explanations are the social comparison approach and the persuasive argument approach. The social comparison approach contends that one outcome of group discussion is a comparison of views. This may lead some individuals to alter their ideas because they are exposed to new or better ideas. The persuasive argument approach contends that during group discussion, people present arguments that are persuasive enough to alter the attitudes of other group members.

In addition to defining boundaries and polarizing positions, group dynamics can also affect the collective self-esteem of group members. Ethnocentrism refers to in-group's belief in its own superiority, whereas xenocentrism refers to belief in the superiority of people outside of one's group. Although it is clear that prejudices can be used to justify the superiority of dominant groups and damage self-esteem among minority group members, there is some disagreement about whether being the target of prejudice has only negative effects on identity and self-esteem. This section concentrated on how being in a group affects the prejudices of group members. In the next section, the focus will shift to the dynamics of relationships between different groups.

INTERGROUP RELATIONS

Intergroup relations refer to how people in different groups or social categories feel about and relate to each other. Prejudice is an intergroup phenomenon because prejudices are formed on the basis of judgments based on perceived membership in a group or category of people. Whether one is the target of prejudice or is using prejudices to interpret the behavior of others, prejudice is involved in how we relate to other groups. In highly individualistic societies such as the United States, people sometimes deny the role of prejudice in interaction. We pretend that we judge people based only on their own behavior and attributes, not on groups or social categories to which they belong. We believe that if only people would disregard gender, race, ethnicity, and class and treat each other as individuals, we would all get along better. But, consider how difficult it would be to interact without being able to categorize people. Suppose, as a small child, you had no experiences or preconceptions to help you interpret what was going on around you. Then, as a child, you would be unable to interpret social situations involving new or unknown people. As a result, you could not make distinctions about how to respond to different people and would likely treat everyone the same. We often note that children have few prejudices, but we also warn children about strangers precisely because they don't have the experience to judge whether a situation or individual is a threat. Children are admonished never to talk with strangers because strangers may be dangerous. We teach children prejudices (albeit inadvertently) when we teach them to be wary of others, particularly people in other groups or from different social categories. A young friend of mine learned prejudices his very first day in the first grade. A schoolmate confided in him that there were two kinds of people you couldn't trust: smokers and black people. Despite the intervention of his mother and the teacher, both a wariness of others and social categorization will probably not diminish as my young friend continues his education. Ridding ourselves of prejudices would indeed make us more like very young children, but that would also make us more vulnerable.

Most people think of prejudice as a personal phenomenon. On this level, the solution to problems associated with prejudice seems simple. Because prejudice involves personal attitudes, just reeducate people and the prejudice will end. According to this view, if people could just unlearn the stereotypes and prejudices they have and be friends, all the problems associated with prejudice and bigotry would disappear. Unfortunately, this idea is rather like telling a person with asthma not to breathe or advising an obese person to give up eating entirely. Like breathing and eating problems, prejudices cannot be entirely eliminated. Like it or not, individuals use prejudices in interaction with others.

The tendency to use an individual perspective (or personal perspective) over a social perspective extends how we view ourselves. While we see ourselves and our close friends and family in terms of our personal identity, we see others less familiar to us in terms of their social identity. A ***personal identity*** is based on the unique attributes and history of each individual. The ***social identity*** we attribute to others is based on the groups and categories to which they belong (or more accurately to which *we think* they belong). For example, if you meet a person of the other gender, you initially relate to that person in terms of their gender categorization. You would make assumptions about that person based on gender, not because you bear any animosity toward them or their gender but because you lack personal information about them.

In contrast to personal identity, which requires at least some experience or knowledge of the individual, indicators of social identity are readily observable. Although social traits, such as gender, age, and race, can sometimes be ambiguous, people make categorical identifications numerous times every day. Whether they are accurate is less important than the impact social identity has on behavior. If I believe a person to be male, black, gay, middle aged, middle class, or Catholic, my beliefs will affect how I interpret the interaction with and my behavior toward the person. If we make mistakes, interaction may become problematic. For example, because professional titles such as "Nurse," "Dr.," and "Professor" do not give any indication of gender, male nurses are often assumed to be doctors and women physicians and professors are assumed to occupy nursing, secretarial, or other staff positions. We make many such errors in everyday interactions. Most do not disrupt interaction because the errors are either not realized or not acknowledged by the people involved.

When we use personal identity to define ourselves and others, there is much more information that can be used to understand interactions and relationships. Because there is more and better information, we sometimes forget or disregard social identity. We usually don't think of our friends and close acquaintances through their social identity. We exempt them from the stereotypes and assumptions associated with their social identity. For example, I don't think of my friend Thais as Brazilian because I have more pertinent information about her. Likewise, my brother-in-law does not think of me as a Yankee because according to him I don't behave like most of them. He says that his knowledge about Yankees does not help him interpret me or his interactions with me. Some years ago I was volunteering to tutor reading in a second-grade classroom. I developed a close relationship with my students. One day the teacher assigned the children to write a short essay about what they loved the most and hated the most. The next day the teacher shared with me the assignment one of my students wrote. I was touched to find that I was who he loved the most but dismayed that he hated "white people" the most. Obviously, I was exempted from the category "white people" in his understanding. My personal identity was so prominent that he did not identify me with the hated social category. Sometimes a personal identity is so prominent that we don't consider the person a member of the out-group at all.

So why can't people just disregard social identities in favor of personal identities, thereby reducing their reliance on prejudices and stereotypes? Aside from the impracticality of having to personally get to know millions of people, prejudices are an intergroup phenomenon. Even if one has personal knowledge of another, social identity can sometimes take precedence over personal identity. There are many factors that affect which identity becomes salient in an interaction. Three of these factors that have been extensively studied are distinctiveness, status, and targeting.

One factor that contributes to the application of a social identity is ***distinctiveness.*** The more distinct we are in a social situation, the more likely the social identity that contributes to our distinctiveness will be used to define us (McGuire et al. 1978). I sometimes refer to this as "the only" experience. Being the only member of a social category or group in a social situation calls attention to our distinctiveness and the likelihood that it will be used to interpret our behavior. For example, being the only white person attending an NAACP meeting or the only man in a Women's Studies class makes that part of the social identity salient.

Studies show that distinctive people are better remembered (Cutler and Cutler 1995; Kleider and Goldinger 2001). When distinctiveness calls attention to a social category or group membership, it not only causes others to remember the distinctive person but can also affect prejudices toward that group or category. One way in which distinctiveness affects prejudice is through ***illusory correlation*** (see Chapter 4). People remember the unusual or atypical. When people notice a distinctive trait or unusual behavior among minority group members, they often overestimate the association between the distinctive trait or behavior and being a member of the minority group (Hamilton and Gifford 1976; Taylor 1981). Thus, being the only member of a group and having distinctive or stereotypical traits can reinforce prejudices.

Interestingly, distinctiveness can also be manipulated in ways that reduce prejudices. Tajfel and Turner's research (1986) suggests that attention to group differences as opposed to their similarities can reduce prejudices. Working with social identity theory Tajfel and Turner contend that the evaluation of one's group is determined through a process of comparison with other groups. Positive discrepancy results in high prestige, whereas negative discrepancy results in low prestige. By focusing on the distinctiveness of groups rather than similarities, competition between groups is decreased. Because individuals derive a substantial portion of their identity from their group affiliations, decreased competition between groups also results in a decrease in prejudices toward out-groups.

Zarate and Garza (2002) contend that attention to group differences reduces prejudice when it is drawn to self-affirmation. ***Self-affirmation*** is the process of defining one's self through comparison with others. In past studies, researchers have found that prejudices can be used to bolster self-esteem by denigrating others (Crocker et al. 1987; Fein and Spencer 1997). Zarate and Garza (2002) asked experimental subjects to either compare or contrast perceived similarities between the subjects' in-group and an out-group. Participants in the comparison condition were asked to rate the out-group on a scale of "extremely similar" to "not at all similar." The participants in the contrast condition were asked to rate the out-group on a scale ranging from "extremely different" to "not at all different." They found that attention to differences in conjunction with self-awareness manipulation reduces prejudice (Zarate and Garza 2002:235). Their findings suggest that a multicultural environment might be more conducive to prejudice reduction.

A second factor that contributes to the use of social identity over personal identity is the relative *status* of the interactants. When a person belongs to a high-status group, they often introduce that status into the interaction. For example, a physician or professor may prefer to use a professional title even in non–work-related situations because the status of their social identity may be more useful than their personal identity. According to the social identity theory, high-status-group memberships are important to people because they elevate both self-esteem and provide social capital within the interaction. *Social capital* refers to connections between people. It is based on social networks, statuses, norms of reciprocity, and benefits that can come from association with powerful individuals (cf. Coleman 1988). Invoking a high-status social identity allows an individual to bring more social capital to bear in interactions with others.

Using a high-status social identity can be used either to promote *bonding* with other high-status individuals (or exclusiveness) and/or *bridging* between groups (or inclusiveness). Bonding has a tendency to reinforce exclusive social identities and create more homogeneous groups. Bridging is used to embrace people across different social divides (Putnam 2000:22). Studies indicate that high-status-group members are likely to favor their own group and denigrate low-status groups (Bettencourt et al. 2001). Members of low-status group are more likely to hold high-status group members in esteem and denigrate their own group (Jost and Banaji 1994). Thus, bridging is most easily accomplished when high-status group members reach out to lower-status groups. When lower-status group members try to bridge the status gap, the higher-status group is more likely to use their status to exclude out-group members.

Finally, a third factor that contributes to the use of social identity over personal identity is *targeting.* Targeting occurs when others call attention to a social category or group membership. When targeting occurs, people are defined in terms of their social identity rather than personal identity. Calling attention to people's group identity makes the targeted social identity salient in the interaction. For example, several years ago I was at a family reunion given by my husband's family. The issue of the Confederate battle flag came up. I was called upon by one of my in-laws to give the Yankee perspective on the flag issue. Suddenly, a social identity that I had not even thought about that day became my prominent social characteristic. Although I begun the reunion simply as an individual who was related by marriage, I was compelled by the targeting into the role of spokesperson for the millions of Americans born or living in the northern states. Not only did my state of origin become my defining characteristic, it also marked me as an outsider. Although this example uses a prejudice that is seldom seen in law suits, the impact of targeting is not a trivial matter. Once targeted, an individual is related to in terms of their social identity. Other personal aspects that create a unique individual are overlooked or ignored. Regardless of what factors lead to my personal opinion about the flag, my comments would be interpreted through my identity as a Yankee. Had I been targeted as a woman, a professor, or a social psychologist, the interpretation of my remarks would likely have been different.

INDIVIDUALISM VERSUS COLLECTIVISM

Just as people can adopt either an individual identity or social identity, cultures vary in the degree to which their norms, values, and beliefs support a more individual or collective identity (Triandis 1995). The United States is a good example of a culture that emphasizes individualism. Individual rights, freedoms, and opinions are paramount in U.S. culture. The United States is one of the most individualistic cultures in the world. Examples of American individualism include our willingness to relocate half a continent away from our family to pursue an educational or career opportunity, our complete rejection of arranged marriage, and the wide acceptance of the idea that personal unhappiness is a valid reason for divorce. China and other eastern cultures have more collectivist cultures, in which group identity and well-being is emphasized (Ho 1995). In contrast to the American belief that individuals are free to pursue any path they choose, eastern societies emphasize responsibility to family and community over personal pursuits. Because of this emphasis, collectivist cultures increase the salience of the social identity whereas individualist cultures emphasize the personal identity.

There is, of course, variation within subgroups of U.S. culture. For example, whites as the dominant racial group are not as cognizant of their group identity as are people of color. Our cultural belief in individualism helps make class, race, and gender privilege invisible. People who have high status, wealth, and power believe they have earned their social position through individual merit. For example, whites are unaware not only of their race privilege, but also of what it means to be white (McKinney 2005). This leads many to the misconception that there is no such thing as white culture or white privilege. The mistake, of course, is that white culture is so powerful and pervasive that it defines every other race and ethnicity by contrast. Indeed, researchers have found that whites do not identify themselves as a racial group (Judd et al. 1995). Judd and his colleagues found that white American participants in their study preferred "race blindness." That is, they reject using race as the basis of a social identity. Part of this can be explained by the relative affluence of their research subjects. The researchers point out that the population from which their white subjects were drawn was a relatively race- and class-segregated environment. In contrast to the race-blind perspective, African American subjects maintain a *cultural pluralism* perspective. The researchers suggest that their African American subjects "have been socialized to respect and value their ethnic heritage and to realize that ethnicity does make a difference in this country" (Judd et al. 1995:78). When they repeated the study using a much more diverse pool of subjects, similar results were found. The differences were especially pronounced for younger cohorts within the study. Judd and colleagues suggest that younger African Americans are being taught to take pride in their race and ethnicity, whereas younger white Americans are learning to de-emphasize racial and ethnic differences (1995:79).

The suppression of stereotypes and prejudices required by the color-blind approach does not mean prejudice and discrimination are a thing of the past. First, as I have mentioned before, there is a gap between attitudes and behavior. Even if self-reports of prejudice are a valid reflection of people's beliefs and attitudes about out-group members, their behaviors may not be consistent with their egalitarian beliefs. Second, the color-blind perspective is basically an assimilationist approach. By insisting that all groups are the same, the norms and values of the dominant group remain the unchallenged standard by which all other groups are measured.

Individualism within the American value system coupled with color-blind socialization makes it more likely that members of dominant groups (e.g., white, male, upper class) will employ a personal identity rather than a social identity. They may fail to see the impact of social groups and structures entirely. This contributes to a fundamental misunderstanding of the relationship between prejudice and the structure of social inequality. People socialized to value a color, gender, or class blind approach may believe that their refusal to hold stereotypes about other groups constitutes a lack of prejudice on their part and a decline in (or even disappearance of) racism, sexism, or classism in society. But, simply denying prejudice does not mean these forms of inequality no longer exists. Ironically, the refusal to acknowledge the different experiences of other racial groups is a form of racism in itself. Of course, this refusal to recognize fundamental differences in the social experience of minority groups is not unique to racism. The same phenomenon occurred a generation ago when girls were raised to believe they could become anything they wanted. Girls and boys, we were told, were equal. In the meantime, the wage gap remains stable, women are woefully underrepresented in public office, and women still bare a disproportionate share of domestic responsibility. Similarly, the myth of a classless American society does not mean there are no classes, rather it justifies economic inequality as a product of effort and ability.

In this section, we have explored prejudice as an intergroup phenomenon. Intergroup relationships are affected by the identities that become salient during interactions. Because everyone has a variety of group identities as well as unique personal characteristics, which identity emerges as important during interaction has an effect on how the interaction is interpreted. Group identity and the prejudices and stereotypes associated with groups can profoundly affect interaction and the meanings attached to the actions and behaviors of others.

Cultural beliefs and values also influence the likelihood of adopting a personal or social identity. In the United States, the value for individualism makes it less likely that people will adopt a social identity. This is particularly true for members of the more powerful dominant groups, such as whites, men, and those in the upper classes. Using the personal identity makes it easier to justify privilege with personal merit while at the same time disguising the structural advantages of race, gender, and class. In the next section, the role of leadership in groups and the potential to manipulate prejudices to maintain leadership will be examined.

LEADERSHIP

Leadership, according to social psychologists, is a process by which a person influences others to accomplish tasks or goals. It involves social influence through the exercise of power linked to a particular position in a group structure. If leadership is a process, a *leader* is a person occupying a leadership position with a group (Shaw 1981:317). Although, given the right situation, almost anyone can be thrust into a position of leadership (Bales 1950; Sherif 1966), there are some personality attributes shared by good leaders. By studying the attributes associated with effective leaders, social psychologists have created leader prototypes (Lord and Alliger 1985; Foti and Luch 1992). Although prototypes vary from group to group, there are many consistent traits. Intelligence, verbal skills, and sensitivity to others are some of these common traits (Kenney et al. 1994). However, because leader prototypes vary depending on the social context and the pool of potential leaders, more recent research has focused on leadership as a social process than as a personal attribute.

Early theories of leadership identified two basic types of leaders: *task leaders* and *socioemotional* leaders (Bales 1950). Task leaders guide and coordinate ideas and information toward the completion of tasks and goals. Socioemotional, or expressive, leaders mediate conflicts, encourage group participation, and provide feedback to group members. Sometimes these roles are assumed by two different people within the group; in formal groups, whose structure designates a single leader, both roles must be accomplished by the same person. Prejudice can be woven into both leadership styles. Task leaders can use intergroup competition to increase productivity and ensure compliance among group members. Socioemotional leaders can appeal to the prejudices of their follows to create group solidarity and support. In other words, prejudice can be used to amplify us–them distinctions.

How does the leadership of a group affect the use of prejudices and stereotypes in intergroup relations? Several theories that we have encountered indicate that leaders have an important impact on prejudice. Contact theory contends that increased contact can reduce prejudices only if the leadership of the group actively endorses the suppression of prejudices and stereotypes (e.g., Gaertner et al. 1994). Although the contact theory hypothesis has been criticized for reducing intergroup conflict to individual ignorance and misunderstanding (e.g., Connelly 2000), its supporters contend that contact between groups can reduce prejudices and facilitate intergroup cooperation when core conditions are met (see Chapter 2 for a more detailed discussion of contact theory). One of these core conditions is that contact must be given legitimacy by having institutional support (Connelly 2000:172). This means that leadership must support intergroup relations and institute that support at both the individual and structural level. Social structures, as well as individual attitudes, must be made conducive to improving intergroup relations.

George Dreher (2003) found support for the link between contact theory and leadership. In a time-lagged study of women managers, he found that as the number of women in leadership positions increases, organizational changes benefiting women will occur. These changes in institutional support for women increase the percentage of women both in management overall and in top-level management. In other words, as more women enter management, the structure of work changed to accommodate women allowing more women to ascend the organizational hierarchy. Dreher suggests that sustained contact and the presence of female leadership will eventually break the glass ceiling allowing women to be better represented at all levels of management.

Social identity theory contends that leadership is a group process generated by social categorization and prototypes based on a depersonalization process (Hogg 2001:184). Social categorization divides the social world into in-groups and out-groups. People in these groups are represented as prototypes. *Prototypes* are generalized sets of attributes that characterize members of that group. *Depersonalization* occurs when people in the in-group and out-groups are not viewed as distinctive individuals, but as representative prototypes (2001:187). As part of the group identification and categorization process, group members with the most prototypical traits exert greater influence on groups. From this perspective, leadership is both a structural feature of groups and contingent upon displaying the normative characteristics of the group. That is, if a person displays traits that are highly representative of the group, they are likely to be seen by others in the group as a leader. Display of prototypical traits acts to validate position within the group and build trust among other group members. Voicing prejudices embraced by the group is one way of displaying prototypical traits.

LEADERSHIP AND SOURCES OF AUTHORITY

Sociologists approach leadership from a slightly different perspective. Instead of focusing on individual personality traits or situational context, sociological studies have focused on the source of authority from which a leader derives influence. Max Weber (1947) identified three sources of authority: traditional, legal-rational, and charismatic. *Authority* refers to the power to influence others that has been *institutionalized. Institutionalized authority* means power is recognized by the people over whom it is exercised and is part of a patterned and predictable social system. In a system based on *traditional authority,* leadership is based on custom and long-accepted practices. For example, in societies governed by absolute monarchies, leadership is based not on personal characteristics or competence, but on inheriting the position. The system continues because "it has always been so." The popularity of the monarch is irrelevant. Even legal codes are irrelevant because the monarch has the ability to decree laws and policies.

Legal-rational authority is based on law. Leaders in this type of system derive their authority from written rules, codes, and regulations. Judges and justices in the U.S. court system draw their authority from the system of laws. The realm and tenure of their authority are defined by the position they hold in the legal system. Like the legislative and executive branches of the government, judiciary leaders derive their power from the U.S. and state constitutions. Although we may hope that elected and appointed members of the judiciary have the technical competence to do their jobs well, their authority does not rest on judicial competence.

Charismatic authority is based on the personal or emotional appeal of the leader. Charismatic leaders can influence others without the benefit of law or tradition. In fact, charismatic leaders often act as catalysts for dramatic social change. They use their strong hold over followers to break with established traditions and legal systems. Elvis Presley used his charisma to launch the rock-and-role movement in popular music; Martin Luther King Jr. used his charisma to further the civil rights movement; and Adolf Hitler used his charismatic appeal to expand the German empire and catapult the world into global war. Of course, charisma is not limited to internationally known leaders. Community leaders, local politicians, and even popular children on the playground can use charisma to influence others to accomplish tasks or goals (cf. Sunwolf and Leets 2003).

Intergroup conflict arises when groups base leadership on differing sources of authority. For example, the conflict between the Citadel and Virginia Military Institute and the federal government was in part a conflict between tradition and law. Both schools argued that the tradition of single-sex military training had value and should be preserved. The third district federal court argued that single-sex public education was a violation of civil rights law (a legal-rational source of authority). Similarly, conflicts between the charismatic leader David Koresh of the Branch Davidian and the Bureau of Alcohol, Tobacco, and Firearms were a clash between charisma and legal-rational authority.

Although leaders are more likely to have personal attributes such as intelligence and attractiveness in common, leadership as a social process is more useful in understanding the relationship between prejudices and intergroup relations. Recent research using the contact theory perspective indicates that when leaders support positive intergroup relations and institute that support at both the individual and structural level, prejudice and discrimination decrease. Research using social identity theory indicates that displaying prototypical traits and attitudes makes it more likely that a group member will be seen by others as a leader. Thus, leaders could be in a position to either increase or decrease out-group prejudices. How a leader uses prejudices is also related to the source of authority from which leadership is derived. For example, leaders using a legal-rational source of authority such as the U.S. constitution could be constrained by the law from discrimination and expressions of prejudice. Thus, even though many people may privately support when politicians express prejudices, the media and public opinion surveys decry such expressions as unacceptable.

Summary

This chapter began with a description of the types of groups, categories, and aggregates that affect human behavior. Group affiliations affect how people understand social situation and even whether they use personal or social identity to understand themselves and others. Prejudices and stereotypes are likely to be used to interpret interaction when people view others as members of an out-group rather than as unique individuals. Other factors that influence the use of social identity over personal identity include distinctiveness, status, and targeting. In highly individualistic cultures like that found in the United States, people believe they are free to pursue any path they choose and are, therefore, responsible for social consequences whether they are good or bad. Individualist cultures emphasize the personal identity, whereas collectivist cultures are more likely to emphasize social identity.

The final section of this chapter addressed the effect leaders and leadership have on prejudices. Although leaders share some general attributes, studies of leadership and authority are more useful in understanding how prejudices are used by leaders. Researchers employing contact theory have found that the support of leadership is important in the reduction of prejudice and discrimination. Research using the social identity perspective has found that group prototypes can both facilitate the selection of a leader and lead to the depersonalization of out-group members. Sociologists view leadership from a slightly different angle. They examine how leadership differs depending on its source of authority.

Key Terms

- Aggregates
- Authority
- Bonding
- Bridging

- Charismatic authority
- Cohesion
- Collectivism
- Depersonalization

- Distinctiveness
- Ethnocentrism
- Formal task group
- Group

- Group cohesion
- Group dynamics
- Group think
- Individualism
- Informal group
- Intergroup relations
- Leadership
- Personal identity

- Persuasive argument approach
- Polarization
- Primary group
- Rational legal authority
- Reference group
- Secondary group
- Social capital

- Social comparison approach
- Social identity
- Socioemotional leader
- Targeting
- Task leaders
- Traditional authority
- Xenocentrism

Taking It Further—Class Exercises and Interesting Web Sites

Individual versus Social identity

People have both an individual identity based on their personal traits and a social identity based on the groups to which they belong. In this exercise, students will discuss what factors influence how they define themselves on both levels. Students will be given two forms. The forms are versions of the "Who am I?" test. On the first form the students should list up to twenty adjectives that describe their personal attributes. For example, I am smart, I am funny, I am serious, and so on. On the second form, they will answer the "Who am I?" question with social roles and group identities. For example, I am a college student, I am an African American, I am middle class, and so on. After completing the form, assemble the students into small groups. Have the groups consider the following questions:

> What have been the major influences in forming my individual identity?
> What are the similarities between what has helped me form my individual identity and the identities of the other people in my group?
> Is there any connection between my individual identity and my social identity? If so what is it?
> Is there a difference between when I employ my social identity and when I use my individual identity?
> If so, how does when you use social identity compared with others in your group?

After re-assembling as a class, the instructor should ask the group if they were able to identify any patterns in what influenced their identities and when they were likely to use their individual and social identities.

References

Adamic, Lada A., and Eytan Adar. 2003. Friends and neighbors on the web. *Social Networks* 25: 211–230.

Asher, S. R., and V. L. Allen. 1969. Racial preferences and social comparison processes. *Journal of Social Issues* 25: 157–166.

Bales, Robert. 1950. A set of categories for the analysis of small group interaction. *American Sociological Review* 15: 257–263.

Bennett, W. Lance. 2003. Communicating global activism: Strengths and vunerabilities of networked politics. *Information, Communication & Society* 6 (2): 143–168.

Bettencourt, Ann B., Nancy Dorr, Kelly Charlton, and Deborah L. Hume. 2001. Status differences and in-group bias: A meta-analytic examination of the effects of status stability, status legitimacy, and group permeability. *Psychological Bulletin* 127 (4): 520–542.

Brand, E. S., R. A. Ruiz, and A. M. Padilla. 1974. Ethnic identification and preference: A review. *Psychological Bulletin* 81: 860–890.

Brauer, Markus, Charles Judd, and Melissa D. Gliner. 1995. The effects of repeated expressions on attitude polarization during group discussions. *Journal of Personality and Social Psychology* 68 (6): 1014–1029.

Brauer, Markus, Patrick Chambres, Paula M. Niedenthal, and Angéélique Chatard-Pannetier. 2004. The relationship between expertise and evaluative extremity: The moderating role of experts' task characteristics. *Journal of Personality and Social Psychology* 86 (1): 5–18.

Burnstein, E., and A. Vinokur. 1977. Persuasive argumentation and social comparison as determinants of attitude polarization. *Journal of Experimental Social Psychology* 13: 315–332.

Clark, Kenneth B., and Mamie Phipps Clark. 1940. Skin color as a factor in the racial identification of Negro pre-school children. *Journal of Social Psychology* 11: 159–169.

———. 1947. Racial identification and preference in Negro children. In *Readings in social psychology,* ed. T. M. Newcomb and E. L. Hartley, 169–178. New York: Holt.

Coleman, J. C. 1988. Social capital in the creation of human capital. *American Journal of Sociology* 94: S95–S120.

Connelly, Paul. 2000. What now for the contact hypothesis: Toward a new research agenda. *Race Ethnicity and Education* 3: 169–193.

Crandall, Christian S., and Amy Eshleman. 2003. A justification-suppression model of the expression and experience of prejudice. *Psychological Bulletin* 129: 414–446.

Crocker, Jennifer, Leigh Thompson, Kathleen M. McGraw, and Cindy Ingerman. 1987. Downward comparison, *prejudice,* and evaluations of others: Effects of self-esteem and threat. *Journal of Personality and Social Psychology* 52 (5), May 1987: 907–916.

Cutler, Steven, and Brian Cutler. 1995. Witness confidence and witness accuracy: Assessing their forensic relation. *Psychology, Public Policy, and Law* 1 (4): 817–845.

Dreher, George F. 2003. Breaking the glass ceiling: The effects of sex ratios and work-life programs on female leadership at the top. *Human Relations* 56: 541–562.

Fein, Steven, and Steven J. Spencer. 1997. Prejudice as self-image maintenance: Affirming the self through derogating others. *Journal of Personality and Social Psychology* 73 (1), July 1997: 31–44.

Foti, Roseanne J., and Carissa H. Luch. 1992. The influence of individual differences on the perception and categorization of leaders. *Leadership Quarterly* 3 (1): 55–66.

Gaertner, Samuel L., Mary C. Rust, John F. Dividio, Betty A. Bachman, and Phyllis Anastasio. 1994. The contact hypothesis: The role of a common ingroup identity on reducing intergroup bias. *Small Group Research* 25: 224–249.

Gray-Little, B., and Hafdahl, A. R. 2000. Factors influencing racial comparisons of self-esteem: A quantitative review. *Psychological Bulletin* 126: 26–54.

Hamilton, D. L., and R. K. Gifford. 1976. Illusory correlation in interpersonal perception: A cognitive basis of stereotypical judgment. *Journal of Experimental Social Psychology* 12: 392–407.

Ho, D. Y. F. 1995. Selfhood and identity in Confucianism, Taoism, Buddism and Hinduism: Contrasts with the West. *Journal for the Theory of Social Behavior* 25: 115–139.

Hogg, Michael. 2001. A social identity theory of leadership. *Personality and Social Psychology Review* 5: 184–200.

Hraba, Joseph, and Geoffrey Grant. 1970. Black is beautiful: A reexamination of racial preference and identification. *Journal of Personality and Social Psychology* 16 (3): 398–402.

Janis, Irving Lester. 1982. *Group think: Psychological studies of policy decisions and fiascoes.* Boston, MA: Hough Mifflin.

Jost, John T., and Mahzarin R. Banaji. 1994. The role of stereotyping in system-justification and the production of false consciousness. *British Journal of Social Psychology* 33 (1): 1–27.

Judd, Charles M., Bernadette Park, Carey S. Ryan, Marcus Brauer, and Susan Kraus. 1995. Stereotypes and ethnocentrism: Diverging inter-ethnic perceptions of African American and white American youth. *Journal of Personality and Social Psychology* 61: 366–379.

Kenney, Robert A., Jim Blascovich, and Phillip R. Shaver. 1994. Implicit leadership theories: Prototypes for new leaders. *Basic and Applied Social Psychology* 15 (4): 409–437.

Kenworthy, Jared, and Norman Miller. 2002. Attributional biases about the origins of attitudes: Externality, emotionality and rationality. *Journal of Personality and Social Psychology* 82 (5): 693–707.

Kleider, Heather M., and Stephen D. Goldinger. 2001. Stereotyping ricochet: Complex effects of racial distinctiveness on identification accuracy. *Law and Human Behavior* 25 (6): 605–627.

Lewin, K. 1941. Jewish self-hatred among Jews. *Contemporary Jewish Record* 4: 219–232.

Lord, Robert G., and George M. Alliger. 1985. A comparison of four information processing models of leadership and social perceptions. *Human Relations* 38 (1): 47–65.

McGuire, William J., Claire V. McGuire, and Pamela Child. 1978. Salience of ethnicity in the spontaneous self-concept as a function of one's ethnic distinctiveness in the social environment. *Journal of Personality and Social Psychology* 36 (5): 511–520.

McKinney, Karyn. 2005. *Being white: Stories of race and racism.* New York: Routledge.

McVeigh, Rory. 2004. Structured ignorance and organized racism in the United States. *Social Forces* 82 (3): 895–936.

Messick, David M., and Diane. M. Mackie. 1989. Intergroup relations. *Annual Review of Psychology* 40: 51–81.

Montera, M. 1986. Political psychology in Latin America. In *Political psychology,* ed. M. G. Hermann. San Francisco, CA: Jossey Bass.

Pederson, Paul B., Robert T. Carter, and Joseph G. 1996. The cultural context of psychology. Questions for accurate research and appropriate practice. *Cultural Diversity & Mental Health* 2 (3): 205–216.

Ponterotto, Joseph G., and Paul B. Pedersen. 1993. *Preventing prejudice: A guide for counselors and educators.* Newberry Park, CA: Sage Publications.

Putnam, R. D. 2000. *Bowling alone: The collapse and revival of American community.* New York: Simon and Schuster.

Shaw, Marvin. 1981. *Group dynamics: The psychology of small group behavior.* New York: McGraw-Hill.

Sherif, Muzafer. 1966. *In common predicament: Social psychology on inter-group conflict and cooperation.* Boston, MA: Hough-Mifflin.

Sunwolf, and Laura Leets. 2003. Communication paralysis during peer-group exclusion: Social dynamics that prevent children and adolescents from expressing disagreement. *Journal of Language and Social Psychology* 22 (4), December, 355–384.

Tajfel, Henri. 1974. Social identity and intergroup behavior. *Social Science Information* 13: 65–93.

Tajfel, Henri, and John C. Turner. 1986. The social identity theory of intergroup behavior. In *The psychology of intergroup relations.* ed. S. Worchel, and W. Austin. Chicago, IL: Nelson Hall Publishers.

Taylor, S. E. 1981. A categorization approach to stereotyping In *Cognitive processes in stereotyping and intergroup behavior,* ed. D. L. Hamilton, 83–114. New York: Erlbaum.

Triandis, Harry C. 1995. *Individualism and collectivism.* Boulder, CO: Westview.

Vinokur, Amiram, and Eugene Bernstein. 1974. Effects of partially shared persuasive arguments on group induced shifts: A group problem solving approach. *Journal of Personality and Social Psychology* 29: 305–313.

Ward, Susan H., and John Braun. 1972. Self-esteem and racial preference in black children. *American Journal of Orthopsychiatry* 42 (4): 644–647.

Weber, Max. 1947. *The theory of social and economic organization.* Translated by A. Henderson and T. Parsons New York: Free Press. Originally published 1913.

Yip, Tiffany, and William Cross. 2004. A daily diary study of mental health and community involvement outcomes for three Chinese American social identities. *Cultural Diversity and Ethnic Minority Psychology* 10 (4), November 2004: 394–408.

Zarate, Michael A., and Azenett Garza. 2002. In-group distinctiveness and self-affirmation as dual components of prejudice reduction. *Self and Identity* 1: 235–249.

CHAPTER

The Role of Prejudice in Interaction

Anticipating and Interpreting Others

The first section of this chapter explores dominant approaches to the study of interaction—symbolic interaction and socialization theories from sociology and the social cognition and perception approaches from psychology. Although attitudes are inaccurate indicators of behavior as demonstrated by social scientists, they are still used in everyday interaction to anticipate and explain the behaviors of others. This chapter will describe why and how prejudices are used to ascertain meaning, interpret interactions, and justify actions.

- Sociological Perspectives
    Socialization and Social Learning
    Symbolic Interaction
- Psychological Perspectives
    Social Cognition
    Social Perception and Attribution Theory
- Changes in How We Perceive and Use Prejudice
    Old-Fashioned Prejudice
    Modern Prejudice
    Symbolic Prejudice
    Aversive Prejudice
    Ambivalent Prejudice
- Summary
- Key Terms
- Taking It Further—Class Exercises and Interesting Web Sites
- References

Recently, a young friend of mine, Jon, had an experience that taught him a lot about how people can come away with very different ideas about what was meant in an interaction. Jon was given a writing assignment in his second-grade class. He was to find a word in the dictionary that describes a classmate and then to write a story about the classmate using the word. Jon was assigned a student who was the class clown and jokester. In fact, Jon had recently been on the receiving end of these jokes.

Searching through his dictionary for a word to describe his happy-go-lucky classmate, he found a perfect word. The definition said this word meant light hearted, merry, and joyful. So he wrote a story about his "gay" classmate. My unwitting little friend was sent to the principal's office, his mother was called, and he was told never to use that word again. Jon learned not only that there was another meaning for gay, but also that the teacher thought there was something wrong or shameful about the other meaning.

Have you ever compared your memories of an event with someone who was present at the same event, only to find that you had a radically different understanding of what was going on? Even relatively ordinary interactions can be interpreted from vastly different perspectives. For example, imagine you are using an outdoor ATM one evening and a stranger walks up behind you. You could reasonably interpret them as another customer waiting in line, but you might also interpret them as a threatening encounter with a potential thief or assailant. Any police officer can tell you that when there are multiple witnesses to an accident or crime, there are also multiple and often conflicting accounts of the event. When witness accounts conflict, people might seek to know what *really* happened. We assume that someone has to be lying or at least deluding themselves. If we could place ourselves in each person's position, we might see the plausibility of their interpretation. However, no one person comprehends the whole truth. That's because the "truth" is not a single explanation. Each person interprets what goes on around them from their own unique perspective. Not only is our perspective influenced by our position relative to the interaction taking place, it is also influenced by myriad other social and personal factors. Whereas some of these factors are situational and particular to the unique interaction we are observing, others are a product of socialization.

As children, we learn to understand human interaction both directly through experience and indirectly when we adopt the interpretations taught to us by family, friends, teachers, and other significant people in our lives. Because no two individuals have the same experiences or are taught exactly the same interpretations, each individual develops a different understanding or perspective on human behavior. "Reality" is not simply a single definitive "truth," rather it is a dynamic process each of us engages in as we try to make sense of the people and events around us.

Just as individuals have different perspectives or ways of making sense of the world and events around them, academic disciplines also represent different perspectives. Sociology focuses on the process of interaction between individuals, group dynamics, and social structures. Psychology focuses on individual traits, cognitive processes, and social perception. Because social psychology is a hybrid discipline with contributions from both sociology and psychology, this chapter will examine perspectives from both disciplines on the role prejudice plays in interaction, perception, and the social creation of reality. Although no single perspective explains every use of prejudice in interaction, each perspective tells us something important about it.

Among social psychologists coming from a sociological background, two approaches have dominated the study of human interaction—theories of socialization and the symbolic interaction perspective. The *socialization* approach studies interaction through the examination of constraints on interaction imposed by rules and roles. Perspectives within this tradition focus on the norms and roles understood by people entering into interactions and how we learn them. The *symbolic interaction* approach explores interaction as a dynamic, open-ended, yet patterned process between self-reflective interactants. Psychological social psychologists understand interaction in terms of social cognition and social perception. *Social cognition* is how we think about the social world, whereas *social perception* explains how we come to understand others.

SOCIOLOGICAL PERSPECTIVES

Socialization and Social Learning

Socialization is the process of learning how to behave according to the rules and expectations of a particular culture. The socialization approach to the study of inter- action emphasizes the rules, roles, and norms of interaction. Even when we interact with strangers in unfamiliar settings, some elements from our socialization provide a structure that enables us to interpret what goes on around us. *Norms* are social rules that prescribe and proscribe behaviors within a social context. For example, college stu- dents are familiar with the norms of conduct for college classrooms. Students know without being told which seats to take and what behaviors are expected from them in the classroom context. Although professors and students may add to or redefine some classroom norms during the course, the basic structure of classroom interaction is made patterned and more predictable because interactants have been taught similar norms. Learning norms through socialization is a process that begins in infancy and continues throughout one's entire life.

Roles and statuses also help create socially regulated and patterned behavior. A social *role* is a set of behaviors associated with a particular social position. A *status* is a named social position. Each individual can occupy multiple roles and have different statuses that can change with the situational context. For example, sitting at my desk typing this sentence I am doing the role that is identified by the status "author." I will shortly walk across the street to pick up my grandson at the university preschool, where I will become "grandma." Both the behaviors (role) and the title (status) will change. How I interpret what goes on around me and how I am perceived by others will be affected by the role and status appropriate to the interaction.

During the process of learning the many different social roles in which people operate, human beings not only learn to perform the roles, they also learn how to inter- pret the behaviors of others and interpret the interaction from a variety of different perspectives. By taking different roles, we learn to step outside of our own individual perspective and imagine how the interaction might be perceived by others. Children switch roles visibly when they play. They may be playing house or school by themselves and switch between the roles of parent and child or between teacher and student. As they switch social roles, they may alter their physical attitude, the pitch of their voice, or the expression on their face to convey the altered social position. Not only does such play allow the child to practice the behaviors that comprise the role, it also allows them to interpret interaction from different social positions. As a person learns the numerous roles they occupy as they move through differing social situations, they are incorporat- ing the roles into their selves. The roles become part of how they define their self. During interaction there is a complex meshing of self and role-taking. The roles we move through in our everyday life are not discrete sets of behaviors that we pick and lay down; rather we develop a network of interactional repertories that become part of who we are (Lindesmith et al. 1999).

The ***social learning perspective*** is a theory of socialization that contends that people learn new attitudes, beliefs, and behaviors through social interaction (Bandura and Walters 1963). According to this theory human behavior is determined by an interplay between elements of a social situation and the individual interactants. There are two processes by which people learn appropriate social behavior: direct learning and observational learning. ***Direct Learning*** involves directly experiencing behaviors and their consequences. Desirable behaviors and attitudes are rewarded whereas those that are undesirable are punished. If a child touches a hot stove, they directly learn not to do so because of the pain they receive as a consequence. We also directly learn attitudes—especially prejudices. Almost everyone has heard little boys being admonished for crying or otherwise acting like a "sissy." Besides being punished for the behavior, the child learns a gender prejudice—males are tough and females are weak.

Indirect learning or ***observational*** learning can be accomplished vicariously by observing the behaviors and consequences of the behaviors of others. This is sometimes called ***role modeling.*** We indirectly learn roles through imitation. Parents are very powerful role models for their children. Children often mimic even the most minute behaviors they observe their parents performing. For example, little girls dress up in their mothers' clothes and little boys work side by side with their fathers using toy versions of the tools their fathers use. When role models express prejudices, the attitudes are incorporated into the self along with the modeled behaviors. For instance, consider the impact of gender prejudices on young children. Many activities are gendered in our society. That means that an activity is thought appropriate for one gender but not the other. Children who cross gender boundaries are sometimes the targets of intense gender prejudices. This is especially the case for boys who cross over into feminine territory. Several years ago my elder grandson was called a "Barbie." by some other boys. From the ensuing conversation, I learned that being a "Barbie" not only implied gender prejudices, but had anti-homosexual connotations as well. His response to the insult was to exhibit more stereotypically masculine behavior and to voice disdain toward all things feminine. Prejudices against women became part of the way he defined himself as masculine.

Although parents, friends, and teachers are powerful role models, the media is an important influence. Books, television, and music expand the range of situations and social context to which people are exposed. For example, movies allow viewers to indirectly experience a wide variety of social contexts that would be otherwise unavailable. When I go to see a *Harry Potter* film, I can imagine what it feels like to be an adolescent boy even though I am not male and have long past that stage of life.

Because movies and other forms of media are carefully staged, they have enormous potential to affect people's attitudes and prejudices. Not only does the media reflect common prejudices, it can also deliver not-so-subtle messages about the acceptability of prejudices. Perhaps the most dramatic example of the media's effect on prejudices is the alarming increase in hate group membership and bigotry generated by hate-group–sponsored sites available through the Internet (cf. Coreno 2002; Duffy 2003; Borgida and Stark 2004). When the rhetoric of hate groups is published on the Internet, it can provide justificatory support for prejudice, discrimination, and even violence.

Even though social learning theory acknowledges the importance of early childhood socialization, it does not restrict the effects of direct and observational learning to the young. Social learning is a process that continues throughout life. Thus, prejudices are learned, altered, and adjusted through social interaction by the reinforcement of behavior, the imitation of others, or both. Some prejudices are so well integrated into our society that people do not recognize them as prejudices. For example, social-class prejudices are so thoroughly normative that most people in the United States do not regard them as prejudices at all. Although most people would recognize racial prejudice, whether they were offended by it or not, many people do not even recognize social-class prejudices. This is partly because social-class inequality is legitimate in a capitalist economic system. The assumption that people with more money, education, and power are better human beings and therefore have a right to exclude others from their social environment is not viewed as a negative prejudgment. Making fun of grammatical errors associated with the lower classes or their taste in clothing, cars, and home decor is not politically incorrect. To the contrary, most people are comfortable using social-class prejudices as a justification for inequality and their position within the class structure.

Symbolic Interaction

Symbolic interaction theory focuses on how individuals use symbolic communication during everyday interaction. Human beings use many and varied symbol systems to communicate. Symbols include words, gestures, written language, and sign language, to name but a few. However, for meaningful interaction to take place, symbols must have shared meaning. This would be much more simple if each symbol has a single, clear definition, but as anyone who has ever opened a dictionary knows, there is seldom just one meaning to anything. Thus, symbolic interaction is a process during which interactants negotiate meaning. The cornerstone of symbolic interaction is the contention that *meaning is in response.* That is, meaning is not a property of a word or other symbol; rather it is constructed through our responses to each other during interaction. Everyone can remember a time when they were talking with someone and became aware that the other person was understanding a different meaning than they had hoped to convey. Some response they observed or heard was inconsistent with the reaction they expected. When this happens, people usually try again to communicate the meaning they intend. They may use different words or another gesture to convey the intended meaning. Not only is the meaning of symbols negotiable, the *definition of the situation* is also established through interaction. For symbolic interactionists, the definition of a situation is how a person perceives reality. Thus, interaction is a process by which humans create and negotiate social reality.

We initially learn how to take part in interaction from our significant others. A ***significant other*** is a person whose responses are very influential in forming your definition of the situation. Usually, significant others are people in our family, close friends, teachers, bosses, and others who play important roles in our lives. Contrary to the popular definition of this term, a significant other is not limited to a romantic partner; in fact, significant others could include enemies as well as allies. Over time, we use the responses and reactions of our significant others to create a ***generalized other.*** Unlike a significant other, a generalized other is not a real person. It is a concept we create to help us anticipate the responses and reactions of others. We create the generalized other from our experiences. We generalize from past responses to apply to the present situations. People use the generalized other to anticipate the likely responses of others, so that we don't have to directly experience every possible reaction to be able to predict likely responses. For example, because I have developed a generalized other, I do not need to wear my pajamas to class to understand the likely reactions of others.

Because the generalized other is constructed through experiences, its usefulness is limited by the extent of one's exposure to others. People who have few experiences outside of their family or community may find it difficult to interpret others from different cultures. Of course, if we engage in an interaction with someone speaking another language, it will be more difficult to establish shared meaning, but even conversing with people from other cultures that use the same language can be challenging. When I first went to England to meet my sister's new in-laws, I had trouble with my generalized other. On the first day morning I was visiting with this new branch of the family, I was asked, "Do you mind faggots?" The question startled me, and I stumbled over a response. Could they be asking me if I was homophobic? As it turned out, they wanted to know if smoking cigarettes bothered me. Fortunately for human beings, the generalized other expands with every interaction.

According to the symbolic interaction perspective, prejudices both emerge from and give meaning to interactions. For example, a child might hear a significant other express a prejudice against people in another group; the child then might use the prejudice to construct a definition of the situation. Thus the child incorporates the prejudice into his or her social reality. Of course, children are not the only ones who adopt the prejudices of other people. We all learn prejudices from a variety of sources, such as friends, family, teachers, movies, books, and even the popular press. Sometimes people are aware that they have acquired and are intentionally employing prejudices. At other times the acquisition and use of prejudice is inadvertent.

We are sometimes unaware that we have acquired a prejudice until it emerges as a response to interaction. During the early 1980s there was an anti-Iranian rhetoric generated by the media coverage of the Iranian hostage crisis. I did not realize how much this had affected me until I showed a prejudiced reaction to a young man I judged to be of Middle Eastern ethnicity. I was having my hair cut at a local salon. A very well-dressed young man arrived in an expensive late-model sports car. He exited the car by jumping over the closed doors of the convertible. He came into the salon and requested a hair cut and manicure. Although I was only a witness to the interaction, I had an unexpected and a negative response to the young man. I suspect my response involved more than one prejudice. It's possible that part of my reaction was a social-class prejudice because the young man was conspicuously displaying wealth by his clothing, jewelry, and automobile. I may have been influenced by gender prejudices because the salon catered predominately to women. But I was undoubtedly also responding to the negative press given to Iranians. Although I had no way of knowing this man's ethnicity, I jumped to the conclusion that he was Middle Eastern. I had an immediate, unfavorable feeling toward the man, which was completely unjustified by my observation. I was surprised and appalled by my reaction, but also intrigued. Where had that prejudice come from? If I use the symbolic interaction perspective to interpret my experience, I would look to both experiences I had with Middle Eastern men and to attitudes expressed about them. Because I had very few experiences, it is more likely that I absorbed the anti-Iranian rhetoric into my generalized other and applied it to anyone who happened to look to me as if they were Middle Eastern. Although it is uncomfortable to admit prejudices, claiming that any human being is without them would only subvert meaningful inquiry. My prejudice triggered stereotypes of oil-rich Middle Easterners as I almost instantaneously and resentfully constructed a scenario of a rich, spoiled, and arrogant person. A symbolic interactionist would focus on how I used the stereotypes to create a justification for my negative reaction and construct a definition of the situation. It is also important to note that I had little experience interacting with Middle Eastern people up to that time in my life. The less experience one has, the more likely a person is to employ stereotypes to create meaning.

Symbolic interaction theory also contends that the self is reflective. This means that people think about or reflect on their own reactions. An instant after I had the prejudiced thoughts, I was reflecting on them. My first reaction was self-critical. I was surprised and disgusted. My next response was to try and suppress and discount the prejudice. However, as we learned in Chapter 4, suppressing prejudices and stereotypes is like trying not to think about white bears (cf. Wenger et al. 1987). Ironically, scanning for the prejudice or stereotype in an attempt to eliminate only draws further attention to it. Although the triggering of prejudice may be inevitable, the application of the prejudice can be avoided (Devine et al. 1991; Devine and Monteith 1993; Dovidio et al. 1997). The application of prejudice occurs when one allows the prejudice to affect how we think or behave. Even people who disapprove of prejudices have been shown to be affected by them (Devine 2001; Devine et al. 2002). However, if the self is reflective as the symbolic interactionists contend, human beings are constantly engaged in a dynamic process of acting and then reflecting on our own behavior and the responses of others. Thus, for the symbolic interactionist, how one responds to self-realization of prejudices is more important than the prejudicial impulse itself.

George H. Mead (1965) describes the reflective self as an internal dialogue between two parts of the self—the *I* and the *me*. The *I* is the part of self that acts; *me* is the objective component of the self. So *I* performs some action or behavior, then *me* thinks about want *I* has just done. The *I* then adjusts responses and behaviors in accordance with the feedback provided by *me*. This endless cognitive conversation allows people to continually adjust and recreate the definition of the situation, as well as the meaning they are constructing. For the symbolic interactionist, the activation of a prejudice is only part of a process. The response to the activated prejudice is where meaning is created.

Thus far the focus of symbolic interaction may be subjective. The prejudice and response to it have been cognitive. But interaction, the responses of others, and our interpretation of those responses are vital to understanding this process. We can never be certain that others understand the situation as we are defining it. We gauge consensus by the similarity between the responses we expect and the responses we observe. However, sometimes meanings are so divergent that we *talk past* one another (Blauner 1989, 1993, 2001). Bob Blauner contends that as Americans become more diverse, the gap in worldviews between people in different racial and ethnic groups will become wider. People in different groups experience the world from different social positions. Therefore, how they interpret those experiences also differ. To put this in terms of symbolic interaction, the definition of the situation differs depending on the social groups to which one belongs. Blauner points out that black and white people in America experience race relations from fundamentally different social positions. He notes that structural explanation of race has little meaning for white Americans because they have never personally experienced the negative consequences of race or racism directed against their group.

My own research corroborates Blauner's interpretation. I interviewed 398 residents of Philadelphia and Meridian Mississippi (Bakanic 1995). I chose these two communities because they experienced some of the worst racial violence of the civil rights era. Despite the past civil rights conflict, most of the people I interviewed, both black and white, indicated little or no support for racial segregation and many prefaced their remarks by disclaiming racial prejudice. However, there were interesting differences in the way the two racial groups interpreted racism and how they remembered their communities' interracial history. Remembering the past was threatening for many whites. They feared that people from other areas of the country would perceive their communities as racist and that perhaps talking about race relations would re-create racial trouble. Black interviewees had a very different view about the past. Many believed that remembering the past was a way to assure history did not repeat itself. Although both groups were asked the same questions, how they interpreted the questions and consequently how they answered differed. Neither blacks nor whites supported racism; however, they still held divergent views about race relations. The majority of whites believed blacks and whites were treated the same, whereas the majority of blacks did not. When people have such divergent perspectives, it becomes more difficult to create a shared definition of the situation. Instead of talking with one another, we talk past each other.

Not only does the symbolic interactionist perspective offer an explanation for the gap between the racial attitudes of blacks and whites, it also offers insight into the gap between attitudes and behavior. In Chapter 5, we explored the weak link between prejudice (an attitude) and discrimination (a behavior). If prejudices predicted behavior, it would be relatively easy to monitor and design strategies to limit discrimination. But, efforts to document this link established only a weak, tenuous relationship. La Piere (1934) and others (Saenger and Gilbert 1950; Kutner et al. 1952; Minard 1952) have demonstrated that prejudice is not a reliable predictor of behavior. Subsequent studies have found several reasons for the weak link. First, the relationship between attitudes and behavior is not a simple unidirectional, causal relationship. There is a difference between attitudes and beliefs and between attitudes and behavioral intentions. Beliefs are much more general, encompassing ideas. Attitudes involve some evaluation of an object, concept, or category. Behavioral intentions are what we think we might do in a specific situation before actually engaging in the situation. Thus, behavioral intentions mitigate the relationship between attitudes and behavior. However, even if one had reliable ways of measuring beliefs, attitudes, behavioral intention, and behaviors, the process of interaction is much more complex than simply adding up the sum of beliefs, attitudes, and intentions. This leads to a second and more complicated reason for the weak link between attitudes and behavior. When people engage in interaction with others, they collectively define the situation, conveying and constructing meanings and negotiating social reality. During ongoing interaction, the attitude–behavior link becomes a complex interactive process, with contextual and situational changes intervening to alter both attitudes and behavior. In other words, during the course of an interaction, the very process of interaction may cause attitudes and behaviors to change.

From the symbolic interaction perspective, prejudices are part of the dynamic process of interaction and cannot be understood as stagnant discrete concepts. If you think of interaction as a river, the problem may become clearer. If you scoop a jar of water from a river, you may have river water, but the essence of the river is its motion, not just the water. Measuring an attitude with a questionnaire or during an interview removes the attitude from the process of interaction. As the jar of river water has been pulled from the context that defines the river (the flow of water), attitudes measured by responses to a questionnaire are separated from the context that defines them (the flow of interaction).

The two perspectives emanating from sociological social psychology share an emphasis on how prejudices fit into social processes. Those using a socialization approach focus on the process of learning how to behave according to the rules and expectations of a particular culture. We learn prejudices and stereotypes during the process of socialization and in turn teach them to others. Prejudices are so well integrated into the culture that we sometimes do not recognize them as prejudices. The symbolic interaction perspective focuses on the process of constructing, communicating, and negotiating social reality. According to this perspective, prejudices emerge from interaction, yet the very process of interaction may cause prejudices and behaviors of the interactants to change. In the next section, two psychological perspectives will be considered: social cognition and social perception.

PSYCHOLOGICAL PERSPECTIVES

Psychological perspectives focus on processes occurring within the individual and social influences that affect the individual. The first approach examined in this section focuses on the internal thought processes that people use when making judgments. The second perspective, attribution theory, is concerned with how people understand, predict, and explain their own and others' behavior. Both perspectives are concerned with how individuals make causal inferences. Prejudices enter the process of making inferences when we use prejudices and stereotypes to help make sense of events around us.

Social Cognition

Social cognition is the process of making judgments from information available in the social environment. In other words, it describes how people make inferences. Human beings reason by identifying patterns through categorizing and grouping information. An *inference* is made when specific information is generalized to a larger group. For example, I observe that my husband and son-in-law consistently choose to watch sporting events in their leisure time; therefore I infer that men in general prefer to watch sporting events. I have generalized from specific observation of two men to men in general.

When making social inferences, people must go through a process of collecting information, deciding what information is pertinent, and integrating the relevant information into a judgment (Taylor et al. 2006). Collecting information is the first step in this process. However, even social scientists don't use scientific methods to gather information in their everyday personal experiences. When people begin to collect information to make a judgment, there are several factors that can prejudice their judgment: prior expectations, biases in the information, and anecdotal evidence.

Prior expectations can be helpful in gathering, organizing, and interpreting information, but they can also lead to inaccurate conclusions. Continuing the example of men and their preference for sports, I might assume that a new male acquaintance is also interested in sports and initiate a conversation about sports with him. Consequently, I may be searching for evidence that confirms my prior expectations. In addition, if information is inconsistent with what I want to believe, I may reject it. So if the hypothetical male acquaintance is uninterested in sports, instead of altering my expectation I may decide he is an exception and continue searching for sports-loving men.

In addition to biases in our own expectations, there may also be biases in the information we collect. When people know the information they are receiving is from a biased source, it can affect their judgment. You need look no further than television commercials for examples. Advertisers choose attractive spokespersons with carefully rehearsed scripts to pitch their products because they know people will make inferences about their product based on impressions they receive from the spokesperson. Even though we know that commercials are inherently biased sources of information, they still influence us. Who hasn't tried a weight-loss product, a stop-smoking method, or other products that promise amazing, instantaneous results, knowing the information about the product is highly inaccurate?

Finally, inferences are more likely to be faulty when they are based on anecdotal evidence. When a very small number or a single incident is used as the basis of an inference, it can produce very biased judgments. How many times have you heard people discount statistical evidence by offering a single contradictory experience? The single contradictory case can be especially persuasive if it is colorful or memorable. Politicians routinely use this to their advantage. Instead of presenting statistics, they often prefer testimonials from constituents. Although people often ignore or discount statistical evidence, few can ignore an engaging anecdote. So while the statistical evidence may be more valid, the anecdote is often far more persuasive.

The second step in making inferences is deciding what information is relevant. This involves sifting through potentially vast amounts of information and experiences to select the things that will be helpful in making a judgment. How do people decide what is relevant? Is it a process of selecting particular incidents and impressions or rejecting information because it doesn't fit? Do we select from only what we consciously recall, or do the events we don't consciously recall also affect this process? Cognitive psychologists have found that our memory for contextual information includes recollection of circumstances and physical features, as well as memory for thoughts and emotional states (Johnson, Hashtroudi, and Lindsay 1993). In other words, we are not limited to recalling only concrete information or articulate impressions. We may recall feelings and make connections between ideas to which we do not fully attend or comprehend. For instance, you may recall your experience when you were aware of some important connection you should be making, but could not articulate it. It may be that later you realized what bothered you, or it could remain a vague sense of unease. The process involved in what we recall and how we decide what is relevant is as complex as it is subjective.

The third step in making social inferences is integrating information to make a judgment. This involves putting sometimes disparate bits of information together to reach a decision. Most of us would like to believe that we are rational and systematic in our decision-making processes. However, researchers have found that humans take a more idiographic or distinctly individual approach to decision making (Broder 2000). That is, human decision making is best explained on an individual or case-by-case level because there is too much variability to assume a consistently rational process. There are several theories that explain how human beings make decisions. Probable Mental Models (PMM) theory contends that because humans have cognitive limitations, they must simplify problems and accept less-than-optimal solutions (McClelland and Bolger 1994).

This leads to the hypothesis that people take the best or most efficient solution given the constraints of the available information (Czerlinski et al. 1999). The problem with trying to fit human behavior to a decision-making model is that human decisions are swayed by an almost infinite array of cultural influences, personal inclinations, and prior experiences. Going back to the example about men's sports preference, even if my observation about my husband and son-in-law's sports predilections are accurate, their decision about what to watch is not a simple matter of preferences. They may not be interested in the teams playing in televised games that day, or they may have responsibilities that interfere with their ability to watch the game, or perhaps they will decide that they have exceeded their wives' tolerance for televised sports. In short, each human being puts together the information they have at hand in idiosyncratic ways that makes predicting the outcome — or even the process — difficult.

Schemas

The process of gathering information, deciding what is relevant, and using that information to make a decision can be time-consuming and difficult. If social cognition is as complex as research indicates, then shortcuts or ways of making decisions more simply are understandably attractive. To make decisions rapidly and efficiently, people often rely on schemas. A *cognitive schema* is an organized, structured set of thoughts about some group, idea, person, or thing. Schemas can be about a particular person, such as your best friend, your little brother, or even yourself. They can be about social roles, such as teachers, police officers, or parents. They can be about events or ideas. However, the schemas about groups and categories of people are among the most important schemas in understanding prejudices and stereotypes.

Schemas often have many different levels. At the most general or abstract level, they include generic information that can be applied broadly. For example, a gender schema for men might include that most men wear pants or shorts, work for pay most of their adult lives, shave or trim their facial hair, and enjoy competition. There are undoubtedly many more characteristics that men share in a gender schema, but we have clear, well-developed ideas about what men in general are like. At the next level of our gender schema, we might have different categories of men, such as boys, old men, fathers, uncles, boyfriends, nice guys, or jerks. Each of these subcategories is distinct and includes specific qualities. For example, boys might be described as energetic, mischievous, and rough. At an even more specific level, we might have specific memories of a particular boy or an event involving boys. Of course, our schemas have to be flexible because we have a variety of experiences and ideas about any category or concept. The schema for boys must be flexible enough to encompass a shy three-year-old toddler, an extroverted athletic ten-year-old, or a gangly teenager.

Information relevant to a schema is more readily remembered and more quickly processed. Information clearly consistent with or clearly inconsistent with the schema is more easily recalled. Information irrelevant to the schema is less likely to be recalled and likely to be quickly forgotten. A *consistency effect* occurs when memory is aided by comparison with a schema. Pezdek and her colleagues (1989) found evidence of a consistency effect when research subjects were asked to recall items in rooms associated with a schema. In this study research subjects entered one of two rooms: a graduate student office or a preschool classroom. Half of the items in each room were consistent with a room appropriate to the schema; the other half was not. In both, same day and next day, interview subjects were better able to recall items in the room that were inconsistent with the schema. In another study, Tuckey and Brewer (2003) examined how witnesses recalled information using a crime schema. They found, over repeated interviews, that schema-irrelevant information was more quickly forgotten than either schema-consistent or schema-inconsistent information.

Because we use schema to process information, we need not think about this process for it to occur. Inferences can occur so quickly that they are virtually automatic. For example, if you meet an attractive young woman with an outgoing manner, you may automatically attribute other favorable traits, such as intelligence or kindness, to her without being aware that you have done so. Automatic activation occurs with negative traits as well. For example, obese people are more likely to be perceived as sloppy, construction workers as sexist, and professors as intellectual elitists.

By now, it should be apparent that according to the social cognition approach, prejudices and stereotypes are a by-product of the way people process information. People often rely on schemas to manage the barrage of information they must process as they interact in a complex social world. People have mental representatives for social categories (Sia et al. 1999). These representations can include attributes and beliefs about the category, norms and values associated with the category, as well as past experiences with the category. These pieces of information serve as ***category exemplars,*** which can be activated when assessing attitudes toward the category (Sia et al. 1999:218). Exemplars can be used to fill in missing information that helps avoid ambiguity thereby allowing people to make more confident inferences. The degree to which the situation matches the exemplar increases the confidence we have in the reliability of the added details. In other words, when we lack information based on observation, we use knowledge from schemas to make inferences. Stereotypes and prejudices are often part of schemas. When people lack information to make judgments about a social situation, they sometimes rely on prejudices and stereotypes to fill in the gaps in their knowledge. This occurs even though people are aware of the inaccuracy and biases inherent in stereotypes and prejudices. Although schematic processing has many advantages, such as speed and efficiency, it also has liabilities. In addition to overrelying on the schema to fill in gaps and the tendency to uncritically accept ideas that fit the schema, there are the dangers of stereotyping and vulnerability to prejudice.

Because cognitive processing is an ongoing dynamic process, schemas are often employed so quickly that they occur without conscious awareness. In other words, some reactions happen so quickly that they are virtually automatic. Patricia Devine (1989) explains how ***automatic processing*** occurs in a rapid, unpremeditated, and unintended manner. She contrasted automatic processing with ***controlled processing.*** Controlled processing includes intentional thoughts of which we are fully aware. Devine's work makes a distinction between explicit and implicit stereotypes. ***Explicit stereotypes*** are those about which the research subject is aware. Because the subject is aware of the stereotypes, they can be measured by self-report. ***Implicit stereotypes*** are a product of cognitive associations that are so ingrained that they are automatic and unpremeditated. Because people may be entirely unaware that they are employing implicit stereotypes, implicit stereotypes are harder to measure. In Chapter 4, we described Implicit Association Test (IAT). IATs use priming words, priming pictures, or ethnically distinctive names as prompts. The amount of time it takes to make the link between the priming word or picture and the positive and negative traits indicates the strength and direction of the bias (Greenwald, McGhee, and Schwartz 1998; Greenwald et al. 2002). Evidence gathered from IATs has consistently shown that although people may report that they hold little or no racial and gender prejudices, there is considerable evidence of racial biases (Fazio et al. 1995; Ottaway et al. 2001) and gender biases (Rudman and Kilianski 2000; Steffens and Buchner 2003) based on the response time for IATs.

There has been some debate about whether implicit measures of prejudices are measuring what the researchers intend them to measure. (Rothermund and Wentura 2004). Studies measuring the validity and reliability of IATs have found relatively strong results (Greenwald et al. 2005; Nosek et al. 2005). However, Blair and colleagues (2002) argue that using physical features to make judgments is not the same as categorizing. They argue that people often find themselves in a situation where they must make a judgment on appearances. The ecological perspective argues that some physical features are valid indicators of other traits: for example, wrinkles indicate age. In contrast, the stereotype perspective contends that judgments based on appearances are used to categorize people and then to apply stereotypes appropriate to the categorization. Blair and colleagues found that having Afro-centric features, regardless of racial categorization, leads subjects to infer stereotypical traits. This argument is particularly important because the cognitive perspective contends that prejudices and stereotypes are a by-product of the underlying cognitive process of categorization. If traits cue the association, rather than categorization being the impetus, then the cognitive process may be even more complicated and the link between prejudice and discrimination (and attitudes and behaviors, in general) more convoluted.

The social cognition perspective helps explain how experiences are mentally ordered, categorized, and given meaning. Social perception refers to the ways in which people respond to social situations. In the next section, we will examine a theory that explains how prejudices are part of how we respond to others and assign motivations to each other's behavior.

Social Perception and Attribution Theory

Our desire to understand others is more than idle curiosity. People must be able to understand the behavior of others to make sense of their interactions with others and to ascertain the social situation. We spend a lot of time and energy trying to understand other people's behavior because it helps us give meaning to what is happening around us and hopefully to predict what may happen next. The study of social perception endeavors to explain how we form impressions of other people and the inferences we make based on those perceptions. Attribution theory describes the way people account for their own behavior and attribute causes for the behavior of others.

When we observe other people, we have many sources of information that can help us interpret them. Facial expressions, body language, and verbal communications are all important social cues that we use to figure out other people. However, understanding other people's behavior involves more than observing what they do. It also involves formulating ideas about *why* they do it. In other words, to what do we attribute their behavior?

According to Fritz Heider (1958), people make both internal and external attributions. An ***internal attribution*** locates the cause of behaviors within the individual. Some individual trait or traits such as personality, moral character, or attitudes causes the observed behavior. Let's suppose your housemate is stomping around the kitchen grumbling loudly while banging pots, utensils, and dishes. If you use an internal attribution to explain the behavior, you might chalk it up to a grumpy personality, being a jerk, or having poor anger management skills. If, on the other hand, you decide it is something in the situation that has caused your otherwise-easy-going housemate to display such behavior, you will search for external attributions. An *external attribution* locates the cause of behavior in the social situation rather than the individual. Perhaps your housemate just broke up with a lover, got fired from a job, made an F on a midterm exam, or had an argument with a good friend. We might behave in a similar manner if any of these things happened to us. Not surprisingly, our understanding of the behavior is very different depending on the type of attribution we make. If an internal attribution is made, we have a very negative impression of the housemate. If an external attribution is made, we assume that anyone in the same position would react in a similar manner.

How do people decide whether to make an internal or external attribution? Heider (1958) observed that people are more likely to make internal attributions because external attributions require much more information about social situations we may not have observed or are difficult to discern. However, we almost always use more than one piece of information when we form attributions. Harold Kelly (1967, 1973) contended that we use patterns of behavior to understand others. He calls this contribution to attribution theory the *covariation model.* In making an attribution, we first recall many pieces of information and then select relevant bits from what we have recollected. We examine the information to discern whether it varies over time and to discern our experiences with the person. Returning to the grumpy housemate example, is this a recurring or usual behavior? Does your housemate behave this way when other people are present? By finding patterns in the variation of your housemate's behavior, you are better able to make an attribution about what has caused the behavior.

Kelly (1967, 1973) identified three kinds of information we need to identify patterns of covariation: consensus information, distinctiveness information, and consistency information. *Consensus information* compares the behavior between the subject and other people when responding to a similar stimulus or situation. Do other people grumble and make a racket in the kitchen when faced with similar impetus or stimulus? *Distinctiveness information* compares how the subject responds in this situation with responses made in other situations. Has your housemate showed displeasure in similar ways toward different people or when in a different place? *Consistency information* refers to how frequently the same person reacts in the same manner across time and conditions. Does your housemate grumble and bang pots regularly and frequently in response to dissimilar situations, and does this occur regardless of whether the house is empty or others are present?

When a clear pattern emerges from these three kinds of information, we can make an attribution. People are more likely to make internal attributions when consistency is high, but consensus and distinctiveness are low. So let's suppose your housemate often grumbles and bangs things regardless of who is present (high consistency). However, you have observed very few other people behaving this way (low consensus) and you have observed this behavior in your housemate's response to other stimuli (low distinctiveness). Thus you are likely to decide that your housemate has some internal trait that caused the outburst. If all three types of information are high, people are more likely to make an external attribution. That is, if you have seen other people respond in a similar fashion, you have seen your housemate behave this way in other situations, and your housemate frequently responds this way when upset, you will conclude some external or situational circumstance has caused the disturbing melee (Kelly 1972).

So far, it sounds as if making attribution is a rational, logic, and systematic activity. However, human beings are only sometimes rational and are inconsistent in their everyday logic. There are several factors that intervene in this process of making rational attributions. Sometimes people are more expedient than logical in their decision making, preferring to take mental shortcuts. Unfortunately, these shortcuts can lead to **attribution errors.** Three types of attribution errors can increase reliance on prejudices and stereotypes. The first type results from a phenomenon known as **correspondence bias.** This is the tendency to believe that people behave the way they do because of the type of internal personality traits they have. For instance, people who break the law have criminal personalities. This attribution error is so common that it has been labeled a **fundamental attribution error.** It occurs when people infer that a person's behavior matches their personality (Heider 1958; Ross 1977).

Another type of attribution error is the **self-serving attribution.** Pretend that you have just received your midterm grade for this course. Congratulations, you got an A! To what do you attribute your success? If you are like most other people, you look for explanations for your success by making internal attributions. You are smart and hard working! Now let's consider the far less likely scenario that you received a D. In this event, you would be more likely to blame your failure on external factors, such as a biased teacher, a terrible textbook, or a fight with your roommate the night before the midterm. When a person's self-esteem is threatened, they are more likely to protect their ego by making self-serving attributions. We take personal credit for our successes while looking to other people and external situations to explain our shortcomings (Pronin, Lin, and Ross 2002).

A third type of attribution error occurs when in-group and out-group distinctions affect attributions. We attribute the positive behaviors of in-group members to internal characteristics and their undesirable behaviors to external factor. The opposite is true for out-group members. When out-group members behave in undesirable ways, we attribute it to internal traits, but when they behave in positive ways, it is attributed to external causes. This is called the **ultimate attribution error** because it exacerbates our predilection for in-group members and our prejudices against out-group members. Not only does the ultimate attribution error promote prejudice and in-group favoritism, it also has an ominous potential for harming inter-group relations (Pettigrew 1979).

It is fairly easy to see how these three attribution errors could facilitate prejudices and reliance upon stereotypes. The fundamental attribution error occurs when people rely too heavily on individual traits and personality characteristics to explain behavior. If one explains poverty by assuming laziness and lack of ambition among poor people, then it becomes easy to attribute these characteristics to the lower classes in general. Not only does this attribution explain the persistence of poverty, it also conveniently blames the victim for their plight.

The self-serving attribution facilitates ego defense by allowing us to take credit for our success while avoiding blame for our failures. The advantages we enjoy are a result of personal attributes, but negative consequences are due to conditions outside of our control. The ultimate attribution error combines the victim blaming implicit in the fundamental error with the self-serving attribution. Consider the following widely held attribution. Welfare mothers deserve their low status and poverty because it is a result of a promiscuous, lazy, and slovenly lifestyle; however, the economic advantages of the middle class are due to hard work and solid family values. Not only does this attitude blame members of the out-group (welfare mothers) for the undesirable consequences of racism, sexism, or classism, it also allows people from dominant social groups to take personal credit for social advantages. To paraphrase this prejudice, the poor deserve their plight because they are failing to take personal responsibility for their choices and behaviors. If only they would act like responsible middle-class people, they would not be impoverished.

The psychological perspectives (cognitive perspective and attribution theories) and the sociological perspectives (socialization and symbolic interaction perspectives) share a focus on how people make sense of their individual world by trying to understand their own and others' behavior. Social learning theory contends that we learn prejudices through the process of socialization. Prejudices can be acquired directly or indirectly through observational learning. For the symbolic interactionist, prejudice is part of a process of negotiating reality in interaction with others. An important point made by symbolic interaction is that one's sense of the situation is derived from observation of and reaction to others. Social cognition theories explore how we process and categorize information from the social environment. Prejudices and stereotypes may be by-products of the categorization process. Attribution theory explains that people use both internal and external attributions in constructing explanation for the behavior of ourselves and others. However, bias and error in attribution can result in the persistence of prejudices and reliance on stereotypes.

Both sociological and psychological perspectives offer explanations for how prejudices influence how people perceive, organize, and give meaning to their experiences. Although there may be some cultural variation in how people categorize people and behaviors, and how they interpret and respond to them, the perspectives described here can be broadly applied. There have, however, been some recent changes in how prejudices in our culture are expressed. In the next section, we will examine varieties of contemporary prejudice.

CHANGES IN HOW WE PERCEIVE AND USE PREJUDICE

According to survey research, racial attitudes in the United States have been moving toward more tolerant and accepting attitudes toward racial minorities (Schuman, Steeh, and Bobo 1985). But, although self-reported racism has decreased, racial discrimination and racial hate crimes have not. Similarly, although attitudes about women and homosexuals have moved toward less rigid gender roles and more acceptance of gays and lesbians, attitudes toward these groups remain negative (Mohipp and Morry 2004). So how can racist, sexist, and homophobic attitudes be decreasing, but negative attitudes, discrimination, and hate crimes toward these groups remain? Obviously, something is amiss. Several theories provide explanations for the emergence of a new kind of prejudice. Whereas overt expressions of prejudice have declined, more subtle forms of prejudice have emerged.

Old-Fashioned Prejudice

John McConahay (1986) noted that there are social and cultural pressures to disclaim blatantly prejudicial remarks. To differentiate between blatant prejudice and more subtle expressions, he coined the terms "old-fashioned" and "modern racism." Janet Swim and her colleagues extended the concept to include other prejudices, such as sexism (Swim et al. 1995). ***Old-fashioned prejudices*** refer to openly expressed animosity toward a group or category of people. For example, men who believe that women are inferior or whites who believe blacks are lazy are expressing old-fashioned prejudices. Although the public expression of old-fashioned prejudices has declined, contemporary forms of prejudice are still very much with us. Researchers have differed in what they call this new, more-covert expression of prejudice. Four theories have emerged to account for this new, more-covert expression of prejudice: modern prejudice, symbolic prejudice, aversive prejudice, and ambivalent prejudice.

Modern Prejudice

McConahay and his colleagues (McConahay and Hough 1976; McConahay 1983) were the first to distinguish between overt and covert expressions of racism. They referred to covert racism as ***modern racism.*** Before World War II, the open expression of racism was normative, and if not exactly acceptable, it was tolerated and seldom challenged. Survey research in the post-war era has shown a steady decline in support for overt expressions of prejudice. Schuman, Steeh, and Bobo (1985) contend that self-reported agreement with racist attitudes has declined to the point that it is no longer useful to ask respondents whether they agree with racism. McConahay (1983) argued that racist attitudes have not disappeared; they have merely changed forms. Modern prejudice has become cloaked in traditional American values. For instance, white people may believe that they are not racially prejudiced, but that black people or other racial minorities violate values such as the work ethic, delayed gratification, and sexual prudence and responsibility. A recent example is the rise of anti-Mexican and anti-immigrant prejudices that have been couched in rhetoric touting respect for immigration law.

The new disguised version of racism includes three integral components: denial, antagonism, and resentment (McConahay 1986). First, perpetrators of modern prejudice deny that discrimination against the target group continues. They may acknowledge that discrimination occurred in the past, but they deny or fail to recognize ongoing discrimination. Second, the purveyor of modern prejudices displays antagonism toward members of the target group who are pressing for equal rights. They do not acknowledge the legitimacy of the fight for equal rights because they do not believe the target group has been denied rights. Finally, those with modern prejudices will express resentment over supposed preferential treatment given to members of the target group. They may even believe that they or members of their group have been the victims of "reverse" discrimination. Despite the resentment and antagonism, people holding modern prejudices do not see themselves as prejudiced. From their perspective, prejudices are bad, and they do not define the attitudes they hold as prejudiced. Rather, they see themselves as moral, hard-working individuals who have, to some degree, succeeded. People who are not successful are not the victims of discrimination; instead they are in some way deficit. From the perspective of those expressing modern prejudices, differences between groups are not the result of racism, sexism, or classism; they are the result of real differences in ability, ambition, and determination.

McConahay (1986) developed the Modern Racism scale to measure the three major components of modern racial prejudice. The scale is constructed from responses to seven self-report questionnaire items. Two items measure the extent to which the respondent denies continuing racial discrimination. Three items measure antagonism toward African Americans. The remaining two items measure resentment for perceived preferential treatment for African Americans. Janet Swim and her colleagues developed a similar scale to measure modern sexism (Swim et al. 1995). Like McConahay, they found that modern prejudices against women include a denial of continuing sex discrimination, antagonism toward women's demands for equal treatment, and opposition toward policies that would help women.

Symbolic Prejudice

David Sears and his colleagues (Sears and Kinder 1970; Sears 1988; Sears and Henry 2003) have a slightly different focus. They contend that prejudice has changed from the overt and relatively straightforward old-fashioned variety to a more complex, insidious, symbolic form. *Symbolic prejudice* occurs when latent negative attitudes toward a group are mixed with widely held values and triggered by political symbols. This form of prejudice is termed "symbolic" for several reasons. First, the prejudice is abstract, ideological resentment of a group rather than resentment based on actual experiences with the group. Another symbolic dimension involves the sense that the target group has violated some underlying, widely agreed-upon social contract. The prejudiced person believes that the target group is not working hard enough, has gained more than they deserve, yet continue to make demands for even more preferential treatment. Finally, symbolic prejudices are overlaid with traditional values. Espousing the traditional values is subtly combined with the suggestion that the target groups' problems stem from their failure to conform to the values rather than from prejudice or discrimination.

Symbolic prejudices are a better predictor of discrimination than old-fashioned prejudices. Because symbolic prejudices hide behind a veneer of widely held American values, people can deny that they are prejudiced. Instead, they resent groups who they believe reject the qualities necessary to achieve social position in a meritocracy. As a consequence, they often express disdain for social policies such as welfare, and affirmative action (Kinder and Sears 1981; Kinder and Sanders 1996).

Symbolic prejudices are also a better predictor of political attitudes than self-interest (Kinder and Sanders 1990; Sears et al. 1997; Henry and Sears 2002). For example, some well-known African American commentators espouse symbolic prejudice with as much, if not more, vehement as whites (cf. Peterson 2000), whereas conservative women have a long history of arguing against women's rights (cf. Freeman 1976, 2000; Schlafly 2002). Kinder and Mendelberg (1995) found that segregation and isolation enhance the impact of prejudice on political opinion. The isolation of working wives from career women and working mother, our increasingly class-segregated society, and our still race and class segregated communities have covertly insinuated prejudices deeply into American opinion.

Aversive Prejudice

Samuel Gaertner and John Dovidio (1986) also note the subtlety of contemporary prejudice, but rather than contrasting old-fashioned prejudice with modern or symbolic prejudice, they contrast two kinds of contemporary prejudice: dominative and aversive. *Dominative prejudice* is the overt, unambiguous, and blatant expression of prejudices toward a group. Dovidio and Gaertner (1991) concede that this type of prejudice is less-frequently expressed. They estimate that only one in five white Americans expresses dominative prejudice. However, the decline in dominative prejudice does not mean that 80 percent of Americans are without racial prejudices. The researchers contend that most white Americans retain negative attitudes toward African Americans because they have been raised in a racist culture. Because the social structure still supports racial inequality, the culture and the language transmit racial prejudice. At the same time, other cultural values support equality. People with ***aversive prejudices*** hold these egalitarian values, while at the same time possessing negative feelings about the target group caused by socialization in a racist culture. These negative feelings are not the virulent hatred expressed by dominative racists. The feelings of an aversive racist are more feelings of unease, awkwardness, and wariness. To cope with this discomfort, people avoid African Americans rather than confront them.

Because aversive racists are committed to egalitarian values, they believe that they are nonprejudiced. They may even abhor dominative racism, but because they are uncomfortable around racial minorities, they discriminate subtly and in ways in which they may not even be aware. How aversive racism is expressed depends on the social context. In a situation where prejudice is discouraged, the aversive racist will work to appear nonracist. However, when the social context is ambiguous or others are expressing justification for prejudice, prejudices are more likely to be expressed.

Several strategies have been used in experimental research designed to reveal aversive prejudice. One experiment coupled emergency intervention and the bystander strategy. This experiment compares the response of white research subjects to unambiguous emergency situations involving white or black confederates posing as victims (Gaertner and Dovidio 1977). In addition, the presence of other witnesses to the emergency is varied. By including other witnesses, the subject could justify their failure to assist black victims by rationalizing that others were present to help. When the subject thought another bystander was present, subjects were much more likely to help a white victim than a black victim (38 percent versus 75 percent). When the subject believed they were the only witness, they helped both white and black victims more evenly (95 percent versus 83 percent) (Dovidio et al. 2002:89).

Dovidio and his colleagues have also used experimental research involving hiring decisions (Dovidio and Gaertner 2000) and college admission decision (Hodson, Dovidio, and Gaertner 2002). The hiring-decision study asked subjects to evaluate candidates for a position in a peer counseling program at their university. When candidate credentials clearly qualified black applicants for the position, there was no discrimination. However, when the black applicant was only moderately qualified, white evaluators did not give them the benefit of the doubt. This was in contrast to moderately qualified white candidates. In other words, while strongly qualified candidates received equal treatment regardless of race, moderately qualified black applicants were treated like weak candidates, although moderately qualified white candidates were treated like strongly qualified candidates.

A similar study compared college admissions decisions for consistently qualified applicants and mixed qualifications (Hodson et al. 2002). Evaluators used SAT scores and high-school records to make their decisions. In the strong and weak conditions, scores on both indicators were consistent. There were two mixed conditions: one with high SAT scores and weak high-school records, the other with a strong high-school record, but low

SAT scores. As in the previous studies, discrimination against black applicants did not occur in the consistently strong or consistently weak conditions. However, when credentials were mixed, black applicants were more likely to be rejected than whites.

According to the theory of aversive racism, contemporary racism is subtle and often unintentional. These unintentional biases affect the ways black and whites perceive and respond to the same behaviors and situations and have different consequences on outcomes for blacks and whites (Dovidio et al. 2002:89). Although aversive racism originated as an explanation for racial prejudice, it has the potential to be adapted to other forms of prejudice, such as gender prejudice and homophobia. The same egalitarian values should deter overt expression of sexism and heterosexism, even though socialization into a patriarchal culture guarantees gender prejudices and heterosexual predilection.

Ambivalent Prejudice

Like the theory of aversive racism, the theory of ambivalent racism identifies value conflict as the problem underlying contemporary prejudice. Irwin Katz and his colleagues (Katz 1981; Katz and Wackenhut 1986; Katz and Hass 1988) point out that people can both feel friendly toward and reject the target group at the same time. The confusion and ambivalence stem from two competing values: individualism and humanitarian-egalitarianism. *Individualism* includes ideas about the Protestant work ethic and individual responsibility. *Humanitarian values* stress empathy and sympathy for others less fortunate than ourselves. *Egalitarian values* emphasize equal treatment and opportunity for everyone regardless of the groups to which they belong. These values sometimes conflict, resulting in jumbled and contradictory feelings. This mixture of benevolent and antagonistic attitudes is termed *ambivalent prejudice.*

When people have ambivalent feelings, their reactions toward the group are more volatile and more likely change as social context changes. To sort out the relationship between racial attitudes and widely held values, Katz and Hass (1988) developed four scales. Two are designed to measure antiblack and problack attitudes, whereas the remaining scales measure humanitarian-egalitarian values and the Protestant work ethic. In the first of two related studies, they found that white subjects agreeing with humanitarian-egalitarian values scored higher on the problack scale, whereas subjects scoring higher on the Protestant ethic scale scored higher on antiblack attitudes. In the second study, they used a priming technique to see if drawing attention to these values affected racial attitudes. First, they activated one set of values by asking questions about it; then they asked questions about racial attitudes. They hypothesized that if they activated humanitarian-equalitarian attitudes, then problack attitudes would increase. However, if they activated Protestant ethic values, antiblack attitudes would increase. They found that priming a given value did raise the corresponding attitude, but did not affect the other racial attitude (Katz and Hass 1988:893). Thus, if humanitarian-egalitarian values are primed, problack attitudes increase, but antiblack attitudes do not change. Similarly, if Protestant ethic values are primed, antiblack attitudes increase, but problack attitudes are unaffected. The independence of the problack humanitarian-egalitarian connection from the antiblack Protestant ethic link underscores the complexity of racial ambivalence.

Katz and Hass (1988) believe that ambivalence creates psychological discomfort. The discomfort makes behavior more responsive to social context and, as such, harder to predict. This can lead to *ambivalence amplification.* Ambivalence amplification occurs when the favorable and unfavorable attitudes toward the target group are juxtaposed. For example, if a white person observes a black person behaving in socially positive ways, they have a tendency to evaluate the black person more highly than a white person engaged in similar behavior. On the other hand, if they observe a black person behaving in socially undesirable ways, they will judge the black person even more harshly than they would a white person in a similar context. Amplified responses are an attempt to balance the discomfort caused by a contradiction between values and racial attitudes. So, when a black person behaves admirably, the ambivalent racist will suppress antiblack attitudes. However, when a black person behaves incompetently, the ambivalent racist enhances antiblack affect.

Like the other theories discussed in this chapter, ambivalent prejudice can be applied to other attitudes besides those about race. Peter Glick and Susan Fiske (1996, 2001) examine ambivalent sexism. They distinguish between hostile sexism and benevolent sexism. **Hostile sexism** includes belligerent, aggressive, and demeaning attitudes. It includes the idea that women are less competent than men and should therefore be subservient to men. It also includes overt antagonism toward women who step out of their gender role or threaten men's domination. **Benevolent sexism** consists of benign and chivalrous attitudes toward women. It includes attitudes that emphasize women's gentler qualities, such as feminine virtue, decency, nurturing, and the need for protection. Although benevolent sexism seems benign in comparison with hostile sexism, it nonetheless puts women on a pedestal. Thus, it limits women to traditional gender roles and reinforces male dominance.

In this section, we have examined some of the ways prejudices have changed. Contemporary prejudices have become more integrated into other attitudes and values. This disguises prejudices allowing people to deny that they harbor any prejudices at all, while at the same time justifying discrimination. Modern and symbolic prejudice both hold that prejudices have changed over time. In addition to denial, modern prejudices include thinly veiled antagonism and resentment toward the target group. Symbolic prejudices are abstract and overlaid with traditional values. They also include a political dimension. Political symbols can be used to trigger and manipulate symbolic prejudices. Often symbolic prejudices are a better predictor of political attitudes than self-interest. In other words, appealing to prejudices may be a more effective way for politicians to secure votes than satisfying the political interests of voting constituents.

Theories of aversive and ambivalent prejudice contend that value conflicts have given rise to more-subtle, less-easily recognized forms of prejudice. However, these contemporary forms are nonetheless prejudices that fulfill the same purposes of justifying and maintaining inequality between social groups.

Summary

This chapter began by making the point that reality is not a single definitive truth. We are engaged in a dynamic process of creating our own realities as we try to make sense of the people and events around us. The socialization approach focuses on how people learn normative behaviors, social roles, and statuses. Prejudices and stereotypes are learned, altered, and adjusted through the socialization process. Social learning theory explains that we learn prejudices through the reinforcement of behavior and the imitation of others. The symbolic interaction approach centers on the process of negotiating and constructing meaning. This is accomplished by interacting with and responding to others. According to this perspective, prejudices are not produced by personal characteristic, but emerge from interactions and vary with the situational context. The social cognition and social perception perspectives explain how prejudices enter the processes of categorizing people, behaviors, and events and the inferences we make from our social experiences.

In recent decades, social psychologists have documented changes in how people perceive and express prejudices. Old-fashioned, overt expressions of prejudices have declined. Contemporary prejudices are hidden beneath a veneer of values and symbols. The suppression of overt prejudice has been so effective that people genuinely believe that they hold no prejudices. However, researchers exploring the modern and symbolic prejudices agree that prejudices still affect our attitudes and behaviors. The aversive and ambivalent perspectives identify value conflict as the definitive difference marking contemporary prejudices. Despite its covert nature, contemporary prejudice remains a part of how we understand others and how we make sense of social interaction.

Key Terms

- Ambivalence amplification
- Ambivalent prejudice
- Ambivalent sexism
- Attribution errors
- Attribution theory
- Automatic processing
- Aversive prejudice
- Benevolent sexism
- Controlled processing
- Definition of the situation
- Direct learning
- Dominative prejudice

- Explicit stereotypes
- External attributions
- Fundamental attribution error
- Generalized other
- Hostile sexism
- Implicit stereotypes
- Indirect observational learning
- Internal attributions
- Meaning is in response
- Modern prejudice

- Old-fashioned prejudice
- Psychological perspectives
- Schemas
- Self-serving attributions
- Significant other
- Social cognition theories
- Socialization
- Social learning theory
- Symbolic interaction
- Symbolic prejudice
- Talking past
- Ultimate attribution error

Taking It Further — Class Exercises and Interesting Web Sites

Modern versus Old-Fashioned Prejudice
When asked about their prejudices, most Americans say they harbor no prejudices toward any group. In this exercise, students will examine their own prejudices by talking about other commonly held American values. Students will assemble in small groups to discuss how prejudices are infused with other values.

Group 1: Class and racial prejudices
This group will discuss their beliefs about meritocracy and the work ethic. Do they believe that people who work hard, are talented, and are intelligent rise to the top positions in school and at work? What does this imply about people who drop out of school or have low-level or no jobs? How might class and race prejudices be related to our beliefs about meritocracy and hard work?

Group 2: Heterosexism and sexism
This group will consider attitudes about gender roles and their reactions toward transgendered and transsexual people. First, this group should discuss some of the ways their behavior is gendered. They might start with the way they dress and groom themselves. They might consider what domestic chores they are most comfortable with and whether those preferences are gendered. After discussing their own

experiences, they should consider how they feel when people violate their gender expectations. For example, does it make them uncomfortable when they see someone cross-dressing? Is this more disturbing when it is a male or a female cross-dresser? How would they react to a women head coach of the men's basketball or football team at their college or university? What reaction would they have to a man teaching home economics in high school? The group should consider their attitudes toward transgendered or transsexual people. In what ways do you think a transgender or transsexual person experiences gender differently? Finally, how do our attitudes about transsexuals fit with our beliefs about gender?

References

Bakanic, Von. 1995. I'm not prejudiced, but . . . a deeper look at racial attitudes. *Sociological Inquiry* 65: 67–86.

Blair, Irene, V., Charles M. Judd, Melody S. Sadler, and Christopher Jenkins. 2002. The role of Afro-centric features in person perception: Judging by features and categories. *Journal of Personality and Social Psychology* 83: 5–25.

Blauner, Bob. 1989. *Black lives, white lives: Three decades of race relations in America.* Berkeley, CA: University of California Press.

———. 1993. Language of race: Talking past one another. *Current* 349: 4–10.

———. 2001. *Still big news: Racial oppression in America.* Philadelphia: Temple University Press.

Borgida, Eugene, and Emily N. Stark. 2004. New media and politics: Some insights from social and political psychology. *American Behavioral Scientist* 48 (4): 467–478.

Bandura, Alfred, and R. H. Walters. 1963. *Social learning and personality development.* New York: Holt Rinehart and Winston.

Broder, Arndt. 2000. Assessing the empirical validity of the "take-the-best" heuristic as a model of human probabilistic inference. *Journal of Experimental Psychology: Learning Memory and Cognition* 26: 1332–1346.

Coreno, Thaddeus. 2002. Anger and hate groups: The importance of structural inequality for the sociology of emotions and social movement research. *Free Inquiry in Creative Sociology* 30: 67–81.

Czerlinski, J., G. Gigerenzer, and D. G. Goldstein. 1999. Accuracy and frugality in a tour of environments. In *Simple heuristics that make us smart,* ed. G. Gigerenzer, P. M. Todd, and the ABC Research Group, 59–72. New York: Oxford University Press.

Devine, Patricia. 1989. Stereotypes and prejudice: Their automatic and controlled components. *Journal of Personality & Social Psychology* 56 (1): 5–18.

Devine, Patricia. 2001. Implicit prejudice and stereotyping: How automatic are they? *Journal of Personality and Social Psychology* 81 (5): 757–759.

Devine, Patricia, M. J. Monteith, J. R. Zuwerink, and A. J. Elliot. 1991. Prejudice without compunction. *Journal of Personality and Social Psychology* 60: 817–830.

Devine, Patricia, E. A. Plant, D. M. Amodia, E. Harmon-Jones, S. L. Vance. 2002. The regulation of explicit and implicit race bias: The role of motivations to respond without prejudice. *Journal of Personality & Social Psychology* 82: 835–848.

Dovidio, John F., and Samuel L. Gaertner. 1991. Changes in the expression of racial prejudice. In *Opening doors: An appraisal of race relations in contemporary America,* ed. H. Knopke and R. Rogers. Tuscaloosa, AL: University of Alabama Press.

Dovidio, John F., and Samuel L. Gaertner. 2000. Aversive racism and selection decisions: 1989 and 1999. *Psychological Science* 11 (4): 315–319.

Dovidio, John F., Kerry Kawakami, C. Johnson, B. Johnson, and A. Howard. 1997. On the nature of prejudice: Automatic and controlled processes. *Journal of Experimental Social Psychology* 33: 510–540.

Dovidio, John F., Samuel L. Gaertner, Kerry Kawakami, and Gordon Hodson. 2002. Why can't we just get along? Interpersonal biases and interracial distrust. *Cultural Diversity and Ethnic Minority Psychology* 8 (2): 88–102.

Duffy, Margaret. 2003. Web of hate: A fantasy theme analysis of the rhetorical vision of hate groups online. *Journal of Communication Inquiry* 27 (3): 291–312.

Fazio, R. H., J. R. Jackson, B. C. Dunton, and C. J. Williams. 1995. Variability is automatic activation as an unobtrusive measure of racial attitudes: A bona fide pipeline? *Journal of Personality & Social Psychology* 69 (6): 1013–1027.

Freeman, Jo. 1976. *The politics of women's liberation.* New York: David McKay Company.

———. 2000. *A room at a time: How women entered party politics.* Lanham, MD: Rowman & Littlefield, c.2000.

Gaertner, Samuel L. and John F. Dovidio. 1977. The subtlety of White racism, arousal, and helping behavior. *Journal of Personality and Social Psychology* 35 (10): 691–707.

Gaertner, Samuel L. and John F. Dovidio. 1986. The aversive form of racism. In *Prejudice discrimination and racism,* ed. J. Dovidio and S. Gaertner. New York: Academic Press.

Glick, Peter, and Susan Fiske. 1996. The ambivalent sexism inventory: Differentiating hostile and benevolent sexism. *Journal of Personality and Social Psychology* 70 (3), March 1996: 491–512.

———, 2001. An ambivalent alliance: Hostile and benevolent sexism as complementary justifications for gender inequality. *American Psychologist* 56: 109–118.

Greenwald, Anthony G., Mahzarin R. Banaji, Laurie Rudman, Shelly Farnham, Brian Nosek, and Deborah Mellott. 2002. A unified theory of implicit attitudes, stereotypes and self concept. *Psychological Review* 109 (1): 3–25.

Greenwald, Anthony G., Brian Nosek, Mahzarin R. Banaji, and Christopher, Klauer. 2005. Validity of the salience asymmetry interpretation of the implicit association test: Comment on Rothermund and Wentura (2004). *Journal of Experimental Psychology: General* 134 (3): 420–425.

Greenwald, Anthony G., D. McGhee, and J. Schwartz. 1998. Measuring individual differences in implicit cognition: The implicit association test. *Journal of Personality and Social Psychology* 74: 1464–1480.

Heider, Fritz. 1958. *The psychology of interpersonal relations.* New York: Wiley.

Henry, Paul J., and David O. Sears. 2002. The symbolic racism 2000 scale. *Political Psychology* 23 (2): 253–283.

Hodson, Gregory, John Dividio, and Samuel L. Gaertner. 2002. Processes in racial discrimination: Differential weighting of conflicting information. *Personality and Social Psychology Bulletin* 28: 460–471.

Johnson, M. K., S. Hashtroudi, and D. S. Lindsay. 1993. Source monitoring. *Psychological Bulletin* 114: 3–28.

Katz, Irwin. 1981. *Stigma: A social psychological analysis.* Hillsdale, NJ: L. Erlbaum Associates.

Katz, Irwin., and R. Glen Hass. 1988. Racial ambivalence and American value conflict: Correlational and priming studies of dual cognitive structures. *Journal of Personality and Social Psychology* 55 (6): 893–905.

Katz, Irwin., and Joyce Wackenhut. 1986. Racial ambivalence, value duality and behavior. In *Prejudice, discrimination and Racism,* ed. J. Dividio and S. Gaertner. New York: Academic Press.

Kelly, Harold. 1967. Attribution theory in social psychology. Nebraska Symposium on Motivation Vol. 15: 192–238. Lincoln, NE: University of Nebraska Press.

———. 1972. Attribution theory in social interaction. In *Attribution perceiving the causes of behavior,* ed. Jones, Kanouse, Kelly, Nisbet, Valins & Weiner. Morristown, NJ: General Learning Press.

———. 1973. The process of causal attribution. *American Psychologist* 28: 107–128.

Kinder, Donald R., and Tali Mendelberg. 1995. Cracks in American apartheid: The political impact of prejudice among desegregated Whites. *Journal of Politics* 57 (2): 402–424.

Kinder, Donald R., and Lynn M. Sanders. 1990. Mimicking political debate with survey questions: The case of white opinion on affirmative action for blacks. *Social Cognition* 8 (1): 73–103.

Kinder, Donald R., and Lynn M. Sanders. 1996. *Divided by color: Racial politics and democratic ideals.* Chicago, IL: University of Chicago Press.

Kinder, Donald R., and O. David Sears. 1981. Prejudice and politics: Symbolic racism versus racial threats to the good life. *Journal of Personality and Social Psychology* 40: 414–431.

Kutner, B., C. Wilkins, and P. R. Yarrow. 1952. Verbal attitudes and overt behavior involving racial prejudice. *Journal of Abnormal and Social Psychology* 47: 649–652.

LaPiere, Richard T. 1934. Attitudes vs. behavior. *Social Forces* 13: 230–237.

Lindesmith, Alfred, Anselm L. Strauss, and Norman K. Denzin. 1999. *Social Psychology* (8th ed.). Thousand Oaks, CA: Sage Publications.

McClelland, A. G. R. and Bolger, F. 1994. The calibration of subjective probability: Theories and models 1980–94. In *Subjective probability,* ed. G. Wright and P. Ayton, 453–482. Chichester: Wiley.

McConahay, John B. 1983. Modern racism and modern discrimination: The effects of race, racial attitudes, and context on simulated hiring decisions. *Personality and Social Psychology Bulletin* 9 (4): 551–558.

McConahay, John B. 1986. Modern racism, ambivalence and the modern racism scale. In *Prejudice, discrimination and racism,* ed. Dovidio and Gaertner. New York: Academic Press.

McConahay, John B., and Joseph C. Hough. 1976. Symbolic racism. *Journal of Social Issues* 32 (2): 23–45.

Mead, George H. 1965. *Mind, self, and society: From the standpoint of a social behaviorist.* Chicago, IL: University of Chicago Press.

Minard, R.B. 1952. Race relations in the Pocohontas coal field. *Journal of Social Issues* 8: 29–44.

Mohipp, Charmaine, and Marian M. Morry. 2004. The relationship of symbolic beliefs and prior contact to heterosexuals' attitudes toward gay men and lesbian women. *Canadian Journal of Behavioral Science* 36 (1): 36–44.

Nosek, Brian A., Anthony G. Greenwald, and Mahzarin R. Banaji. 2005. Understanding and using the implicit association test: II. Method variables and construct validity. *Personality and Social Psychology Bulletin* 31 (2): 166–180.

Ottaway, Scott, Davis C. Hayden, and Mark A. Oakes. 2001. Implicit attitudes and racism: Effects of familiarity and frequency in the implicit association test. *Social Cognition* 19 (2): 97–144.

Peterson, Jesse Lee. 2000. *From rage to responsibility.* St. Paul, MN: Paragon House.

Pettigrew, Thomas F. 1979. The ultimate attribution error: Extending Allport's

cognitive analysis of prejudice. *Personality and Social Psychology Bulletin* 5: 461–476.

Pezdek, Kathy, Tony Whetstone, Kirk Reynolds, Nusha Askari, and Thomas Dougherty. 1989. The memory for real-world scenes: The role of consistency with schema expectations. *Journal of Experimental Psychology: Learning, Memory and Cognition* 15: 587–595.

Pronin, Emily, D. Y. Lin, and Lee Ross. 2002. The bias blind spot: Perception of bias in self versus others. *Personality and Social Psychology Bulletin* 28: 369–381.

Ross, Lee. 1977. The intuitive psychologist and his short comings: Distortions in the attribution process. In *Advances in experimental social psychology,* ed. L. Berkowitz, Vol. 10: 173–220, Orlando, FL: Academic Press.

Rothermund, Klaus, and Dirk Wentura. 2004. Underlying processes in the implicit association test: Dissociating salience from associations. *Journal of Experimental Psychology: General* 133 (2): 139–165.

Rudman, Laurie A., and S. E. Kilianski. 2000. Implicit and explicit attitudes toward female authority. *Personality and Social psychology Bulletin* 26: 1315–1328.

Saenger G., and C. Gilbert. 1950. Customer reactions to the integration of Negro sales personnel. *International Journal of Opinion and Attitude Research* 4: 57–76.

Schlafly, Phyllis. 2002. United Nations treaty on women. *Eagle Forum,* May 22. http://www.eagleforum.org/column/2002/may02/02_05_22.shtml.

Schlafly, Phyllis. 2003. *Feminist fantasies: Essays on feminism in the media, the workplace, the home, and the military.* Dallas, TX: Spense Publishing.

Schuman, Howard, Charlotte Steeh, and Lawrence Bobo. 1985. *Racial attitudes in America: Trends and interpretations.* Cambridge, MA: Harvard University Press.

Sears, David O. 1988. Symbolic racism. In *Eliminating racism: Profiles in controversy,* ed. Katz and Taylor. New York: Plenum Press.

Sears, David O., and P.J. Henry. 2003. The origins of symbolic racism. *Source Journal of Personality and Social Psychology* 85 (2): 259–275.

Sears, David O., Colette Van Laar, Mary Carrillo, and Rick Kosterman. 1997. Is it really racism?

The origins of White Americans' opposition to race-targeted policies. *The Public Opinion Quarterly* 61 (1): 16–53.

Sia, Tiffany L., Charles G. Lord, Kenneth A. Blessum, Jennifer C. Thomas, and Mark R. Lepper. 1999. Activation of exemplars in the process of assessing social category attitudes. *Journal of Personality and Social Psychology* 76 (4): 517–532.

Steffens, Melanie C., and Axel Buchner. 2003. Implicit associations test: Separating trans situationally stable and variable components of attitudes toward gay men. *Experimental Psychology* 50 (1): 33–48.

Swim, Janet, Kathryn Aikin, Wayne Hall, and Barbara Hunter. 1995. Sexism and racism: Old-fashioned and modern prejudices. *Journal of Personality and Social Psychology* 68 (2): 199–214.

Taylor, Shelley E., Letatia Anne Peplau, and David O. Sears. 2006. *Social psychology* (12th ed.). Upper Saddle River, NJ: Pearson Prentice Hall.

Tuckey, Michelle Rae, and Neil Brewer. 2003. The influence of schemas, stimulus ambiguity, and interview schedule on eyewitness memory over time. *Journal of Experimental Psychology: Applied* 9 (2), June 2003: 101–118.

CHAPTER

9

Reducing Prejudice

This chapter begins by considering whether prejudice can or should be eliminated. Strategies for prejudice reduction will be explored at the micro, mezzo, and macro-levels and the plausibility of such strategies will be critically examined. Students will explore changes induced by education, pressures for social conformity, and legislative solutions The chapter also explores what happens to subverted prejudice. When prejudice is hidden, denied, or ignored, there are still consequences for both individuals and the entire society.

In Chapter 8, I told a story about my young friend Jon who used the word "gay" to describe a classmate. Let's consider what Jon learned about antigay prejudice from that interaction. In addition to learning that the term had another meaning, he learned a lot from the reactions of his teacher, the principal, and his mother. Let's assume that the teacher was trying to suppress prejudice against homosexuals by her reaction. Did punishing Jon for using the word "gay" accomplish that? I am sure Jon will think twice before he uses the word again, but does that mean the prejudice has been reduced? One could argue that reactions of the adults taught Jon the very prejudice they sought to suppress. Simply teaching people that expressing prejudice is socially incorrect is not the same as reducing or eliminating prejudice. As we learned in Chapter 8, modern prejudices have become subtle and covert. So in this climate of denial, how do we reduce prejudice?

IS PREJUDICE DECLINING?

According to survey researchers, the vast majority of Americans claim they are not prejudiced (Schuman et al. 1997). Levels of self-reported prejudices have been declining steadily since the 1940s. Yet hate crimes are up and small towns are passing laws targeting employers, businesses, and landlords who provide jobs, services, and housing to illegal Latino immigrants. (Box 9-1) Are prejudices in the United States declining? There is no simple or clear answer to this question. Certainly, when one looks at the trends recorded by survey research, people are less likely to admit racial prejudices. So, on the surface, it appears that prejudice has declined. However, research measuring automatic biases indicates that many Americans are still affected by deeply ingrained preferences and prejudices. Several contemporary theories of race and gender prejudices contend that racism and sexism have not declined, as much as they have taken different forms (see Chapter 8). Today's prejudices are more often cloaked in values and disguised by political rhetoric. If old-fashioned prejudice may have been blatant and crude, contemporary prejudice is subtle, but no less demeaning and oppressive.

Regardless of whether prejudices are actually declining, there is broad consensus in contemporary American society that expressing racial prejudice is not socially acceptable. This is evidenced by the widespread denial of racial prejudices (Schuman et al. 1997). Almost no one admits to holding racial prejudices. Although gender prejudices and homophobic prejudices are less likely to be denied, people in our culture are becoming increasingly sensitized to the negative impressions they generate (cf. Herek 2000, 2005). Between 1970 and 2000 there was a slow but steady decline in old-fashioned antigay prejudices (Sherrill and Yang 2000). However, the recent trend is inconsistent (Herek 2002) and seems to have reversed (Brewer 2003). Only class prejudices still fall outside of the scope of social and political correctness. Because social class and economic inequality are legitimate in a capitalist economy, people are not protected from discrimination based on social class. Thus, prejudices based on class are at least less objectionable, if not completely acceptable.

BOX 9-1

Hazelton, Pennsylvania

In July 2006 Hazelton, Pennsylvania, passed an ordinance aimed at making it a difficult place for illegal immigrants to live and work. The Illegal Immigration Relief Act (IIRA) says that a landlord can be penalized for renting to an illegal immigrant and that businesses will be fined for hiring one. The American Civil Liberties Union and the Puerto Rican Legal Defense and Education Fund challenged the constitutionality of the law on behalf of Hazelton business owners, landlords, Latino groups, and four anonymous plaintiffs. Is the law blatant discrimination against Latinos or local enforcement of immigration law? Mayor Louis J. Barletta insists that he is protecting the legal taxpayer. According to Mayor Barletta, race has nothing to do with his policy, he simply wants to "get rid of the illegal people" (*Washington Post,* August 22, 2006).

Despite the widespread denial of prejudiced attitudes, there is plenty of behavioral evidence to the contrary. If one looks at hate crime as an indication of prejudice-induced violence, prejudice would be on the rise. According to the U.S. Bureau of Justice (Harlow 2005:1) a yearly average of 210,000 hate crimes were reported between July 2000 and December 2003. During that period racial hate crimes were most frequently reported (55 percent) followed by ethnic hate crimes (29 percent). According to the FBI an analysis of the 7,160 single-bias incidents reported in 2005 revealed that "54.7 percent were motivated by a racial bias, 17.1 percent were triggered by a religious bias, 14.2 percent were motivated by a sexual-orientation bias, and 13.2 percent of the incidents were motivated by an ethnicity/national origin bias. Nearly 1 percent (0.7) involved bias against a disability" (Federal Bureau of Investigation 2005). According to the Council on American Islamic Relations (CAIR 2005), anti-Muslim hate crimes rose by more than 50 percent between 2003 and 2004. The Anti-Defamation League (ADL) reported that there was a 17 percent increase in anti-Semitic incidents from 2003 to 2004.

Hate crime based on homophobia and misogyny is more difficult to measure. Victims of hate crimes based on sexual orientation may avoid reporting that they have been victimized because of the stigma attached to homosexuality. Even so, hate crimes based on sexual orientation accounted for 18 percent of the hate crimes reported between 2000 and 2003 (Harlow 2005:1). Although the Hate Crime Statistics Act of 1990 did not initially include gender as a reporting category, a 2004 amendment attempted to add gender to the list of groups to be tracked. Data on hate crime toward women is difficult to distinguish because of the overwhelming number of crimes against women that involve domestic violence. Imagine the task of trying to separate crimes induced by hatred toward women from those caused by domestic disputes!

Of course, the problem of segregating the various crimes comprising hate crime has been difficult because of the difficulty involved in determining the motivation of the crime. The National Crime Victim Survey (NCVS) requires corroborating evidence of hate motivation. In the NCVS research, the criteria for hate crime include hate expressed through words and symbols that are used by the offenders during and immediately after the commission of the crime. Using this criterion, NCVS reports an annual average of 210,430 victims of hate crime, of which 91,630 reported the incident to law enforcement (Harlow 2005:2).

If we look at the history of social relations between people in different groups and categories, we see that from the earliest period of U.S. history people have employed prejudices to justify social inequality (Erikson 1966; Segal and Stineback 1977). Very recently, social norms emerged prohibiting the expression of certain prejudices. This has made people censor and deny their prejudices. Unfortunately, this denial makes determining the actual reduction of prejudices and the problems prejudices cause more, rather than less, difficult. Prejudices wax and wane according to the history of intergroup relations. Prejudice between Puritans and Quakers that characterized our early history is no longer a social problem. However, new prejudices have emerged. Since 2001 there has been a rapid increase in hate crimes against people who are or who are perceived to be Arab, Muslim, or Middle Eastern. Anti-Hispanic and anti-Latino prejudices are also increasing as immigrants spread from border states into the interior of the United States. There is also evidence of a resurgence of prejudice based on sexual orientation, fueled by gains in civil rights activity by the gay rights movement (McMahon et al. 2004; Wilkerson and Roys 2005).

In this last chapter, we will consider strategies to reduce prejudices and some solutions to the problems caused by prejudices. Theories about what causes prejudice are based on three levels: micro, mezzo, and macro. So, we will consider prejudice reduction strategies on each of these three levels. First, we will examine micro, or individual, level strategies. These tactics emphasize individual motivation to control or suppress stereotypical thinking and prejudiced attitudes. Next, we will explore group-based interventions. Contact theory is the primary theory behind most of the interventions that have been attempted at this level. Finally, we will address macro-level solutions. Macro strategies are based on the premise that prejudice cannot be eliminated as long as the social structures they justify persist. In other words, as long as our social institutions and policies promote racial, ethnic, sexual, and class inequality, prejudices will continue to flourish.

MICRO-LEVEL STRATEGIES

Micro-level strategies focus on how individual thoughts, values, personality attributes, and interactional constraints make people more or less liable to express prejudice. Because micro-level theories contend that prejudices are ingrained and embedded in individuals, intervention strategies must also center on individuals and the interaction between individuals. In this section, we will explore three strategies geared toward individual intervention and self-control: suppression, self-regulation, and interactional strategies.

Suppression

Have you ever had one of those nights when you simply could not sleep because you were worried or anxious? No matter how many times you told yourself to quit thinking about it, you simply could not shut out the unwanted thoughts. Unfortunately, the harder one tries to control one's thoughts, the more the unwanted thoughts consume consciousness. In Chapter 4, we learned that attempts to suppress thoughts can result in a **rebound effect** (Wegner et al. 1987; Wegner 1994). This rebound effect results from two processes. The first is a self-monitoring process. Imagine that you have a midterm examination tomorrow morning for which you are not prepared. It's too late to begin studying now and you have decided that getting a good night's sleep is your best strategy. You give yourself the instruction to forget about the midterm and go to sleep. Unfortunately, having given yourself the instruction, your mind scans for the unwanted thought. Ironically, giving yourself the instruction to forget the exam guarantees that the exam will continue to occupy your thoughts. Now, the second part of the process begins: you try to distract yourself from your pretest anxiety by distracting yourself with less-vexing thoughts. You decide to think about something pleasant, like the spring break trip you are planning. But, these happier distracting thoughts aren't effective because you are still monitoring for unwanted thoughts about the impending exam. This keeps the unwanted thought in your mind, so that it is repeatedly recalled. Paradoxically, the harder you try to forget your upcoming exam, the more you think about it.

The rebound effect makes it difficult to simply tell yourself not to be prejudiced. However, several researchers have found that suppression can succeed provided a person is highly motivated (Monteith, Spicer, and Tooman 1998). People who hold strong personal beliefs that prejudice and stereotyping are wrong are more successful at suppressing stereotypes and avoiding rebound. Monteith and Voils (1998) found that in addition to motivation, distraction plays a role in successful suppression. In a series of three studies, they examined the relationship between prejudice, discrepancy in values, and response to derogatory racial jokes. In the first two studies, they found that when respondents had a discrepancy between their values (what one should do) and their behavior (what one would do), they were more likely to express general discomfort with self-consciousness, social anxiety, and social desirability. In the third stage of their study, the researchers examined whether discrepancies between what they should do and what they thought they would do had any effect on their responses to racial jokes. Respondents who held low-prejudiced responses toward blacks were compared with respondents holding high-prejudiced responses toward blacks. Participants were led to believe that they were participating in a study about humor. They were then exposed to jokes that made fun of blacks. Participants rated the jokes on a "HA-HA meter." The meter ranged from "Boo" (the participants did not like the joke at all) to 7 "HAs" (they found the joke extremely funny). To measure distraction, participants were assigned to high and low cognitive load conditions. In between listening and responding to jokes, participants were shown eighteen objects on a monitor. Those in the high cognitive load condition were asked to count the number of pairs of objects on the screen and to find the object that appeared four times and remember both the object and the total number of pairs. Those in the low cognitive load condition were asked to find the object that appeared four times on the screen and remember that object. High-prejudice participants evaluated the racial jokes more positively. In addition, it was found that neither the high nor low cognitive condition affected how funny they found the jokes. However, the low-prejudice participants were more likely to rate the jokes favorably if they were in the high distraction condition and had a high discrepancy between what they should and would do. The distraction manipulation did not affect those with both low discrepancy scores and low prejudice. This means that if the commitment to low prejudice is strong and consistent, people can successfully suppress prejudiced reactions even under highly distracting conditions (Monteith and Voils 1998:914). So although suppression is difficult and rebound likely, there is some evidence that suppression is effective for highly motivated individuals. Not only does this give hope to highly motivated, low-prejudiced people, it also suggests that the presence of strong social norms against the expression of prejudices may actually foster real, albeit long-term, reduction of prejudices.

Self-Regulation

The research concerning suppression resulted from experiments in which participants were given the instruction to suppress stereotypes and prejudices. The self-regulation strategy relies on the internal motivation of individuals both to be aware of and to regulate their own prejudiced responses. In other words, they must give themselves the instruction to recognize and reduce or eliminate their prejudices. However, the temptation to use prejudices and stereotypes is often overwhelming because prejudices are easily accessible and provide cognitive shortcuts.

One potential motivator to induce self-regulation is guilt. The use of guilt to reduce prejudice was first used by Gordon Allport (1945). Allport noted that negative reactions among participants in an eight-hour minicourse on race relations used hostility toward the instructor as a way of protecting their own racial status and projecting guilt about the advantages of race. He suggested using guilt as a method for inducing insight among students for race relations. The idea of using guilt re-surfaced nearly half a century later in the work of Patricia Devine and her colleagues (1991). In studies concerning attitudes toward blacks and gay men, feeling of discomfort, guilt, and self-criticism were induced in research participants. Participants with higher levels of prejudice experienced only discomfort, whereas low- and moderately prejudiced subjects experienced guilt and self-criticism. As we found earlier when reviewing research on suppression, self-regulation seems to be more effective for people who are low prejudiced and already motivated to reduce prejudices.

Leanne Son Hing (2002) looked at ways that inducing feelings of hypocrisy might be used to reduce prejudices among more-prejudiced respondents. She found that aversive racists (i.e., subjects who were low in explicit prejudices, but scored high in implicit prejudices) responded to a hypocrisy-induction procedure with a reduction of prejudicial behavior. She suggests that consciousness-raising might motivate aversive racists to self-regulate their prejudiced responses. In other words, if people are made aware of their prejudices and the inconsistency between their other values and prejudice, they become motivated to reduce or suppress their prejudice.

The research concerning self-regulation confirms that this strategy is effective in low- to moderately prejudiced subjects who are motivated to reduce prejudices. However, there is little evidence to date that inducing either guilt or hypocrisy has any effect on highly prejudiced individuals. Monteith and Walters (1998a,b) suggest that highly prejudiced individuals who hold egalitarian ideals might be induced to reduce prejudice in an attempt to decrease cognitive dissonance. That is, it may be possible to motive people to reduce prejudices if it can be demonstrated to them that their prejudices are at odds with their egalitarian values. As with any problem, getting people motivated to solve the problem is the first and most difficult step.

Interactional Strategies

Symbolic interactionists explain how prejudices affect both our reaction and other people's reaction to stigmatized identities. You may remember from Chapter 3 that *stigma* is a deeply discrediting social identity (Goffman 1963:3). Any person or group that possesses characteristics that are devalued can become stigmatized. People possessing stigmatized traits are identified primarily by the stigmatized trait even if the trait or behavior is no longer in evidence. For example, an alcoholic retains the label even if he or she has not had a drink in years. Stigmatized people are treated differently, but ironically it is the reactions of others, rather than the stigmatized attribute, that create the problem.

Roschelle and Kaufman (2004) argue that stigma management strategies are used by stigmatized individuals to decrease discrimination and to protect their sense of self. They observed homeless children during a four-year ethnographic study and identified two varieties of stigma-reduction strategies: strategies of inclusion and strategies of exclusion. Strategies of inclusions are defensive tactics and include passing, covering, and forging friendships. Passing and covering are both attempts to conceal the stigmatizing trait. Forging friendships is a strategy that uses alliances with others to mitigate the full effect of the stigmatized identity. Strategies of exclusion are offensive tactics that include verbal denigration and posturing. Rather than waiting for nonstigmatized individuals to exclude or rebuke them, homeless children used aggressive tactics to discourage others from targeting them.

One major difference between stigma management and the other micro-level strategies we have discussed is that stigma management is addressed to the targets of prejudice. Both suppression and self-regulation focus on the prejudiced person rather than the target. One advantage of the stigma management approach is that it empowers the victims of prejudice. Rather than being the passive recipients of negative attitudes and discriminatory behavior, people can employ stigma management strategies to mitigate and reduce the negative effects of prejudice.

The three micro-level strategies presented in this section depend on individuals who are motivated to control or change their own thoughts and reactions. Suppression requires individuals not only to constantly monitor for stereotypes and prejudiced thoughts, but also to recognize and resist the rebound effect. Self-regulation strategy also depends on individuals monitoring for and suppressing prejudices and stereotypes. In addition, it relies on individuals to motivate themselves to maintain their own cognitive vigil against prejudice.

There is some evidence that highly motivated individuals can reduce their levels of prejudice and use of stereotypes, but thus far there is little evidence to suggest that highly prejudiced individuals can be motivated to undertake such relentless activity. Stigma management differs from the other two strategies in that it focuses on the targets of prejudice rather than the perpetrators. One advantage of this approach is that it does not rely on altruistic motivations. The targets of prejudice have a self-serving interest in avoiding stigma. However, stigma management tactics have consequences for self-esteem and intergroup relations. It is possible that attempts to avoid stigma can be as disruptive as the prejudices themselves. In the next section, we shall address strategies that manipulate contact between groups and intergroup relations as a method of prejudice reduction.

MEZZO-LEVEL STRATEGIES—GROUP INTERVENTION

Contact Theory

In Chapter 3, we noted that when people become friends they cease to be representatives of groups. We see our friends as individuals with unique characteristics. Contact theory contends that physical and social separation, which reduces contact between groups, promotes ignorance. Ignorance increases reliance on stereotypes, negative beliefs, and hostility between groups. Thus, increasing intergroup contact works to decrease reliance on stereotypes, reduce prejudices against other groups, and reduce hostility between groups.

We also learned in Chapter 3 that contact must occur under very specific conditions to result in a decrease in prejudice and an improvement in intergroup relations. If not, contact can lead to greater, rather than less, intergroup hostility. Five conditions must be met for contact to reduce intergroup prejudices. First, contact must be sustained. Brief or sporadic contact has little or no effect on prejudice. Second, the contact must involve cooperation. Groups must rely on each other to accomplish their goals. Third, the contact must involve more than casual acquaintance. In other words, there must be more than superficial interaction for meaningful improvement in intergroup relations to occur. Fourth, the contact between groups should have the support of legitimate authority.

Finally, the setting in which the contact occurs should bestow equal status on both groups (Jackman and Crane 1986).

Probably the most widespread application of contact theory has been the attempted desegregation of the public school system in the United States. The U.S. Supreme Court ordered the desegregation of public school in its landmark verdict in the *Brown v. Board of Education of Topeka* (1954). In the more than fifty years since the verdict, there has been what amounts to a massive natural field experiment testing some of the major tenets of contact theory. After all this time, did school desegregation reduce prejudice? Unfortunately, because school desegregation was not a true experiment, it did not have carefully controlled conditions. Thus, the results are not conclusive. First, despite the Supreme Court ruling calling for desegregation to occur "with all deliberate speed" (1954), many schools and school districts remain segregated fifty years later. The federal government began the long process of implementing school desegregation in 1957 when President Eisenhower ordered federal troops to protect students at Central High School in Little Rock, Arkansas. In the same year nine of the seventeen states and the District of Columbia had begun integration of their school systems. Yet by end of the twentieth century 66 percent of African American public school students and 70 percent of Latino students attended predominately minority schools, whereas white students attend schools that have over 78 percent white students (cf. Orfield et al. 1997; Orfield and Yun 1999; Reardon and Yun 2001; Orfield and Lee 2004). Orfield and Yun (1999) argue that schools are actually in the process of resegregating, not only by race, but perhaps more importantly by socioeconomic class.

When desegregation has been implemented it has seldom met the conditions under which contact is hypothesized to improve intergroup relations. The first condition indicates that contact must be sustained, but even when schools have a diverse student body, students are segregated by ability, tracking within the school. (Conger 2005). Within school tracking is associated with race and socioeconomic status. Students tracked into different ability and vocational tracks have little contact with students outside of their track and thus outside of their race and class.

The second condition for successful intergroup contact is cooperation. Although some pedagogies used in public schools do encourage team work, the methods of instruction most often used in public schools encourage competition rather than cooperation. The third condition requires this interaction go beyond superficial acquaintance. Although some students make friends across race and class boundaries, segregation caused by academic tracking results in little opportunity for more than superficial contact between students in different tracks. Some research has suggested that extra curricular activities may provide opportunity for contact outside of the tracked curriculum. One study suggests that extra curricular activities are also segregated and can worsen race relations among high school student (Goldsmith 2004). Another study found that participation in integrated high school sports teams improved racial and ethnic relations (Chu and Griffey 1985).

The fourth condition for contact to reduce intergroup hostilities stipulates that contact must be sanctioned and supported by legitimate authority. In her study of workplace contact, Cynthia Estlund found that managerial authority helps facilitate intergroup interaction (2005). She contends that when people are compelled to get along by workplace structure and culture, racial integration works well. However, public schools have a different authority structure than work places. Unfortunately, school integration has often been opposed by members of the community and forced on reluctant school boards, administrators, and politicians. Finally, contact theory specifies that contact must take place under conditions in which the groups have equal social status. Even if all other conditions of contact theory had been satisfied, this last requirement cannot be met until social and economic inequality in the wider society is reduced.

Because public school integration has not conformed to conditions specified by contact theory, it has yielded inconsistent results (cf. Campbell 1977; Goldsmith 2004; Zirkel and Cantor 2004). Goldsmith (2004) found that segregated academic tracks, few minority teachers, less group work, and segregated extracurricular activities worsen racial relations among high school students. However, Zirkel and Cantor (2004) reviewed the effects of interracial and ethnic contact in education fifty years after *Brown v. the Board of Education.* They found that contact can lead to attitude and behavior change toward out-group members and improve developmental outcomes for all students. Campbell (1977) found that the inconsistent effects of school desegregation are due in part to a failure to appreciate the complexity of interracial contact. He identified three factors that mitigate the effects: family, peer group, and school environment. Campbell concluded that economic and social deprivation were better predictors of intergroup relations than contact.

Because school desegregation has never been implemented in ways consistent with contact theory, it should come as no surprise that school desegregation is associated with increases in prejudice more often than decreases (Stephan 1978). Although desegregation turned out to be a failed opportunity as a prejudice reduction strategy, there have been other smaller programs that have demonstrated more success. In the next section, we will examine less ambitious, but more controlled programs designed to utilize the principles of contact theory.

Cooperative Learning

Cooperative learning programs are classroom pedagogies designed to improve intergroup relations by requiring students to work together to achieve common goals. Elliot Aronson and his colleagues (Aronson et al. 1978; Aronson and Thibodeaux 1992) developed one such program called the *jigsaw method.* This exercise requires each student to contribute to the completion of the project. The instructor divides the class into six member groups. The lesson is also divided into six parts. Each student is given an opportunity to become an expert on one part of the lesson and teach that part of the lesson to the others in their group. Because no student is an "expert" in more than one part of the lesson, the students are dependent on each other to learn the material (Jones 1992:177). Not only does the academic performance of students improve with this method, the children also improve conflict management skills. Cooperative learning also increases friendship across racial and ethnic groups (Banks 1995) and improves the self-esteem of minority group children (Walker and Crogan 1998).

Other Group-Level Strategies

There are, of course, many other strategies employing intergroup contact. Walter and Cookie Stephan (2005) discuss several other strategies including multicultural education, diversity training, and intergroup dialogues. *Multicultural education* is an approach for transforming educational curriculum into one that addresses disadvantages and discriminatory practices in our system of education. It is based upon a value for social justice and education equity. Multicultural education bridges the gap between group-level strategies and macro-level, or structural, strategies. Ultimately those advocating multicultural education seek to use the educational system to transform society and eliminate racial and ethnic oppression and injustice.

Diversity training is a training provided by an organization, usually with the stated purpose of treating diversity as an opportunity and promoting the ability of students and workers from a great variety of backgrounds to cooperate productively and make as great a contribution as possible to organizational goals. Most employers and educators use one of three strategies to promote diversity: diversity training and feedback; designating organizational responsibility for diversity; and policies that aim to reduce the social isolation of minority employees (Kalev et al. 2006). In their analysis of federal data on private sector workplaces, Alexandra Kalev and her colleagues found that strategies using diversity training and feedback were the least effective at increasing the proportion of women and minorities in management. Policies that reduced social isolation through mentoring and networking produced some increases in diversity; however, designating organizational responsibility for diversity produced the highest increases in diversity.

Intergroup dialogues are programs that bring together small groups of students and work colleagues from diverse backgrounds to share stories about their life, education, and work-related experiences. The goal of intergroup dialogues is to promote social empathy. Biren and Zuniga (2003) studied the effectiveness of intergroup dialogues facilitated in face-to-face interactions among college students from diverse social backgrounds. The results of their study indicated that the programs were only effective for increasing the students' awareness of the importance and centrality of racial group membership. However, students who indicated that they valued the dialogue process also exhibited increases in how much they said they thought about racial group membership, their ability to take the perspective of other racial groups, their comfort communicating across groups, and their interest in bridging differences between groups.

Group-level interventions have a long tradition in the social psychology of prejudice. Gordon W. Allport's (1954) seminal work on prejudice included group-level strategies as the most promising area for reduction of prejudices. Although school desegregation was initially heralded as an unprecedented opportunity to reduce prejudices and intergroup bias, it proved a naïve assumption because the conditions whereby contact leads to improved intergroup relations were never met. Cooperative learning strategies have been effective, but on a much smaller scale. Other strategies designed for the classroom and the workplace also have the potential to decrease intergroup hostilities. If individuals are not personally motivated to decrease their prejudices, group-level strategies sponsored by workplaces, schools, communities, and religious organizations are promising avenues to collectively reduce prejudice and foster intergroup communication. In the next section, we will review macro-level strategies and consider how to bridge the gap between micro, mezzo and macro solutions.

MACRO-LEVEL STRATEGIES—STRUCTURAL CHANGES

Marco-level strategies are based upon the assumption that social values and attitudes, including prejudices, are used to justify and support the social order. Prejudices are embedded in a larger social, economic, and political hierarchy in which individuals and groups have unequal access to material resources, education, and political power. Sociologists call systemic inequality *social stratification.* Basically, stratification is layering of people and groups according to their access to scarce resources, status, and power. According to macro-perspectives, prejudices cannot be eliminated as long as social stratification and inequality provide the structure of social order. The United States has one of the most complex and dynamic stratification systems in the world. Because the social structure is dynamic, the targets of prejudice, the intensity of prejudices, and social tolerance for prejudice vary as the stratification system shifts and changes. The United States is an especially intriguing society in which to study prejudices because it has always been a nation of immigrants. As each wave of immigrants has been replace by even newer arrivals, the stratification system becomes more complex and multilayered. Thus, the prejudices that justify social stratification also become more complex and prolific.

Assimilation versus Multiculturalism

Two very different strategies for coping with minority groups have developed in response to the constantly changing demographics of the United States: assimilation and multiculturalism. *Assimilation* requires that newly arriving immigrants learn the language, norms, and customs of the host culture and eventually blending into and becoming indistinguishable from the dominant group. It is a process by which the various immigrating groups have, over the history of the United States, merged to create one society.

Assimilation occurs in two phases: acculturation and integration. *Acculturation* is a process by which a minority or immigrant group takes on the characteristics of the dominant group. This is sometimes voluntary and sometimes forced. The "melting pot" metaphor so often used to describe American culture casts assimilation as a voluntary process that includes sharing, inclusion, and the eventual amalgamation of immigrant group into the dominant group. However, assimilation is not always benign. First, not all assimilation is voluntary. Assimilation in the United States has often been coercive and one-sided (Healey 2006). The requirement that immigrants speak English to become U.S. citizens is an example of forced assimilation policy. Another, even more coercive, policy required the children of Native American Indians to attend federally financed and operated boarding schools, often hundreds of miles from their tribe and family. Children attending these schools were forbidden to speak their native languages or practice their religions.

Another way in which American assimilation departs from its benevolent "melting pot" image is the one-sided adoption of the dominant culture. Assimilation in the United States encourages *Anglo-conformity* or *Americanization.* Instead of blending components from the diverse immigrant cultures, newly arriving groups are pressed to adopt the English language, follow legal systems patterned after British law, and adopt an Anglo-American culture. Although some characteristics of the immigrant groups are absorbed into the dominant culture, as evidenced by the number of non-English words used in the American vocabulary, assimilation creates cultural homogeny by imposing the dominant culture upon immigrating groups.

Finally, not all groups—especially racial and gender groups—can fully assimilate. Because the characteristics that define some groups include physically distinctive traits, group members can never blend into patriarchal Anglo-American culture. Although there have been some sensational cases of racial minorities and women who have passed as whites and men, the overwhelming majority remain distinct and are never completely assimilated. (Box 9-2) Whereas many individuals and groups have eagerly adopted American culture, one consequence of assimilation has been the erosion and gradual loss of their cultural heritage.

The second stage of assimilation is *integration,* or structural assimilation. Structural assimilation occurs in two stages. The first stage is *primary structural integration,*

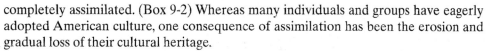

BOX 9-2

The Double Life of Billy Tipton

Imagine the coroner's surprise in 1989 when the cadaver he was doing a routine job with, jazz musician and entertainment agent Billy Tipton turned out to be a woman. So came down the curtain on a brilliant deception spanning over fifty years, when an aspiring young lady named Dorothy Tipton decided to remake herself over as a man and lived that way for the rest of her life.

At the age of nineteen in 1933, Dorothy (who had already taken to calling herself "Tippy" in high school) obtained legal documents listing her as a man and began dressing in traditional male clothes and calling herself "Billy." Friends knew this, and it was no big deal, even as Billy went on to marry the first of five wives. Playing in Jazz clubs throughout Kansas City and then other parts of the country, Tipton built a small name as an accomplished performer and writer. Several opportunities arose over her life to take the lead position in several clubs, but she turned them down, possibly to avoid publicity.

In fact, nearly all of Tipton's moves are fascinating in the pure mechanics of the fraud, with the different parts of her life clicking into place like an Agatha Christie mystery novel, all clear in retrospect. Her marriages were common law, her three sons adopted. Four of the five wives had no idea they'd married a woman; Billy claimed a medical condition required wearing a truss that concealed the truth from them. As time went on, this process must have gotten easier and easier, until it was effortless. After playing Jazz for nearly fifty years, Billy moved into agency, representing clients in Spokane, Washington, although the practice naturally declined as well.

This is not to say that Tipton's life was a complete and utter success; no life is. She ended every marriage she got into, had a habit of occasionally being absent as a father and spouse, and the necessary aspects of maintaining her male status made some parts of life very difficult indeed. Most problematic was her refusal to take Social Security or Medicare toward the end of her life, accelerating health problems more than they might otherwise have; and we can only imagine how many doctor's visits she avoided that might have made a cold or other illness less prolonged. Billy's need to avoid the spotlight means that ironically her place in Jazz, the very music she made all these difficult choices to be able to follow, was destined to be minor, at best.

But all told, this is less a "hoax" than someone who made a decision early on how they wanted to live and held to that choice for the rest of their life. The fact that it required a decades-long dance of carefully chosen words and subtle glances just makes it fascinating for the rest of us.

SOURCE: Soylent Communications/Rotten.com

which involves public integration in areas such as employment, education, and other public institutions. The second stage of integration is ***intimate integration.*** It includes private, personal, or emotionally close associations, such as friendship and intermarriage (Healey 2006:243–244.) The United States made great strides toward primary structural integration during the second half of the twentieth century. Civil rights legislation and judicial decisions opened most areas of public life to all people regardless of race, religion, national origin, or gender. Intimate integration has also increased, albeit more slowly. For example, over 70 percent of Americans claim to have good friends of another race (Thernstrom and Thernstrom 1997). Interracial, interethnic, and interfaith marriages are also increasing (Benokratis 2008).

Whereas assimilation promotes consensus and homogeneity, pluralist strategies encourage maintaining cultural distinctiveness and diversity. ***Multiculturalism*** is a version of cultural pluralism that encourages groups to maintain their distinctive identity and stresses respect and tolerance for other groups. ***Cultural pluralism*** occurs when a group has not fully acquired the language, norms, and values of the dominant culture. The group maintains its language, traditions, folkways, and values in cultural enclaves. ***Cultural enclaves*** are geographic regions or sections within cities where ethnic minorities form cultural communities. Although some groups maintain cultural pluralism by geographic isolation (e.g., tribal reservations, Amish communities), other groups maintain ethnic enclaves in the middle of cities (e.g., China town).

Structural pluralism occurs when a group has acculturated but not integrated into the dominant group. The group practices the same culture as the dominant group. Members speak the same language, internalize the same norms, and hold the same values and goals as the dominant culture. However, they do so in parallel, but separate institutions. The most obvious example of structural pluralism in the United States is our practice of religion. Churches are the most segregated institutions in America. Often African American, white, and Latino churches of the same denomination exist within very close geographic proximity. They say the same prayers, sing the same hymns, hold the same beliefs, and send representatives to the same governing bodies, but they attend different churches (Healey 2006:51).

The United States has implemented policies that encourage both assimilation and multiculturalism. The celebration of African American, women's, and Hispanic history months are clear examples of multiculturalism. On the other hand, recent attempts to enforce English-only instruction in states with large Latino populations are an assimilationist strategy. This inconsistency mirrors the debate over whether acculturation and integration should be a societal goal. Critics of pluralist strategies, such as multiculturalism, worry that cultural distinctiveness will prevent structural integration. Critics of assimilation lament the cultural loss that accompanies the disappearance of racial and ethnic boundaries. The goal of both strategies is to produce social harmony between groups in a heterogeneous society. Which strategy works best is not a simple question. It depends on the history of conflict and cooperation between groups, demographic changes caused by immigration patterns and birthrates, and the intensity of competition for scarce resources under current economic conditions.

Antidiscrimination Legislation

In Chapter 5, we considered several legislative solutions for public discrimination. The assumption underlying legislative strategies is that reducing—and, hopefully, eventually eliminating—discrimination will lead to a reduction in prejudice. Because attitudes have affective, behavioral, and cognitive dimensions, change in any one of the dimensions of prejudice produces the impetus for change in the others. Changing the law changes people's behavior; changing people's behavior changes their attitudes. Changes to the legal structure are used to change other aspects of the social structure that eventually changes the values and attitudes which justify and reinforce social order. Thus, although there may be initial resistance, the new norms created by antidiscrimination laws eventually reduce prejudice.

The civil rights movement of the mid-twentieth century revolutionized social justice and antidiscrimination legislation. Through a series of judicial verdicts and federal legislation, civil rights were greatly expanded. However, since the early 1980s there has been a reversal in the trend toward more civil liberties and protection from discrimination (Steinberg 1995). There have been setbacks in employment and education policies, gay rights, and civil liberties. Throughout the 1990s there were numerous attempts to curtail affirmative action and other antidiscrimination policies. Although the gay rights movements seemed to have some limited success in extending civil rights to nonheterosexuals in the early 1990s, reaction to gay marriage has resulted in even more restrictive legislation. The Patriot Act of 2002 has limited civil liberties at an unprecedented level. It has had a negative impact on civil liberties issues ranging from racial profiling, religious liberty, freedom of speech, criminal defendants' rights, and equal opportunity in both education and employment. A number of social scientists, political analysts, and civil rights organizations have suggested that the Patriot Act is undermining the principles of democracy that have, for more than two centuries, expanded civil rights (cf. Etzioni 2004; Abele 2005; Van Bergen 2005). Contrary to the assumptions of many Americans, the current trend is to remove legal protection from discrimination. This bodes ill for reduction of prejudices in the future. Indeed, there have been recent increases in anti-immigrant prejudices (Wilson 2001), anti-Latino prejudice (Houvouras 2001), and anti-Arab prejudice (Johns et al. 2005).

CAN PREJUDICE BE ELIMINATED?

Throughout this text we have examined the ways prejudice manifests in our thoughts, our emotions, and our behaviors. It may seem that the cognitive processes, groups dynamics, and social forces that promote prejudices make it inevitable. Cognitively, we use prejudices to make decisions quickly and simply. At this level, prejudices and stereotypes are so deeply embedded in our cognitive schema that we are often unaware of either the process or the particular prejudices. At the group level, intergroup dynamics often exaggerate differences and increase conflict and animosity between groups. Finally, the racism, sexism, and classism embedded in our social structure perpetuate discrimination and the prejudices that emerge to justify social inequality. It would seem that at all three levels of prejudice are inevitable.

Before we end the discussion on eliminating prejudice, let's look at the other side of this picture. Although there are many psychological, group, and social forces that promote prejudice, there are also many strategies that can be used to reduce, or possibly even eradicate, it. Perhaps the most optimistic path toward nonprejudice is at the individual level. Earlier in this chapter, we learned that prejudices can be reduced at the individual level if people are motivated to do so. Although individual strategies work one person at a time, highly motivated individuals can reduce their prejudice, react to prejudice expressed by others, and promote nondiscriminatory policies. Working from the individual level, those committed to nonprejudiced attitudes can create widespread social change.

Mezzo-level strategies have also had some success at reducing prejudice. Several educational strategies have the potential to improve intergroup relations. Cooperative learning, multicultural education, and intergroup dialogues increase awareness of and empathy for people from other groups and cultural backgrounds. The hope is that as these strategies become embedded in school curriculum and workplace policies, reliance upon prejudices both inside and outside of these institutions will decrease. If schools and workplaces compel intergroup contact and cooperation, the barriers between groups may become less formidable in the wider society.

Macro-level change is difficult, but essential if prejudices are to be reduced. Sociologists contend that prejudices justify and support social inequality. As long as racism, sexism, and classism exist within the structure of society, there will be race, sex, and class prejudices. According to this perspective, any attempt to reduce prejudice without decreasing social inequality is at best temporary and ineffectual. It is rather like Sisyphus' task. Just as the mythic king was condemned to forever roll a giant bolder uphill only to watch it return to the bottom, without structural change individuals would have to be taught and motivated to suppress prejudices one individual at a time and one situation at a time. Even though changing the social structure seems overwhelming, we must remember that people create and re-create social order everyday through ongoing interactions between individuals. Macro-structures are ultimately human constructions, and we can and do alter them.

However, for every step forward, we seem to take a step backward. The inconsistent and sometimes contradictory policies of federal, state, and local governments toward our increasingly diverse population has stymied efforts to create a more equal and inclusive social structure. Forced assimilation co-resides with the celebration of multiculturalism. For example we celebrate Hispanic history month in schools that enforce English-only instruction policies. Antidiscrimination legislation achieved by the civil rights movement has yielded to charges of reverse discrimination and the dismantling of policies designed to reduce discrimination against women and minorities. There is increasing public and judicial support for color-blind policies that operate on the flawed assumption that failing to officially record and take race into account is the same thing as eliminating the effects of racism. Reaction to gains made by the gay rights movements has created a backlash of legislation prohibiting same-sex marriage. It is not coincidental that prejudice against homosexuals is increasing after over a decade of decline.

Part of the problem is that, both collectively and individually, we fail to see the bigger picture. Our strong value for individualism has led to a myopic view of social responsibility. We justify blaming the victims of social inequality under the banner of personal responsibility, while at the same time we attribute prejudices not to ourselves, but to some ill-defined group of anonymous bigots. If we do not stop denying that we have prejudices, we cannot hope to eliminate them. If we do not acknowledge that our social, legal, and economic systems are grossly unequal, we cannot hope to rid ourselves of the attitudes that justify and thereby perpetuate inequality.

Although it seems overwhelming, and perhaps unrealistic, to believe prejudices can be eradicated, it is well within our powers, both individually and collectively, to reduce both the quantity and impact of prejudice in our society and around the world. America has been called the sleeping giant. We have tremendous impact on cultures around the world through the diffusion of global capitalism. As our material culture spreads, so does our ideology. If that ideology uses prejudices to justify inequality and advantage, our prejudices will expand both within our culture and to other cultures. As long as individuals deny their prejudices and remain unaware of their advantages, it is unlikely that we as a culture will be motivated to make the structural and individual changes necessary to accomplish the goal of eliminating prejudice. Prejudice can be reduced, but only by individuals and societies motivated to do so.

Key Terms

- Acculturation
- Americanization
- Antidiscrimination Legislation
- Assimilation
- Cognitive suppression
- Cooperative learning
- Cultural enclaves

- Cultural pluralism
- Diversity training
- Integration
- Interactional strategies for reducing prejudice
- Intergroup dialogue
- Intimate integration
- Multicultural education

- Multiculturalism
- Primary structural integration
- Rebound effect
- School desegregation
- Self-regulation of prejudice
- Stigma
- Structural pluralism

Taking It Further — Class Exercises and Interesting Web Sites

Evaluating Racists Anonymous

Below is a 12-step program modeled on the Alcoholic Anonymous program. You know from reading Chapter 9 that it is possible for motivated individuals to suppress their prejudices, but that the total elimination of all prejudices is an unrealistic goal because people use prejudices in their cognitive processes and in everyday interaction. Have student assemble in small groups and consider the difficulties in following a 12-step program to reduce their prejudices toward a racial out-group.

A 12-Step Program for Racists in Recovery

1. We admit that we are negatively affected by our own racism and that of others, that our lives have been damaged by racism and that we have damaged the lives of others.
2. No one can overcome racism alone. It requires a *Higher Power*. That *Higher Power* can be a spiritual entity or it can be the power of collective cooperation. We believe that together with our *Higher Power* human beings can reduce and eliminate racism.
3. We make a commitment to become anti-racist and to turn our lives over to changing ourselves and our world one day at a time and one action at a time.
4. We make a searching, fearless, moral inventory of our racist beliefs and discriminatory actions.
5. We admit to ourselves and at least one other human being the exact nature of our racist wrongs.
6. We are ready to remove the defects of character which have caused and are caused by our racism.
7. We humbly seek to reduce and eliminate our own racism.
8. Each person will make a list of all persons and groups that we have harmed and commit to make amends to them all.
9. Each person will make direct amends to people we have harmed whenever possible, except when to do so would harm them or increase racism.
10. We will continue to monitor our thoughts, words and actions for racism and promptly admit to it.

11. We will seek through personal reflection and meditation to improve our conscious contact with fellow human beings and seek the knowledge, courage and stamina to work actively against racism.

12. Having had an awakening to the pain and suffering caused to the human race by racism we will carry this message to other racists, and practice these twelve principles in all our affairs.

Mapping Hate Groups at Tolerance.org

The Southern Poverty Law Center Web site includes a map of hate groups around the United States. Students can go to http://www.tolerance.org/maps/hate/index.html to find out how many hate groups are identified in their state.

Film Recommendations

The Color of Fear (90 minutes) Stirfry Productions

"*The Color of Fear* is an insightful groundbreaking film about the state of race relations in America as seen through the eyes of eight North American men of Asian, European, Latino, and African descent. In a series of intelligent, emotional, and dramatic confrontations, the men reveal the pain and scars that racism has caused them. What emerges is a deeper sense of understanding and trust. This is the dialogue most of us fear, but hope will happen sometime in our lifetime."

Source: http://www.stirfryseminars.com/pages/coloroffear.htm

References

Abele, Robert P. 2005. *A user's guide to the USA Patriot Act and beyond.* Lanham, MD: University Press of America.

Allport, Gordon W. 1945. Catharsis and the reduction of prejudice. *Journal of Social Issues* 1 (3): 3–10.

Allport, Gordon. 1954. *The nature of prejudice.* Cambridge, MA: Addison-Wesley Pub. Co.

Anti-Defamation League. 2004. Annual audit of anti-semitic incidents.

Aronson, Elliot K, N. Blaney, C. Stephan, J. Sikes, and M. Snapp. 1978. *The Jigsaw classroom.* Beverly Hills, CA: Sage Publications.

Aronson, E., and R. Thibodeaux. 1992. The Jigsaw classroom: A cooperative strategy got an educational psychology course. In *Cultural diversity and the schools.* ed. J. Lynch, C. Modgil, and S. Modgil, 231–256. London: Falmer Press.

Banks, James A. 1995. Multicultural education and the modification of students' racial attitudes. In *Toward a common destiny: Improving race and ethnic relations in America.* ed. D. Hawley Willis and Jackson, Anthony Wells, 315–339. San Francisco, CA: Jossey-Bass.

Benokratis, Nijole V. 2008. *Marriages and families: Changes, choices and constraints* (6th ed.). Englewood Cliffs, NJ: Prentice Hall.

Biren, Nagda, and Ximena Zuniga. 2003. Fostering meaningful racial engagement through intergroup dialogues. *Group Processes & Intergroup Relations* 6 (1): 111–128.

Brewer, P. R. 2003. The shifting foundations of public opinion about gay rights. *Journal of Politics* 65: 1208–1220.

Brown v. Board of Education of Topeka, KS. 1954. 347 U.S. 483.

Campbell, Bruce A. 1977. The impact of school desegregation: An investigation of three mediating factors. *Youth & Society* 9 (1): 79–111.

Chu, Donald, and Griffey, David. 1985. The contact theory of racial integration: The case of sport. *Sociology of Sport Journal* 2 (4): 323–333.

Conger, Dylan. 2005. *Understanding within-school segregation in New York City elementary schools.* Dissertation Abstracts International, A: The Humanities and Social Sciences, 659 (7), January: 2554-A.

Council on American Islamic Relations. 2005. Post 9/11 hate crime trends: Muslims, Sikhs, Hindus and Jews in the U.S. http://www.pluralism.org/research/profiles/display.php?profile.

Devine, Patricia G., Margo J. Monteith, and Julia R. Zuwerink. 1991. Prejudice with and without compunction. *Journal of Personality and Social Psychology* 60 (6): 817–830.

Erikson, Kai T. 1966. *Wayward Puritans: A study in the sociology of deviance.* New York, Wiley & Sons.

Estland, Cynthia. 2005. Working together: Crossing color lines at work. *Labor History* 46 (1): 79–98.

Etzioni, Amitai. 2004. *How patriotic is the Patriot Act?: Freedom versus security in the age of terrorism.* New York: Routledge.

Federal Bureau of Investigation. 2005. *Hate Crime Statistics 2005.* http://www.fbi.gov/ ucr/hc2005/pressrelease.htm (accessed August 19, 2007).

Goffman, Erving. 1963. *Stigma: Notes on the management of spoiled identity.* Englewood Cliffs, NJ: Prentice Hall.

Goldsmith, Pat Antonio. 2004. Schools' role in shaping race relations: Evidence on friendliness and conflict. *Social Problems* 51 (4): 587–612.

Harlow, Caroline Wolf. 2005. Hate crime reported by victims and police. Bureau of Justice Statistics Special Report November 1005 NCJ209911.

Healey, Joseph F. 2006. *Race, ethnicity, gender and class: The sociology of group change and conflict* (4th ed.). Thousand Oaks, CA: Pine Forge Press.

Herek, G. M. 2000. The psychology of sexual prejudice. *Current Directions in Psychological Science* 9: 19–22.

———. 2002. Gender gaps in public opinion about lesbians and gay men. *Public Opinion Quarterly* 66 (1): 40–66.

———. 2005. Sexual prejudice: Understanding heterosexism and homophobia. http:// psychology.ucdavis.edu/rainbow/html/ sexual_prejudice.html.

Houvouras, Shannon Krista. 2001. The effects of demographic variables, ethnic prejudice, and attitudes toward immigration on opposition to bilingual education. *Hispanic Journal of Behavioral Sciences* 23 (2): 136–152.

Jackman, Mary R. and Marie Crane. 1986. Some of my best friends are black.... *Public Opinion Quarterly* 50: 467–486.

Johns, Michael, Toni Schmader, and Brian Lickel. 2005. Ashamed to be an American? The role of identification in predicting vicarious shame for anti-Arab prejudice after 9-11. *Self and Identity* 4 (4): 331–348.

Jones, Melinda. 2002. *Social psychology of prejudice.* Upper Saddle River, NJ: Prentice Hall.

Kalev, Alexandra, Erin Kelly, and Frank Dobbin. 2006. Best practices or best guesses? Assessing the efficacy of corporate affirmative action and diversity policies. *American Sociological Review* 71 (4): 589–617.

McMahon, Brian T., L. West Steven, N. Lewis Allen, J. Armstrong, Amy, and Joseph Conway. 2004. Hate crimes and disability in America. *Rehabilitation Counseling Bulletin* 47 (2): 66–75.

Monteith, Margo, and I. Corrine Voils. 1998. Proneness to prejudice responses: Toward understanding the authenticity of self-reported discrepancies. *Journal of Personality and Social Psychology* 75 (4): 901–916.

Monteith, Margo, and L. Gina Walters. 1998a. Egalitarianism, moral obligation, and prejudice-related personal standards. *Personality and Social Psychology Bulletin* 24 (2): 186–199.

———. 1998b. Egalitarianism, moral obligation, and prejudice-related personal standards': Erratum. *Personality and Social Psychology Bulletin* 24 (4): 442.

Monteith, Margo, C. Vincent Spicer, and J. D. Tooman. 1998. Consequences of stereotype suppression: Stereotypes on and not on the rebound. *Journal of Experimental Social Psychology* 34: 355–377.

Orfield, Gary, D. Mark Bachmeier, R. David James and Tamela Eitle. 1997. Deepening segregation in American public schools: A special report by the Harvard project on school desegregation. *Equity & Excellence in Education* 30 (2): 5–24.

Orfield, Gary, and Chungmei Lee. 2004. Brown at 50: King's dream or Plessy's nightmare. Harvard Civil Rights Project. www.civilrightsproject.harvard.edu/ research/reseg04/brown50.pdf.

Orfield, Gary, and T. John Yun. 1999. Resegregation in American schools. Harvard Civil Rights Project Report. Cambridge, MA.

Reardon, Sean F., and T. John Yun. 2001. Suburban racial change and suburban school segregation, 1987–95. *Sociology of Education* 74 (2): 79–101.

Roschelle, Anne, and Peter Kaufman. 2004. Fitting in and fighting back: Stigma management strategies among homeless kids. *Symbolic Interaction* 27 (1): 23–46.

Schuman, Howard, Charlotte Steeh, Lawrence Bobo, and Maria Krysan. 1997. *Racial Attitudes in America Trends and Interpretations.* Revised edition. Cambridge, MA: Harvard University Press.

Segal, C. M., and S. Stineback. 1977. *Puritans, Indians and manifest destiny.* New York: Putnam.

Sherrill, K., and A. Yang. 2000. From out-laws to in-laws: Anti-gay attitudes thaw. *Public Perspective* 11: 20–23.

Son, Hing, and S. Leanne. 2002. Inducting hypocrisy to reduce prejudicial responses among aversive racists. *Journal of Experimental Psychology* 38 (1): 71–78.

Steinberg, Stephen. 1995. *Turning back: The retreat from racial justice in American thought and policy.* Boston, MA: Beacon Press.

Stephan, Walter G. 1978. School desegregation: An evaluation of predictions in brown vs. the board of education. *Psychological Bulletin* 85: 217–238.

Thernstrom, Stephan, and Abigail Thernstrom. 1997. *America in black and white.* New York: Simon & Schuster.

Van Bergen, Jennifer. 2005. *The twilight of democracy: The Bush plan for America.* Monroe, ME: Common Courage Press.

Walker, Iain, and Mary Crogan. 1998. Academic performance, prejudice, and the Jigsaw classroom: New pieces to the puzzle. *Journal of Community & Applied Social Psychology* 8 (6): 381–393.

Wegner, D. M. 1994. Ironic processes of mental control. *Psychological Review* 101: 961–977.

Wegner, D. M., D. J. Schneider, S. Carter, and L. White. 1987. Paradoxical effects of thought suppression. *Journal of Personality and Social Psychology* 53: 5–13.

Wilkerson, Wayne, and Andrew Roys. 2005. The components of *sexual orientation,* religiosity, and heterosexuals' impressions of gay men and lesbians. *Journal of Social Psychology* 145 (1): 65–83.

Wilson, Thomas C. 2001. Americans' views on immigration policy: Testing the role of threatened group interests. *Sociological Perspectives* 44 (4): 485–501.

Zirkel, Sabrina, and Nancy Cantor. 2004. 50 years after *Brown v. Board of Education:* The promise and challenge of multicultural education. *Journal of Social Issues* 60 (1): 1–15.

Glossary

Acculturation A process by which a minority or immigrant group takes on the characteristics and adopts the culture of the dominant group.

Affective attitudes The feelings or emotional response a person has toward an object, person, group, or behavior.

Affirmative action Refers to policies requiring that constructive or proactive steps be taken by employers to ensure equal employment and educational opportunities.

Aggregate A collection of people who are grouped together, but not necessarily sharing any traits. They are simply a category of people with no common bond, no goal, and little or no interaction. An aggregate may be a group of people waiting to buy tickets to a concert or the occupants of an elevator. They are in the same place at the same time, but have no common connection to each other.

Aggregated data Information gathered from a large number of subjects showing a common characteristic. Rates of discrimination are measured aggregately so that patterns of inequality can be discerned.

Ambivalence A mixture of benevolent and antagonistic attitudes.

Ambivalence amplification This occurs when the favorable and unfavorable attitudes toward the target group are juxtaposed. For example, if a white person observes a black person behaving in socially positive ways, they have a tendency to evaluate the black person more highly than a white person engaged in similar behavior. On the other hand, if they observe a black person behaving in socially undesirable ways, they will judge the black person even more harshly than

they would a white person in a similar context.

Anglo-conformity When minority groups conform to the culture of the dominant white race.

Antidiscrimination legislation Laws created to eliminate or mitigate certain types of discrimination.

Antigay prejudice Prejudice targeting homosexual, lesbian, bisexual, transsexual or transgendered people.

Antiracism A strategy to decrease racism by publicly and actively reacting to prejudice, discrimination and other components of racism.

Assimilation A strategy that encourages or compels members of the minority group to adopt the language, customs, and culture of the dominant group, eventually becoming indistinguishable.

Attitude A set of beliefs and feelings toward an object that predisposes the person to act in a certain manner when confronted by that object.

Attribution errors Mistakes made when inferring causality. There are three types of attribution errors that can increase reliance on prejudices and stereotypes: correspondence bias, self-serving error, and ultimate attribution error.

Attribution theory Attribution theory explains that people use both internal and external attributions in constructing explanation for the behavior of themselves and others. Attribution bias, or errors in attribution, can result in the persistence of prejudices and reliance on stereotypes.

Authority The power to influences others has been institutionalized. That is, authority is power that is recognized by the people over whom it is exercised and is part of a patterned and predictable social system.

Authoritarian personality A theory first espoused by Gordon Allport that explains that some people integrate prejudices into their personality to justify control and domination of others.

Automatic processing The activation of stereotypes without conscious attention to the process.

Aversive prejudice People who hold egalitarian values while at the same time possessing negative feelings about the target group caused by socialization in a racist culture. These negative feelings are not the virulent hatred expressed by dominative prejudices. The feelings associated with aversive prejudice are more feelings of unease, awkwardness, and wariness.

Axiom Highly abstract and untested assertions.

Axiomatic format The axiomatic format is hierarchal. Propositions and specific hypotheses are derived from these axioms that predict how an event should occur if the axioms are indeed true. This format is used more often with experimental research.

Behavioral attitudes Tendencies toward action connected to an object, person, group, or behavior.

Benevolent sexism Benevolent sexism consists of benign and chivalrous attitudes toward women. It includes attitudes that emphasize women's gentler qualities, such as feminine virtue, decency, nurturing, and the need for protection. Although benevolent sexism seems benign in comparison with hostile sexism, it nonetheless puts women on a pedestal. Thus, it limits women to traditional gender roles and reinforces male dominance.

Bonding Reinforcing exclusive social identities and social ties to create more homogeneous groups.

Bono Fide Occupational Qualification An occupation that requires a special trait possessed only by members of a particular group or category.

Bogardus scale Emory Bogardus created a scale that measures social distance. The Bogardus scale asks people how willing they would be to interact with members of various groups in specific situations.

Bourgeoisie A term from conflict theory that refers to the group that owns or controls the means of production.

Breeching experiments A kind of field experiment in which everyday ordinary social rules are violated to understand how people construct social reality.

Bridging Bridging between groups (or inclusiveness) is used to embrace people across different social divides.

Category A grouping based on a shared characteristic. Members of a category need not interact or share an awareness of group membership. Race and sex are both categories used to sort people.

Causal format A causal process format is like a flow chart that maps the effects of variables on each other.

Charismatic authority Authority based on the personal or emotional appeal of the leader. Charismatic leaders can influence others without the benefit of law or tradition. Charismatic leaders often act as catalysts for dramatic social change.

Chattel A moveable piece of personal property.

Civil Rights Act of 1964 A pivotal piece of civil rights legislation that says neither the United States nor any state may discriminate on the basis of race, color, creed, national origin, or sex.

Class consciousness Class consciousness is an awareness of common economic and political interests among a group of people.

Classism A structure that ranks socioeconomic classes in a hierarchy of advantage. The entire complex of roles, statuses, norms, organization, and institutions that creates and perpetuates advantages for the dominant social class and disadvantages for other social classes.

Close ended questions A question that lists a limited number of responses from which the research participants must choose.

Cognitive attitudes The ideas and beliefs a person has about an object, person, group, or behavior.

Cognitive formation function When attitudes help us simplify and integrate complex, rapidly changing information.

Cognitive neoassociationist view This perspective suggests that exposure to aversive events generates negative feelings. Negative feelings can trigger aggression in some and flight or withdrawal in others. This is an offshoot of the **frustration aggression theory.**

Cognitive schema An organized, structured set of thoughts about some group, idea, person, or thing.

Cognitive suppression Attempting to consciously suppress thoughts about a specified subject.

Cognitive theories Theories that explain human behavior as a by-product of how human being process thoughts.

Cohesion Cohesion is collective solidarity. Cohesive groups tend to display homogeneity among members.

Colorism A form of intraracial racism. Lighter-skin members of minority races are advantaged in a hierarchy based on the absence of racial characteristics, such as skin, hair, and eye color, facial feature, and hair texture.

Compunction theory According to compunction theory, there is a distinction between stereotypic knowledge and personal beliefs. Exposure to stereotypes and a social context in which stereotypic responses are supported can compel people to use stereotypes. For people with low- or anti-prejudiced personal beliefs,

this causes a compunction, or feeling of uneasiness and guilt, for behaving in ways that are inconsistent with their personal beliefs.

Conflict perspective This theory contends that social order arises from conflict. Society is composed of competing groups with conflicting interests. Social order arises from the process and the resolution of these conflicts. Conflict theory is built on the theoretical foundation laid by Karl Marx and Friedrich Engels and the philosophy of George Hegel.

Consensus information A comparison of how the subject behaves with the behavior of other people responding to a similar stimulus or situation.

Consistency effect Part of the process of social cognition whereby memory is aided by comparison with a cognitive schema.

Consistency information This refers to how frequently the same person reacts in the same manner across time and conditions.

Contact theory The basic premise of this theory is that intergroup contact can break down stereotyped notions and reduce prejudices against other groups.

Control group A group not exposed to the experimental treatment.

Controlled observation research Allows the researcher to control extraneous factors that might affect the phenomenon being studied. Also known as *laboratory research.*

Controlled processing Controlled processing includes intentional thoughts of which we are fully aware.

Constitutional Amendments Changes to the U.S. constitution. The 13th amendment prohibits slavery and has been interpreted by the courts to prohibit public or private racial discrimination in the disposal of property, employment, and in the making or enforcing of contracts. The 14th amendment specifies that all persons born or naturalized in the United States are citizens and that no state can make or enforce any laws that abridge the rights of citizens. The 14th amendment also guarantees every citizen equal protection under the law. The 15th amendment specifies that the right to vote cannot be denied or abridged "on account of race, color, or previous condition of servitude."

Corporate welfare (or wealthfare) Government programs aimed at subsidizing business and industry.

Correspondence bias This attribution error is the tendency to believe that people behave the way they do because of the type of internal personality traits they have. Also known as *fundamental attribution error*.

Cultural beliefs Shared ideas that describe how our culture operates.

Cultural pluralism Cultural pluralism occurs when a group has not fully acquired the language, norms, and values of the dominant culture. They maintain their language, traditions, folkways, and values in cultural enclaves.

Cultural stereotypes Widely shared beliefs about groups that emerge not from direct experience but from popular knowledge or what we sometimes refer to as *common sense*.

Definition of the situation A concept from symbolic interaction that explains that the definition of a situation is how a person perceives reality. It is a process by which humans create and negotiate social reality.

Dependent variable The variable in which variation is explained by one or more independent variables.

Deprivation–Frustration–Aggression theory of prejudice This theory contends that troubling or stressful events trigger aggressive impulses. These impulses are directed at convenient and vulnerable out-group members, regardless of whether the person or their group is responsible for the troubling events. It follows that, in times of economic, political, social, or personal stress, prejudice and discrimination should increase.

Depersonalization A process that occurs when people in the in-groups and out-groups are not viewed as distinctive individuals, but as representative prototypes.

Dialectic According to Hegel, ideologies are born of a dynamic process in which an initial idea or set of ideas (the thesis) is challenged by another set of ideas (antithesis). Conflict between ideologies inevitably results in a blending of ideas (synthesis).

Direct institutional discrimination Prescribed, intentional actions that have become institutionalized.

Direct learning Directly experiencing behaviors and their consequences. Desirable behaviors and attitudes are rewarded whereas those that are undesirable are punished.

Discrimination Treating people unequally based on their identification or association with a group or category of people.

Dispersion inaccuracy Refers to how widely or narrowly the trait is dispersed throughout the group in comparison to other groups. This is commonly referred to as *overgeneralization*.

Distinctiveness The more distinct we are in a social situation, the more likely the social identity that contributes to our distinctiveness will be used to define us.

Distinctiveness information A comparison of how the subject responds in this situation with responses made in other situations.

Diversity training Training provided by an organization, usually with the stated purpose of treating diversity as an opportunity and promoting the ability of students and workers from a great variety of backgrounds to cooperate productively.

Dominant group The group that has the most political, social, and economic power.

Dominative prejudice The overt, unambiguous, and blatant expression of prejudices toward a group.

Double consciousness A dilemma experienced by people with conflicting social-class and racial group interests. Also known as *dual consciousness*.

Egalitarianism A value that contends that equal treatment and opportunity should be extended to everyone regardless of the groups to which they belong.

Ego-defense function The ego-defense function refers to using prejudices to bolster self esteem.

Environmental justice The equitable distribution of environmental benefits and harms. The environmental injustice movement primarily involves protecting the poor and minority groups from a disproportionate exposure to environmental hazards.

Ethnocentrism The tendency to see in-groups more positively than out-groups.

Ethnomethodology The study of the body of commonsense knowledge and the range of procedures and the methods by which ordinary members of the society make sense of and act on the circumstances in which they find themselves.

Evaluative roles Evaluative roles involve the sorting of objects, experiences, and people into good or bad.

Experimental group An experimental treatment group that is exposed to the phenomenon that is being tested.

Experimental research Experimental research is designed to demonstrate causality. There are many types of experimental designs, but true experiments have the strongest causality. (See *True experiment* for the criteria of a true experiment.)

Explicit stereotype Explicit stereotyping occurs when a person is aware of the stereotype and their decision to employ it.

External attribution Locates the cause of behavior in the social situation rather than the individual.

False consciousness A term from conflict theory that refers to convincing people that are harmed by an ideology to nonetheless embrace it.

Field research Observational research projects conducted in a particular setting or environment outside of the laboratory.

Formal task group Formal task groups have established goals that define the group.

Freedom Summer The summer of 1964 was dubbed "Freedom Summer" because a coalition of civil rights groups organized volunteers recruited from college campuses to come to Mississippi to help register African Americans to vote.

Frustration aggression hypothesis Deprivation and frustration lead to hostile impulses and the need to scapegoat blame upon less powerful groups.

Functionalism The functionalist perspective has also been called an order, or consensus, theory because one of its basic premises is that social order arises out of consensus or agreement. According to this theory, patterns of social behavior are created and perpetuated because they perform functions for society. In other words, they meet some social need. Society is made of many interdependent parts. These parts are interwoven, such that a change in any part of the society affects every other part. Each part of society performs functions within the social system.

Functions of attitudes Prejudices help serve functions both at the individual level in our interactions and understanding of others and at the societal level by supporting and justifying the social structure. Micro level-functions include cognitive formation, value expression, ego-defense, and utilitarian functions. Mezzo-level functions include the social functions and the group justification function. Macro-level functions include system justification.

Gender insults Comments intended to embarrass individuals into gender role compliance.

Generalized other A compilation of accumulated experiences and expectations used to anticipate and understand the behavior of others.

Group Two or more people who interact and are conscious of their identity as a group.

Group cohesion The level of bonding or attraction of group members to each other. The cohesiveness of the group is very important because it affects group stability and endurance.

Group dynamics Group dynamics refer to the social processes that affect the outcomes of interaction within and between groups.

Group justification function Using prejudices to help foster collective self-esteem.

Group polarization The tendency of groups to make more extreme or polarized decisions than individuals. After taking part in group discussion, group members shift to views that are more extreme.

Group think A process that severely alters the decision-making capacity of the group. There are three indicators of group think. First, group members believe that the decision they make cannot possibly be wrong. They believe themselves to be infallible. Second, they discredit, ignore, or destroy information that is inconsistent with the group's position. Third, members of the group are unwilling to contradict or question the group's position.

Hierarchal roles Ranking of members according to domination and submission. Not only does a status hierarchy emerge within a group, out-groups are ranked in relation to the in-group.

Heterosexism Heterosexism is part of a sexist system of inequality. It is an entire complex of ideas, values, norms, policies, and organization that gives advantages to heterosexuals and withholds them from all other sexual orientations. It is a social structure embedded within the patriarchal structure.

Heterogeneity *Heterogeneity* literally means different (*heter*) kind (*genos*). Members of a heterogeneous group have different characteristics.

Homogeneity *Homogeneity* literally means same (*homo*) kind (*genos*). Members of

homogeneous groups share very similar characteristics.

Homophobia The fear and loathing of gays, lesbians, bisexuals, or transsexuals.

Hostile sexism Hostile sexism includes belligerent, aggressive, and demeaning attitudes. It includes the idea that women are less competent than men and should therefore be subservient to men. It also includes overt antagonism toward women who step out of their gender role or threaten men's domination.

Humanitarianism Humanitarian values stress empathy and sympathy for others less fortunate than ourselves.

Ideology A body of beliefs and values that guides individuals, groups, organizations, and social institutions. It shapes how people understand their society and how they as individuals fit into the social order.

Ideological hegemony The dominance of one ideology over all others. Hegemony occurs when an ideology explaining and justifying the power of an elite groups is accepted even by the oppressed.

Illusory correlation When people notice a distinctive trait or unusual behavior among minority group members, they often overestimate the association between the distinctive trait or behavior and being a member of the minority group. This perceived association is referred to as an illusory correlation.

Implicit Association Test This measure records the amount of time research subjects take to make pairings between attributes and groups. Computer programs are used to administer and record the tests. The research participants are presented with sequences of positive and negative attributes that are to be paired with different groups of people. The participants are first asked to pair positive attributes with one group and negative attributes with the other. Then the association is be reversed; that is, the group previously paired with the positive attributes is paired with negative ones. As words and images flash on the computer screen, participants' reaction times and errors in pairing are measured. These measures record the subtle cognitive process and prejudices of which the participants may be unaware.

Implicit stereotyping Implicit stereotyping occurs when a person is not aware that a stereotype is influencing their interpretations and reactions.

Intimate integration The second stage of integration in the assimilation process. It includes private, personal, or emotionally close associations, such as friendship and intermarriage.

Incorrigible proposition An idea that people persist in believing despite overwhelming evidence to the contrary.

Independent variable A variable used to explain variation in a dependent variable. The experimental treatment is always an independent variable.

Index A composite measure that adds together multiple indicators of a concept.

Indirect institutional discrimination Policies, practices, or organizational procedures that are not a product of prejudices or intended to harm or handicap anyone, yet they have unequal and deleterious impact on some groups.

Indirect learning Learning that can be accomplished vicariously by observing the behaviors and consequences of the behaviors of others. This is sometimes called *role modeling* or *observational learning.*

Individualism The belief that a person is responsible for their actions and the consequences of those actions. Individualism includes ideas about the protestant work ethic and individual responsibility.

Individual intervention Strategies to reduce prejudice geared toward individual intervention and self-control. They include suppression, self-regulation, and interactional strategies.

Individual stereotypes Beliefs and expectations about a group that derive from personal experience with members of that group.

Informal task group Informal task groups are highly flexible. They are often temporary and the roles of its members tend to change according to the situation. Norms within the informal group are emergent and also subject to change with the situation. Goals for informal groups are short-lived and are not central or necessary for group formation.

Interactional strategies There are two varieties of stigma reduction strategies: strategies of inclusion and strategies of exclusion. Strategies of inclusions are defensive tactics and include passing, covering, and forging friendships. Passing and covering are both attempts to conceal the stigmatizing trait. Forging friendships uses alliances with others to mitigate the full effect of the stigmatized identity. Strategies of exclusion are offensive tactics that include verbal denigration and posturing. Rather than waiting for nonstigmatized individuals to exclude or rebuke them, homeless children used aggressive tactics to discourage others from targeting them.

Integration The first stage of assimilation. The first level of integration is primary structural integration. It involves public integration in areas such as employment, education, and other public institutions. The second level of integration is *intimate integration.* It includes private, personal, or emotionally close associations, such as friendship and intermarriage. Also known as *structural assimilation.*

Intergroup dynamics Social processes that affect how people behave when interacting in groups.

Intergroup relations Intergroup relations refer to how people in different groups or social categories feel about and relate to each other. Prejudice is an intergroup phenomenon.

Internal attribution When people attribute the cause of behaviors within the individual.

Some individual trait(s) such as personality, moral character, or attitudes causes the observed behavior.

Intersection of race, gender, and class The points at which disadvantages and advantages caused by the overlapping systems of structured inequality are amplified.

Institutional discrimination Polices and regulations, rather than personal prejudices, compel a person to discriminate. There are two types of institutional discrimination: direct and indirect.

Isolate discrimination Intentionally harmful actions carried out by an individual member of a dominant group against one or more persons in a minority group. It's called isolate because it occurs without the imminent support of a large group or organization.

Labeling theory This theory explains how people come to have deviant identities. In each stage of the labeling process, individuals see themselves differently and are seen differently by others. When an individuals accepts the deviant attribute as part of their self, they have established a deviant identity. Also known as *societal reaction theory*.

Leadership A process by which a person influences others to accomplish tasks or goals. It involves social influence through the exercise of power linked to a particular position in a group structure.

Legal-rational authority Authority based on law. Leaders in this type of system derive their authority from written rules, codes, and regulations. Judges and justices in the U.S. court system draw their authority from the system of laws.

Liberal capitalism The blending of democracy and a capitalist economic system. Liberal philosophy, which reached its zenith in the eighteenth and nineteenth centuries, challenged inherited rights and privileges.

Likert scale Likert-scaled questions ask respondents to decide whether and how much each of them agrees or disagrees

with an item. Several different statements about the same issue and using the same response categories may be arranged in a matrix. Five response categories are normally employed, ranging from "strongly agree" to "strongly disagree."

Looking glass self A concept from symbolic interaction theory that explains how people incorporate the reactions of others into how one understands and defines themselves.

Macro-level An individual-level analysis.

Male identified A term from Marxist-feminist theory that explains how some women distance themselves from the negative attributes of own their groups by contrasting their personal attributes with stereotyped attributes of women.

Meaning is in response A concept from symbolic interaction. Meaning is not a property of a word or other symbol; rather it is constructed through our responses to each other during interaction.

Meritocracy The ideas that those who demonstrate the most merit will rise to the top ranks of society.

Mezzo-level A group-level analysis.

Micro-level A societal-level analysis.

Minority groups Groups with less power and access to resources.

Model minority Positive images of minority groups have been used in the media and by politicians who present the groups as model minorities. The contrast of "problem" versus "model" minorities had detrimental effects on both model and other minorities.

Modern prejudice This theory explains that prejudiced attitudes have not disappeared, but have merely changed forms. Modern prejudice has become cloaked in traditional American values, such as meritocracy.

Multiculturalism A strategy for coping with a heterogeneous population that encourages subcultures to retain their distinctiveness while fostering respect and tolerance for other groups. Multiculturalism is a version of cultural pluralism.

Natural experiment The reaction of people to a natural disaster or other naturally occurring event. Because the event could not be anticipated, it is not possible to have pretest measurement.

Norm Norms are social rules that prescribe and proscribe behaviors within a social context.

Observational research A qualitative method of gathering data that involves observing people while they go about their normal activities.

Old-fashioned prejudice Refers to openly expressed animosity toward a group or category of people.

Open ended question A question that allows the participant to respond in their own words.

Out-group A group to which one does not belong.

Out-group homogeneity People have a tendency to see out-groups as homogeneous, while at the same time noting the individuality and diversity within our in-groups.

Participant observation Research in which the observer joins in the setting that is being observed.

Patriarchy A hierarchical form of social organization that occurs in a large number of social institutions in which men dominate.

Personal identity The part on a person's identity determined by their individual traits.

Persuasive argument approach This theory contends that during group discussion people make arguments that support their views. Some of these arguments are persuasive enough to alter the attitudes of other members of the group. As more members of the group are convinced by the persuasive arguments, the attitude of the group shifts toward that view resulting in the polarization of attitudes.

Phenomenological A perspective that concerns how individuals define their social world.

Plurality The group with the highest percentage of the population but not a numerical majority.

Pluralism A strategy in which many different groups co-exist and retain their cultural or group differences.

Predilection A preference for or positive prejudice about a person, group, place, or thing.

Prejudice A negative attitude about a person, group, place, or thing.

Primary discrimination Discrimination against traditional minorities and women.

Primary group A small intimate group in which closeness and a sense of belonging are forged through the intimacy and relative permanence of the group. People in primary groups have direct, extensive, and extended contact with other group members (e.g., a family or group of close friends).

Primary structural integration An assimilation process that involves public integration in areas such as employment, education, and other public institutions.

Proletariat A term from conflict theory that refers to the working class.

Quasi experiments Experimental designs that lack one or more of the components of a true experiment.

Random assignment A systematic, unbiased method of assigning research subjects to experimental or control conditions.

Random selection A systematic method (based on probability) of selecting members of a population for the sample.

Racism A structure that ranks racial and ethnic groups in a hierarchy of advantage. Racism refers to the entire complex of roles, statuses, norms, organization, and institutions that creates and perpetuates advantages for the dominant racial or ethnic group and disadvantages for other races and ethnic groups.

Realistic conflict theory A contemporary hybrid of the conflict perspective and psychological research on intergroup relations.

According to this theory, groups can have incompatible goals and be in competition for scarce resources. This extends the uses of prejudice beyond the tactics of false consciousness. The conflict is "real" in the sense that the groups have distinctive interests that generate conflict between them.

Rebound effect Increased attention to a topic following a task in which it was suppressed.

Relative deprivation A hypothesis from deprivation-frustration theory. Relative rather than absolute deprivation is more likely to trigger frustration and aggression.

Reference group A group used as a standard for evaluating behaviors and attitudes. One does not have to be a member of the group to use a group as a referent.

Reverse discrimination Setting aside a number or percentage of positions for members of a minority group may have been intended as a remedy for discrimination against that group, but it is actually a requirement to discriminate against all other groups.

Sample A subset of cases drawn from a larger population.

Sampling unit The element used to select cases from a larger population.

Scale A more sophisticated composite measure of a theoretical concept. Several items are constructed to measure different aspects of the concept. The items that make up the scale must measure distinct aspects of the concept and must be interrelated with the other components used to construct the scale.

Scapegoating Blaming troubling events on out-group members who have nothing to do with events.

Secondary groups A group which is more formal, more impersonal, less permanent, and organized around a limited set of tasks or goals (e.g., a class of students).

Self-fulfilling prophecy When expectations about how someone will behave actually causes the anticipated behavior. This concept is part of labeling theory.

Self-report The most direct and simplest way to measure attitudes. It includes all procedures by which a person is asked to report their attitudes.

Self-serving attribution error The tendency to blame failure on external factors, while crediting successes to internal traits.

Semantic differential scale Typically a seven-point scale used between two antonyms. Respondents are asked to indicate where on the scale a concept belongs to by putting a check mark in one of the spaces between the polar opposites.

Sexism A structure that ranks people by their sex and sexual orientation in a hierarchy of advantage. The entire complex of roles, statuses, norms, organization, and institutions that creates and perpetuates advantages for the dominant gender group and disadvantages for other genders. In the United States heterosexual men are the dominant group.

Significant other A person, such as a parent, a close friend, a teacher, or a mentor, whose responses to the social world influences our own understanding and the meanings we give to the world around us.

Small group discrimination Deliberately malevolent actions taken by a small group of individuals from the dominant group who act collectively against members of a minority group. Hate groups, vigilante groups, and terrorists engage in this type of discrimination.

Social-adjustive function When the social constraints of a face-to-face interaction inhibit our actions and the expression of attitudes.

Social capital This refers to connections between people. It is based on social networks, statuses, norms of reciprocity, and benefits that can come from association with powerful individuals.

Social category A social category is composed of people who share a common characteristic (such as race, national origin, gender, or age), but do not necessarily interact with each other.

Social class A ranking of individuals according to access to socioeconomic resources in a hierarchy of economic, social, and political advantage.

Social cognition How people think about the social world. It is the process of making judgments from information available in the social environment.

Social comparison approach This theory contends that before group discussion most individuals within a group assume that their views are as good as or better than other members of the group. However, one outcome of group discussion is learning that one's own views may not be nearly as good or well thought-out as first imagined. This process of social comparison shifts the position of the group toward more consensus.

Social distance theory This theory describes under what conditions people avoid contact with people from other groups.

Social Dominance Orientation An orientation toward antiegalitarian values, competitiveness between groups, preference for hierarchies, and a desire for in-group dominance over out-groups. Abbreviated SDO.

Social function of prejudice Using prejudices to identify with and gain acceptance to social groups.

Social Identity The part of a person's identity that comes from membership in social groups.

Social identity theory This theory contends that part of our sense of self derives from group memberships.

Social institution A network of roles, statuses, groups, and organizations designed to accomplish a basic social goal.

Social learning perspective A theory of socialization that contends that people learn new attitudes, beliefs, and behaviors through social interaction. According to this

theory, human behavior is determined by an interplay between elements of a social situation and the individual interactants.

Social organization A configuration (or network) of social roles and positions.

Social perception The process whereby people come to understand or perceive others and the social situations in which we interact.

Social roles A set of behavioral expectations attached to a social position. Roles often have statuses as well as behavioral expectations.

Social status The relative positions of persons in a social hierarchy. Social status is a named social position that implies the relative prestige of that position. It is often measured as occupational prestige.

Social structure The basic framework or architecture of social order. Social structures provide the social context in which interaction between individuals takes place. Among its many components, social structure includes social roles, statuses, norms, forms of organization, cultural beliefs, and values.

Socialization The process of learning how to behave according to the rules and expectations of a particular culture.

Socialization approach This perspective studies interaction through the examination of constraints on interaction imposed by rules and roles. Perspectives within this tradition focus on the norms and roles understood by people entering into interactions and how we learn them.

Socioemotional or expressive leaders Leaders who mediate conflicts, encourage group participation, and provide feedback to group members.

Stereotype Widely held beliefs and expectations about people that allow us to quickly categorize people and make sense of them based on social categorizations.

Stereotype activation When stereotyping is precipitated by association with a group or category of people. In other words, just noticing attributes such as a person's age, race, or gender can trigger the stereotypes.

Stereotype application When stereotypes affect our thinking or behavior. But, whereas stereotype activation may be virtually automatic, application of stereotypes is not inevitable.

Stereotypic inaccuracy A measure comparing the prevalence of the attributes in the target group compared with other groups.

Stigma Any social attribute that is deeply discrediting to an individual's identity.

Stratification The layering of people and groups according to their access to scarce resources and power.

Structural discrimination A corollary of structured inequality. It refers to the existence of institutionalized bias. Race and ethnicity, gender and sexual orientation, and social-class discrimination are products of our stratification system.

Structural Inequality Structural inequality occurs when the unequal treatment of people based on the groups to which they belong has become embedded in the social structure.

Structural pluralism Structural pluralism occurs when a group has acculturated but not integrated into the dominant group. The group practices the same culture as the dominant group. They speak the same language, internalize the same norms, and hold the same values and goals as the dominant culture. However, they do so in parallel, but separate institutions. The most obvious example of structural pluralism in the United States is our practice of religion.

Survey research A research design that selects and analyzes information from a defined sample and generalizes that information to a larger population.

Symbolic interaction The basic premise of symbolic interaction theory is that people create and negotiate the meanings they apply to objects, events, and people through a process of interaction.

Symbolic prejudice A theory of contemporary prejudice that explains that latent negative attitudes toward a group are mixed with widely held values and triggered by political symbols. This form of prejudice is termed "symbolic" for several reasons. First, the prejudice is abstract, ideological resentment of a group rather than resentment based on actual experiences with the group. Another symbolic dimension involves the sense that the target group has violated some underlying widely-agreed-upon social contract. Finally, symbolic prejudices are overlaid with traditional values. Espousing the traditional values is subtly combined with the suggestion that the target groups' problems stem from their failure to conform to the values rather than from prejudice or discrimination.

System justification function When prejudices are used to maintain and help justify existing social structures.

Talking past People from different groups often "talk past" each other. That is, their experiences and the understanding are so different that although they may be using the same language they are not sharing meaning.

Target group A group that receives prejudices or discriminatory treatment.

Task leaders Leaders who guide and coordinate ideas and information toward the completion of tasks and goals.

Theory A set of ideas that helps us explain and predict what happens in our world.

Theoretical concepts They denote phenomena. That is, they define, distinguish, and clarify ideas.

Theoretical formats The most common formats for social theories are the inductive and deductive causal formats.

Theoretical statements Statements that specify how concepts are related to each and are systematically organized.

Thurstone scale A complex scale measuring attitudes. First, the researcher collects a large number of statements that represents an extreme range of attitudes toward the subject in question (e.g., social class, gender, or race). Next, a large group of judges are recruited (approximately fifty). Each judge is asked to sort the statements into an odd number of piles (seven, nine, or eleven), the middle pile being neutral. Then the judges are asked to place each item along a continuum from one extreme to another, but not to let their own opinion about the subject influence the placements. After all the judges have ranked the items, a median (half the placements were lower, half were higher) is calculated for each individual item by using the pile numbers to which it was assigned. Items that had a wide range of placements or were ambiguous to the judges are discarded. The researcher then selects from the remaining items those that are most equally spaced along the entire range of the continuum. The selected items are then included in a questionnaire. The order of the statements is deliberately mixed, so respondents will not notice the continuum. Respondents are asked to check all the items with which they agree.

Title The legal evidence, justifications, and specifications used to establish a legal right. Subsequent antidiscrimination policies have been written under the authority of one or more of these titles. For example, title V of the 1964 Civil Rights Act outlaws employment discrimination.

True experiment A strong causal design that must meet four conditions. (1) It must have both control and experimental groups. (2) Subjects must be randomly assigned to control and experimental conditions. (3) There must be a pretest measurement of the dependent variable. (4) There must be a posttest measurement of the dependent variable.

Traditional authority Leadership is based on custom and long-accepted practices. For example, in societies governed by absolute monarchies, leadership is not based on personal characteristics or competence, but on inheriting the position. The system continues because "it has always been so."

Ultimate attribution error An attribution error that occurs when in-group and out-group distinctions affect attributions. People tend to attribute the positive behaviors of in-group members to internal characteristics and their undesirable behaviors to external factors. The opposite is true for out-group members. When out-group members behave in undesirable ways people attribute it to internal traits, but when they behave in positive ways it is attributed to external causes.

Utilitarian functions of prejudice Using prejudices to obtain rewards or avoid sanctions.

Valence inaccuracy This refers to how one judges the central tendencies of a group compared with other groups. Valance inaccuracy is related to ethnocentrism.

Values Standards that people use to decide what goals and outcomes are desirable.

Value expression function Allows people to express important components of personality.

Variables Empirically defined concepts that must vary and can be measured.

Work ethic The belief that hard work not only leads to success, but is also a reward unto itself.

Xenocentrism The belief that groups to which one does not belong are superior to one's own group.

Index